**HOW SKEPTICS DO ETHICS**

AUBREY NEAL
# *HOW SKEPTICS DO ETHICS*

A Brief History of the Late Modern Linguistic Turn

UNIVERSITY OF
CALGARY
PRESS

© 2007 by Aubrey Neal.

Published by the
University of Calgary Press
2500 University Drive NW
Calgary, Alberta, Canada T2N 1N4
*www.uofcpress.com*

No part of this publication may be reproduced, stored in a retrieval system or transmitted, in any form or by any means, without the prior written consent of the publisher or a licence from The Canadian Copyright Licensing Agency (Access Copyright). For an Access Copyright licence, visit *www.accesscopyright.ca* or call toll free to 1-800-893-5777.

We acknowledge the financial support of the Government of Canada through the Book Publishing Industry Development Program (BPIDP) and the Alberta Foundation for the Arts for our publishing activities. We acknowledge the support of the Canada Council for the Arts for our publishing program.

Canada Council   Conseil des Arts
for the Arts         du Canada

Canadä

LIBRARY AND ARCHIVES OF
CANADA CATALOGUING IN
PUBLICATION

Neal, Aubrey, 1946–
How skeptics do ethics : a brief history of the late modern linguistic turn / Aubrey Neal.

Includes bibliographical references and index.
ISBN 978-1-55238-202-8

1. Skepticism.
2. Ethics.
3. Philosophy – Language.
4. Philosophy, Modern.
I. Title.

B837.N42 2007     149'.73
C2007-900012-6

Cover design, Mieka West.
Interior design & typesetting,
Jason Dewinetz.

# TABLE OF CONTENTS

|  | 1 | INTRODUCTION |
|---|---|---|
| *One* | *19* | **HUME'S PREDICAMENT** |
|  | 20 | Hume's Fork |
|  | 28 | Sentiment |
|  | 38 | Kant's Critique of Hume |
| *Two* | *65* | **HEGEL'S PREDICAMENT** |
|  | 74 | G.W.F. Hegel |
|  | 92 | Wilhelm Dilthey |
| *Three* | *113* | **THE LINGUISTIC TURN** |
|  | 115 | Friedrich Nietzsche |
|  | 120 | Ferdinand de Saussure |
|  | 128 | Ludwig Wittgenstein |
| *Four* | *153* | **THE MODERN PREDICAMENT** |
|  | 163 | Maurice Mandelbaum |
|  | 174 | Hempel's Covering Law |
|  | 187 | Leonard Krieger |
|  | 197 | Kant and Marx |
| *Five* | *209* | **POSTMODERNISM** |
|  | 210 | Martin Heidegger |
|  | 233 | Jacques Derrida |
|  | 242 | Michel Foucault |
|  | 256 | Understanding Postmodernism |
|  | 273 | NOTES |
|  | 297 | BIBLIOGRAPHY |
|  | 311 | INDEX |

*For Joan*

> *The normal wrongly assimilates us.*
> – GEORGES CANGUILHEM

# INTRODUCTION

> *I am a very conservative person.... The constancy of God in my life is called by other names.*[1]
> — JACQUES DERRIDA

**ABOUT TWENTY YEARS AGO,** a prominent Canadian social theorist told me the 1960s had been "a wonderful time" for him. "I announced to myself God was dead and so all things were possible," he explained. He declared his loss of traditional faith with the unalloyed confidence of Europe's historical Enlightenment. He was the skeptical attitude incarnate. Those famous words, "God is dead" are the gauntlet of a fully fledged, out of the closet, skeptical scion of the modern age. The declaration did not surprise me. I had reached a similar conclusion at about the same time in my own life. It was the word "wonderful" that caught me by surprise. That was one of the last words I would have used to describe the loss of traditional religious faith. The social theorist was a successful public intellectual. His work was grace under pressure; he was a player, a doer, and a leader in his field. I appreciated his position. Our differences were not professional. They were more a matter of personal emphasis. I was surprised to find I was not as "modern" as he. I was, colloquially, not as "with it." I still liked the old tunes. In spite of my doubts, I still enjoyed the old creeds. I missed the traditional meaning of the old words and I still enjoyed trying to truth-say in the old unequivocal ways.

Reflection and study indicated a complex history lay behind our differences. If the theorist knew the history, it did not seem to bother him. I decided it bothered me. Martin Luther had been the first to propound the "death of God" in his theological quarrel with the Nestorians. G.W.F. Hegel had been the first modern philosopher to use the phrase with unequivocal skeptical intent. He had shed crocodile tears of "infinite grief that God himself has died" in 1804. Friedrich Nietzsche turned Hegel's grief into a sound byte in *The Gay Science* (1882). Nietzsche's madman stood in a town square screaming "who has drunk up the sea?" Like most well-read skeptics, the theorist knew Nietzsche's sound byte, but he did not seem to know or seem to care about Hegel's grief. Informal solicitation of the opinion of friends and colleagues came down solidly with the theorist. There was not a mourner among them. Friends were indulgent, colleagues looked askance, and my wife stopped taking me to parties.

Hegel's grief was not in evidence among friends and colleagues with whom I broached the topic. Their discretion was monolithic. To me, it was amazing. Hegel's grief was a metaphor for a significant historical event. Hegel had felt the first deep impact of science and materialism on daily life in modern Europe. He had experienced firsthand the crossover from metaphysics to materialism at the end of the Enlightenment. His grief reflected the emotional trauma of skeptical Enlightenment in modern history. My friends and colleagues were as incredible to me as a group of feminists who had forgotten about the pill. Fascination with Hegel's "grief" became the determination to do a project sometime in the early 1990s. The university has a remarkable tolerance for navel gazing. The formal phase of the project began with an unstructured feeling of emotional difference. Inexplicit differences are not pleasant. If language is the home of man, Hegel's grief has no home. Finding an expository style for the project was difficult. Finding the appropriate tone for the project took a long time. A few readers have expressed doubts it took long enough.

Hegel's grief is not a conventional topic for historical research. In the majority view, as far as I could see, a sorrow like Hegel's is a latent sign of eccentricity or, even worse, unpublishability. The majority point is: Hegel got over it. His "grief" was temporary. Hegel grieved during a transition stage in his development as a philosopher. When he overcame his grief for God, Hegel was able to abandon superstition and embrace science. When Hegel became a religious skeptic and an historical positivist, his thinking rose to a new level. His career as a philosopher took off. He grew confident in his new faith. He realized history did not threaten the substance of the old religions. The moral practices of the old religions remained alive, but their violent side was eliminated from modern history in the West. Why mourn the absence of religious fanaticism and political intolerance? Transcendental categories of right and wrong distilled from epochs of traditional religious experience were still available for reflection.

History, in the West, had shorn religion of its violence and preserved what was valuable. The moral anthropology of modern life draws on the practical wisdom of traditional ethics in a new and progressive environment. Ideally, the old wisdom gives politics a conscience. The religious heritage balances the coldness of the scientific view and humanizes the predatory nature of states. Hegel's grief was a stage in getting the modern balance right. The educated secularist in the modern Western tradition is a happy, well-adjusted example of the Hegelian phenomenology of mind minus the grief. History has done us the service of eliminating the prejudices of the old traditions while confirming their proprieties.

Describing the modern philosophy of history is easier than criticizing it. History permeates public discourse like the soft buzz of a fluorescent light. Readers like the light, they get used to having it on, and so they barely notice the noise. History supplies politics with its store of popular anecdotes. Politicians like the stories, accept the conventional wisdom and hardly notice a downside. One of the practical difficulties which separated me from most my friends and colleagues was over this cozy nineteenth-century view of modern history. Hegel's philosophy of history did not seem to me to include Hegel's loss of traditional religious faith. Hegel's grief was still alive to me. I believed, on the basis of my personal experience, Hegel's grief was still active in subtler ways than modern historical idealism was able to comprehend. Hegel had an emotional experience powerful enough to change his philosophy of life. Hegel was important so Hegel's grief had to be important. Given the importance of his philosophy, Hegel's "grief" must have reflected a general convulsion. God's metaphorical "death" seemed a research path into a social history traditional scholarship had neglected.

The documents subsequent to 1804 do not show any grief. If Hegel still felt it, it stayed a private matter and did not affect his influential theories of dialectic, consciousness, and political right. I decided, as much for my own purposes as any other, that traditional scholarship was not satisfactory in this area. The traditional scholarship seemed to reflect an inadequacy in the traditional method. Hegel had expressed and then repressed an important emotional experience. I believed he had committed a kind of philosophical sin deep down in the heart of his philosophy. Hegel got over his grief by building a boisterously secular tradition into the heart of the old theology. I subsequently discovered David Hume was Hegel's silent partner in the hostile takeover of dialectics from the church. Hegel was as silent about Hume as he was about his grief. His hostile takeover of Christian dialectics looked like corporate business practice or a military campaign. Nothing indicates he was worried about the *ad hoc* political alliances the death of God had let him make. Hegel's secularization of history was like the "Machiavellian moment" John Pocock describes in the Renaissance.[2] All that was good congealed into politics. All that was noble melted into air. Skeptics have to accept the moment, but surely they could be indulged a few modest regrets. It seemed to me Hegel's system or, alternatively, the system for which he spoke, was in denial. Hegel used history to side-step his grief over the political take-over of all that had been holy. That was my side. The psychological and emotional side of modern history intrigued me. Hegel's grief had a history. I was sure of it.

Jürgen Habermas is one of the most respected critical theorists of the twentieth century. Moral conscience and history are two of his recurrent themes. In his view, the modern West is torn emotionally between its moral duty to others and its historical obligation to democratic politics. His eponyms for the two sides of the schism are Kant and Hegel. Kant is the ethicist and Hegel is the politician. Habermas wants his work to relieve us of the Hobson's choice between Kant and Hegel.[3] He hopes Western history can gather its senses and develop a conscience without having to curtail its traditional freedoms. Habermas raises the heritage issue of moral practice in secular terms. The complexity of the task is reflected in his Germanic prose. I turned to Habermas because skeptics who refuse to mourn the loss of the old certainties may have ethical issues with their politics. I thought the ethics of side-stepping the death of God might show up in what Habermas calls, "communicative behaviour."

Habermas believes the fundamental social issue in modern public life since the Enlightenment is how skeptics can even do ethics. Like Freud commenting on his children, he is amazed we remain, basically, decent people. Habermas chooses high-profile protagonists to illustrate his arguments. He often returns to the moral puzzle of Marxist politics. Logically, Marxist politics is reasonable, but Marxist moral indignation is a paradox. A materialist has no standard of comparison for how things could be other than the way they are. Logically, a materialist is a well-adjusted realist. S/he has no measure for behavioural anomaly outside the norm and no higher standard than politics by which to make general moral judgments. Injustice might concern her as a matter of policy, but Marx is angry. Why would a materialist be angry, Habermas wonders? Habermas supports Marxist politics in practice, but his philosophical side wants to know how they are possible. Jürgen Habermas is a very complicated man. The complexity of the modern moral problem, as he sees it, indicates the old religions are not obsolete.

In the early nineties Habermas conceded:

> I do not believe that we, as Europeans, can seriously understand concepts like morality and ethical life, person and individuality or freedom and emancipation without appropriating the substance of the Judeo-Christian understanding of history ... Without the transmission through socialization and the transformation through philosophy of any one of the great world religions, this semantic potential could one day become inaccessible.[4]

Old Hegel comes through clearly in phrases like "understanding ... the substance ... of history" and "Judeo-Christian understanding of history." The world spirit moves through the "great world religions." Any of the great historical religions can be an instrument of "freedom and emancipation." Modern history makes progress using the collected wisdom of the traditional texts of all historical peoples. The last eight words are the cutting edge of the passage. Habermas is afraid the "semantic potential" of religion "could one day become inaccessible." He is candid. He has not backed off from the modern problem. He puts it obliquely, but there it is. The world still needs ethics. The prospect is not pleasant to Pangloss skeptics who want the best of all possible worlds without paradox, sorrow, and political inconvenience.

The last eight words of Habermas's concession pose a serious general issue for a skeptical society that uses history to conserve its moral heritage. In a world where "God, himself, has died," skeptical realists are left with only the "semantic potential" of the old wisdom. From this perspective, good intentions are not their only responsibility. They are keepers of the language. Since they are morally responsible for the substance of the traditional wisdom, they have to do more than keep the old language in play. They have to keep it alive. Habermas expresses concern the wisdom of the great world religions will die unless their "semantic potential" is preserved. Protecting the full semantics of the heritage religions is part of the skeptical challenge in late modern life. Habermas believes the semantic heritage is as important as the physical environment. The deep green skepticism of scientific doubt has just as much responsibility for the language environment as it does for the physical one. Habermas feels obliged to protect the semantic heritage from pollution by power politics and other less thoughtful aspects of "the public sphere." He believes the modern tradition assaults the language of traditional moral reflection at a number of key points. In his view, the conflict between the modern tradition and the moral tradition has caused a "legitimation crisis" in modern life. What should be done cannot often be plausibly defended. The right and just in the old moral traditions are not legitimate issues in the modern one.

The ethical paradox Habermas describes has an ambivalent pedigree. Immanuel Kant (1724–1804) and G.W.F. Hegel (1770–1831) are the German idealists who founded the tradition in which Habermas works. They are irreconcilably different in their approaches to the problems of knowledge and belief. Kant is the founder of modern aesthetics, and Hegel is the father of philosophy of history. Kant is a moral idealist, and Hegel is a political idealist. Continental philosophy has wrestled with the warring angels of these two traditions for almost two hundred years. Habermas aroused my curiosity about these two giants. The plainest difference between them is the way they treat the act of reflection. Kant sees the world as a reflection of mind. Hegel sees the mind as a reflection of world. After my project was underway for a few years, my confidence in Habermas ebbed. His skill remains an inspiration. His goal of reconciling Kant and Hegel now appears to me to be futile. One philosopher has to take precedence over the other in any organized discussion of modern intellectual history. The attempt to adjudicate their respective claims led this project to postmodernism and the late modern linguistic turn. My conclusion is that postmodernism was a Continental act of philosophical adjudication between the competing claims of Kant and Hegel. From the postmodern perspective, Kant won, hands down.

Let me sketch how it happened from a postmodern perspective. The most significant details and their implications make up the body of the narrative. In 1768 Immanuel Kant looked at himself in the mirror and saw something he had never noticed before. He realized he could interpret the left/right reversal of a mirror image without being conscious of it.[5] Kant's reflection changed Western moral philosophy forever. His reflection convinced him the mind is the first ordering principle of the world. The difference between himself and his reflection made him a transcendental idealist. In truth, he did not need a lot of convincing. His last short publication in 1770 announced his intention to rethink his approach to philosophy:

> It is one thing to conceive for oneself the composition of the whole.... It is another thing to represent the same concept to oneself in the concrete by a distinct intuition.[6]

Until 1770 Kant had thought of philosophy as an intellectual process of logical construction. Philosophers built up large and inclusive concepts about things in general from simple propositions about things in particular. After seeing himself in the mirror for the first time, he decided modern philosophy was looking through the wrong end of the telescope. Its historic task was the opposite of the one it had set itself since classical times. The major task of philosophy was to discover the simple propositions behind the complex process of logical perception. Kant called his new insight a "Copernican Revolution" in thought.

The reflection paradox convinced Kant knowledge was not a linear progression and philosophy should not be a series of linear propositions. Knowledge was a complex function of two related, but fundamentally different, mental operations. Philosophy's new task was to explain the complex relation between two contrasting operations going on simultaneously in the human mind. The mind conceives and reflects. Knowledge requires a concept *and* a concrete intuition of the concept in external form. Kant claimed our concrete intuitions of the external world were a spontaneous reflection of our own purposes. The world is there but we give it order. Spontaneous intuitions which suit our own purposes take place beneath the threshold of consciousness. Kant did not use the word *unconscious*, but he said our intuitive capacity operated spontaneously and it was beyond the scope of all critical philosophy at that time. Kant reflected on what he thought he had discovered for eleven years. He broke his silence with a book many philosophers consider the greatest single intellectual achievement in the history of Western civilization. Kant's *Critique of Pure Reason* opens with the following words:

> There can be no doubt that all our knowledge begins with experience.... How then should our faculty of knowledge be awakened into action?

Kant's answer is the beginning of postmodernism and the late modern linguistic turn. It is, simply put, the way skeptics have to do ethics. We are categorically responsible for the order of things. The meaning of life, history, and human culture is in our hands. We moderns have given the world a logical order which suits our physical purposes. When that world or any part of it goes awry, the blood is on our hands.

Kant was not as dramatic as my summary. He was the consummate professional at all times. Kant's baby-step approach to the problem of a skeptical ontology continued as follows:

> But though all our knowledge begins with experience, it does not follow that it all arises out of experience.... If our faculty of knowledge makes any addition [to experience], it may be we are not in a position to distinguish it from the raw material.[7]

Skeptics have to sort out what they know from how they know it. Knowledge itself is dialectical. The conceptual half of an experience is analytical, i.e., rational and, hopefully, enlightened. Analytical concepts are pure. The synthetic reflection of concepts is not pure. The human mind plays tricks with its own reflections. It surreptitiously organizes experience to suit its concept of it. *The synthetic process of empirical reflection is hidden from us. It does not belong to the conscious mind.* Kant called the hidden process a synthesis *a priori*. He believed ethics were the only way to verify the empirical process of spontaneous reflection. Since our mind routinely plays tricks on us, the standard of judgment we apply to ordinary experience has to be categorical. The conceptual world must rigorously mirror a universal experience. We cannot measure the validity of experience by our view alone. A concept of experience is not valid unless every ordinary experience *of that category* can be reflected within it. Kant's theory of skeptical reflection prohibits privilege, special cases, and political expediency. One world, one system of thought, one common human experience – these are the cornerstones of the Kantian system. He thought they were as permanent and fixed as the starry sky.

*World* is the governing term in the Kantian moral epistemology. Kant refused to stop his *Critique of Pure Reason* at any point smaller than the whole world. When we see the world whole and entire, then we see the world from a moral perspective. Ethics are the one and only way a human being can concretely intuit the world whole and entire. An ethical world is the only intelligible world. It is the only world where we can trust our senses. The moral freedom of an intelligible world is unexceptional. It sees every part of the world in the same way. The same laws apply to all parts of the world in all places at all times. There are no acausal holes in Newton's scientific universe, and there were no behavioural holes in Kant's moral one:

> *Synthesis* does not come to an end until we reach a whole which is not a part, that is to say, [until we reach] a WORLD.[8]

The unflinching congruence between abstract concept and concrete, sensory intuition has been the ground and rule for secular moral theory ever since Kant. I believe Kant's moral epistemology provides an answer to the Habermas question about Marx. How can a materialist have moral indignation? Kant's approach provides a relatively simple answer. Marx can be angry at the bourgeoisie because, arguably, they commit the fundamental intuitive error which Kant confronted in his own reflection. The bourgeoisie let their mind play tricks on them. They conceive the world one way and they experience the world in another. They conceive the world in terms of spiritual growth, peace, prosperity, and economic development. The world they conceive is not the world reflected in most people's experience. Marx claimed bourgeois values hid a concrete world of exploitation, imperialism, and double standards. His charge was polemical, but, by Kant's standards, his logic was impeccable. Karl Marx understood the way skeptics have to do ethics.

The American version of Continental philosophy is called *pragmatism*. The name which Charles Sanders Pierce and William James gave to the study of "things" (*pragmata*) stuck to the tradition of American philosophy that was continued by C.I. Lewis, Willard van Orman Quine, Hilary Putnam, Nelson Goodman, J.L. Austin, George Lakoff, and Mark Johnson.[9] They took William James's psychological "pragmatism" and applied it to the study of philosophy. Charles Morris expanded pragmatism into cultural studies at the same time C.I. Lewis was re-grounding it in Kant. Lewis's *Mind and the World Order* (1929) argued that the "action orientation" of expressive concepts had to be understood historically in terms of what he called "their temporal spread."[10] Lewis criticized the practical effect of interpretive systems, including (by implication) American historical studies. It was Lewis, in the American tradition, who was the first to articulate Kant's moral epistemology in plain language. He called the concrete sensory side of knowledge an "action orientation." Modern life has "action orientations" which are learned from childhood on up. The learning only ceases when we die. Jobs, politics, and interpersonal relationships continue the learning process after the period of formal education. Lewis refused to stop his evaluation of the "action orientations" in modern life short of anything smaller than the whole world. Lewis laid the foundation for plain language moral philosophy in the United States. Plain language is the approach which will be favoured here.

"We live in an age of skepticism," Lewis explained in 1955.[11] The glassy stare of fish-eyed skeptical doubt had been a central fact in his long professional life:

> Men have become doubtful of any bedrock for firm belief, any final ground for unhesitant action, and of any principles not relative to circumstance or coloured by personal feeling or affected by persuasions which may be only temporary and local.[12]

The skeptical attitude only needs "principles relative to circumstance" and "persuasions which may be only temporary and local," Lewis continued. The flexibility of the skeptical attitude fares brilliantly in the hard sciences. It encounters some difficulties when the same habits of mind are introduced into the traditional questions of ethics, faith, and religious belief. Protecting the good in the temporal and local faces a number of procedural problems. The largest one, according to Lewis is:

> Objects do not classify themselves and come into experience with their tickets on them.... Knowledge must always concern principally the relations which obtain between one experience and another, particularly those relations into which the knower himself may enter as an active factor.[13]

Lacking guidance from a higher spiritual entity, all judgment is relative. It may even be trivial. Issues of time and place have to be left to time and place to decide. Skeptical social skills may be high, but the skeptical moral situation is dubious. The skeptical observer has no higher authority than history. His historical perspective is part of the skeptical moral problem. How can history awaken skeptical reason to the need for *principled* action? History only stipulates something happened. It makes no value judgments.

Lewis's work was continued in the United States by Hilary Putnam. The redoubtable Putnam enlisted a colleague for service in the cause:

> Hartry Field says we have *low standards* in theory of language; and we ought to have the same standards that we have in other natural sciences, especially if, as good physicalists, we view language as a natural phenomenon.[14]

Field expressed this disagreeable possibility in the William James lecture at Harvard University in 1974. Field had trouble getting even so prestigious a lecture published and Putnam used Field's unpublished manuscript during the writing of his in 1978. Putnam found Field's message "fascinating" because, he thought, "it illuminates an issue that has been submerged in philosophy for a long time, and that has surfaced in the twentieth century."[15] Field thought a theory of language might be the best way to discuss a skeptical moral perspective. The conceptual bridge between language and life might be an entry point for a plain language approach to this relatively abstruse topic.

Field's theory of language was Kant's mirror to Putnam. He was fascinated by the complexity of an everyday event he had always taken for granted. The simple one-to-one correspondence between words and things had no essential foundation in reason, truth, or history. For Putnam, the "crisis" Habermas belabours boiled down to a less caustic question. Putnam was not directly concerned with grand issues like materialism, religion, and history. He said he simply shared the general interest of all academics with regard to the matter of scholarly references. Putnam wondered if it was entirely clear how scholars and writers do them. With the apparent soul of innocence, he asked:

> Is *reference* just ... a relation which is as much a part of the natural-causal order as the relation, "is chemically bonded to"? Is it to be studied in the same way?

And then, the bombshell:

> If not, are we viewing language as something transcendental?

Field had said, "Yes," language has become something transcendental to people, many of whom do not otherwise believe in transcendence. In a skeptical society, references to the world are made in the language of the same world. References are circular. Words mirror whatever is the case; the relation between words and things is taken from the use for things at hand. Words have no innate "bond" to a higher truth. The "catch," Putnam writes, "is that the concept of truth is *not* philosophically neutral."[16] Formal reference is reflexively loaded with unspecified pragmatic assumptions. Those who share the assumptions understand the reference.

Putnam's way of speaking is less dramatic than Habermas's, but his position covers the same range of issues. For example: In the West, wealth exists prior to our discussion of it. Western Europe and the United States have accumulated large quantities of capital over the last 250 years. Most Europeans and North Americans grew up with it. Those who do have it see it all around them. Wealth induces a sophisticated form of political reflection among those whom it benefits. The majority of people in Western Europe and North America are relatively rich by world standards. They tend to see the larger world pulled through the looking glass of their own personal experience. They hold well-tutored economic and political expectations of what the world is like. Their affluent environment is the mirror in which they see the rest of the world. From a non-Western view, these well-tutored expectations reverse the correct relation between morality and politics. In the West, politics looks like a religion and religion is just a lifestyle choice.

In the previous example, the developed and the non-developed world are made to show diametrically opposite points of view. The example is pejorative, but not irrelevant. The "reference problem" is not about who has the most evidence to support their point of view. The "reference problem" is not a problem of proof. Putnam uses the word reference to denote a question of discourse – hopefully an amicable one. Putnam is concerned human cultures do not discuss differences very well. He surmises one of the reasons they disagree obdurately, at times, is because words are confused with the real process of reflection. The best things in life are not about words. They are about the relationships the words imply. Confusing the word with the thing can cause severe misunderstandings. The Continental tradition has produced several philosophers who were very excited about these kinds of problems.

"Here," Jean-Paul Sartre said, "we must face that unexpected revelation, the strip tease of our humanism. There you can see it, quite naked, an ideology of lies, a perfect justification for pillage; its honeyed words were only alibis for our aggressions."[17] Sartre called his autobiography *The Words*. He believed his life had been a morbid history of honeyed words. Near the end of *Being and Nothingness* (1943), Sartre screams into print the primal pain of a war-torn Europe:

> Thus the passion of man is the reverse of that of Christ, for man loses himself as man in order that God may be born. *But the idea of God is contradictory* and we lose ourselves in vain. Man is a useless passion.[18]

Sartre's cry is the anguish of a history without god, grief, or ethical introspection. Sartre's pain is the existential torment of a sensitive soul imprisoned in a culture of bad faith. It is impossible to be innocent in such a place. Existentialism is no longer in fashion. Sartre's philosophy may be passé, but his *Nausée* (1938) is not. Sartre's nausea is the emotional sickness of denied grief. His vertiginous sense of nothingness is the symptom of extreme moral paradox. His visceral longing for moral certainty is a symptom of the legitimation crisis in late modern life. Sartre's anti-hero, Roquentin, confronts the most personal of all reference problems in the form of a chestnut tree just outside Bougainville. The feeling Sartre describes is the visceral self-loathing of a man facing his own complicity with evil:

> It was the chestnut tree. Things – you might have called them thoughts – which stopped halfway, which were forgotten, which forgot what they wanted to think and which stayed like that, hanging about with an odd little sense which was beyond them.... And I was inside, I with the garden.... I hated this ignoble mess ... filling everything with its gelatinous slither.[19]

Roquentin's melodramatic depression mirrored the disillusionment of many Europeans after World War I. Roquentin's rant fails as philosophy, but it excels as an honest confession of grief. It succeeds as a sensory illustration of the difficulty Habermas and Putnam were trying to warn us about. Roquentin's emotional breakdown is the primal scream of a modern skeptic whose language has failed. The semantic potential of his church, his politics, his art and culture are no longer sufficient for his life. He has no thoughts of his own. Normative adjustment has degraded his spirit. He is a creature of time and place. Roquentin is that most desperate of human beings – a man absolutely alone – a man without a soul in the world to share his pain.

Michel Foucault called Sartre a terrorist thirty years before the word was in fashion. Sartre's nausea terrorized Foucault. My perspective is that Continental philosophy is the Kantian unconscious of modern history. It is the moral mirror of a bourgeois history the Romantics turned inside out and then tried to deny altogether. The late modern linguistic turn was taken by real-life people like Roquentin who believed their language had been robbed of its moral power. They were sickened by the violence politely mirrored in the politics of their time. Roquentin's "nausea" is the reason for postmodernism and the late modern linguistic turn. The semantic heritage of modern history is Roquentin's spiritual disease. He is sick from its honeyed words. The word world weighs heavily on his heart. The word pictures of modern progress have not comprehended the violence and suffering which have accompanied them. They have trapped him in their coils. The sweet dreams of history have him in their grasp. Roquentin's revulsion at seeing himself mirrored in the violence of history reverberates across half a century. He is sickened by the sight of what he has become and sickened by the fact he became it all unawares. He was guilty before he realized it. The world had turned him inside out and he had never seen it coming. Roquentin is the existential heir of Hegel's infinite grief. He cannot stomach what history has done to the heritage he once thought he knew and knows, with certainty, he still loves. Roquentin was a direct inspiration for the postmodern movement in France. He was also the historical product of a great collective grief. Roquentin is the modern voice of that deepest and maddest of sorrows. He is the grieving skeptic for whom words have failed. He is Hegel without the opiate of history.

Roquentin dramatizes the guilty side of the Kantian moral conscience. Kant's ethics are the background of the novella. Sartre could not have published *Nausée* if Europe's leading intellectuals had not been reading Kant. The intellectual history behind the dramatism is, I hope, at least as useful as Roquentin's morbid suffering. The history of Roquentin's grief goes back to Europe's historical Enlightenment. David Hume was the greatest skeptical philosopher of the Scottish Enlightenment. He had bouts of suicidal depression which he called "the academic disease." History saved him from it. Hume believed in history and he made a relatively good living writing it. Hume's expository brilliance was audacious at the time. He believed modern history had given the old moral theology a scientific foundation. Hume's secular faith in modern history was the perfect foil for a moralist like Immanuel Kant. Kant thought modern history was the enemy of moral progress. Hume and Kant were divided by their attitude toward modern history. The division between them was touted by the Romantics of the next century. The Romantics wanted a world rigidly divided between history and ethics. They chose Hume over Kant and Hegel over the whole pre-modern moral tradition. Hume and Kant were divided over history, but they were united in their opposition to the perspective which prevailed in Europe in the next century. Hume and Kant wanted ethics to be a practical force in modern history. They both wanted a unified world united in peace.

In many ways postmodernism and the late modern linguistic turn are a return to the great moral debate between Hume and Kant. Most of the characters discussed here have re-read the Hume/Kant debate and rejected the conventional interpretation of it. Their "deconstruction" of modern intellectual history is difficult to penetrate because their critical premises are not widely discussed. This extended essay defends postmodernism and the linguistic turn. It suggests postmodernism grew out of a widespread dissatisfaction with Hume's and Hegel's confidence in modern history. This essay suggests the premises for the "post-" this and that movements of the late twentieth century were a positive reaction to a fundamental misreading of modern intellectual history. The Romantics of the nineteenth century entrenched their conventional explanations of how skeptics do ethics in modern academic culture. Postmodernists wanted to change the way skeptics do ethics so they had to challenge those conventional explanations. Their topics and their writing style reflected the perceived failure, in their minds, of modern ethical theory and moral practice at the most basic level of modern life.

From the perspective developed here, modern intellectual history is not a footnote to Plato, as Whitehead imagined. It is a seminar on Immanuel Kant. Major conceptual problems with the skeptical attitude were openly admitted in the eighteenth century. Kant summed them up. His secular summae were seriously bowdlerized in the Romantic era which followed the French Revolution. Hegel is the arch-villain of this piece, even though his grief is honest and his hopes are humane. Hegel mugged Kant's ethics and bequeathed to us a moral pabulum of predigested political aestheticism. The most contentious and misunderstood issues in modern intellectual history derive from the aesthetic reading of Kant's philosophical opus passed down to us from the Hegelians at Marburg University in the 1860s. It may be crediting academics with too much influence, but I believe they have been instrumental, in some instances, in driving the world mad.

Immanuel Kant believed science was "intelligible." He did not say "right" or "corresponding to reality." He said it was intelligible because it was internally coherent with itself from top to bottom in all parts of the known universe, with no exceptions, no exclusions, and no special exemptions. The ultimate measure of "intelligibility" was what Kant called a "categorical imperative." The "intelligibility" of science was a "categorical" fact. Kant tried to make the logical standards of modern science into a secular standard for the modern moral life. He believed a moral life was intelligible from top to bottom in every place, in every time with no exceptions, no exclusions and no special exemptions. Kant thought men of science had to live up to their own intellectual standards because it was the only way they could live a moral life. Lampe, Kant's moody manservant, is said to have complained Kant's philosophy was destroying his faith. Kant assured Lampe he wanted "to make room for faith."[20] Kant's faith is moral faith. Kant believed the ethical philosophies of the world's great religions were compatible with science. Science could not prove the existence of God, but it could prove the truth of God's moral teachings. Kant understood a personal grief like Hegel's. He knew the deracinated moral life would be a life of loneliness and despair. His "categorical imperative" is a prescription for psychological and emotional health in a skeptical world that does science.

Modern intellectual history has shown less attention to these old Kantian questions than they deserve. Kant explicitly believed in science. He did not hide his faith. What do the moderns believe in? What are the explicit categories of their diverse and disputed faiths? What gods govern the word world wars of late modern culture? The late modern linguistic turn and postmodernism saw the language of modern public life as a categorical problem. Low language standards had made slogans, shibboleths, and buzzwords the measure of modern faith. Language had, as

Field and Putnam concluded, become something transcendental. Words with a meaning in themselves had become corrosive to ethical philosophy and moral practice. Rhetoric had replaced faith. Talismanic words became the highest measure of mutual understanding. Modern language became the magic mirror where soft-core solipsists saw only their personal view of the world. Obligation was unsayable, ethics were unintelligible, and traditional morality was all but impossible in the chaos of a world where words rule and reason is speechless.

This book reflects a condition of chronic consternation I have felt all my adult life. On the up side, the research gave an old skeptic the opportunity to scrounge intellectual history for the long-lost solace of his childhood faith. On the downside, it has not repaired the innocent idealism which seemed so palpable when I was young. If I could go back in time before the race riots, the Vietnam War, the Nixon shocks, Iran, Afghanistan, Reaganomics, and the Bush men, I would tell that innocent idealist to take Kant's advice: "Make room for faith." In the immortal words of Miracle Mets relief pitcher, Tug McGraw: "You gotta believe," kid. What religious traditionalists, philosophical realists, and political idealists call utopian, a skeptic calls survival. The no-gloss, full-time skeptic has no other world but this one. S/he had better believe it can work. The shortest and fastest route to nausea is lost faith in the only world for which there is credible evidence. In a skeptical world room for faith is room for everyone. The leading exponents of a consistently skeptical position have all believed the human race can live in peace. They believe the economy and the spirit can coexist. They have all been deep green boosters of a better world. Violent superstition is difficult for a no-gloss, full-time skeptic to comprehend. Pious citizens of the economically developed world have no reason to be proud. Among the most violent of modern superstitions their political abstractions have prominence of place. Western politics (absent the God its politicians claim to worship) has made a secular trinity of democracy, freedom, and global development. These Molochs of modern political correction have been drafted into the service of every violent double standard in the world. They illustrate a practical reason for Putnam's theoretical concern. The language of modern politics has become something transcendental. Those interested in avoiding the existential forest around Bougainville might appreciate the story of how it happened.

The challenges of this project require a cautionary paraphrase from Theodore Adorno. He often warned about the implications of discussing qualitative terms like ethics, truth, and culture. Discussing them does not mean, perforce, you have them. I must emphatically repeat Adorno's warning. The story here has become, Dan McAdams might say, the story I live by. However, like Proust's "poor old Swann," I think about it more often than well.

I owe an expression of gratitude to several people. Doug Sprague, Dawne McCance and Lionel Steiman commented patiently on early drafts. Sprague helped me put the philosophy in plain language. Klaus Klostermaier was the first reader to realize the modern language problem is an ethical problem. Brian Wiebe called my attention to the importance of Wittgenstein. David Manusow helped me see the whole thing more clearly. The editors at University of Calgary Press have been unflaggingly patient. I am grateful. I trust the *demarche* described in this book has not yet degraded common sense to the point of blaming these generous people for my errors and omissions.

CHAPTER ONE:
# *HUME'S PREDICAMENT*

> An individual, assumed to be the standard exemplar of an invariant humanity, faces his world. How can he think it, conceptualize it, comprehend it? ... In the end, the greatest classics articulating this vision will remain David Hume's Treatise of Human Nature and Kant's three Critiques.[1]
>
> — ERNEST GELLNER

**IAN HACKING (1975)** is concerned about the public appropriation of Enlightenment thought for general use in situations for which it was not intended. Hacking makes a strong case for one of the central concerns of this extended essay. Language matters to history *and* philosophy because the language of Enlightenment philosophy has become the language of democratic politics. The problem is particularly acute in the United States. Since words do not have a timeless meaning and modern times require so many words, Hacking believes the essential link between words and things has come unglued.[2] "It is widely held among modern analytic philosophers that such writers as Locke and Berkeley ... were working on something structurally similar to our problems," he observes. Hacking believes the prevalent opinion is an anachronism. In fact, modern thought has not taken the trouble to reconstruct the original frame of reference in which the early rationalists were working. Contemporary thought uses Enlightenment ideas in a different context from the one for which they were intended. "We have replaced [their] mental discourse by public discourse and 'ideas' [in their terms] have become unintelligible," Hacking concludes.[3]

The "mental discourse" which modern politics blandly appropriated was concerned with perception and whether the senses could be trusted. This problem was finally articulated in its modern form by Hume. Hume's formulation still presents major difficulties for philosophical realists, theologians, and philosophers of history. W.V. Quine believed, "On the doctrinal side, we are no further along today than where Hume left us. The Humean predicament is the human predicament," he explained. The crux of the predicament is "Hume's fork." It has systematically sapped the moral courage of politics and piety for two hundred years. The plain language philosopher, J.L. Austin, warned it has remained "inexplicit" in modern history of ideas. A.J. Ayer said, pointedly, it left us "unable to accommodate mental events." On account of it, Michael Dummett calls modern language "incomplete." C.I. Lewis made the behavioural effects of Hume's fork the fundamental issue in American pragmatism. These warnings would appear to merit historical consideration.[4]

### HUME'S FORK

Hume's *Treatise of Human Nature* (1739–40) was not well received, so he split it into two "Enquiries" which were shorter and easier to read. One studied "human understanding" (1748) and the other looked into ethics and morals (1751). The latter is considered the lesser of the enquiries. *An Enquiry Concerning Human Understanding* holds Hume's most famous and enduring contribution to modern thought. He proceeds there, no less, to the skeptical destruction of cause and effect in all relations concerning matters of fact. Hume begins his nonplussed destruction of the very foundation of Aristotelian certainty with a simple division of knowledge known as Hume's fork:

> All the objects of human reason or enquiry may naturally be divided into two kinds, to wit, relations of Ideas and Matters of Fact.[5]

Ideas are principally the truths of mathematics and logic. Hume believes them to be discoverable by "the mere operation of thought." Matters of fact are not discoverable by thought. They are the "truths" about how people actually behave and how physical nature really works. Hume called these areas of study the "natural sciences." Hume's natural science includes the "social sciences" of sociology, psychology, history, anthropology, and political studies. There was no sociology, psychology, or academic anthropology in Hume's time. Hume denied the "natural sciences" were understandable theoretically. Matters of fact could only be understood by observation. All facts are distinct matters and do not cohere by nature or in and of themselves. Matters of fact are contingent truths which only *seem* to be founded on an absolute relation. Hume then blithely proceeds to destroy the credibility of our normal perception of the causal relation between ideas and events.

Hume's destruction of cause and effect poses the largest general problem in modern thought. He bases his critique on a simple analogy from the game of pool:

> When we look about us towards external objects and consider the operation of causes, we are never able, in a single instance, to discover any power or necessary connexion.... The impulse of one billiard ball is attended with motion in the second. This is the whole that appears to the outward senses. The mind feels no sentiment or inward impression from this succession of objects.... The power of force which actuates the whole machine is entirely concealed from us, and never discovers itself in any of the sensible qualities of body.[6]

The skeptical modern mind of which so many proper people have been rather improperly proud was invented in a poolroom. "In a word, then," Hume wrote, "every effect is a distinct event from its cause.... Ultimate springs and principles are totally shut up from human curiosity and inquiry."[7]

We see the billiard balls collide and learn to expect similar outcomes. Our proud tower of reason is but a habit to which we have been conditioned. We never "see" a cause nor know a quality that, in itself, is recognizable as the "effect" which the cause has added to an object. Hume's mechanical reductionism is the philosophical culmination of Descartes' egoistical detachment. David Hume completed the Cartesian project of radical doubt by demonstrating that cogitation does not have to account for history, society, and law. "Natural necessity forces reason in the direction of a society. The need to survive will create a culture. Hume replaces God in the Cartesian Christian system of radical doubt with "natural necessity" and the brute, physical drives that constitute "human nature."

In his *History of Scepticism* (1979), Richard H. Popkin identifies Hume as the first philosopher to systematically doubt both faith and knowledge. All the major skeptics in the modern tradition before him had accepted one side or the other of the major division in the modern concept of truth.

They were either fideists who doubted knowledge in order to cling to faith or they were rational theists who used knowledge to prove the efficacy of faith. Popkin writes, "It was not until Hume that someone appeared who was both a religious sceptic and an epistemological sceptic."[8] Hume knew total skepticism could not sustain human community or historical continuity unless there were constants in the new relative universe of human experience. He thought he had an intellectual ace up his skeptical sleeve. He believed there was a type of knowledge which needed neither faith nor philosophical first principles. The practical knowledge which cut a middle way between religious dogma and philosophical opinion was history and the practical effect of that knowledge was a trustworthy public record and a morally responsible political debate.

History records the stability of habit and the goad of necessity, but "ultimate springs and principles are totally shut up from human curiosity and inquiry," Hume opines.[9] People study history to understand custom and necessity. "Nor have philosophers ever entertained a different opinion from the people in this particular," Hume believed. "What would become of history ... *politics* ... *morals* ... *criticism* ... without acknowledging the doctrine of necessity," he asks? The maxim of necessity governs our "*inference* from motives to voluntary actions, from characters to conduct."[10] Progress is inevitable. The progress of reason will be driven by human misery and our "mutual dependence" for each other. Metaphysical speculation and moral abstractions about duty and conscience are unnecessary in the real historical world reason has opened up before us. There is a powerful and appealing pragmatism to Hume's argument. In a world dominated by church and aristocracy the plain truth helped the majority escape from what Kant called "self-incurred tutelage." A famous skeptic in the next century would call the same condition "false consciousness."

Hume put the substance of the matter for him in two sentences:

> Mankind are so much the same, in all times and places, that history informs us of nothing new or strange in this particular. Its chief use is only to discover the constant and universal principles of human nature.[11]

Human nature was Hume's bottom line. The poets and historians of the next century would revel in it. Hume revelled in it for a different reason. Hume thought the historical record "proved" the futility of the aristocracy and the church. History was the record of how "real people" have coped. Hume has complete confidence in the customary coping strategies of the people. It was obvious the life habits, attitudes, and values of ordinary people were infinitely more survival worthy than the puffed-up virtues of priests and landed aristocrats. Hume's common sense attitude addressed a rigid class society. It was not articulated for the mass culture which begins with the industrial revolution.

In *A Treatise of Human Nature* the great skeptic exclaims:

> Take any action allow'd to be vicious: Wilful murder, for instance. Examine it in all lights, and see if you can find that matter of fact, or real existence, which you call vice. In which-ever way you take it, you find only certain passions, motives, volitions and thoughts. There is no other matter of fact in the case. The vice entirely escapes you, as long as you consider the object.

Stephen Darwall cites this passage as an example of "Hume's challenge" to traditional metaphysics. A disquieting event like a wilful murder can be broken down into an infinite number of observable matters of apparent fact. Add all the facts up in as great a detail as you like and you still will not reach a qualitative total that adds up to interpersonal regard and moral concern. The sum of the qualities which make a wilful murder vicious [cruel, horrible, repugnant, mean, etc.] is not a matter of fact. Hume's question is: Where does a categorical quality like cruelty originate? "It lies in yourself, not in the object," Hume explains.[12]

Where do ideas come from, Hume asks? From necessity, the effect of material need and human drives on mutual experience. History shows Hume:

> The mutual dependence of men is so great in all societies that scarce any human action is entirely complete in itself or is performed without some reference to the actions of others.

The more complicated a society becomes, the more men depend on "a greater variety of voluntary actions which ... cooperate with their own."[13] We have to realize, Hume contends, that principles like cause and effect, freedom and necessity are merely verbal representations of physical experience. They are not "secret forces" which constitute the nature of experience. Behind experience is the brute disposition of our physical bodies. Discussing the physical impressions lodged upon our senses is the only way progress can be made and vapid quarrels over chimaeras can be ended.

> It seems certain that, however we may imagine we feel a liberty within ourselves, a spectator can commonly infer our actions from our motives and character.[14]

Our motives are physical need and our character is a social construct. Hume's concept of experience is strictly physical. The imagination cannot correctly infer anything beyond the customary connections to which physical experience has conditioned it.

The philosophical term for inferring big ideas from everyday experiences is called "induction." Hume has destroyed private induction in theory and left history as the plain proof only groups can do it. Hume conceded that "the conjunction between motives and voluntary actions is as regular and uniform as in any part of nature,"[15] but he added, casually, "this transition of thought from the cause to the effect proceeds not from reason."[16]

> *Such is the influence of custom* [my italics] that where it is strongest it not only covers our natural ignorance but even conceals itself, and seems not to take place, merely because it is found in the highest degree.... We are apt to imagine that we could discover these effects by the mere operation of our reason, without experience.... The mind can never possibly find the effect in the supposed cause by the most accurate scrutiny and examination. For the effect is totally different from the cause, and consequently can never be discovered in it.[17]

So, according to Hume, freedom, ethics, value, and reason are naturally conditioned. We get used to environmental conditions which we call by these exalted names. Law and culture are historical structures generated by necessity and chance just like the final configurations of the "colliding billiard balls" on his infamous pool table. They have vast relevance, but very little of the transcendental significance often associated with them. The human mind plays infinite tricks on itself, distilling the virtues of group survival down to short-hand terms that it then praises to the skies.

Hume admits the "skeptical solution" to these "doubts" might have something to do with the failure of language:

> It might reasonably be expected in questions which have been canvassed and disputed with great eagerness, since the first origin of science and philosophy, that the meaning of all the terms, at least, should have been agreed upon among the disputations, and our enquiries, in the course of two thousand years, been able to pass from words to the true and real subject of the controversy.[18]

The sly old fox knows fully well what he is up to and reading him is still an intellectual pleasure. Hume's world is of eggs, and the gout, billiard balls, milk, and bread. If anyone wants proof that boxcar logic is not an indispensable ally of criticism, read David Hume.

In common practice, "men begin at the wrong end of the question," Hume continues. They should not start with an idea, but with the brute experience of necessity and see where that leads them:

> Let them first discuss a more simple question, namely, the operations of body and of brute unintelligent matter; and try whether they can there form any idea of causation and necessity, except that of a constant conjunction of objects, and subsequent inference of the mind from one to another. If these circumstances form, in reality, the whole of that necessity which we conceive in matter … the dispute is at an end; at least must be owned to be thenceforth merely verbal.[19]

Hume's *Enquiry* attempts to lead us to admit that "regular conjunction produces that inference of the understanding, which is the only connexion that we can have any comprehension of."[20] The truth about history and philosophy, for Hume, is that people never take action against habit and custom except under compulsion. Hume believed the compulsive element need not discourage reason from pursuing its own Enlightenment. Metaphysical objections to the evident logic of necessity were merely "verbal inconveniences." A clear understanding of the role of language in public life would correct these difficulties. Reason had nothing to fear from admitting its dependency on the material and the real. In fact, by framing our mutual dependency in the right language, reason would be assured.

History was supposed to be the right language in which to discuss how people actually live. In the eighteenth century Voltaire, Hume, Gibbon, Millar, Robertson, and Moser wrote political history in the style of the old church chronicles. Material and political progress was their new church. Historical study was the literary rage of the eighteenth century. Hume described historical study as "the easy and obvious philosophy."[21] It was the preferred form of critical reflection for people with a practical bent. Hume conceded there might be a problem:

> Were the generality of mankind contented to prefer the easy philosophy to the abstract and profound, *without throwing any blame or contempt on the latter*, it might not be improper to comply with the general opinion [emphasis added].[22]

Hume criticized "the easy philosophy" with disingenuous reluctance because, he said, people were inclined to use it *against* the "abstract and profound" philosophy. "The easy philosophy" could be used to obstruct more profound investigations into the principles of human understanding.

Hume was not being candid. He did not really believe the "easy" and the "abstract" were in conflict. Hume wanted to prove the conclusions of abstract philosophy were just common sense. He thought history was a resource for the skeptical simplification of his era's most arcane debates. Hume had no idea the "easy and obvious philosophy" would become a political force in its own right. He could not anticipate nationalism, mass culture, media, and status consumption. The skeptical antagonism between "the easy" and "the abstract" philosophies brings us to some hard truths about the history of more recent times. Hume had no way to foresee the history that was to come and the role his language would play in it. His own approach was direct, honest, and designed to defend everyday values that had changed little in over five hundred years.

Hume said philosophers of the 'easy' way:

> Paint virtue in the most amiable colours; borrowing all helps from poetry and eloquence.... They select the most striking observations and instances from common life; place opposite characters in a proper contrast; and alluring us into the paths

of virtue by the views of glory and happiness, direct our steps in these paths by the soundest precepts and most illustrious examples. They make us *feel* the difference between vice and virtue; they excite and regulate our sentiments; and so they can but bend our hearts to the love of probity and true honour.[23]

Given these high hopes, "It may be a subject worthy of curiosity, to enquire what is the nature of that evidence which assures us of any real existence and matter of fact, beyond the present testimony of our senses," Hume is slyly asking what easy principle bends our feelings to the same noble ideals as the old abstractions and profundities?

His answer is relatively obvious from the kind of writing Hume himself often did. The history which Hume wrote to keep the wolf from his door was easy and obvious. It was not social or intellectual. It was political. Hume turned to political history after he was denied tenure for the second time.[24] The popularity of the English translation of Voltaire's *Century of Louis XIV* (1739) gave Hume the idea for a similar career coup in England.[25] His history of England appeared in 1754. Popkin and Norton point out that Hume's attitude toward history and historical philosophy was always cavalier. He refused to have his 1741 essay, "Of the Study of History" included in the later editions of his collected works. It could "neither give Pleasure nor Instruction – a bad imitation of the agreeable Trifling of Addison," he complained.[26] David Hume had a use for history, although he did not believe his theory of history should be included among his collected works.

Hume's use for history was its profoundly impressive documentation of the mutual dependency of humankind. He used history to argue that we can "infer" the motive of an action or the likely action that will follow upon a given condition because "the *union* betwixt motives and actions has the same constancy as that in any natural operations, so its influence on the understanding is the same" [as in any other natural operation].[27] Therefore, Hume continued:

> In judging of the actions of men we must proceed upon the same maxims, as when we reason concerning external objects. When any phenomena are constantly and invariably conjoin'd together, they acquire such a connection in the imagination, that it passes from one to the other, without any doubt or hesitation.[28]

From reading history, Hume comes to the unequivocal conclusion that human beings never act under the influence of ideas and never really know what they are doing. He continued with sanguine aplomb:

> All inferences from experience are effects of custom, not of reasoning.... Without the influence of custom, we should be entirely ignorant of every matter of fact beyond what is immediately present to the memory and senses.[29]

Discussing matters of fact involves human beings in the use of misnomers like "reason," "understanding," and "cause and effect," which most people do not understand at all. There is even the possibility, Hume continued, that "while we study with attention the vanity of human life ... we are, perhaps, all the while flattering our natural indolence, which, hating the bustle of the world and drudgery of business, seeks a pretence of reason to give itself a full and uncontrolled indulgence."[30]

## SENTIMENT

Hume answers the moral dilemma of his skeptical fork with a direct defence of sentiment. Hume thought ethics were safe from harm because "morality is determined by sentiment." The skeptical attitude awoke the viewer to the great wisdom of ordinary life. It broadened the affections and made them susceptible to real events affecting the here and now. Skepticism had no negative effect on morals because the impartial attitude saw "virtue to be whatever mental action or quality gives to a spectator the pleasing sentiment of approbation, and vice the contrary." Moral sentiment "arises entirely from ... the structure of human nature," Hume had concluded. By structure, Hume means the social structure – the everyday structure of human association. Human affections are schooled by association with others. No philosophical doctrine (even his own) could ever injure ethics because:

> The ultimate ends of human actions can never, in any case, be accounted for by reason, but recommend themselves entirely to the sentiments and affections of mankind, without any dependence on the intellectual faculties.[31]

Sympathy for others comes naturally as a result of the human condition. The sympathy for others that is a natural characteristic of society protected skeptical philosophy from consorting with any issue pernicious to the general good.

In "Why Utility Pleases," in *An Enquiry Concerning the Principles of Morals* (1751), Hume explains, "The intercourse of sentiments, therefore, in society and conversation, makes us form some general unalterable standard, by which we may approve or disapprove of characters and manners." Though individuals may feign eccentricity and indifference, social structure determines the general character of free debate, "being sufficient, at least, for discourse, [to] serve all our purposes in company, in the pulpit, on the theatre, and in the schools." History is a record of those sentiments learned in common and common to us all. Hume believed, "The perusal of a history ... would be no entertainment at all, did not our hearts beat with correspondent movements to those which are described by the historian."[32]

Hume left history with a Romantic fallacy the next era was quick to use without a footnote or an asterisk. Hume believed in a structure of feeling common to all human beings. He did not extend his ruthless destruction of ideas to the acquisition of moral sentiments. Hume found a significantly modern escape clause for his otherwise absolute indifference to abstract ideas. Language is a pivotal ambiguity in Hume's moral system. He opens his *Enquiry Concerning the Principles of Morals* (1751) with the following disquisition on language:

> There has been a controversy started of late ... concerning the general foundation of morals; whether they be derived from reason, or from sentiment.... It is needless for us, at present, to employ farther care in our researches concerning it.... *The very nature of language guides us almost infallibly* [my italics] in forming a judgment of this nature.... It is probable, I say, that this final sentence depends on some internal sense or feeling, which nature has made universal in the whole species. For what else can have an influence of this nature?[33]

From passages like the above, one might believe Hume answered his own paradox. One might conclude Hume anticipated the Romantic reaction to Enlightenment skepticism.

Hume's use for sentiment foreshadows a major difficulty in modern intellectual history. There are two related issues. Hume identified both issues without explaining the problematic intertwining of them. The issues are language and sentiment. Language identifies matters of fact and sentiment influences the relations of ideas. Language, then, in Hume's account bridges his skeptical fork. Language permits human life to go on in coherent and intelligible ways even though we are thoroughly and pre-consciously conditioned by the brute forces of our physical environment. David Hume turns to the distinctively human phenomenon of language for an answer to his skeptical moral dilemma. His easy and obvious salve for the deep body blow skepticism had given philosophy is easy to defend, but not easy to justify, nor can the inherent intelligibility of his solution be considered obvious.

When Hume split the *Treatise of Human Nature* into two parts, he also reorganized the argument. He posed a devastating practical problem for reason in *An Enquiry Concerning Human Understanding*. Reason, properly, has no word for how ideas *should* be used. Reason has no con-science. Hume concluded the first *Enquiry* with an upbeat defence of science and empirical observation. Reason can bridge the gap between fact and value, but it must use the same patient skills of observation and organization that were beginning to pay such vast dividends in applied science. Everything else must be "consigned to the flames." Hume left the first enquiry dangling over a moral dilemma. He answered the dilemma in the second and lesser half of the rewritten *Treatise*.

The second and lesser half of the rewritten *Treatise* is *Enquiry concerning the Principles of Morals*. History provides the "scientific" evidence that morals are not threatened by skepticism and science. History was not moral by any means, nor should homilies be constructed from its examples. History was just a scientific record like astronomy and zoology. History accumulated evidence for studying the moral world just like astronomy had accumulated evidence for the Newtonian revolution in modern physics. Hume's casual confirmation of an easy and obvious answer to the skeptic's moral difficulties foreshadowed a dubious public practice in the eras to come. The language of traditional moral values and civic virtue was granted an historical life of its own. The qualitative terms of more credulous eras (from a skeptic's point of view) were declared still in force. God might have departed the known universe, but his language had not.

Consider this passage from *An Enquiry concerning the Principles of Morals*:

> From the apparent usefulness of the social virtues, it has readily been inferred by skeptics, both ancient and modern, that all moral distinctions arise from education, and were, at first, invented, and afterwards encouraged, by the art of politicians, in order to render men tractable, and subdue their natural ferocity and selfishness....

Hume's cynical paraphrase is as familiar to contemporary readers as it was to readers during the Enlightenment. To save virtue Hume has to find a disinterested explanation of why moral concepts persist. The passage continues:

> That all moral affection or dislike arises from this origin, will never surely be allowed by any judicious enquirer.

Rational inquiry into the matter of social virtue and personal morality has not been conducted fully and the empirical test of reason has not been extended to this important issue. Unprejudiced observation of the social virtues confirms common sense regarding the matter. When virtue is regarded as a natural phenomenon on the same order as sunrises and billiard balls all reasonable doubts regarding the efficacy of such virtues are laid to rest. The social virtues would not be universally acknowledged among all peoples in all times,

> Had nature made no such distinction, founded on the original constitution of the mind.

Unless a natural connection existed between

> The words, *honourable* and *shameful*, *lovely* and *odious*, *noble* and *despicable*, [they would] never [have] had a place in any language. Nor could politicians, had they invented these terms, ever have been able to render them intelligible, or make them convey an idea to the audience.

Thus the case was closed for David Hume. The historical evidence across cultures and eras indicates conclusively:

> Nothing can be more superficial than this paradox of the skeptics.[34]

The virtue of "an already formed language" saved skepticism from being gored on its own fork. Civic virtue, personal piety, and community values were safe from skeptical depredation because the language of virtue was hard-wired into the human mind.

Hume's solution to his skeptical moral dilemmas is problematic. He believed the sanctity of moral language written in virtual stone gave public access to private virtue on a global scale. Obviously, the world had nothing to fear from science, skepticism, and political demagoguery. Hume's faith in the language of public virtue is the easy and obvious mistake that carried a host of language "tricks" into modern public life. His easy answer to an obvious problem made politics and history the easy and obvious arbiters of civic virtue. The long-term social effects of this position have entailed a huge range of consequences in modern public life.

Hume's facile solution to the skeptical moral dilemma was a personal solution for the moral dilemmas of skeptics like himself. An honest, open-hearted person like Hume could not have anticipated the bad faith, commercialism, and petty chauvinisms of the nineteenth and twentieth centuries. Hume's world was a pre-industrial world of small businessmen, a rustic work ethic, and an obsolete aristocracy. He had little inkling of the double standards and bad faith in the extended and influential social circles that were to come. The natural language of social virtue he explains in the second *Enquiry* worked for Hume and the Scottish Enlightenment. The "mutual need" for social virtue was evident to them and they simply assumed the language of modern society was the natural topsoil where the old Christian virtues could still be cultivated.

In later years, politics and the economy eroded the sense of "mutual need" and the traditional virtue of the old language. When "mutual need" became a mass market, David Hume's staple language of social virtue was blighted. When the language of personal probity became the hype of modern nation-building, the "natural" connection between the mind and the old moral vocabulary was broken down. Hume's social world is gone, but his facile solution to the moral consequences of skeptical doubt remained behind. Public language in the modern democracies has not been saved from the devastating moral consequences of Hume's fork. Democratic due process faces its public moral problems across a devastating chasm between how things are and how things, arguably, ought to be. The sentiments invested in the keywords of the old moral vocabulary did not and cannot, in themselves, close the gap. The practical moral dilemma of Hume's naïve faith in language and the modern reluctance to face it is the reason for the late modern linguistic turn.

In Hume's homely world of pool, milk, bread, and the gout, "an already formed language" carried the everyday wisdom and practical traditions of a self-reliant and sociable folk culture. Hume believed ordinary language protected ordinary people from the abstruse and difficult abstractions of modern philosophy. The Humean predicament did not, in his opinion, affect daily life. The philosophical predicament he described mutates in the nineteenth century. It metastasizes in a direction Hume never anticipated. Industrialization and the emerging global economy did not suck up the healthy values of the folk community into the geo-political industrial context. What happened was an opposite and entirely untoward effect. The attitudes, values, and behaviours of geopolitics trickled down into ordinary life. The language of folk community is retained, but the meaning of many keywords was slowly transformed. Duty, virtue, strength, health, help, work, honour, loyalty, and the like took on a life beyond the horizon of most people's lives. The healthy honesty of "an already formed language" could not, in itself, protect daily life from the global realism, impersonality, and vast mutual suspicion that has become one of the most indescribably dispiriting aspects of the modern age.

To put Hume in context let us look at the way the world appeared to the great skeptic in the 1730s and 1740s when he was formulating his fundamental ideas. Hume's *A Treatise of Human Nature* had been received with incomprehension and derision. In an anonymous defence of it (1740), Hume said that his only wish was "that some expedient were fallen upon to reconcile philosophy and common sense."[35] It seemed only common sense to Hume that the everyday values of those who dug the ditches, did the work, fought the wars, and invented the new machines must triumph over useless pretension and mindless superstition. Hume's theory of sentiment was a "common sense" argument for the inevitability of freedom. The language of real work, real business, and real invention had to defeat the arrogant abstractions of elite philosophy and aristocratic culture. Hume's moral sentiments were simply common sense in the early eighteenth century.

The moral quandary for practitioners of Hume's common sense comes later. Hegel, in particular, took Hume's theory of sentiment out of context. In his historical context, Hume expected the real needs of a scarcity economy to overcome the imaginary needs of aristocratic class and religious superstition. He could not anticipate a world of effulgent plenty where status needs would take over from economic fundamentals. Hume's common sense is part of the early age of opposition to the perceived tyranny of kings and priests. Hume's defence of sentiment was common sense in opposition to superstition and scarcity. Hume's sentimental common sense is not wisdom for mass politics and popular culture in a society of post-scarcity plenty. Emotional and moral quandaries creep into them through the common language of popular history and public debate. Late modern skeptics can still share Hume's confidence in history, but they cannot share Hume's sentimental confidence in the language of history. History still writes large lessons for all segments of the public sphere to study and learn, but the language of history is no longer the language of common sense. The lessons of history are no longer the simple lessons of opposing a healthy everyday world to the sclerotic traditions of aristocracy and church. The everyday world in the developed democracies is now a status world of professional services, status consumption, and psychological need. Mass politics, popular culture, and middle-class values are the developmental norm held or desired by most of the world's people. After the French Revolution and the harnessing of steam, Hume's theory of language needed revision. The "structural" connection between human nature, sentiment, and key words like honourable, shameful, lovely, and noble needed to be revised. The words, themselves, were shifted in and out of currency like clothing styles, but the "structural" connection allegedly extant in mind and nature was rarely re-evaluated and never re-evaluated in the mainstream cultural canon.

Hume applies the skeptical knife to the raw nerve of aristocratic politics: "This principle is Custom or Habit," Hume concludes.[36] Vice is novelty. Virtue is habit. Other realists of the Scottish Enlightenment like Thomas Reid, Dugald Steward, and Francis Hutcheson doubted habit had a conscience. They tried to find a moral dimension for history in natural law or an implied social contract.[37] Hume thought history supported Pufendorf's theory of natural law and answered the pessimism of the contractarian debate Hobbes had begun. To cover his optimism Hume extended the Enlightenment idea of natural law debate in an unwarranted way. He resorted to an unintelligible sleight of the cultural invisible hand. It has been favoured by secular optimists ever since.

The next step for a gentle skeptic like Hume appeared so innocent and likely it has not been seriously questioned for over two hundred years. Hume declared the spoken and written languages of European public life were a direct reflection of human nature and a concrete correlate of progress. It was an innocent step, apparently warranted by common sense. Human nature was a constant in history. Material and political progress were constants in public life. The record of human progress reflected the same constancy. Hume thought human language – its mastery and public use – was the quantum rope bridge across his infamous skeptical fork. The relation between ideas and matter of fact found a constant and fulfilling presence in the language of ordinary experience. Hume adapted Locke's empiricism to the language of historical progress. By studying and debating what we have actually done, we give words a meaning that transcend their relative context. In the language of literature, politics, and the pulpit, Hume found a solution to the skeptical dilemmas of moral solipsism and emotional isolation.

The turn to language was so easy and obvious, its philosophical dimensions were not remarked upon in a systematic way until much later. The truth about history is Hume had embarked on a quantum leap of secular faith. His sentimental appeal to modern language is a cornerstone of democracy and humanities studies at the university. Hume's linguistic turn gave new art forms like the novel and the new public language of the coffee houses a dignity they had not, heretofore, enjoyed. Hume gave the language of history the same significance in public life as the language of numbers in nature. He gave literacy the same relevance in history that mathematics had in physics. He believed the application of history to human nature would be just as effective as the application of mathematics to problems of a physical nature. History would, in time, build an "easy and obvious" language for resolving the political and moral enigmas of modern life.

Anthony Flew has summarized the skeptical predicament for Hume. Classical philosophy held that we are:

> Supposed to be able to settle all questions about what *ought* or *ought not* to be done by an appropriately intellectual inspection of

the incorporeal Ideas; realities which are in Plato's own words, "a pattern laid up in heaven" [arché-type].[38]

Flew explains that:

> Hume provides the first inspiration in modern times for all those who believe that value cannot be, and is not, embedded in the structure of things, but instead is, and must be some sort of projection of human desires and human needs.[39]

The definitive disconnection of whatever *is* the case from a critical idea things *ought* to be different is the deductive triumph of Hume's "fork." It is commonly called, "Hume's law."[40] The modern era is conceived under its sign and the public sphere proceeds under the burden of its ubiquitous interrogations.

Hume merely articulated what most Western literati already felt informally to be the case. In practice, everyday language crosses between the tines of Hume's fork everyday in every way imaginable. Flew uses the evolution of the common law as an example of how it happens. Presumed innocence evolved naturally from the conservative rule of custom by which Hume comprehends everything. "Until and unless we find particular reason to change our minds, we presume that the conservative rule holds true," Flew says.[41] Hume would not invite us to change our minds on the basis of an ideal indictment of anything for the simple reason that we have no way to know what an "idea" might be. The only thing that changes our minds is a new "is."[42] The presumption of innocence rests on the skeptical assumption derived from experience that most people are creatures of habit. Conformist attitudes are the reality inside most social groups. Since most people conform, most people are probably innocent of crimes. There is no idealism here. Presumed innocence is the habit of mind that comes from the normal conformist attitude.

The habitual and natural attitude is that most people cooperate and few commit crimes. We presume innocence on the basis of our habituation to the natural attitude. Flew writes:

> If this rule is accepted, then its built-in defeasibility can be most properly paraded as a trophy of Hume's philosophical investigations.[43]

External realists like Hegel, Ranke, Dilthey and the American intellectual historian, Leonard Krieger, wanted to display Hume's "natural attitude" as a spiritual idea. The alleged spirit of the laws has a fundamental ethical problem. Hume's faith in natural law is gold-plated natural conformity.

The presumption of innocence is not based upon the career of an idea come down to earth from some higher more inclusive Platonic heaven; it is based upon the preservation of convention. In Hume's world, resumed innocence is not an idea, it is a habit. The crime which breaks into the habit of social cooperation must be punished and prevented from happening again. In the skeptic's logic, change, deviation, uniqueness, and autonomy are conditions leading to crime. History raises consciousness when it describes ideas and events that are evidently in violation of the norm. The *ancien regime* shocked normative sentiment that was habituated by necessity to another, more realistic and, probably, more ethical "is." Hume's fork could be tuned to the contrasts between aristocracy and the people in the great age of Enlightenment levelling. The contrast between practical Plebeian "is" and fulsome aristocratic "is" constituted an *exposé* in the eighteenth century. The resulting indignation created the gold-plated illusion of an "ought."

Hume thought the mind of the masses was naturally healthy by virtue of living in close, real connection with others. The solidarities of physical need, local community, and natural sentiment protected them from the metaphysical illusions of the upper class. The norms of daily life among the masses of people did not pose a problem for the affable, personable, and agreeably extroverted philosopher. He did not foresee the dilemmas that were to come after industrial revolution and the rise of the modern nation state and the global political economy. He did not expect that the norms of daily interpersonal life could be influenced, even distorted, by the demands of national politics and a consumer economy. A late modern skeptic encounters difficulties Hume never imagined. They centre on norms, i.e., practical everyday attitudes and actions which have the force of habit and seem to arise from natural necessity. In the late modern global context of nations, consumers, and media, common sense encounters seemingly insurmountable ethical conundrums when the norm is the problem.

A mass society of relative plenty has no sentimental immunities against the metaphysical illusions Hume scorned in the *ancient regime*. The earthy wisdom of Hume's enlightened skepticism is foreclosed to late modern experience because of an obvious fact that simply has not been adequately factored into modern intellectual history. Hume's historical world was pre-industrial. It was a world of handicraft, local community, and traditional labour. Hume's emotional and psychological world held some differences from ours. The modern skeptic experiences Humean difficulties which need to be factored into intellectual history. Kant walked the midnight streets of Königsberg alone by memory without a light and without molestation. Adam Smith took it for granted no one would stay in business in London after they had made enough money to retire to the country. Machines were a product of cottage ingenuity and Blake's dark, Satanic mills had not yet despoiled the heart of faith. Squire, shire, heir, and looms still guided much of the countryside. The security of habits, rituals, and practices accumulated over centuries protected the people's sanity and morality. The French and industrial revolutions changed all that. Hume's skeptical faith in the language of the people was taken over by consensus politics and a consumer economy. The external and material realisms of power politics began a linguistic looting of Hume's innocent social virtues.

### KANT'S CRITIQUE OF HUME

Immanuel Kant called Hume "the acute man" to whom he owed "the first spark of light."[44] He made his famous admission in *Prolegomena to any Future Metaphysic* (1783): "I openly confess my recollection of David Hume was the very thing which many years ago first interrupted my dogmatic slumber and gave my investigations in the field of speculative philosophy a quite new direction."[45] Kant said it was "positively painful to see how utterly Hume's opponents, Reid, Oswald, Beattie and Priestley ... so misconstrued Hume's valuable suggestions [and so] that everything remained in its old condition, as if nothing had happened."[46] Reid, Oswald, Beattie and Priestley had not faced the skeptical moral predicament. Hume had made "valuable suggestions" which could not be ignored. Hume realized the world had changed and he had tried to change philosophy along with it. Kant had much more respect for Hume than for Hume's opponents. Hume's detractors wanted everything to remain the way it had been. They denied the world had changed and they denied that modern philosophy needed to change along with it.

Kant's insight is simple, but the consequences of it are vast. Hume thought individuals learn directly from experience. Kant's better insight is that individuals *do not* learn directly from experience. They do not absorb life lessons directly from head-on dialectical collision with the world. "The crooked timber of humanity" resists adversity *and* wisdom with equal determination. "Nature is very far from having adopted man as his special darling," Kant wrote. "Man is not only subject to plague, famine, flood, frost and attacks from other animals; but his own absurd natural predispositions land him in further troubles that he thinks up himself."[47] Hume's convivial optimism was not warranted by the facts. History showed Kant a "self-tutored" humanity with an heroic capacity for self-destruction.

Were traditional piety, duty, and spirituality even possible after David Hume? Did the modern world have room for ethics and ideals? Had science and history scrubbed the new world clean of all its old apprehensions – including the noble ones? What was to become of the old Christian values after the devastation of Hume's relentless fork? Kant boiled his concern down to three simple questions: "What, then, can we know?" "What ought we to do?" and "What can be hoped?"[48] These three questions from the first critique are basic to Kant's mature work. Each question corresponds to one of the great Critiques. What can be known is discussed in *Critique of Pure Reason*. What we ought to do is discussed in *Critique of Practical Reason* and what can be hoped was addressed in *Critique of Judgment*.

Hume's misunderstanding of his own predicament rested, for Kant, on a fourth question which Kant only raised in his university courses on logic. Hume was not able to answer the question, "What is man?"[49] Hume did not think he had to answer that question. History and the common sense of daily life would work out an answer in due course. Kant was disturbed by Hume's blithe optimism. In Kant's opinion human beings could not trust history to solve their problems. To make his concerns clear, Kant attacked Hume's logic. Hume was not thinking clearly, in Kant's opinion, because Hume did not understand the nature of experience. Hume believed empirical sensation was real and ideas were derivative. Kant took the opposite position. Kant took the position ideas are real and experience is based on our idea of it. Kant took this controversial position because he feared the moral and social effects of Hume's carefree optimism.

"Where Hume erred, or seems to have erred, both Kant and Wittgenstein had the better insight," P.F. Strawson concluded.[50] Experience is a fact given in the world outside of us, but we create what experience means for us by the way we sort, organize, and analyze it. The human mind has natural grids or pathways it uses to focus stimuli and synthesize impressions. They operate like psychological cisterns to catch, store, and organize the "sensory manifold" into practical patterns for everyday use. Thus, Kant concluded, we only know objects in the way the mind perceives them. We do not know objects in themselves. "Phenomena" belong to selective "categories" of organized impressions. What we know tells us more about ourselves than the fundamental nature of world. Attacking Hume for his radical empiricism lets Kant approach his devastating fork from a new angle. The nature of perception lets Kant introduce critical introspection into Hume's radical optimism.

Kant will, if he can, force Hume back to his Socratic roots. If Kant's theory of perception is correct, then self-knowledge remains the most important knowledge. If self-knowledge is the most important knowledge then Hume's fork is bridged. When we understand how the mind works, then we understand each other at a level that permits the heritage wisdom to work in ordinary daily life again. Self-knowledge at the basic level of how human beings filter, sort, and file information lets us understand each other. Epistemological self-knowledge permits us to learn from our shared experience and share what we have learned. It completes the gap between how things 'are' (for us) and how things 'ought to be' (for everybody). From Kant's perspective, Hume had overlooked these points.

Drawing on the work of his friend Crispin Wright, Paul Abela calls the famous "categorical imperative" nothing more than simple "empirical realism." Kant's "imperative" is a function of the mind. It is imperative for human beings to sort, organize, and analyze sensation. The mind is set up to perform these functions. They are basic to human life so they become reflexive. In competently socialized adults, sorting, organizing, and analyzing sensation involves a series of complex involuntary judgments just as vital and no less complex than the act of breathing. Competent adults are continually recreating the world with every word they utter and every act they undertake. The famous "categorical imperative" is not governed by an intuition of a higher good existing in some ethereal Platonic world of noumenal mind. It is the fundamental thought process that distinguishes the human mind. Categorical organization of sensation turns physical stimuli into experience. In human beings, the systematic categorization of sensation has replaced instinct in the lower animals. All human activity relies on reflexive categorical judgments. The world of categorical order is the real world human beings share. We do not share the world as it is, in itself. We share a world *which we have given ourselves*. Since we have created the world ourselves, we have moral responsibility for it. Good judgment is required to make the world logically coherent, universally inclusive, and mutually satisfactory.

The prior organization of sensory experience by what seems to us to be an 'intuitive' form of judgment is the strong force in human life. The effect is so powerful, Abela writes, that we accept it as a part of human nature, outside history and society. Hume committed this simple error of potentially devastating proportions. He took the order of history and society to be the order of nature. Kant foresaw a world of incredible pain if Hume's error were permitted to stand. To let daily life determine the quality of our judgment would be fatal to freedom, law, and the moral heritage of Western culture. "It would in essence be no better than the freedom of the turnspit," Kant warned. "Once wound up it would carry out its motions by itself."[51] An organized act of perception is involved in everything we do. Human beings have to nurture their ability to see the world in coherent patterns every day in every way during the course of ordinary life. The categorical imperative to develop good judgment is the psychological link between Kant's phenomenology of mind and the way skeptics do ethics.

Hume's 'easy and obvious' philosophy made the modern quality of judgment a casual affair. Human nature follows the path of least resistance and like water will seek its own level. Science and the people protect the stream of ordinary consciousness. Nothing is to be feared from history or human nature because progress is inevitable. Hume spoke for a new culture whose members claimed to see no danger in his devastating empirical skepticism. The morally devastating gap between what empirically 'is' and what logically 'ought' to be was a conceptual paradox with no real effect on daily life.

Kant's "categorical imperative" is the basic psychological criticism of Hume's skeptical position. Kant said that fundamentally we do not see the world the way Hume said. His radical criticism of Hume is one of the fundamental insights in modern intellectual history. P.F. Strawson (1959) credits Kant with achievements

> So great and novel that, nearly two hundred years after they were made, they have still not been fully absorbed.[52]

Kant made all conceptual understanding dependent on subjective categories of mind. The categories may be found on page 212 of the Cambridge edition of *Critique of Pure Reason* (1998).[53] The four general categories are quantity, quality, modality (states of being), and relation. They break down into sub-categories. Kant gives three each. One has the impression the categories may be sub-divided many times.

Strawson calls the categories an "empty I" and says they define no principle of unity between them.[54] Having the theoretical capacity to make up a world does not guarantee it will be fit for human habitation. Good judgment is required for the development of a human habitat. To develop some specie of plausibly good judgment we must habitually organize our perceptions of the world in the broadest and most logically inclusive way. We are, therefore, delivered by human nature into a world of freedom. We are free to create a world fit for human habitation. That is our only freedom. It is also our greatest potential threat to the viability of our species.

Hume built his view of the world from a diametrically opposite perspective from Kant. Paul Abela has summed up the philosophical position of a culture educated in the tradition of David Hume. His pithy motto links Hume's blithe optimism to the cynicism of modern culture. In a skeptical culture, Abela writes, "necessity is encoded in the mode of representation." This is Hume's predicament. He makes the normal into a necessity. He sells off moral, emotional, and intellectual freedom to pay for political and economic progress. He writes up philosophy and history in a way which makes history inevitable and moral freedom an illusion. His mode of representation is shallow and incomplete. It is damaging to everyday life, personal relationships, and the peaceful evolution of law. Ethics plays no substantial role in it. Ian Hacking calls Hume's predicament, "the depth knowledge of our time."[55] Abela, Strawson, and Hacking back Kant against Hume. They call Kant's categorical theory of perception realistic. They believe Kant saved the traditional capacity for moral judgment from destruction on the dialectical dilemma of Hume's disastrous fork. All skeptics who persist in the attempt to exercise moral judgment use a variation of the categorical approach to human perception first articulated by Kant.

Kant saw a danger in Hume's naïve idea of necessity. If raw experience ever became the arbiter of human life, there would be no moral judgment – no transcendental concepts, no truth, God, freedom, beauty, duty, right and wrong. The dignity of daily life would be destroyed. Individuals would be the pawns of historical forces on a global scale. Moral courage and personal responsibility would be subjective illusions long since left behind by the physical and social sciences. Kant did not live to see how or whether Hume's easy and obvious attitude caught on. Permit me, if you will, to cut to the proverbial chase. *It did!* Hume's "easy and obvious philosophy" defeated the more abstruse and abstract reflections on the subject. His lesser enquiry, *Enquiry Concerning Morals* now speaks for the times. It has become part of the "depth knowledge" of modern history. It has been put to a public use Kant could not have anticipated, but which he certainly would have deplored.

Hume's theory of language in the lesser enquiry on morals was the hook, line, and sinker that would catch up modern history in a self-taught crisis of blithe submission to perceived historical necessity. Hume left behind a sentimental system of moral complicity with the empirical data of raw history. Hume's naïve theory of language hauled up critical reflection from the depths of theology and philosophy to be boated, filleted, processed, and packaged for easy consumption. "The original constitution of the mind" guaranteed words like honourable and shameful, lovely and odious would always retain their power even though their meanings were undergoing continual change. The modern era did not need to nurture the process of meaning underwriting these and similar qualitative terms. Qualitative shibboleths from a previous age would serve modern politics, commerce, and empire with equal success. Kant could not foresee the language problem in a mobile, media society of science-based skeptics, but he foresaw a possible crisis. The crisis he foresaw was the moral surrender of human freedom to the raw forces of economics and history.

*The Critique of Pure Reason* (1781 & 1787), is Kant's first response to Hume's naïve theory of necessity. Kant hoped to end it there. He wanted to expose and close Hume's fork with one masterstroke. The first critique was intended to be hearth, anvil, and hammer with which a final answer to Hume was forged. Kant called *Pure Reason* "the elaboration of the Humean problem in its greatest possible amplification."[56] His hopes were not realized. *Pure Reason* was not well received. Most readers found it too dense. The two subsequent critiques were answers to the critics. He re-wrote the "Transcendental Deduction" of the first critique (1787) and published *The Critique of Practical Reason* (1788). *Practical Reason* tried to make the skeptical moral predicament 'easy and obvious' in a language reminiscent of Hume. *Practical Reason* has succeeded with generations of readers but the connection with *Pure Reason* has remained obscure. In the third critique, *Critique of Judgment* (1790) Kant tried to connect the first two. *The Critique of Judgment* is Kant's last attempt to warn the Enlightenment against the blithe optimism of David Hume.

I want to proceed with *Critique of Judgment* first, because it represents Kant's most strenuous effort to explain his work to his critics. In the opening pages of *The Critique of Judgment*, Kant explains the difference between the key terms *transcendental* and *metaphysical*. The normal use of the words was still Aristotelian. Kant undertook to re-think them. He points out the active verb difference between the two words. An individual may "transcend" in the sense of overcoming an obstacle or extricating herself from a difficulty. One does not "metaphysic" anything. The metaphysical is external to the physical world. Kant continues with a slight, non-controversial, emendation of Aristotle:

> The principle by which we cognize bodies as substances and as changeable substances is transcendental if it says that a change in them must have a cause; but it is *metaphysical* if it says that a change in them must have an *external* cause.[57]

Kant then applies his explanation of the difference between the transcendental and metaphysical to Hume's theory of causation. Hume's theory combines two contrasting concepts into one experience. Ordinary causation, like Hume's billiard balls is transcendental. Human beings invented it to describe serial changes in the quantity, quality, and intensity of the physical sensations they receive from the external world. When he explains transcendental causation, Hume has only addressed one form of causation in human experience. He has reduced all causation to its transcendental form. The neurological accuracy of Kant's distinction between the transcendental and the metaphysical is not historically important. What is important is the issue he confronted.

Kant has two significant concerns and they parallel his emendated distinction between the transcendental and the metaphysical. He calls one concern *practical* and he calls the other concern *pure*. His practical concern is duty. Duty comes from within. It is transcendental in the sense Kant uses the word. His pure concern is the law to which duty is obligated. The law, to be effective, must have metaphysical force. It must seem to come from a higher authority than ourselves. Human beings can create transcending ideas and transcendental moments. They cannot create the metaphysical. That must come from beyond the world of human experience. Hume's only metaphysical realm was the physical realm of brute necessity. In classical terms, Hume has introduced a dreadful fork into human experience. He has separated duty from the law. Hume has explained the world in a way such that duty is no longer relevant to a larger, higher and more inclusive world.

Kant realized the logical separation of duty from the moral law could have negative consequences on civil society and personal life. His solution was to look at Hume's predicament from the inside out rather than the outside in. He called his solution a second Copernican revolution. If he can demonstrate transcendental concepts like causation are natural functions of the mind, he can defend metaphysical concepts like God, immortality, and freedom as the natural extension of mind beyond our existence in a state of physical nature. Whatever their real standing as existents in some unknown "noumenal" universe, God, immortality, and freedom are the guideposts in our heads which indicate to us, in ordinary situations, the right thing for human beings to do. Even Hume's world is subject to this higher order of categorical considerations. Even Hume must obey the injunctions of his own mind. If the Humean mind has a higher order of regularity than mere individual response to stimuli, then Hume's devastating fork is closed and a brave new world of moral freedom is re-opened for enlightened skeptics in a science-based society.

Hume thought words were a natural connection between noble sentiments and social virtue. A natural feeling for the social virtues was excited by words like *honourable* and *shameful*, *lovely* and *odious*, *noble* and *despicable*. Kant completely disagreed. He distrusted feeling altogether and had no use for it as a defence of virtue and truth. "Feeling is not a faculty whereby we represent things, but lies outside our whole faculty of knowledge," Kant argued.[58] Reason could never disprove "a necessity which can only be felt," Kant concluded.[59] Feelings, for Kant, are "a logical peculiarity" we have. Kant only discusses feelings because of their powerful influence on judgment. Kant, personally, does not care for them. He once called marriage the legal right to rent another person's genitals. Feelings in private life and in high Rococo art, were merely sensations. They had to be understood as phenomena and then assigned consciously to the appropriate category of experience before they could be discussed.

Feelings had little practical use until philosophy deduced their "transcendental" foundation. (Remember, the "transcendental" is the idea which we give ourselves according to the natural function of our own minds.)

Kant was as plainspoken as he could be that:

> Virtuosi of taste, who not just occasionally but apparently as a rule are vain, obstinate and given to ruinous passions, can perhaps even less than other people claim the distinction of being attached to moral principles.... I am indeed quite willing to concede that an interest in the *beautiful in art* ... provides no proof whatever that a way of thinking is attached to the morally good, or even inclined toward it.[60]

Section 42 of *Critique of Judgment* continues by developing the pedagogical tone on which *Critique of Practical Reason* closed. Kant is not interested in the progress of art and the beautiful; he is interested in the "progress of the power of judgment."[61] He wants to use the language of Wolff, Baumgarten, and Leibniz to develop "the reflective power of judgment."[62] The power of judgment can build or destroy ideas. At this point, Kant felt his culture was morally challenged. Its collective power of judgment was weak. Classical debates over art and the ideal of the beautiful were the best examples of transcendental debates his society had to offer. They were sadly lacking in logical rigour, in Kant's opinion, but there you are: the aesthetic provided a place for a much-misunderstood moral philosopher to begin. The quality of ordinary, practical judgment is the point of the great critiques and aesthetics are Kant's primary example of how such a practice is constructed.

Kant's analysis of aesthetic judgment is often taken for a defence of the higher world of feeling. Holy art points human beings to a higher world. This reading is not supported in Kant's own words. Kant thought aesthetics provided clear anthropological proof human beings have the abstract capacity for transcendental judgment. The inexplicable (to Kant) brouhahas over fine art indicated how the power of aesthetic judgment works. Aesthetic judgment has the extreme peculiarity of bridging the transcendental and metaphysical worlds of experience. It appears externally as a law and internally as a source of duty. Aesthetics show an emotional commitment to a completely historical discourse that human beings have fabricated for themselves. It is both inside and outside the knowing subject. *Aesthetic judgment has both transcendental and metaphysical effects.* Aesthetics prove that human beings can create abstract principles to which they have fervent emotional allegiance in complete disregard, if not defiance of custom and necessity. People exercise this "strange" and "unusual ability" in theology and politics, frequently to their discomfiture.[63] They also do it in the arts. What they need to do in all such cases is understand the "discursive principles" at the foundation of the immense emotional regard they show for imaginary entities. With this advice and counsel, discourse theory enters modern intellectual history.

Kant was not artistically inclined. In his discussion of *Kant's Conception of Moral Character* (1999) G. Felicitas Munzel observes that, "Kant never treats beauty as the symbol of morality."[64] Peter Gay discovered that, "Kant found music irritating and painting boring – an engraving of Rousseau was the only picture in his house."[65] Kant thought that:

> If we search for a principle of taste that states the universal criterion of the beautiful ... then we engage in a fruitless endeavour.... I cannot dispute the preponderance of evils that the refinement of our taste to the point of its idealization, and even the luxury of sciences as food for our vanity, shower on us by producing in us so many insatiable inclinations.[66]

Kant entered this fray in order to falsify the skeptical position from within its own system of knowledge. Kant is the source of Karl Popper's theory of falsification. The only way, then and now, skeptics can be moved to action is to show them they themselves are the cause of their own problems. Skeptics believe only in what they have done or seen done. The appeal to an ideal world leaves the skeptical attitude cold.

*Critique of Judgment* attacks the skeptical attitude from inside its own intellectual vanity. If you are so objective, realistic, and "natural," Kant's argument runs, then how do you explain your irrational aesthetic "judgments of taste"? You admit, even boast, they "cannot be determined by a presentation of an objective purpose."[67] How then, do they come about? Kant's critique of judgment is not a defence of feeling. It is the classiest polemic in the history of Western philosophy. Kant invokes aesthetics to prove that Hume's radical empiricism forgets (conveniently) it is the author of its own aesthetic laws. Kant uses the language of Wolff and Baumgarten (the leading philosophers of Kant's time) to show how art is an example of self-legislated knowledge *a priori*. Art shows human beings can make up worlds and then regard them as if they were the most obvious and self-evident fact of nature. The aesthetic process turns transcendental (internal) experience into metaphysical (external) fact. The whole process is imperceptible to us. It happens before we notice it. Philosophy has to criticize resolutely the extended effects of this unusual ability on all aspects of civil, social, and economic life. Kant called that resolute criticism, "the critique of judgment."

Kant took the position a concept of the good could be built up in the same manner as a judgment of taste. This "strange" aesthetic ability we have could be used for something "practical." He believed the existence of art proved we can do this. That he outlines his system as a polemic against Hume's devastating fork does not preclude its compatibility with revealed religion and traditionally organized piety. Kant is devoted to dialogue. He wanted the practical effect of the critiques to transcend sectarian schism.

The sensory forms we use to represent the world become, in their practical effect, "principles of the *possibility of experience*," Kant points out.[68] Elsewhere Kant says that

> Upon them (as heuristic fictions), we may base regulative principles of the systematic employment of the understanding in the field of experience.[69]

Kant called the "principles of possible experience" by which competently adjusted people read their world "an a priori determining ground of the will."[70] He warned the culture vultures their "principles of possible experience" had to be coherent and taken from the real world. They had to be cared for and maintained like a corpus of "pure practical law." By "law" Kant meant an intelligible, historical law just like the civil and criminal law. He meant that skeptics have to give themselves intelligible forms for the organization of sensory experience just as surely, confidently, and competently as they do when they debate torts and precedents or lay down rules for portrait painting and musical composition.

In a sub-section to the "Transcendental Aesthetic" added to the second edition of *Critique of Pure Reason* in 1787, Kant warns against the moral effect of confusing nature with our organization of it for our own purposes:

> If we ascribe *objective reality* to these forms of representation, it becomes impossible for us to prevent everything being thereby transformed into mere *illusion*.[71]

The ethics of necessity will not awaken reason to action in a scientific society. Ethics based on the nature of mind will awaken reason to action, Kant believed, if mind is understood at its most basic, and powerful level. Truth, beauty, and justice beaming down from a Platonic world could never awaken the sleep-walking conformist to duty in the real world of Hume's devastating skepticism.

Kant believed formal structures have a "motivating drive" because they function as a schema for the organization of sensation.[72] Nature provides the sensory building blocks; the human mind creates an experience. The structure of an experience is portable. The mind moves successful schemas from place to place, sets up shop and processes the world all pre-consciously – *a priori* – while getting on with its conscious tasks. Schematic structures like poetry and music are not to be understood through the feelings they arouse. Formal structures exert their strongest force when abstracted from all interest. Kant argues we routinely do this. We routinely transpose formal structures of knowledge from one domain to another. Emotional attachment to a system of knowledge makes it available for use across the boards. Kant's theory of perception is, for this reason, rightly regarded as epistemological not aesthetic.

Kant used aesthetics as an example of how systems of knowledge work. Kant concluded that, "The hypothetical employment of reason has, therefore, as its aim the systematic unity of knowledge, and this unity is the *criterion of the truth* of its rules."[73] Kant's criterion of truth is its inclusiveness, not its beauty. The meaning of an experience is borrowed from the schematic whole of which it must be a part. Experience is impossible without the memory sorting it out and assigning it (all *a priori*, you understand) to a category of experience. The rational mind is "architectonic" to Kant. Since Kant we should have known that systems of knowledge inform our "habits of the heart." They are the "metaphors we live by," "the stories we live by," and they structurally determine "the politics of language."[74]

Hume had used differences in "taste" as concrete examples of skeptical relativism in "The Skeptic" from *Essays, Moral and Political* (1741–42). Kant quotes Hume:

> You will never convince a man who is not accustomed to Italian music and has not an ear to follow its intricacies that a Scots tune is not preferable.[75]

Hume revelled in the indisputable fact that some people prefer the bagpipes to Italian opera. It was a statement guaranteed to rankle Rococo sensibilities in the 1740s. Kant has not the slightest concern that some lowbrow might prefer a Scottish reel to a classical aria. Kant was aesthetically indifferent, but art was a "mental event" which the skeptic had to admit s/he could not account for. Hume's smart-aleck relativism only showed that everyone enjoys some liberating form of this peculiar mind-game. The sensory content of the game does not matter to Kant. In Kant, it is always the form that determines the meaning. Show me the form of a judgment, Kant cries, and I will show you a metaphysical meaning, a personal turnspit – one man's self-imposed determining ground for the will.

In reference to Hume's earthy aesthetic preferences, Kant remarks:

> Hence, although, as Hume says, critics can reason more plausibly than cooks, *they still share the same fate.*[76]

Art was a shared sign-system of sensory schema for which there was no natural necessity, yet skeptics accepted its existence as if it were an act of nature. Kant viewed aesthetics and the whole art-crit industry as a startling phenomenon. The high-brow critic and the ordinary reveller shared the same fate. From high to low, human nature revealed its most subtle secret in the moral anthropology of modern art.

Kant could not help noticing the existence of the art-critical world contradicted the foundational assumption of the skeptical attitude. Why would one have a preference in these matters at all? Why should anyone care about the difference between these intuitive forms of logical impossibility? Kant's philosophical interest is not the "right" aesthetic values. Kant's question is why aesthetic values exist. The skeptical position admitted no logical place for aesthetic values. Neither habit nor necessity could have created the Fine Arts. If left to necessity, they would likely come to an end. Yet even skeptics like the great Hume defended an aesthetic preference. Kant observed in the Fine Arts, "Man's aptitude in general for setting himself purposes." Fine Art illustrates the fundamental relation between man and nature. Man is continually "using nature as a means in conformity with the maxims of his free purposes generally."[77]

The Fine Arts proved to Kant that:

> It must be possible to think of nature as being such that the lawfulness in its form will harmonize with at least the possibility of ... freedom.[78]

The laws of artistic expression are not categories of metaphysical experience available to us through intuition. We know lawfulness because we see laws in operation in the world around us. Nature is a lawful system. Art proves that human begins can also create lawful systems. The ability to create law defines the nature of freedom. We are neither disembodied spirits nor Stygian shades. We are born law-givers and we had best take our human nature seriously.

Self-legislation in complete harmony with the well-being of others is, for Kant, the highest expression of freedom. The moral law, self-legislated and entire, brings together the formal patterns of regularity in physical nature with the categorical operations of human mind. Science, art, and ethics are congruent experiences in that they have the same categorical structures. Their inner logics obey the same master plan. Kant calls such congruencies, "the paralogism of pure reason." A completely intelligible experience is compatible with the way the mind functions. Our freedom, the integrity of our laws, culture, and politics – all these fine, high-minded things – consist, in practice, of being true to ourselves.

It is clear, Kant argues, that we give ourselves the Fine Art, Capital C Cultural world in plain defiance of the fact that it is just about the furthest thing from a natural necessity that a skeptic could possibly imagine. Equally clear is the fact that we must do it. The development of good judgment requires practice in self-legislative acts like art and law:

> The concept of the purposiveness that nature displays ... is a subjective principle that reason has for our judgment.... The principle is regulative (not constitutive), but it holds just as necessarily for our *human judgment* as it would if it were an objective principle.[79]

The art industry proves human beings have the capacity to live and love by acts of purely abstract judgment. For Kant, this fact was a source of unlimited hope.

"Experience consists not merely of feeling," Kant concluded, "but also of judgments."[80] Ideas, in time and space, provide unity for "empirical knowledge in general" and hold that knowledge "secured within its own limits."[81] He explained:

> One concept cannot be combined with another synthetically ... [without] a third something, namely, the condition of time-determination in an experience.... [These] discursive principles are therefore quite different from intuitive principles.[82]

"Discursive principles" constitute the mediating concepts in Kant's system and they are determined in time.[83] Feelings are rationally connected to objects by coherent "discursive principles." The principles are relative. They are the internalized history of the regulative principles civilized societies have composed for themselves. They are carried from person to person like any other rule-governed system. The rules change, the objects change, but the love of order, regularity, and pattern goes on. Even today, in non-representational art, the old language of aesthetic value still goes on. One wonders if the opportunity to externalize our feelings in real objects in real time and space has not always been the reason for art.

Kant's use of the phrase "discursive principles" does not refer to discourse in the same sense as Heidegger, Derrida, and Foucault. It anticipates them, but in Kant the word "discourse" means the regulatory laws that organize expression and make social life and civilized society possible. Structure and law are formal parallels in Kant's theory of mind. "Culture is intended solely to give a certain kind of skill and not to cancel any habitual mode of action already present," Kant observed.[84] Hume never said it better, but Kant went a step further. Even in aesthetics, he all but chortles, the skeptic, "must proceed when reflecting on the objects of nature with the aim of having thoroughly coherent experience."[85] The skeptic is loyal to discursive principles taken from history and society. Her discursive principles are also emotional principles and they have a regulatory force s/he cannot explain in Hume's terms.

The skeptic can offer no external cause (i.e., metaphysical cause) for discursive principles. Hence culture, not happiness is "The Ultimate Purpose

That Nature Has as a Teleological System." Culture, on this account, shows that, "the principle of the purposiveness of nature (in the diversity of its empirical laws) is a *transcendental* principle," i.e., internal and self-imposed.[86] Discursive principles in art, law, theology, etc. 'feel' metaphysical, but a close examination indicates they are derived from the culture. Culture is man-made. Human beings invent and systematize categorically binding laws which they then accept as their culture. Culture shows that human beings can freely invent and freely apply coherent, intelligible principles. Human beings are *free* to invent systems. They can make up their own structures of law, art, and philosophy. They can and do routinely make up worlds. If one begins philosophy with an understanding of this fact, then moral philosophy becomes much easier and more *practical*.

The most controversial part of Kant's critical philosophy concerns "purposiveness as a transcendental principle." Kant's critics accused him of reducing science and ethics to heuristic fictions. Kant was the first modern intellectual to be charged with nihilism, because his theory of self-legislating intellect logically denied objective truth.[87] In Kant's account, human beings should act "as if" God, science, ethical theory, and moral action were true. Most of these same charges were levelled against Kierkegaard, Schopenhauer, Nietzsche, Wittgenstein, and the postmodernists two centuries later. The relativity of all knowledge, the reduction of truth to appearances and the destruction of standards are charges that were first levelled against Kant. Kant saw a problem his detractors, then and now, had overlooked. All theories of objective metaphysical truth are subject to Hume's disastrous fork in a skeptical society that does science.

Kant was the first philosopher who understood the practical effect on human societies of Hume's disastrous fork. He admonished the West it had a public choice to make about the kind of society it wanted to be. It could have objective metaphysics in a society of sycophantic conformity or it could embrace its freedom and have a society of thoughtful and independent republics. A skeptical society which does science cannot have both. Hume's naïve theory of experience had the practical effect of justifying conformity. Kant saw the problem. The emotional attraction of the species for rule-governed systems like art, law, and religion could lead societies to act "as if" transient social constructions were ordained by God. Human beings forget, if they ever knew, that art, law, and religion are schemas they have invented. Their truth and force comes from the efficacy of their own collective intelligence. Kant's caution does not negate the existence of God. He was as plain as he could be that his philosophy is a critique. Kant's concern is Hume's willingness to accept temporal rules as timeless laws. Kant's concern is that God, nature, and natural necessity get blamed for human stupidity. Kant was concerned that future generations of skeptics like Hume would not take moral responsibility for the "cosmopolitan" systems they were likely to create. *Critique of Pure Reason* failed to get this point across. When the reviews of *Critique of Pure Reason* were negative, Kant put his concerns in a more accessible form.

"Man must have a *motivational drive* that puts him in motion *before* a *goal* can be set for him," Kant reminded his first two important reviewers. Christian Garvé and J.G.H. Feder gave the *Critique of Pure Reason* its first major review. The Garvé/Feder position was that Kant's dull and weighty "deductions" led to solipsism. They added nothing to Berkeley's subjective idealism almost a century before. Garvé had been a good friend before the negative review. Kant swallowed his personal disappointment and wrote a public letter to Garvé collegially chiding him for missing the point.

In *On the Old Saw: That May Be Right in Theory but it Won't Work in Practice* (1783), Kant explained the critical role of the "transcendental deduction." Without a "transcendental deduction" of the "determining ground of the will," empirical experience is only "the crudest, most legible script ... that flows from the principle of self-interest."[88] The prior determination of the will "concerns the *form of the right*, not the matter of the object to which I have a right," Kant advised (emphasis added).[89] Formal representation carries "a motivational drive." The "drive" behind the rule is what Kant called a "maxim." The maxim is the determining ground of the will. Rules are crude legalisms. To understand human behaviour we must "deduce" the transcending purpose human beings imagine they can see behind the rules. The system in which the rules are represented provides the driving force behind obedience to the rules. The system always appears to us as if it were metaphysical i.e., external and beyond our control.

Human beings have the strange ability to detach rules from one system and apply them elsewhere. This "maximization" of the rules is fundamental to the moral life. Ethical behaviour is not just behaviour which conforms to the rules. Hume's system is like that, but no civil society can survive unless it believes it "should" either obey the rules or invent better ones. In *The Old Saw* he accused Garvé/Feder of defending "the vulgar understanding" which could only follow "the cruder idea of duty, based upon certain benefits expected."[90] A crude calculation of self-interest cannot do ethics. It cannot resist the motivating drives of modern discursive systems and their corresponding complexes. Self-interest is easily manipulated and the mind is highly susceptible to its natural affection for order, regularity, system, and law.

Kant's open letter stated, in an accessible form, the major direction of his final philosophical work. *On the Old Saw* begins Kant's last warning about the *a priori* power of order, regularity, system, and law on human behaviour. These last statements are a synopsis and a redeployment of the pure and practical critiques. They repeat the major points of a lifetime in an attempt to convince enlightened readers human understanding does not learn directly from experience. Human understanding is able to "intuit" the rules and principles by which experience is organized. The most controversial of Kant's critical deductions is that human understanding "intuits" formal unities of experience prior to their conceptualization and then applies these formal unities *a priori* and all unawares.

Kant had spent at least half his time in *Critique of Pure Reason* explaining how human understanding routinely recognizes *and acts upon* relatively complex perceptions without a conscious concept (an interest) in mind. Identifying and explaining this complex 'intuition' at length in the pure and practical critiques created the opportunity for Kant to outline a critique of judgment. The logical force of all three critiques warns us that the socialized modes of perception which exist prior to personal experience come at us with *metaphysical force*. They "drive" us toward the norm. Rule systems are the metaphysics of modern life. The integrity of the moral life requires the metaphysics of modern life be subjected to a rigorous categorical critique.

In Kant's final synthesis, feeling is not a reliable guide to moral action. Feeling organizes experience, but it does not make experience rational, lawful, practical, and fair. Just like the laws of gravity in Newtonian science, the schemas which inform moral judgment are not available to our senses. Their effects are experienced by the feelings, but their logical structure is not felt. The existence of a logical structure behind our natural affinity for art, law, and science must be deduced. We must learn to criticize the aesthetic grounds of art, law, and culture. The famous phrase "categorical imperative" refers to this inescapable moral obligation.[91] The categorical imperative awakens reason to critical moral introspection. Assuming they want to survive, "even a race of devils" must know their own minds, Kant advised.[92] "Devils" may not call self-knowledge "moral," but the group will have to act in coherent and mutually intelligible ways if they propose to survive.

It would be strange indeed, if logical grammars, artistic forms, and systems of law were not precious to human beings. Our minds have a natural affinity for order. The species has thrived by bringing order, structure, and regularity to the world. Human aptitudes for cooperation, order, and system invest the natural world and permit art, language, science, and law. Where the mind finds order, it intuits an intelligible will. The broadest and most inclusive regulatory systems were always attributed to God in pre-scientific societies. Kant calls these antiquated "cosmological" arguments "antinomies," bottomless debates that can never be resolved.[93]

Kant believes good will is more important than arguments over God's will.[94] Kant's determination to quiet the wrangling of "the schools" led him to his famous moral injunction: "So act so that the maxim of your will could always hold at the same time as the principle giving universal law."[95] Eckart Förster believes Kant's concept of maxims "is motivated by considerations similar to those that motivate Wittgenstein's discussion of the roles of words."[96] The logic of the law is not the same as the behavioural effect of the maxim behind the law. Förster links Kant with Wittgenstein on this point. All laws imply a schematic system of knowledge. The law is part of an intelligible world. Kant was the first moral philosopher to investigate the moral force of the logical system in which laws were entrenched. When Wittgenstein extended Kant's maxim to include the "roles of words," the linguistic turn was taken and a new critical system was born.

"Formal relations prescribe maxims without reference to an object," Kant believed.[97] Human beings "maximize" knowledge. We try constantly to extend successful areas of experience into other areas of experience in order to make our daily life more orderly, predictable, and safe. A competent critique of judgment criticizes how effective knowledge is maximized. It criticizes the extension of the rules from one experience to another. That is all Kant means. The social relation Marx found concealed in the "commodity fetish" is pure Kant. Husserl's "intentionality," Heidegger's "Logos," Derrida's "supplement" and Foucault's *episteme* are clarifications of a theme begun by Kant. Kant's concept of the maxim begins the way skeptics do ethics. Fine art, law, and the sublime in nature are nothing in themselves. They can only be understood as part of a larger, patterned system. Twentieth-century critical philosophy added language to Kant's discussion of the "maxim" behind the law. In a consensus society of commodity production, political democracy, and mass media, language is the most important patterned system. It affects every part of modern life.

The clearest summary Kant gave of his mature thought on system, structure, and behaviour is *The Groundwork of the Metaphysics of Morals* (1785). *Groundwork* is the most cited of Kant's work because it has most of the famous references. It contains the passages on a good will, repeats the categorical imperative from *Critique of Practical Reason* and defines Kant's "golden rule," i.e., the famous kingdom of ends.[98] Although these concepts are often discussed, they are not as often cited in relation to the cautions Kant built around them. Sandwiched between the logical imperative to act in accordance with maxims that could become a universal law and the moral necessity to treat others as an end in themselves, Kant warns against "deriving" these concepts "from the special property of human nature."[99] The maxim behind the law must be deduced. It can never be simply felt. The maxims of law, art and society are all determined in time. They are all historical. The maxims of art, law and culture must be deduced, so that they can be consciously affirmed or logically amended.

Understanding the maxims behind our actions and sensing our duty accordingly are not special properties of human nature. To warn his readers against a naïve faith in history and human nature, Kant invokes Hume. Hume's skeptical destruction of the moral law defines the spiritual limit of the known universe. No natural connection exists between the relation of ideas and matters of fact. Kant reminds us of the universal skeptical axiom of his era and ours. What *is* a fact, and what *ought* to be a fact are not intrinsically joined in Heaven, Hell, or human nature. Yet, civilization requires the existence of a connection. Ideas and events must combine in a predictable, orderly, and decent world. Kant warns, "In order to discover this connection we must, however reluctantly, step forth, into metaphysics."[100] History harbours 'forces' which feel like spiritual or "metaphysical" forces outside us. Human beings who are pro-social and emotionally adjusted are adept at "reading" these forces and using them to define the behavioural horizon of their daily lives. We have " a strange ability" for living cooperatively with others. How can this be and how can we understand it?

In the passages of the *Groundwork* which follow the warning about trusting human nature Kant summarizes how phenomenal beings can have what is, to them, a metaphysical experience. Remember that metaphysics is the perception of a cause which we have not given ourselves. It comes from outside us.[101] Kant says the will to obey the law comes to us (or at least *appears* to come to us) from outside our own internal, self-legislated (read: transcendental) perceptions of the world. It appears to come to us from outside our inner world of personal freedom. Appearances are deceiving. By covert and ingenious means, we give the metaphysical law to ourselves just like we give ourselves a fine art. The implications of these thoughts have opened up a large late modern philosophical debate.

In *Groundwork*, Kant appears to be admitting, cautiously, that the determination of the will is not, usually, a motivating drive we give to ourselves. The power of the human will appears to us to come from outside the domain of our personal life experience. He had thought otherwise, Kant admits, until Rousseau "corrected him" in this. The personal will is part of a general will which is derived from social life. The will to obey the law comes to us, Kant says, from inside the general sensory world, but from outside our personal sensory world. In Kant's terminology, phenomenal beings who know nothing of "things in themselves" discover shared rational purposes in religion, culture, and law. They approach common goals as if these goals exist in heaven or the nature of things. They debate cosmological issues "as if" such issues are external to them and inherent in things themselves.

Kant's metaphysics begins the late modern debate on the social construction of reality. It is, properly understood, an attempt to construct a formal ecology of mind. Kant introduces a skeptical feedback loop into the sociology of knowledge and the way human beings understand the world. Self-legislated norms at work over time get institutionalized into "aesthetic" systems like fine art, law, and theology. The group forgets they made it all up and begin to worship the rules as if they were the will of a God or inherent in things like history and the economy. Kant criticizes the way human beings divest themselves of moral responsibility for a world they themselves have created. The way they divest themselves of moral responsibility is ingenious. In *Groundwork* he warns, "The will is thought as a capacity to determine itself to act in conformity with the *representation of certain laws*."[102] The representation of the law is just as important as the law. This fact is apparent in the aesthetic debates of the late Rococo. "Good will" is under continual attack by formal adherence to the social order which determines the letter of the law. The spirit of the law cannot be trusted. It must be continually brought to consciousness and reformed. Any law, like any other work of art, is a categorical representation of a specific order. Human beings grasp the inner duality of the law in the way it is *represented*. The system of representation cues them into the kind of society a law implies.

A good will, which must, by definition, also be a moral will, can be undermined by the way the law, an otherwise reasonable law, is *represented*. The system of representation provides the "motivating drive." Socially competent adults 'read' the reasoning behind a law in the way the rule is represented. The discursive system has an *a priori* effect on behaviour. No skeptic admits the existence of metaphysical principles. To salvage pro-social behaviour from a world of brute necessity the clever skeptic smuggles in metaphysics through the epistemological back door. For skeptics in a science-based world of empirical facts and brute necessity, *the representation of the law has metaphysical force*. The system of representation sanctions a higher wisdom and a better world. The skeptic's discursive principles are the schema she uses to invoke her freedom and acknowledge the possibility of a better world.

Kant's choice of words in *Groundwork* is clear. It is not the content of the law which determines the will. It is the way the law is represented. The power of aesthetic judgment connects the law with the capacity for judgment. The system of law is external to the skeptical world of personal freedom. The switchback from inner to outer and back again is intuitive in act, but logical in fact. Here, in the *Groundwork*, is Kant's last refutation of Hume. Language i.e., "discursive principles" cannot sustain moral judgment. Words, in themselves, are the last metaphysical illusion of a skeptical society. They hide the logical system of the society behind a fig leaf of social feeling. A prior understanding of the way the system works gives keywords the illusion of a meaning in themselves. The spontaneous ability to put words in context is at one and the same time our highest intellectual achievement and our greatest emotional vulnerability. Ethics requires us to cultivate the achievement and face the vulnerability in the full light of a critical consciousness.

This "strange ability" to read the poetry of daily life forces us to develop good judgment.[103] Human beings take their "motivational drive" from the schemas, pattern, system, and architecture of things. We abstract patterns of experience from the way one thing is normally combined with another in our everyday world. In this way our abstract categories of perception are filled up with empirical details. Creating and decoding categories of experience so as to recognize, maximize, and legitimize them is the categorical imperative in general. We must maximize our most important experiences to be human. The ordinary ways we "schematize" or "categorize" our world determines what heritage words like "duty," "spirit," "nobility," "honour," and "truth" mean. The normative "schemas" of our lives set the boundaries for how inclusive, universal, and fair our discursive principles are.

Kant's final warning lays the foundation for what is likely the last and most important metaphysical consideration a skeptical, science-based society needs to discuss. To link the universal law with a personal good will; to graduate from documenting how things are to an agreement over how things ought to be; *to be ethical* in public and private life; a just society pays fundamental attention to how it represents the law. A system which maximizes conflict, profit, popularity, and knee-jerk chauvinisms diminishes the legitimacy of the law and depletes the stock of good will in public life.

Like Hume, Kant confines us to the phenomenal world where we are free to invent, sustain, and destroy ourselves. He generalized his argument so well that it still stands. It does not stand as a "great interruption" of Christian humanism or as a "Romantic reaction" to the Enlightenment. Kant's metaphysical critique of the power of judgment applies to all systems of knowledge. No "phenomenal" object, as it appears, can be a guide to right action. No flag, no event, no trauma, no great day, key word, song, or slogan can provide a maxim for sober judgment. We do not understand a word, work of art, law, or event until we have deduced the system which gives it "maximal" meaning. The system must be deduced. It is not felt. It is not emotionally available to our critical power of understanding.

Human begins have always created cosmological systems for themselves, so in the grand historical sense, all systems of knowledge "transcend" the immediate and the everyday. Kant argued skeptical enlightenment had not changed the most fundamental fact about history and human nature. It had only liberated human nature from its "self-incurred tutelage." The traditional "spiritual" problems of history and human nature remain in force, but they have to be discussed in a new way more appropriate for how a science-based, skeptical society discusses everything else. In a science-based society "metaphysics" has become "epistemology." The critique of knowledge is the skeptical correlate of theology in a skeptical world.

Kant's final warning could hardly be clearer. Fine Art, religion, and philosophy are orderly systems of representation. These systems operate on the moral life at two levels. At the most obvious level, they prescribe rules of conduct, composition, logical exposition, and the like. At a second, less obvious level, they maximize a point of view. The logical "architecture" of any system can be "abstracted" from the rules normally associated with it and used "without interest" in other areas of experience. Incomplete, inadequate, and poorly constructed systems teach "maxims" that impair good judgment.

We have "a strange ability" to read the cognitive architecture of our world. Given this fact, the moral life is the most "practical" of concerns. A moral life is a life where the law and the way the law is represented produce a good will. Without good will, society is impossible. "The interests of humanity" will be lost. Kant's insights have retained their relevance. They are fundamental to critical theory and the deep green politics of the radical left. The Kantian critique of judgment is the winter seed from which late modern thought has sprung. It was the taproot and spring water of phenomenology, existentialism, and the late modern linguistic turn.

In 1798 Immanuel Kant wrote a long scholarly letter to the Prussian censor. "The Conflict of the Faculties" singled out clergymen, magistrates, and medical doctors for special criticism. He was worried the best and brightest of Prussian society were, for the most part, not supporters of good government and did not have "the interests of humanity at heart." His criticism was far from intuitive or emotional. In his critique of the professional classes Kant applied his longstanding argument with skeptics like Hume to civic affairs. Kant described the majority of clergymen, magistrates, and doctors as "businesspeople." They were rational, intelligent, and diligent, but they were not ethical. Kant claimed they "welcomed transgressions of the law as occasions for showing their great art and skill in making everything as good as ever." They used political crisis to advance their fortunes and enhance their authority. Kant accused the professional "businesspeople" of exploiting fear of the world situation to further their own interests. He advised the censor not to be so concerned about protecting the masses and more concerned about the moral integrity of the professional classes.

Kant was also worried about the "awe" with which the public regarded these "businesspeople." He thought an overly credulous public was letting the professional classes spread secular superstition among them.

They were creating cults of ritual practice without the faith needed to sustain them. Kant made a critical distinction between religion and faith and accused the professional classes of spreading a new religion without cultivating the moral convictions associated with the tenets of the old faith. To redress the problem he asked the censor to create a new critical faculty at the university. Kant believed history and philosophy should be invited to criticize the professional classes. They should "work together to deny the magic power that the public superstitiously attributes to these businessmen," Kant said. Working together, history and philosophy could break down the hold the "businesspeople" had on the rest of the people. The people would then support their government and work together to build a more prosperous and peaceful society. An Enlightened criticism "is a better means for achieving government ends than its own absolute authority," he advised.[104]

The Prussian censor ignored Kant's proposal. Kant's quaint and radical idealism was not one a government would be likely to appreciate. To raise a moral protest against clergymen, doctors, and lawyers would alienate many of the government's most influential supporters. Nor was the government the only obstacle to Kant's "critical faculty." For a university to support Kant's critical faculty, it would have to sanction interdisciplinary cooperation and resist powerful groups of alumni. Kant's critical faculty would have required the administration of the university to address methodological and philosophical issues affecting the faculties; and, more to the point; it would have to address its duties in relation to government. Together, the university and the government would have to distance themselves from the "businesspeople" in the interests of the public good. None of these practical eventualities were likely to occur.

Kant's advice to the Prussian censor was his last attempt to make pure reason practical. Allowing for the impatience of old age and physical infirmity, his suggestions are remarkably topical. From the perspective being developed in this extended essay, I believe one must consider the relation between "awe" for the "businesspeople" and Hume's theory of language. Hume treated language as a natural weapon in an abstract stone age of primary politics. Considerable empirical evidence has accumulated in the history of the twentieth century to indicate Hume was in error. Words do not litter the landscape with a democratic potentiality falling naturally out of the ordinary discourse of daily life. The greatest moral dilemma of mass politics is the assimilation of language. The key words Hume absolved from complicity with the norm have been drafted into daily duty by Kant's "businesspeople." Resisting the "awe" they inspire is the categorical duty of the moral life in the modern world. "Freedom" is the prize and the issue at stake in the debate.

CHAPTER TWO
# *HEGEL'S PREDICAMENT*

> *Expression and intention penetrate one*
> *Another. Cunning consists in exploiting*
> *The distinction.*[1]
>
> — HORKHEIMER AND ADORNO

**IN 1802, JUST FOUR YEARS** after Kant's modest proposal to the Prussian censor, a young G.W.F. Hegel (1770–1831) announced the futility of all moral philosophy. Hegel dismissed Kant's concerns as subjective quibbles. Philosophy must and should be the handmaiden of history, he announced. Categorical speculations like Kant's were antiquated. They had no place in modern life. Hegel lined up German idealism with Hume. In so doing, he drafted Hume and history into the service of the "businesspeople." The Hume-Hegel hybrid has been a formidable adversary to moral philosophy ever since. It was a forced hybrid Hume himself never intended and likely would not have condoned. The combination of Hegel, Hume, and modern political history distorted secular moral judgment with a cognitive force not yet played out. It left behind an inaccurate idea of Enlightenment and skewed the modern political debate toward an unhealthy political realism that almost forbids conscientious attention to the older philosophical realism of classical philosophy and traditional theology.

Hegel led the charge against the idea of secular moral imperatives in the brave new industrial world of nation-states and economic empires. Hegel's philosophy of history affirmed the defeat of public conscience, business ethics, and political integrity with the most dramatic metaphor in Western intellectual history. Moral philosophy was dead, because "God, himself, has died," Hegel explained.[2] No idea or constellation of ideas could possibly mount a resistance to history because the only force powerful enough to give history a moral purpose had been eliminated from the universe.

Hegel's philosophy of history granted moral immunity to Kant's "businesspeople." History was their get-out-of-jail-free card. Secular moral philosophy in the modern public sphere was silenced forthwith. History had corked the lethal tines of Hume's disastrous fork. When they finally realized what Hegel's Gordian knots of dialectical abstraction actually meant, Kant's "businesspeople" rejoiced.

The "death of God" usually attributed to Friedrich Nietzsche, appeared first in Hegel's *Faith and Knowledge* (1802). The aetiology of the metaphor is important. Hegel offered it as the practical answer to enlightenment moral speculation. The "death of god" made the historical way straight and plain for self-made men of action in the new industrial economy. Hegel knew what he was saying and he calculated astutely its probable effect. Kant's critical faculty – indeed the whole Enlightenment project – required what philosopher's call a "critical ontology." Enlightenment required a platform of natural laws which were absolutely free from relativism. The "death of God" meant no such platform existed in moral philosophy. By any ethical standard, Hegel's drastic announcement *did not* end the great interruption of moral philosophy that had been caused by skeptical Enlightenment. It *did not* restore a temporal balance between head and heart. On the contrary, the triumph of Hegel's historical thinking broke Western culture in two. It ended the Enlightenment's unfinished moral project. After Hegel, the critical coalition between modern history and moral philosophy was as stone cold dead in modern public life as old Jehovah God had been to Napoleon and the Marquis de Sade.

Napoleon had just been elected first Consul when Hegel confessed his "infinite grief, which existed historically.... God, himself, has died."[3] Hegel's obituary for God was a brilliant summary of modern intellectual history to date. It captured superbly the ecumenical sorrow of a disillusioned Enlightenment. Not only Jehovah God, but the Goddess reason, the Deist God of divine clockwork, Newton's God of nature, and all the muses – they were all gone. Humankind was infinitely alone. Hegel grieved the death of transcendence, the death of absolutes, the death of utopia, and the perfectibility of man. The traditional guarantee for all custom, tradition, manners, and mores was dead. If God were dead, so was the absolute measure for every intangible quality in the universe. The "death of god" snapped the scholastic cord which had linked ideas with events in Western history since Augustine. Without a God to guarantee its meaning, history was free from moral obligation. The very existence of right was now indeterminate. Hegel had expressed the modern experience with a metaphor most educated readers could easily understand.

An elated Enlightenment deflated rapidly during the Napoleonic wars. Hegel lived through it. He blamed the Enlightenment for the excesses of the Napoleonic regime. He believed the Enlightenment had worshipped the image of reason and destroyed the spirit of it. Hegel blamed the failure of Enlightenment thought on "formal ... or more properly, psychological idealism."[4] The "intellect" which results from Enlightenment idealism, "is human intellect, part of the cognitive faculty, the intellect of a fixed Ego-point," Hegel warned.[5] Hegel's "infinite grief" was accompanied by a stern suspicion of Enlightenment individualism. Without a higher faith, reason turned into terror. Hegel's problem was, "faith in what?" He, himself, had lost his traditional faith in the Christian god. Where was he to turn?

With his soul in sackcloth, Hegel turns to the memory of God in history. The historical effect of God on the lives of ordinary people was an historical fact. Hegel is the prophet of the new historical consciousness. He will save the dead God's memory and keep the old God's positive accomplishments alive in the modern world. "The conception of God constitutes the general basis of a people's character," Hegel explains.[6] To bring God's legacy over into history without God himself, Hegel introduces the state. Hegel's concept of the state "is based on Religion.... Religion must be brought into the state – in buckets and bushels as it were – and impressed upon people's hearts," Hegel wrote.[7] God died from buckets and bushels of the "cognitive intellect" that supports a "fixed Ego-point." No matter, Hegel continues:

> God has died – God is dead – this is the most frightful of all thoughts, that everything eternal and true is not, that negation itself is found in God. The deepest anguish, the feeling of complete irretrievability, the annulling of everything that is elevated, are bound up with this thought. However, the process does not come to a halt at this point; rather, a reversal takes place: God, that is to say, maintains himself in this process, and the latter is only the death of death. God rises again to life, and thus things are reversed.[8]

History has resurrected God. God lives again in his moral legacy and the Western tradition that was founded in his name. Hegel's historical positivism saves an external meaning for the deity even while admitting the death of deity as an external force. Deity internalized is the new historical tradition and defines the new direction of modern thought.

Hegel's generic response to Kant's moral idealism is ground zero for modern intellectual history. Hegel's word, "god is dead" was a metaphor. It might mean many things and what it meant to Hegel is not entirely clear. What it meant about the culture in which Hegel lived is relatively clear. The metaphorical death of God meant the non-cooperation of philosophy and history. Before the modern era, philosophy had worked closely with or against a theological perspective on history. God's active providence in the affairs of humankind was the core of pre-modern philosophical debate. The metaphorical "death of God" announced the impossibility of any ultimate purposes in history. The old system of categorical debate was foreclosed. Philosophy and history became the two sides of Hume's disastrous fork. Philosophy took possession of the "relation of ideas". History took possession of "matters of fact". In agreement with Hume, no logical relation between the two domains was possible. The death of God was the death of Kant's "critical faculty" before it even got started. The death of God meant the end of a two-thousand-year tradition in the intellectual history of the West. The language of mutual reflection on truth, ethics, good, and evil was as dead as Hegel's old pietist God. Hegel, considered by most as *the* philosopher of history, was not historically minded enough to consider the real effects on daily experience foretold in the death of a whole critical faculty. A critical tradition had been lost and one might expect the loss to be recorded as a grievous event. Hegel's generation did not grieve for very long before they chocked up another notch on their test tubes. God's death was just collateral damage. The old tradition He represented had been surpassed. History was now able to stand alone. Matters of fact had surpassed the power of ideas. The accurate description of events would promote traditional ideas of the good far better than the worship of God. Hegel's Miltonic metaphor was hubris on a scale unlikely ever to be seen again.

Hegel claimed his grief for the late great God of his fathers was "infinite," but he made no effort to address the void so great a grief must cause. His reaction was not "realistic" in the contemporary use of the term. Hegel gave Kant's proposed critical faculty over to historical events. Philosophy proper became the internal overseer of a fragmented stream of overexcited consciousness. After God's "death" every disciplinary sub-section of the arts and sciences developed its own philosophy. Professional solidarities inside carefully demarcated areas of scholarship replaced an interdisciplinary overview. The Ph.D. degree becomes the last anachronism of the old time when philosophy cooperated with all knowledge in the pursuit of a unified truth. The death of God left philosophical feudalism defending the modern Balkanization of experience.

Hegel believed historical events would educate the "businesspeople" to their moral duty far faster than critical speculation. Hegel deeded the brave, new industrial world to the businesspeople; but it was a probate without probity. The "death of God" was a sly slogan in league with the "businesspeople" whom Hegel held in awe. A word war in the world of scholarship and the arts began here. Hegel's obituary for traditional faith immunized the new business economy from moral criticism. It left the real the final arbiter of the good, and it left political history the final arbiter of the real. Hegel's trenchant metaphor captured the moral corrigibility at the foundations of modern historical study.

Strip Hegel's alleged 'idealism' of its boxcar language and his ideas are simple. Hegel said the forces driving history had changed, but the structure of history had remained the same. No one needed to be concerned because the same approach to ideas and events which had worked during the credulous eras of religious superstition would still work. No one needed to change their thinking about anything in the practical spheres of politics and the economy. The world was still moving toward redemption by a fitful path which the human mind was unable to grasp. The only difference between now and then was that history, not God, moved in mysterious ways its wonders to perform. Politics had replaced God as the world's guiding spirit. The prime mover was now secular, not sacred. Political history had taken care of God and now it was taking care of God's former people. Hegel was happy to report that a minor change in the board of directors had not altered the progressive course of history. History was the rational foundation for a modern social science now cured of abstract speculation and transcendental bogey-men. Hegel and his heirs believed the dialectic in history guaranteed a more practical, durable, and inclusive public sphere.

Hegel thought modern history could sustain the older tradition of moral realism and ethical criticism. What had been an unconscious movement toward the light could now be carried on in the full light of day. Hegel had overlooked something. Old Jehovah-God in Hegel's own

European religious tradition was not a trickster. He might bluster and rant; but he obeyed his own natural laws. The idea of natural laws which even the deity chose to obey was the richest and most fruitful cultural insight in the world. It has paid so many dividends so many times over in the West that its simple origins have been filed away and forgotten.

The Western God's strict adherence to his own laws guaranteed the intelligibility of a real world and *that was not all*. God's rational self-discipline guaranteed the timeless integrity of names. Jehovah God's world was a nominative world. It could be described once and for all and for all time. Its laws could be written in stone with no fear they would ever have to be changed. God guaranteed the historical covenant between words and things. *When God, 'died' the indelible connection between words and things died with him.* The intellectual difficulty with language after the "death of God" is the most basic issue in Western history. The indeterminate connection between words and the objects to which they refer has been the occasion for a modern history of bad faith, ethical incompetence, and emotional despair. When politics became the new world spirit, politics also become the new author and emendator of the modern experience. Politics after Hegel was not just the environment in which the great traditional issues were discussed; politics was the crucible in which key words like "truth," "freedom," "democracy," "honour," and "duty" *were defined*. From the perspective of modern intellectual history, the integrity of the name is the biggest problem in modern life. The most fundamental issues in modern intellectual history are not democracy, progress, and freedom, but what democracy, progress, and freedom actually mean. The integrity of the name was disrupted by the syndrome of secular events which Hegel dramatically dubbed the death of God. He and his heirs, quite casually, overlooked the problem.

The managerial elites in whom Hegel had vast confidence were not and are not concerned with even the possibility that the modern world is building on semantic quicksand. What Kant's "businesspeople" were reluctant to know was relatively evident to ordinary people at the social and subsistence levels of daily life. After God's 'death,' God's former people could *not* be confident their emotional impressions of right and wrong were real. The rich and powerful, as a class, could hardly have cared less, but ordinary people noticed the loss immediately. Their practical problem was with qualitative expressions like care, compassion, duty, and obligation. These terms had been thrown into question. There was no longer a categorical frame of reference underneath such expressions. In a world without Jehovah God's old philosophical covenant in place, all qualitative contents were locally defined and all meanings were relative to their historical context.

A sardonic irony twisted around the philological power of the new politics. Power and wealth provided the perfect language for business and diplomacy, but it was the devil's own language of conscience and moral responsibility. The indeterminacy of ethical speculation and moral critique in the modern era was the tragedy from which Kierkegaard worshipped the absurd. It drove Marx into philippics from exile and Nietzsche into madness. It has eroded a tradition of moral idealism active in Western culture since Moses and the Hebrew prophets. The old words for right and wrong were made historically relative in the new political economy which emerged in Europe soon after the Napoleonic wars. Modern historical 'idealism' has played a significant role in the process. Only the most courageous and sensitive were prepared to announce the true tragedy of modern history in unadulterated terms. Most members in good standing of the new secular culture fled in droves from the truth.

The anomy of modern culture drove the affluent scuttling to Plato's cave in numbers unmatched since the fall of Rome. Nineteenth-century reactionaries congratulated themselves for rectifying the sadistic intellectual detachment of Enlightenment. They thought the treasures of Plato's cave would save them from their bold secular covenant with the gods of war. In the Hegelian reading which survived him, Kant was enlisted in support of a culture and a moral practice which his last published works had openly scorned. Schiller, Coleridge, Pater, and Matthew Arnold identified Kant as culture vulture number one. In this carefully adapted reading, Kant's critical philosophy began the inner immigration of the 'businesspeople' into the private world of spiritual contemplation and recreational high culture. The centrality of Kant's rejoinder to Hume was downplayed. His defence of natural law went unheard. His critique of judgment was neutralized and his denunciation of the "businesspeople" was suppressed. Nineteenth-century sweetness and light seduced modern moral philosophy. Ethical rigour drowned in the cathartic tears of Romantic culture. An exhibitionist middle class has been exposing itself to art, history, and culture ever since.

*The Meaning of Meaning* (1923) defends modern literature against the moral pretensions of the modern social sciences. Ogden and Richards begin their classic defence with an attack on Hegel. "There is no greater

defect in Hegel's system than the want of a sound theory of language....
[His] language is a duplicate, a shadow-soul, of the whole structure of
reality," they advised.⁹ To Ogden and Richards, Hegel's flawed theory of
language is the reason for modern literature. History *à la* Hegel leaves
the reader mired in reality, buried by the normal, unable to escape the
overbearing power of the empirically real. The turf war they announced
in 1923 is still going on. It uses the terms "narrative," "semantics," and
"discourse" to include literature and history in a larger issue. Narrative
is the normative term, semantics holds the neutral centre, and discourse
is the radical term preferred by the postmodern left. One general conclusion is clear. History *and* literature have both been problematized in
the twentieth century. They appear to be part of a larger problem with
the cultural role of narrative language in late modern experience. The
larger problem is one Kant would have called "practical." Modern public
language in both fact and fiction does not appear to represent the emotional and behavioural stresses of contemporary life very well. A general
problem with language and what language means affects politics, the
arts, and everyday interpersonal relationships. It is one of the abiding
and besetting problems of the age.

Peter Seuren (1998) has reviewed the history of modern semantics.
His book is a centrist report on the modern language question. He traces
the language debate from Plato and spends a considerable time on Hegel.
Hegel is the renowned idealist whom Karl Marx allegedly "turned on his
head." Why does Seuren include Hegel in a history of semantics? Because,
Seuren explains, the modern world has discovered through bitter experience that one of its oldest fundamental assumptions about language is
wrong. Seuren explains the modern discovery in non-partisan terms:

> The grammatical subject-predicate division of a sentence and the
> cognitive structuring of a thought as a mental act of assigning a
> property to a given entity most of the time *do not run in tandem*
> (emphasis).[10]

Hegel thought they did. The semantic representation of experience (I
have, did, hope, think, feel, etc.) is not intrinsically connected to any pre-
existing system of representation. Hegel thought it was. He thought the
objective representation of events (in words) paralleled the subjective
perception of them. Seuren points out there are no natural schemas for

the system of representation favoured by Hegel. The connection between representation and experience is not secure. Seuren agrees with Ogden and Richards that the historical cover-up of this soul-jolting narrative pothole begins with Hegel.

Seuren notes that Hegel's semantics received no theoretical attention until the twentieth century. By that time the Hegelian tradition was ensconced like a stone inside the standard language practices of modern historical studies. A plain language explanation of Hegel's semantic problem was rendered difficult by the Hegelian dominance over the style, form, and system of explanation favoured in the modern research university. Hegel's philosophy of history took shape at the beginning of the age of Romantic reaction, European ethnocentrism, and economic *laissez-faire*. Its narrative format, literal research methodology, and indirect approach to ethical issues represented nineteenth-century culture and politics in a positive light. Hegel's philosophy of history transmitted nineteenth-century ethical norms into the next century. Fundamental concepts that Hegel was the first to codify in their contemporary public use still inform the everyday notion of how history, politics, culture, and society are represented.

Hegel's illusive misapprehension that events and ideas run "in tandem" is formalist and goes back to Plato. It was an endearing myth as long as the people who practised it were not fully-fledged, science-oriented Humean skeptics. When Platonic language became common practice in the democratic politics of large, pluralistic societies, the myth began to have mood swings. The full range of possible difficulties flowing down to us from nineteenth-century semantics has not been adequately explored.

In *Principia Ethica* (1903), G.E. Moore described a "very contradictory doctrine" in modern thought. He blamed Hegel for an "ambiguous language" of "the supreme good" that was so "contradictory, no practical maxim in it can possibly be true."[11] A temporal politics of the timeless good was a destructive contradiction bound to destroy any practical idea of the good. "This very contradictory doctrine ... pervades almost the whole of modern philosophy," Moore added.[12] Moore's answer to Hegel's "ambiguous language" was the exalted "states of consciousness" induced by intellectual conversation and the classical fine arts.[13] Moore's aesthetic state was overwhelmed by the politics of state in the twentieth century. Hegel's ambiguous language survived the hot, cold, and colonial wars. Moore never asked why.

Margaret Urban Walker provides an indirect explanation of Hegel's triumph over sweetness and light. She concludes her contribution to the anthology, *Moral Epistemology Naturalized* (2000), with the following question:

> We cannot but ask ourselves what we know best about science, morality and social life, and how we know it. Yet here it is epistemically and morally urgent that we open the question that Moore would never have asked: who are "we"?[14]

Hegel's ambiguous language survived because 'we' who benefit from it refuse to ask what it has done to us. What 'we' know 'best' about science, morality, and social life, in Margaret Urban Walker's terms, is how much they benefit those of us fortunate enough to live in the developed world. What we know 'worst' is who we are and what we have become in Hegel's world of dialectical thuggery and knee-jerk loyalty to the state. Hegel's representation of history began a selective edit of the past in favour of naturalistic survival and moral indifference to the suffering of others. The system he and Wilhelm Dilthey etched on the modern mind maximizes conflict and minimizes morality. It suppressed Kant and began a secular religion that has turned the heritage culture into a handmaiden of the corporate state.

### G.W.F. HEGEL (1770–1831)

"Whether we know it, or like it, or not," Paul de Man wrote, "most of us are Hegelians and quite orthodox ones at that.... Few thinkers have so many disciples who never read a word of their master's writings."[15] It is Hegelian to see literature as the synthesis of opposing cultures. It is Hegelian to systematize art according to style and period and, most famously, Hegel began the modern view of history as the progress or regress of objective mind. In the Introduction to *The Philosophy of History* (1822), Hegel suggests a fourth way we have come to be like him whether we know it, or want to admit it, or not.

The fourth way I want to emphasize here is Hegel's answer to the formalist problem Seuren described in his book on semantics. Hegel knew that state politics were a moral dilemma for the older, heritage culture. Classical philosophy and both stages of the Christian synthesis were suspicious of secular history, distrusted the state, and insisted on the primacy of the law. A philosophy of secular progress faced the moral objections of Greek philosophy and Christian ethics. Hegel defended his sanguinary, secular realism in terms very similar to the older language of religious belief in which he had been raised. The nineteenth century still couched its most important ideas in the traditional language of idealist philosophy and Christian theology. Hegel adapted the language tradition of his day to the new, secular study of history. Here are his words:

> The revelation of the divine being must ultimately advance to the *intellectual* comprehension of what was presented in the first instance, to *feeling* and *imagination* [Hegel's italics].[16]

Hegel believed the intellectual comprehension of history explained the sentiments associated with religious piety. "What is commanded in the Holy Scripture," he admonishes. "That we should not merely love, but know God.... The science of which we have to treat [i.e., history] proposes itself to furnish the proof."[17] The "cunning of reason" in history is the real architect of moral progress.[18] History, rightly understood, justifies the old ways of God to the new ways of men.

Hegel claimed he understood God's laws and was sympathetic to their development. What he did about them casts suspicion on the depth of his understanding and the authenticity of his motives. He did not review the history of the problem. He did not concede, like both Hume and Kant, that skeptical philosophy, science, and logic were limited to the phenomenal world. Hegel led the way in declaring a double duty for history that is morally ambiguous. He declared history both the cause and the cure for the skeptical moral dilemma. He blamed history on the one hand and then exempted history on the other. "The world is in itself falling to pieces," Hegel warned.[19] That tragedy and its social consequences were the way history made progress. Those with moral concern and social vision had to have faith in dialectical conflict and the world spirit. The old providence of God no longer moved through history. It resided in history. The forces of history were now the supreme mover of the world. Hegel has Hume's predicament without being aware of it.

Laurence Bonjour (2002) calls Hegel's solution to Hume's predicament an externalist view of knowledge. "On externalist views, the factor in light of which a belief is likely to be true may be wholly or partially external to the believer's own cognitive perspective." In this perspective a true believer may not understand why an idea is true and, worse still, does not need to know why it is true. Bonjour points out the difficulty with a boisterously external perspective like Hegel's. The believer does not need to *justify* the truth. S/he trusts circumstances to justify the truth for her. Hegel's "epistemological" problem is what Kant called "intelligibility." Hegel's secular faith is not coherent. It does not add up to a systematic perspective on any of the old ideals upon which Western civilization was grounded. Hegel's secular faith supports policy not people. It is a system of representations which undermines the anonymous dignities of everyday life. Citizens in Hegel's state are deracinated souls whose only remaining heritage is the theory of state.

Hegel had no problem with the emotional and cognitive dilemmas posed by his global, secular faith. He believed history was the answer to the skeptical predicaments debated by Kant and Hume. Bonjour doubts Hegel's answer is adequate. He suggests, "The claim that externalism makes it possible to avoid skepticism ... turns out to be largely empty; and internalism remains the only viable approach to the deepest and most important [skeptical] epistemological problems."[20] Ordinary decency, interpersonal concern, everyday kindness, and the larger coherencies normally associated with moral action and ethical theory are "the deepest and most important" of the problems to which Bonjour refers.

William H. Dray (1993) concedes, "When Hegel secularized the Christian idea of providence ... providential theories passed over into theories of linear inevitability." Dray excuses Hegel from any turpitude he may have occasioned. Secularizing the idea of providence was merely an innocent figure of speech. "The notion of inevitability is often used by historians simply to express the idea of one thing necessarily following another," Dray remarks. The language of providence is not to be taken literally. The great value of history lies in adapting language to explain events in a way most people can understand.[21] Dray (1993), Taylor (1975), Gadamer (1976 & 1985), Krieger (1989), and Wood (1990) disagree with Bonjour, Seuren, de Man, and Moore. They respect Hegel for giving history philosophical respectability. They believe Hegel explained, once and for all, how historical narrative could be the logical equivalent of moral philosophy and theological casuistry. The Hegelian philosophy of history bridged the great disruption of skeptical Enlightenment and linked modern progress with the older humanism. History, post-Hegel, links modern thought with the wisdom of the past.

The link is purely semantic. Hegel's philosophy of history uses language his theory of history cannot sustain. Hegel expropriates the language of the older humanism and adapts it to support industrial growth and state power. The Hegelian philosopher Charles Taylor (1985 & 1989) calls language "the most powerful agent in the construction of a modern identity.... Language realizes man's humanity," he says. It is the "source of the self" in modern life. Human beings "discover" their higher potentials in the language of history, politics, and literature. "Thinking is essentially expression," Taylor believes. "It is particularly illuminating to see Hegel's philosophy of mind through this perspective," he advises.[22] Through historical study the "expressive self" discovers the moral truths political participation uncovers in practice. "History reminds us of the context of practices in which ideas are embedded." Ideas "interweave with their practices in various ways" and history reveals this process to us.[23] Our mutual involvement in history develops each individual "expressive self" to the highest degree. Taylor speaks for a powerful range of opinion that still holds to a boisterous externalism most moral philosophers oppose.

Lawrence Dickey (1987) has described the Duchy of Württemberg where Hegel was born as an insular province, which after turning Protestant in 1534, was rife with religious enthusiasm, mysticism, and Hermeticism. Hegel's historicism is an amalgam of personal genius and parochial traditions on which he was raised. His language is dense, but its content is relatively traditional. Hegel hides his lost religious faith in history. The boxcar clauses of his steam train dialectics are the bereaved meditations of a lonely heart. Glenn Magee (2001) calls the Swabians, "*the* mystical people of Germany." Franz Wiedmann (1968) writes of the Swabians, "Reserved and uncommunicative, they conceal deep within themselves a quiet faculty for brooding and meditating."[24] Hegel turned to history to save the memory of his childhood faith.

In his youth, Hegel had intended to enter the religious ministry, but he was a poor orator so he turned to the fulltime study of philosophy, instead. Kant's *Religion within the Limits of Reason Alone* (1793) was particularly influential on Hegel's development. In response to it he wrote *The Spirit of Christianity*, which was not published until 1907. Hegel breaks with Kant's claim that Christian ethics are rational. Hegel's anti-semitism and his dualism come together in a defence of the "spirit" of Jesus' moral teaching. Jesus broke with the Jews because they were overly rational. His insights into history and the human condition were higher than the Jewish race was capable of appreciating. From racism, Hegel moves to Romanticism. The Christian kingdom is a dual kingdom. One side is material and the other spiritual. The two kingdoms can only be united in the history of great men and great peoples. Legalistic rationality of the Jewish, popish and Kantian sort are unable to comprehend the historical development of Christ's supermundane kingdom here on earth.

Hegel bases his petty mysticism on passages from St. John. Spirit and flesh cannot be reconciled in any one life. Church and state, worship and life, piety and virtue, spiritual and worldly action can never be resolved in personal experience. Individuals are forced to live in a perpetual state of continual becoming. Personal life is always a work in progress and the direction of our lives is not within our own control. Hegel's choice of the word *geist* reflects the unresolved inner dualism of his thought. The word means "mind" as well as "spirit." The ambiguity of the two meanings is Hegel's stock and trade. He plays mind and spirit off against each other, never having to chose, never having to decide which side of Christ's super-worldly historical kingdom must finally have priority over the other.

History was the only concept big enough to cover the ambiguity in Hegel's system. Hegel cannot defend his grieving and fragmented spirit, but he can defend history. Hegel defended history as the bridge to a higher philosophy in his lectures on the philosophy of history from 1810 to 1822. Originally, Herodotus and Thucydides "changed the events, the deeds, and the states of society with which they were conversant, into an object for the conceptive faculty," Hegel wrote.[25] History stayed the same, in Hegel's opinion, until the "critical mode of treating history, now current in Germany."[26] Trusting the "conceptive faculty" had been the great mistake of the Enlightenment. There was no innate and universal "conceptive faculty." The faculty differed greatly from person to person. Trusting the psychology of the individual to be categorically the same (as Kant had argued) left each individual detached, ostracized, and isolated from his historical community. Hegel thought the Germans had solved this problem.

History was the only dependable link between the "conceptive faculty" in each individual and the universal human spirit made flesh in the Gospel of St. John. The state in history was the new body of Christ. The Germans had discovered the truth about God's last revelation in history. German language, art, and high culture reflected the national historical experience. Through its culture, political traditions and military power the German state transcended the infinite subjectivities of the individual. Human consciousness was only truly happy under the administration of a strong national state. Hegel had to sell his power perspective to a society of religious enthusiasts and regional chauvinists. He turned to the language arts as a co-underwriter for his new church of national redemption. Hegel drew on the prestige of all the classical Fine Arts, leaning heavily on the language arts, in particular. Historians translate experience "in the same way the poet operates upon the material supplied him by his emotions; projecting it into an image for the conceptive faculty." The only difference between historians and poets is that historians "find statements and narratives of other men ready to hand."[27] History is the poetry of everyday life. History is real, so its ideas are not merely "psychological." The evidence of history amalgamates the higher emotional senses developed by high culture and the Fine Arts.

Poets and historians use the "heritage of an already-formed language," Hegel explained. Both poets and historians "owe much" to this heritage even if it is "merely an ingredient."[28] Hegel's readers did not find the equation of poetry and historiography unusual in the early nineteenth century. They were educated to an aesthetic tradition where "succession of time is the domain of the poet." The great Enlightenment critic and aesthetician Gotthold Ephraim Lessing had held both "poetical and prosaic painters" to the same task. They both "paint bodies, but only by way of indication, and through the means of actions."[29]

Hegel's philosophy of history founds a school of prosaic painting that saved the language of the heritage culture without having to investigate its new contents. History was a secular parable about the parallel worlds of sweetness, light, and *power politics*. Simple, historical word pictures were the interface between the old faith and current events. History gave the modern world logical integrity and communicative competence. Under the new dispensation Hegel had given them, the old words were as ambiguous as the new dialectic. They functioned like magic in the nineteenth century. Words were both in history and outside of history at the same time. Hegel defined the essential relation between language and history in Volume One of *The Science of Logic*: "It is a joy for speculative thought to find words which in themselves have a meaning," Hegel exulted.[30] History proved the meaning of the old words. The heritage language was made flesh in history. Historical events fulfilled the prophecy of the old texts. History was the spirit come down to dwell among us. The logical link between spirit and history for Hegel was the same as for Hume. The constant presence in history which gave foundation and intelligibility to modern progress and politics was language. The truth revealed by words "which in themselves have a meaning" was a constant truth through time which human consciousness first saw dimly as through a glass and then finally (through history) were now seeing it fully revealed.

Hegel claimed his *Logic*, or, as he sees it, the dialectical development of logic, was sustained by the inner logic of language. He believed semantic logic itself, though revealed historically, was as non-relative and timeless as geometry and mathematics. History was fundamentally discursive. The recovery of history was semantic. The language of historical description connects a people with "the presentation of God as he is in his eternal essence before the creation of nature and a finite mind." Hegel described the logic of history as "the course of truth as it is without veil in and for itself."[31] A timeless logic which was, at the same time, historically revealed depended upon language being an invariant guide to historical experience. A universal secular philosophy required a universal guarantor of truth to replace the old Jehovah God. An inherently logical language is, for Hegel, the spiritual guarantor of the new secular God's old, traditional revelation. Hegel's claims for his philosophy have close affinities with Romantic culture. The easy dismissal of the Hegelian *gesamtgeistwerk* hides the subtle affinity Hegel had with his era, its politics, and its need for easy answers to difficult moral questions.

Hegel's timely, timeless logic rests on a covert theory of language. The pseudo-science of Hegelian history hides a Cabbalistic faith in magic words. One of the earliest fragments from Hegel's *nachlass* contains the following reference to language:

> Every individual is a blind link in the chain of absolute necessity, along which the world develops. Every individual can raise himself to domination over a great length of this chain only if he realizes the goal of this great necessity and, by virtue of this knowledge, learns to speak the *magic words* which evoke its shape.[32]

Hegel could not save his faith in God; but he retained his faith in God's words. History revealed a "mythology of reason" still active in the world. In one of his earliest speculations, he was naive enough to use the phrase, "magic words." He soon stopped talking about magic words, but he never gave up on their magical effect.

Historical events were the everyday process which revealed the esoteric truths of philosophy in a plain language everyone could understand. The natural adaptation between philosophy and events proceeds spontaneously, in tandem. Glenn Magee traces Hegel's faith in magic words to the hermetic traditions of rural Saxony. In the mysticism of Bruno, Benz, and Oetinger, "magic words" were the way mortals "recollected" what had been forgotten since the fall of Adam.[33] Hegel's discussion of the historical importance of language in *The Phenomenology of Mind* is the resurrection of Swabian mysticism in modern public life. Here is Hegel:

> We see Language to be the form in which spirit finds existence. Language is self-consciousness existing *for others*; it is self-consciousness which as such is there immediately present, and which in its individuality is universal.... The content, which language has here obtained, is no longer the self we found in the world of culture, perverted, perverting, and distraught. It is spirit which, having returned to itself, is certain of itself, certain in itself of its truth.... Moral consciousness, on the other hand, remains dumb, shut up within its inner life; for self has no existence as yet.... For universal self-consciousness stands detached from the specific act which merely exists: the act means nothing to it: what it holds of importance is the conviction that the act is a duty: and this appears concretely in language.... Actual conscience ... is universal ... its very language pronounces its action to be recognized duty.[34]

Life is universal self-expression in history. Conscience is mute before the universal truths of history. The language of history instructs the moral conscience. Only in history is the solitary self reminded of her necessary relations with others.

History gives human reason its only critical reasons. Hegel advised:

> Thus the passions of men are gratified [in history]; they develop themselves and their aims in accordance with their natural tendencies, and build up the edifice of human society; thus fortifying a position for Right and Order *against themselves*.[35]

The moral progress of two thousand years had been consummated by the "cunning of reason" in history.[36] History has reasons which the individual cannot comprehend. History works behind the backs of individuals to realize its larger purposes over against the selfish competition of finite egos. Hegel had such boisterous confidence in history, he bragged:

> What experience and history teach is this – that peoples and governments never have learned anything from history, or acted on principles deduced from it.... Amid the pressure of great events, a general principle gives no help. It is useless to revert to similar circumstances in the Past. The pallid shades of memory struggle in vain with the life and freedom of the Present.[37]

History, for Hegel, proves the futility of theoretical speculation on deeper causes or fundamental principle. History shows in dramatic relief the good sense of getting on with it. History gives us confidence that nothing in the present can be as bad as "the French" try to pretend.[38] "Disgusted by such reflective histories, readers have often returned with pleasure to a narrative adopting no particular point of view.... We Germans are content with such," Hegel announces proudly.[39]

Well, a satisfying national entertainment that puts the French in their well-deserved place may not seem like the beginning of an era to most people and they should be right. Unfortunately, Hegel's conjoined philosophy of mind and spirit begins the modern political era. Good, realistic moderns (like Hegel) are moral and intellectual formalists. They act "as if" ideas and events move in tandem. They trust political debate to simulate the conscious power of a moral philosophy. Hegel's language describes history with a boisterous externalism. His fallacies implicate Western individualism in a crucial moral paradox. Hegel's objective idealism "presents us with a rational process" without having to admit to any particular point of view or justify any particular sense of right and wrong.[40]

The fallacy of an already-formed language provided Hegel with a scholarly escape from the hard grind of ethical Enlightenment. Words which, in themselves, had a meaning were the historical harvest of old Jehovah God's culture, theology, and law. Hegel's semantic 'joy' made God the first historical organ donor. Literally, over God's dead body, Hegel transplanted the moral sentiments of the Christian religion into the new political language of consensus politics. German historical idealism, British political liberalism, and Jacksonian democracy in the United States were culturally specific expressions of the same facile joy. The linchpin of what seemed practical common sense in each social context was the inseverable connection between history and an already formed language. Political debate uses the right words. In Hegel's perspective, political debate must, on account of its mastery of the language, be a world historical process in pursuit of ultimate truth.

Peter Seuren (1998) indicates Hegel's theory of language was part of a theological enterprise that had been going on since the sixth-century Latin Grammarian Priscian. The success of the missionary church rested four squarely on the perceived plausibility of its message. In the Christian gospel, any perceived change in the nature of the good always occasioned a scholastic tinkering with the language of the good. If language were to be an instrument of institutional continuity, language and practice had to be continually refitted. Language, as used by those with moral authority, had to be a dependable mediator between the temporal and spiritual worlds. Seuren explains, "the point of this enterprise was to demonstrate that linguistic categories are really a direct reflex of cognitive categories (which in turn are assumed to reflect ontological categories in a straightforward way)." He then notes all such attempts place the language user firmly in a scholastic camp that modern skepticism routed in the eighteenth century. In the linguistic history of the Christian era in the West, the scholastic theory of language "agrees naturally with the tradition known as analogism in Antiquity and renamed 'formalism' here," Seuren says.[41] A culture in which the secular superstition of language is being entrenched has turned classical "formalism" into an empty shell – the form no longer serves the moral and emotional needs of the community. The word "formalism" in late modern culture often denotes the empty promise of merely going through the motions without understanding the deeper meanings that might be involved. Hegel's political faith in the dead God's old formal language is formalism. It is an empty shell, a mere language-game. Its promises are heart-breaking delusions for those who trust the process and absolve themselves from responsibility for the results.

Seuren indicates Hegel adapted the institutional linguistics of the Church to modern politics. The political use of a language tradition borrowed from Church history had no guarantee for the integrity of its use over time. Voltaire and Hume had used history to scourge the upper classes. Hegel made history the comfortable pew of the new economic upper classes. Historical description, free from God and guilt, provided men of means with the moral and emotional detachment required for empire, class culture, and the White Man's burden.[42] Its lessons took deep root in the United States during the era of westward expansion. History was "the science of the ways in which knowledge appears" to the white, male, European middle-class.[43]

The pseudo-science of plain language historical description provided ordinary realists a special exemption from *both* the conviction of sin *and* the logic of radical doubt. The constancy of language made the dialectical clash of wills in history impregnable to critique. It assured the state, the bourgeois political economy, and its institutional infrastructure would continue *even after their moral collapse.* Deliberated or not, the brazen bad faith of it is worthy of a Borgia or a tobacco company. Heinrich Heine called Hegel the Louis XVIII of philosophy. He was the monarchist principle restored to life after the great age of revolutionary upheaval. Hegel was, secretly, the great conservative. The great return of the old traditions in new robes, with new backers and a new bankroll.[44] Hegel's morally ambiguous language survived on wings of song. It plays well, but the aesthetic sense and the moral sense are not synonymous. Truth is not beauty. Truth and roses both have thorns.

Hegel's 'joy' is a rhetorical trope which Paul de Man called a "metalepsis," i.e., "the exchange or substitution of cause and effect."[45] De Man took the word, "metalepsis" from Nietzsche's lectures on rhetoric. The "metaleptic" confusion between language as a cause and language as an effect was the germinal seed for de Man's *Allegories of Reading: Figural Language in Rousseau, Nietzsche, Rilke, and Proust* (1979). Hegelian history is the "figural language" for a Dick and Jane version of situational self-assertion that lets Dick and Jane be morally mindless. History decides the big issues, wisdom follows history, and philosophy anticipates the way history is going. Time reasons, so people do not. Facing questions of distributive justice, global development, environmental degradation, and the spiritual quality of our everyday lives, most competently adjusted Westerners default to a language process conceived and implemented by Hegel's Romantic flight from infinite grief. The bad faith of Hegel's historic turn is part of a deep and pervasive tradition that controls the very language in which the problem could and should be discussed. The circularity here between history and language is an existential complex of destructive negations at the heart of honesty, community, and interpersonal concern.

The happy historical consciousness moves in history like a fish in water and sums of the will of the world spirit it finds there. History eliminates the need to worry about one's neighbour. History takes over responsibility for issues of ethics and morals which pre-Enlightenment culture had taken to be fundamental to philosophy. Prior to the era of mass communication and computer enhancement Hegel invented the first virtual reality. The meaning and integrity of a life lived in association with others is a projection of history. History represents ethics, culture, and social values. Hegel is so confident in the absolute right of historical reason that he denies the need for ethical reflection. He calls ethics a "merely formal point of view." Its uselessness is evident in politics. He objects to traditional ethics because they can be used to support incredible sophistries. Some Christian moralists have been so audacious as to claim "instances of bravery, courage, magnanimity, self-denial, and self-sacrifice, are found among the most savage and the most pusillanimous nations." To even suggest the Negro or the Indians of the New World show "as much of social virtue and morality as the civilized Christian states, or even more" is unthinkable.[46] This French sophistry shows the morass to which psychological idealism of the Kantian sort can lead. Heaven forbid! Rational Europeans have history. Universal ethical questions are abstract questions of "formal rectitude – deserted by the living Spirit and by God," Hegel contends.

When you open questions about ethics and morality, you have opened a bottomless pit of nonsense, Hegel declares.[47] He announces:

> On these grounds a doubt has been suggested whether in the progress of history and of general culture mankind have become better; whether their morality has been increased – morality being regarded in a subjective aspect and view, as founded on what the agent holds to be right and wrong, good and evil.[48]

History shows that "social virtue" stands "in opposition to [this] false morality," Hegel declares. History puts "social virtue" on a "higher ground than that on which morality has properly its position." Moral philosophy,

> Must not be brought into collision with world-historical deeds and their accomplishment. The Litany of private virtues – modesty, humility, philanthropy and forbearance – must not be

raised against them. The History of the World might, on principle, entirely ignore the circle within which morality and the so much talked of distinction between the moral and the politic lies.⁴⁹

History justifies us, "not only in abstaining from judgments ... but in leaving individuals quite out of view and unmentioned," Hegel concludes.⁵⁰

Hegel thought "State-power and national wealth" were "the supreme purposes of its [the spirit's] strenuous exertion."⁵¹ There is a difference between Hegel's dangerous fascination with the nation-state and the equivalent fascination in twentieth-century form. Hegel does not make the political an end in itself. Politics is to Hegel as the sublime is to Kant. Politics shock the individual into recognition of a higher faculty of reason. Hegel continues,

> But its [spirit's] gaining acceptance thus is itself vain.... Only by self-consciousness being roused to revolt does it know its own peculiar torn and shattered condition; and in its knowing this it has *ipso facto* risen above that condition.⁵²

The purpose of the spirit's dialectical struggle is that ego, first for itself and then for the state, is overcome.

Through political struggle the ego discovers "pure insight...all the one-sidedness and peculiarity of the original self-existing self is extinguished."⁵³ The *experience* of the "pure insight" of the other realized through confrontation "is the simple ultimate being undifferentiated within itself":

> This pure insight is, then, the spirit that calls to every consciousness: be *for yourselves* what you are all essentially *in yourselves* – rational.⁵⁴

Hegel's political optimism makes politics a process of moral growth and personal self-discovery. The hurly-burly of modern politics teaches humility. Personal ego must, by virtue of the encounter with history, must be driven to "see" a higher truth. Political practice was Hegel's moral arena in which egotism and vanity were overcome. In Hegel's theology of the great new word being made flesh, the fragmentation of consciousness leads the ego to politics. Politics leads to a rational understanding of history. When the individual sees her life in the light of world history all is revealed. "Thereby the sole and only surviving interest is done away with; and individual light is resolved into universal insight.... By marking this feeling [of political participation] as a moment of the supreme Idea, the pure concept ... [overcomes] the empirical being" Hegel concludes.[55] This philosophy can, in truth, be called idealism; but it cannot itself be called truth.

"The term history ... comprehends not less what has *happened*, than the *narration* of what has happened," Hegel happily concluded.[56] He continued:

> This union of the two meanings we must regard as of a higher order than mere accident.... It is an internal vital principle common to both [events and language] that produces them synchronously.[57]

God originally guaranteed the emotional and intellectual union between two meanings. Hegel recognized the need for an internal principle of unity still existed after the skeptical takeover of public life during the Enlightenment. The language of politics provided this link for Hegel.[58] Hegel's idea of language is the first modern "linguistic turn." Hegel's covert theory of language is the golden calf of modern media and mass politics. The political dialectic in history is the new modern graven image. Political consensus is Hegel's god.

We cannot understand Hegel's language unless we understand what Hegel's language was designed to do. Hegel's philosophy of language saves a traditional manner of speaking without saving its moral content, sense of community, and interpersonal obligation to others. He leaves "Words which in themselves have a meaning" as the foundation for a new metaphysics. His theory of language re-grounded classical thought in a new faith for the age of mass culture, consensus politics, and commercial capitalism. "It is apparent we should grasp a knowledge of cause from *the origin*," Aristotle observes [emphasis added]. Hegel gives the Aristotelian principle of origin a new foundation. The origin of Hegel's philosophy is the new middle class. The knowledge it proffers is a faith and knowledge in the new industrial system. Aristotelian *arché* becomes an ethos driven by words, a way of life driven by self-advertising. It is a splendid system of tropes for a middle-class who will avoid, if possible, the harm, damage, and aggressive misunderstandings its politics have sown.

Aristotle had resorted to dialectical arguments as a negative proof for the existence of qualities that could not be proven directly. He wanted to establish the first principles of "the science of being as such ... by means of a refutation of the premises contrary to these principles.... The necessity of scientific statements, which is demonstrable in the case of essential attributes [like physical motion], is indemonstrable in the case of the first principles each individual science presupposes," Richard Bodéüs explains. Aristotle resorted to dialectical argument because no direct argument existed with which to secure the first principles of his ethics and physics. Bodéüs explains that "this dialectical attempt at securing first principles is an integral part of a larger project that paved the way for many philosophical paths and was later to be called 'metaphysical.'"[59]

Aristotle's discussion of origin and cause was a formal process of negative induction. It was an eristic method for defending the essential in life from skeptical relativism. Aristotle left his principles standing in negative relief by showing "contrary premises necessarily lead to contradictions." The Medieval theological perspective developed from Aristotle's negative proof. God had to exist or else the world was unintelligible. It was impossible to conceive good and evil without an absolute presence whose power was "real." Hegel carried the classical debate over essentials into modern history. His adaptation of the Aristotelian negative proof was so successful, metaphysics continued without even being recognized as such. The old conversation of the West continued with political debate taking the place of angels, ectoplasm, divine reason, and pure form. In Hegelian history an occult pantheon of unseen paganisms moves toward redemption through an ironic sequence of *felix peccata*.

Stephen Priest suggests Hegel's philosophy of history is not intelligible by contemporary standards of logic. Hegel's "examples are open to Quine's objection to analyticity based on synonymy," Priest points out.[60] Priest is referring to the Quine-Duhem thesis that any statement can be true providing you make enough changes to the background system. History is an excellent background system for flux and change. The early Church used history to adapt its language to new ideas. It assimilated pagan feasts and non-Christian rituals by explaining ideas and events in historical parallel. History can always be re-written in such a way that current ideas and events appear to move in tandem. Hegelian history is the malleable background for the Quine-Duhem thesis in action. In Hegel, "Geist is not the cause of what is," Priest observes. Geist "is what is," he advises.[61] The ethical dilemma should be obvious. In a system where spirit is synonymous with history, anything real is, arguably, full of the spirit. Historical continuity shows the spirit of the times and the spirit of the times is, by definition, the spirit of the good. Shlomo Barer identifies this discovery as the turning point in the intellectual development of the young Marx. In the first and most revealing of Marx's surviving letters, he explained to his father, Heinrich, how "Hegel's subtle dialectic preserves the 'is' even while changing it into the 'ought.'" Although he did not admit it to his father, "he was actually about to make philosophy his chief concern," Barer concludes.[62]

Ethics are suppressed by Hegel, but not directly. Hegel suppresses the moral content of the heritage culture by appropriating its theory of language. The Esperanto of world commerce and the global political economy is not likely a foundation for what a less skeptical society would have called "spirit." Robust empirical evidence indicates consensus politics do not usually sustain the community traditions of elementary decency and ordinary kindness normally associated with a moral life. Modern intellectual history faces the failure of its own self-denying philosophical flight from infinite grief. Words which, in themselves, have a meaning are the foundation for political correctness, professional detachment, and bureaucratic indifference. They will not and cannot assuage the "infinite grief" of a history without a warrant for ethics, moral responsibility, and interpersonal concern. Hegel's theory of language was the linchpin holding together the dual worlds of a new secular spiritual incarnation. The defence of Hegel's language was the next step in spreading Hegel's "joy" over words to the rest of the European world.

Hegel's philosophy of history was welcomed by the conservative concert of Europe after the Napoleonic wars. After twenty-five years of revolutionary tumult, Hegel's stately dialectic was an idea whose time had come. Hegel gave philosophical dignity to the boom and buzz of ordinary events. The world spirit in daily life touched every man with its cunning, wisdom, and grace. Even the humblest were included. Even the smallest life was, in some small way, part of the great pageant of historical progress. Europe was an event history had created for the ultimate edification of the rest of the world. Hegel's 'joy' for history was the apostle's creed for the new gospel of progress.

Hegel's philosophy of history defeated the Kantian critique of judgment in the battle for the hearts and minds of the new, upwardly mobile, industrial middle-class. World history was turned into a vocational education in political economy and national politics. Hegel's dialectical dream was institutionalized by Leopold von Ranke (1795–1886). Ranke is considered the father of modern historical method. Ranke was Hegel's organization man. He franchised Hegel's dream to every college and university in the Western world. Ranke took his research method from Barthold Georg Niebuhr's *The History of Rome* (1812), but he took his philosophy of history from Hegel. Ranke viewed history as a "dialogue, coming from kindred hearts ... which lovingly guides contemplation ever higher until it finds God and general truth....The inherence of the eternal in the particular need not be demonstrated – it is the religious ground which our historical effort assumes," he explained.[63] Ranke's secular faith in history gave Hegel's morally suspect "cunning of reason" a scholarly method. Ranke's method gave scholarly respectability to Hegel's stratospheric abstractions. Hegel's "joy" over words which have a meaning in themselves was confirmed by modern scholarship. Ranke insisted repeatedly that history "is not a denial but fulfillment of philosophy."[64] The philosophy being fulfilled is unmistakable. Ranke's functional faith in history as the language of religious providence lets him imply *the* philosophy, *the* reason, and *the* history as if history were a ceiling to floor showcase for spiritual truth.

*The* philosophy which history "fulfills" is Hegel's philosophy of state. History builds complicity with the state into the language of fact. Historical descriptions which in themselves allegedly have a larger, more inclusive meaning are the universal language of political cunning. Ranke completes the fundamental intuition inherent in Hegel's turn from pietism. Ranke makes the transition from theology to history concrete. The politics of the nation-state stand in for theology in the new historicist system. History "fulfills" theology by incarnating the great philosophical questions of truth, knowledge, ethics, justice, ideals, and the law in the modern political process.

Ranke received his first university appointment at the University of Berlin in 1825 when he was thirty years old. He wrote that his success would never cause him to forget, "the knowledge ... of the God of our nations and of the world."[65] He said that he believed that, "One must experience everything in order to understand, or rather to know that one does not understand.... It is all a mystery: marriage and birth, life and death; behind and with sensory appearance appears the Divine, as in the Lord's Supper.... Without an absorption in divine things, man is a shadow on earth, passing through in the haze."⁶⁶ Nostalgia for "the old God" coloured his writing and shaped his thoughts.⁶⁷

The historical and the religious threads in Ranke's intellectual life come together in the following passage from a letter Ranke wrote to his younger brother Heinrich in the spring of 1820:

> I can only assure you that I am very lonely. My heart is so numb that it does not even complain much about it. But there is a dialogue, coming from kindred hearts ... which lovingly guides contemplation ever higher until it finds God and general truth.... This dialogue I miss.... The fog of enveloping habitual error still gives way but little.... If I only had your faith! If I only were firm!⁶⁸

It was in this mood that Ranke turned to historical study. History, for Ranke, was the study in which he hoped to find "a union of God and the world which he could find neither in religion nor in classical education."⁶⁹

Rankean history was the fulfillment of pre-Enlightenment faith, not the fulfillment of post-Enlightenment science. Ranke thought that an historian can "attain the perception of spiritual elements through mere research." "The historian," he wrote, "is but an organ of the general spirit which realized itself through him." In this spirit, Ranke reiterated his famous historical formula from 1824 again in the early 1840s with an important qualification:

> Only from a spiritually combined series of facts does the event result. Our task is thus to inquire into what really happened [*was eigentlich geschehen ist*] in the series of facts ... in its sum.⁷⁰

Between 1819 and 1822, when he began writing his first historical book, Ranke rejected orthodox Christianity and replaced it with his ever-stronger belief in history as "the uninhibited truth of the inner sense."⁷¹ His life was retracing the biographical experience of his philosophical mentor. The turn to history to cover the loss of traditional faith is hidden by his historical method. No deeper explanation is given for a shallow secular faith easily washed away by the skeptical tide of current events in the next century.

An early manuscript which Ranke finished in 1831 was published in 1878 under the title *History of Italian Art*. Its companion piece, *History of Italian Poetry*, had been finished in 1835 and was published in 1837. It shows Ranke was a cultural idealist. When he told historians to write *wie es eigentlich gewesen war* (as it actually was), he was invoking Hegel's old "conceptive faculty". He believed historians and poets shared the same fundamental language. Things "as they actually were" would enlighten the moral spirit and kindle a traditional hope for the good of humanity in every human heart. Historical description was a scientific art. Ranke's method was a joyful marriage between rational words and Romantic sentiments. Enlightenment reason and religious faith come together in the Hegelian church of timeless words, political worlds and spiritual becoming.

By the turn of the twentieth century Hegel's infinite grief had been overcome in a manner of speaking. Modern professional historians no longer remembered the emotional orientation of these old debates. They did not recall accurately and with respect the time when most people still believed conscience, ethics, and individual moral agency "transcended" politics. The language of modern history "forgot" Hegel's grief. By the turn of the twentieth century, Hegel's "joy in words" had become an article of secular faith with no warrant other than political success. Theoretical legitimacy did not lag far behind political success. The owl of Minerva flew for Hegel just as he predicted. After Hegel and Ranke joined the pantheon of the liberal arts, Wilhelm Dilthey summed them up. His widely-accepted theory of historical "understanding" stood uncontested in the modern research university for almost a hundred years.

### WILHELM DILTHEY (1833–1911)

José Ortega y Gasset called Wilhelm Dilthey "the most important philosopher in the second half of the nineteenth century." Gasset credits Dilthey with making history a "moral science." Dilthey expanded history to include a whole way of life, Ortega explains.[72] Ortega's view was the traditional view of Dilthey for most of the twentieth century. The moral "expansion" of the social sciences Ortega praised depended on a move which has been made problematic in late modern thought. Dilthey's "expansion" of historical understanding rested squarely on Hegel's "joy" over words "which in themselves have a meaning."

Robert Chia and Ian King (2001) criticize Dilthey for ignoring the ethical and political dimensions of language. Dilthey makes "language the organizational template which actively constructs social reality," they point out. Robin Cooper (1983) emphasizes that Dilthey's theory of historical understanding "is a form of covertly willed prior knowledge for validating conventional knowledge."[73] The skeptic's classical dodge around the "minor" and merely "subjective" consideration of ethics becomes a pseudo-science with the linguistic structuralism of Wilhelm Dilthey.

What is at stake in Dilthey's theory of history is the first and original meaning of the word, "structuralism". The hermeneutical meaning of "structure" as used for over a century in literature and history refers to a Romantic theory of "objective mind" which rested solidly on Hume's and Hegel's theory of language. Dilthey's "structuralism" or "formalism" stipulates all human minds have the same cognitive structure. History, literature, and the Fine Arts provide the human cognitive structure with the stimuli it needs to realize its full potential. History is the keystone in Dilthey's theory of human development. Literature and the Fine Arts play a similar role in parallel schools of structural interpretation. The turf war over structure and structuralism is a fraternal tempest in a Romantic teapot. They all assert an emotional link between cognitive and moral development. Historical description, literature and the Fine Arts edify human beings because people have an innate emotional ability to react morally to what they see. In the nineteenth century the moral development of the mind ran parallel to progress in science and the economy. The moral development achieved through history, literature, and the arts compensated for the more aggressive side of modern life. Classical structuralism was kind to the fact-based banalities of history. The emotional link between cognitive and moral development gave the study of history a powerful claim to be the "queen" of the human sciences.

Since watching could make you moral; reading, listening, and going to art galleries could make you good. It was a neat theory, highly appealing to the elite classes of the Romantic era. It let them endow schools and enjoy the arts without being overly concerned about the physical suffering of others. The metaphysics of knowing soothed their social conscience. It assured them they were the best because their spirits had been nurtured on the best that had been written and thought. Adam Smith and the Scottish Enlightenment used "the spectator theory of value" to justify the moral indifference of dons, squires, and aristocrats to the plight of the peasantry during the enclosure movement. Wilhelm Dilthey carried "the spectator theory of value" one stage deeper into the social psychology of his era. He gave the infamous invisible hand of *laissez-faire* economics the power to genuflect before the state and worship economic progress.

Dilthey's amalgam of Romanticism, nationalism, and popular psychology has had remarkable staying power. Many reflexive assumptions about the efficacy of culture and intellectuality are traceable to Dilthey and his generation of German idealists at the end of the nineteenth century. They spawned a popular idea of cultural irradiation which has been dragging reluctant husbands to the opera for over a century. The general theory was that an emotionally educated person is sensitive to quality. Good taste, when fully developed, runs the gamut from décor to morality. Kant's casual observation that "Taste is morality in external appearance" was their motto. History was the linchpin holding together the more imaginative cognitive disciplines. History showed how far humanity had developed, and history also indicated how far we still had to go. History illustrated qualitative differences to which the cultured and educated had been sensitized. The qualitative difference between how things were and how things ought to be was revealed to them by their educated feelings. Seeing, sensitively, with senses that had been educated by history, literature, and the arts had closed Hume's devastating fork. The skeptical gap between the relations of ideas and matters of fact was no longer a threat to public morality. The old German word for Dilthey's vicarious social conscience was *Bildung*, literally life in the image of the culture. The vicarious life of culture and learning could awaken the dullest sensibility from its potentially devastating skepticism. Emotional education would resolve the perennial skeptical moral predicament. The sight of history falling short would stimulate the greater good. Language was the master key to the complex tumblers of Dilthey's Biedermeier brain. His classy theory of bourgeois values was hard-wired with Hegelian 'joy.' Words which in themselves have a meaning linked the vicarious moral life of private sensitivity to the suffering of others.

Dilthey was another pastor's son who had studied theology in preparation for the ministry. Dilthey's career shift from theology to philosophy of history was symptomatic of the modernization process in Western Europe. Change was so evident and progress was so real, the older questions of traditional theology and classical philosophy seemed almost antiquated. His son-in-law Georg Misch recorded Dilthey's disillusionment with theology. The history of medieval Christianity destroyed Dilthey's tolerance for "the beyond" in general. Dilthey complained:

> The historian of Christianity has to endure the tortures of Tantalus.... I struggle in vain to wring any inner life from this

alien material.... This mistrust of human nature in its wholesome serenity – that nature which has always been an object of highest admiration to me; this haste towards the beyond and towards transsensual knowledge ... this sectarianism, which I find simply incomprehensible.... I hate it thoroughly.[74]

Modern history and the study of history contributed to Dilthey's loss of faith. He was, in his emotions, in solidarity with millions of like-minded moderns since the Renaissance. He believed deeply, passionately, in the traditions of his culture. He wanted, more than anything, to save the roots of his childhood faith from destruction by nationalism and the industrial revolution. He found himself a promising intellectual in his late twenties whose life, education, and experience had stranded him on the barren rock of skeptical empiricism in a materialistic age. Like Kant, he refused to abandon the moral traditions of the old faith. Like Hegel, he was unwilling to be non-conformist and leave the established church. Wilhelm Dilthey was trapped in the triple bind of science, faith, and social conformity. To save faith and face, Dilthey tried to give the elementary structures of traditional religious life a new, scientific foundation.

In 1860, the twenty-seven-year-old Dilthey professed, "His vocation was to grasp the innermost essence *of the religious life in history* and to provide a moving portrayal of it in our time, a time which is concerned exclusively with the state and with science."[75] Dilthey turned from theology to philosophy of history because he believed "seeing" history would raise moral consciousness. That had been his personal, biographical experience, and he believed what had worked for him would work for others. On the basis of his own deeply personal experience, Dilthey concluded "this world" could do better service for the spiritual life than the old "transsensual knowledge" of "the beyond."

Dilthey's historical stature as a thinker is greater than Schiller, Pater, Arnold, and the other aestheticians of his day. Dilthey directly addressed the moral weakness of Hegelian historicism and skeptical philosophy. He answered Hegel and Hume with one system. It combined the two areas of major visibility in nineteenth-century culture – art and history. Dilthey rejected Hume's theory of necessity as a plausible foundation for moral values. Dilthey's answer was an aesthetic reworking of the skeptic's favourite ethical labour-saving device. He built up Hegel's "conceptive faculty" until it included a traditional moral dimension. Dilthey defended the

Hegel's historical idealism from Hegel's moral relativism. According to Dilthey, the old Godly connection between words and things was still in force. The living link between subject and object was still guaranteed by secular history. Hegel should not have dismissed ethics, but he need not have defended it, either. The structure of the human brain meant ethics could fend for itself. The vicarious shocks of modern history resonated so deeply in the soul, that moral progress was inevitable.

Otto Pöggeler describes Dilthey's "metaphysics" as a new secular holy spirit. He notes:

> The shortcoming of [Dilthey's] metaphysics is that it conceives of thinking as a "seeing" and of Being as a constant being-in-view, a constant presence [*ousia*]; thus it cannot ascertain the realization of factical-historical life itself.[76]

Dilthey is no more able to stand outside his own history than the old Christian martyr could stand outside his faith. Pöggeler believes Dilthey smuggled in a metaphysical perspective without admitting it. He did not eliminate the need for metaphysical properties within the skeptical point of view. He introduced a new one suitable for the attitudes and values of his time. Dilthey's new metaphysics was a camouflage spirituality cut whole-cloth from the moral values of a previous era.

The skeptical Achilles' heel is ethics. Dilthey believed history could teach ethics because history and human nature showed parallel processes of development. History showed the progress of culture and culture showed the progress of human nature. Each half of human experience ratcheted up the other in a continual cycle of mutual uplift. The modern philosophy of history and the Fine Arts has slogged in Dilthey's hermeneutical circle for a century. Like an old elephant at the fair, the great beast carries its children at ground level, its ponderous legs deep in the trench dredged by stolid and unthinking decades of mindless labour.

History, Dilthey explained, was the source and solace for Hegel's infinite grief. Happily, he concluded, history had broken its ties to theology in the modern age. The modern "inner life" no longer needed guilt or grief. The fruitful and productive side of religion (its tranquility and compassion) could be learned from the study of history. The guilt, fear, and grief of traditional theology could be left behind. The "inner life" of the old theology was transported from the sacred to the secular by Dilthey's

Romantic affirmation of human nature. In turning to history from religion, Dilthey tried to keep the forgiving core and peel away the guilt and sin from the traditional Christian attitude toward life. Ramon J. Betanzos notes Dilthey's lengthy list of worldviews (over sixty) does not mention anyone who is primarily a religious thinker. He says virtually nothing about Christ or Moses, the patriarchs, prophets, apostles, or evangelists. Even his interest in Schleiermacher [who invented hermeneutics] is tangential. "It is ironic that one whose life was dedicated to historical studies, especially *Geistesgeschichte*, should leave this giant lacuna in this survey of significant worldviews," Betanzos remarks.[77]

Dilthey thought he had discovered, "the fixed system of relations in which our self stands to other persons and to objects outside us." Difference was not a world problem or, even, a local one. Apparent contradiction was an illusion. No theologian ever proved God, no Freudian ever defended repression, and no imperialist ever honoured the dominions with a more topsy-turvy logic than Dilthey on culture. A "limitless variety of systems and the claim of each system to be universally true was a contradiction which supported the skeptical attitude more effectively than any systematic argument," he concluded.[78] The contradictions and quarrels between dozens of particular points of view did not concern Dilthey. He believed the invisible hand of cultural conflict was harmonized by the universal regularity of the human mind. Innate structures of feeling would reflexively harmonize the dozens of competing perspectives openly shared among the brightest and best. Dilthey used the many different examples of what we now call faiths and cultures as proof for one fixed psychic system at work in all times and places. He reduced the diversity of world history to one similar, psychological process. His psychological deduction of a universal historical process was compatible with the mainstream thinking of the time.

David Hume had coolly stipulated human nature was constant and unchanging just like Newton's laws. It was, in Hume's opinion, constantly conniving, self-centred, and pleasure-seeking. Dilthey turned Hume's skeptical constant on its head. He saw in history a categorical capacity for a diametrically opposite set of qualities from the ones Hume had specified. Dilthey reasoned since all white, European male "inner lives" were psychologically the same, the progress of Western society proved their values were objectively "true." Apparent cultural and philosophical contradictions were being brought together by the grand dialectic Hegel had analyzed. History revealed "the 'I' in the 'Thou'" to thoughtful readers of modern history.[79] Dilthey's portmanteau term for the secularization of the spirit was *verstehen*, i.e., "understanding." The new "inner life" of historical "understanding" was synchronized with public progress. Its conflicts were the high road to Plato's utopia. Conflict led to self-discovery, self led to others and solidarity with others led to inner peace, public wealth, and the rule of law. Empire, class conflict and psychological distress were but way stations on the road to the good life.

Dilthey explained the new historical "understanding" of man and the spirit means:

> Man knows himself only in history, *never through introspection*; indeed, we all seek him in history.... Man is only given to us at all in terms of his realized possibilities.... The extension of our knowledge of what is given in experience takes place through the interpretation of the objectifications of life and this interpretation, in truth, is only made possible by plumbing the depths of subjective experience.... The mind rediscovers itself at ever higher levels of connectedness [emphasis].[80]

Dilthey's secular hermeneutics was so dominant in Europe that the German verb "to understand" (*verstehen*) became the professional term among historians for the special knowledge which the study of history affords those who follow its muse.

The best study of Dilthey is Rudolf A. Makkreel's *Dilthey: Philosopher of the Human Studies* (1975). Makkreel observes that:

> Among the major philosophers of the late nineteenth century, none has contributed more to the understanding of historical life than Wilhelm Dilthey.[81]

"Human Studies" is Makkreel's translation of Dilthey's word, *Geisteswissenschaften*. It means literally, "spiritual science." Ironically, Dilthey intended *Geisteswissenschaften* to be the German translation of J.S. Mill's "moral sciences."[82] Dilthey appreciated Mill's intentions, but he felt that a moral science modelled exclusively on the natural sciences had been the flaw in Hume and Hegel. The link between the outer world and the inner life was indefinite in a world without God. To build scientifically on the good start superstition had left us with, a special faculty of knowledge had to be added to the skeptical view.

To save the "moral sciences" from skeptical destruction, Dilthey argued history is a distinct and separate way of understanding the world. Its hermeneutical laws are exempt from logical criticism and the demand for internal consistency to which every other modern body of thought is accountable. Makkreel writes, in support, that:

> Dilthey's primary aim is to argue that the methodology of the *Geisteswissenschaften* must be different from that of the *Naturwissenschaften* (natural sciences).[83]

To salvage moral integrity from skeptical destruction Dilthey took a methodological step which is highly problematic. "Dilthey proposed that we expand the self in order to uncover the transcendental conditions of intersubjective understanding," Makkreel explains.[84] Inside the charmed circle of affluent swells Dilthey's hypothesis was a lovely excuse for war, plunder and naked aggression. Even in Dilthey's own terms, the "expansion" of the "self" was a double expansion between two selves or aspects of the self which were morally incompatible. One self was the allegedly timeless one resident inside all white, straight, Christian and middle-class males. The other was an historical self, subject to the parochialisms of the time. Dilthey did not try to sort out the difference between these two equally expandable inner lives.

Dilthey's timeless "self" is being historically "expanded" for ulterior motives. His structuralist theory of "historical understanding" lets modern history do its work without facing moral guilt and ethical responsibility. Dilthey has not explained how the "spiritual values" of history produce idealism and moral principles outside, above, and beyond the times and places of real, empirical history. Dilthey refers all questions about history to history, itself. History was the grain of sand and the mind was an oyster. The irritations of history had grown over the course of four thousand years into a pearl of enormous wisdom. He, Dilthey, was an Hegelian Dr. Johnson. He refuted all skeptical doubt thus: Kick the facts and the pain is your proof. The historical evidence for parallel paths of moral and scientific progress is conclusive. There could not be a better time or place to live than Europe in the nineteenth century. More people live better there than they have ever lived anywhere else before. The historical process is total and irrevocable. The moral life and material progress are one. They are the grand cunning of history working behind the backs and over the heads of the people. The dialectic in history lets Dilthey deduce what could not be proved otherwise. The human mind and the moral spirit are historically aligned.

If the subsequent facts of world history are any guide, Dilthey's transcendental understanding of history did not "understand" history and moral development very well. Considerable factual evidence in the twentieth century suggests Dilthey's split-world paradigm of intuitive "understanding" alienated the moral life from modern politics. Dilthey's neatly structured world of parallel development was class-biased, gender-biased, and ethnocentric. The late modern global world of liminal cultures and marginal peoples finds Dilthey's intuitive fun house a heartbreak hotel of smoke and mirrors. His expanded "self" was an imperialist. Dilthey's hermeneutics generated an enthusiasm not seen since Plotinus.

"In Hegel, Dilthey discovered the most powerful embodiment of nineteenth-century historical accomplishments," Makkreel notes.[85] Dilthey's psychic sense of historical "understanding" made Hegel a psychological property of the human mind. External contradiction was the secret signpost pointing the way toward an internal harmony of spirit. Only the edified and cultured could know this, but they were the chosen ones. Their insights into the nature of history and human nature were the only ones which really counted. Ethics, as always, was the principle casualty of Dilthey's happy hermeneutical system. The "is" and "oughts" of history were an emotional dissonance for the viewer/knower. The facts of history set the external "cunning of reason" at work inside the human heart. Dilthey's edified theory of historical "understanding" provided modern historians with their still standard reason for not needing Kant, theology, or simple, moral consistency. History does not need theology or philosophy. History holds up its mirror to the human heart. The human mind interprets what the heart understands. Mind and heart together have a natural aptitude to see in history the power of ideas. Biography was the best way to study history in Dilthey's opinion. Ideas and events came together naturally in the lives of famous men.

Dilthey wrote, "the peculiar contribution of 'understanding' in the human studies lies in this: the objective mind and the power of the individual together determine the mind-affected world. History rests on the understanding of these two." Dilthey's explanation of the "conjunction" between individual and world posited two coexistent modes of alternative experience *which run in tandem.* Their connection in the unified life of the spirit was an "objective mind" viewing events from outside the fray. Historical events were an *a priori* conjunction of body and mind, which Dilthey called a "composite structure."[86] The unity between the inner laws of the psyche and the outer laws of history assured a moral "understanding" of events was the inevitable by-product of a good education.

Russell Jacoby, frontline reporter of the culture wars, notes cautiously that:

> Dilthey in his uncertainty, oscillation and desperation foreshadowed a crisis.... In the throes of that crisis, the German intellectual world turned to the interpretation of history and life in a skeptical and relativistic mood.[87]

Jacoby's shadows lean in the wrong direction. Dilthey's interpretation of history does not foreshadow anything. It is the culmination of a moral crisis in modern thought that was already there. Dilthey's theory of objective mind completes the denaturing of religion in the West and its transformation into patriotism. His theory of spiritual *"verstehen"* defines a critical chiasmus in secular thought *which already occurred* by 1905. With Dilthey, historical studies accepted a metaphysical assumption that retrofitted history for the ulterior purposes of the present. Grief was out and progress was in. Guilt was out and consensus was triumphant. The crisis was here. History stood in for theology among the managerial elites of the nineteenth century. The only one of the old religious essentials it retained was language. Lacking God, grief and moral introspection, history had become a secular casuistry for industrial progress, economic empire and the invisible hand.

Hegel, Ranke, and Dilthey foreshadowed a crisis in one important sense. They were far-sighted fundamentalists who turned to politics and history after they lost their traditional religious faith. Probably, they anticipated a class crisis among the affluent bourgeois in subsequent decades. If Hegel, Ranke and Dilthey represent an early crisis in modern intellectual history, then one element in their crisis requires mention. The social history of their precipitate conversion to politics is a Kantian problem in the social history of ideas. From Kant's perspective, faith cannot be wrong. The wrong lies in the form in which faith is expressed. The secular faith of Hegel, Ranke and Dilthey was unintelligible. Their secular faith meant the old language of the good remained in play even though the idea of the good had changed. If government and civil administration were to discuss truth, law and moral obligation, the discussion had to be free from the skeptical politics which determined it. Consensus politics could not affect the meaning of the noble words most politicians like, ever so fondly, to use. Hegel's, Ranke's and Dilthey's secular faith is a modern Shaman's faith in mantras and magic words. They had converted to an antinomy, a bottomless argument, a knot, a bind, and a logical short-circuit from which no truth could ever be drawn. The language of business, public administration and politics is impregnated with stories of fame and wealth. It describes wealth and power, but it cannot describe how to live. I believe the crisis foreshadowed in Dilthey is an emotional and psychological crisis in the daily life of most Western adults. Over the long run, Dilthey's theory of language failed to sustain daily life. The loneliness and moral anomy of a world without God, grief or moral introspection collapsed into the therapeutic culture of the late twentieth century. I suspect the minority experience of the early Hegelians became a majority experience a century later. In this sense, Dilthey's crisis anticipated a general crisis in secular society and the industrial states.

The Romantics said they wanted history *to save their world* from the "skeptical and relativistic mood" of eighteenth-century Enlightenment. One may suspect they also wanted to save their world from their traditional moral conscience. The contemporary cultural unease which Russell Jacoby attributes to Dilthey's "oscillation and desperation" was part of a century-long attempt to deny the immorality of Hegel's historical cunning. A double standard was at work in the social sciences and it was just as pernicious as the racial, gender, and economic double standards also pervading the same historical era. Hegel, Ranke, and Dilthey wanted the freedom of Enlightenment skepticism without any of the uncomfortable behavioural questions honest skeptics like Hume and Kant had raised. They wanted the best of science and the best of faith without debating first principles. They wanted to practice skepticism without admitting the skeptical ethical predicaments in which their politics, economy and daily life were involved.

In his typically combative style, Marx had diagnosed the dilemma by the time Dilthey was born. The moral crisis foreshadowed in Hegel's philosophy of history had already happened. Dilthey built the crisis into the language of literary criticism and political philosophy. Marx believed:

> The bourgeois philosophers have nothing of Hegel's dialectics but language.... They do not directly state that bourgeois life is for them an eternal verity. They state it indirectly by deifying the categories which express bourgeois attitudes in the form of thought.... This mistake arises from the fact that the bourgeois man is to them the only possible basis of every society; they cannot imagine a society in which men have ceased to be bourgeois.[88]

Dilthey's language suits a public arena from which God, grief, and moral introspection have been banished. Dilthey's theory of historical "understanding" is a temporal conjunction which fits into the nineteenth century like a fish in water. His optimism is founded on an ulterior convocation of literati and imperialists. Dilthey wants history to bear his personal burden of ontological grief and sum up his public burden of moral responsibility. History "shows" philosophy in action and relieves him of his duty to others. It records the great lessons of the past and explains how they could not be any other way. In a democracy, the public burden of moral responsibility is paid when the history is written. No one is responsible for the political will required to change history. A solitary human being cannot take the sins of the world on her shoulders. Personal responsibility ends with "understanding" the truth about history.

"Understanding", in Dilthey's sense of the term, limits moral responsibility. The charity of the Victorian mind found a public voice, and a political excuse. The inner duality of the system emaciated traditional virtue. *Verstehen* brings opprobrium to the high culture of the late nineteenth century. Quentin Skinner traces its shame back to the British constitutionalists of the restoration period two centuries before. He sees politics replacing moral will in Western culture at that time. The erosion of personal responsibility is in part seduction by wealth, but, in greater part, it is seduction by consensus. After the civil war, personal responsibility was surrendered to the politicians. British citizens let politics define "liberty".[89] From this time forward the language of modern public life moved inexorably toward a moral silent spring. The plots it hatched were too thin to nurture life. The accumulation of behavioural anomalies in the economy and public administration are demoralizing to ordinary life outside the archives of government. Understanding history meant understanding politics. The carrot of wealth and the club of complexity drove the old virtues underground.

In the discourse Darwinism of modern intellectual history, the cunning of reason has it both ways. It can criticize with moral impunity. Observers who understand history can slipstream the order of things and feel privileged to follow in its wake. The literati who have been schooled to Hegel and Dilthey have no moral responsibility higher than consensus. One may debate Marx's violence. He is a prophet of dialectical thuggery schooled in the nineteenth century academy of Romantic will. Withal, one timeless value will always be connected with his ringing dissent from the moral cowardice of his day. Marx knew his culture had lost its public sense of right and wrong. He realized modern, industrial society had lost its moral sense. His appeal to the proletariat was a call to pick up the fallen standard of a venerable argument. Politics without moral standards, ethics, and a rigorous system of personal accountability was a return to a classical problem Marx hoped had died with Rome. He is correct about the foundations of nineteenth-century philosophy, even if he excludes himself from his own fruitful observations. The philosophy of Hegel and Dilthey cannot conceive of society in any way other than it is. From inside a secular metaphysics like theirs, Hume's disastrous fork is an iron law. The gap between is and ought has been sealed like the gates of Hell. Whatever is the case *is* what ought to be.

Dilthey gave the political culture of ethical avoidance which Hegel began a 'scientific' status. The "crisis" Dilthey's work "foreshadows" was the inevitable moment when economic empires, gender chauvinism, and class hypocrisy would be unmasked. Above all else, the triumphant middle class had to forestall its inevitable reckoning with the ethics of its violent, free enterprise world. The "crisis" Dilthey "foreshadowed" was the return of moral questions which nineteenth-century optimism had repressed. Dilthey's "crisis" foreshadows nothing other than having to admit imperialism, racism, gender chauvinism, and class culture were morally insupportable. The "crisis" Jacoby saw is the ethical crisis internal to Dilthey's concept of history. Dilthey's concept of *"verstehen"* is a mind-game of the modern middle class. It is the intellectual hypocrisy of a culture that has killed God but still wants to look like it obeys the old God's moral laws.

The nineteenth century was not embarrassed by its smarmy elegance. It applied a double standard to culture and history just as it applied double standards to race, gender, capital C, Fine Art Culture, and the economy. Dilthey's structuralism was a culturally specific pedagogy of conformist attitudes and consensus practices. It seemed as natural to educated nineteenth-century elites as empire, Christianity and white, European, male superiority. Dilthey's aesthetic link to history was definitive for the age. One can read its narrow purposes in Dilthey's definition of history. "History is the expressions of life which have become part of the objective mind," he concluded.[90] Europe has discovered the 'objective' life of the mind. Applied science and Western culture are the two sides of this historic revelation. History records their composite interaction. Modern history is the new metaphysics for the new skeptical age. The expansion of the West and the expansion of "objective mind" are one and the same.

Dilthey thought he was responding to, "the great crisis of the sciences and European culture which we are now living through." The crisis had "so deeply and totally taken possession of my spirit," he wrote, "that the desire to be of some help in it has extinguished every extraneous and personal ambition."[91] Dilthey thought his theory of interpretation had solved the "great crisis of the sciences and European culture." Leonard Krieger's editor, Michael Ermarth points out that Dilthey's system stands or falls on its use of language. He writes that "hermeneutics, not psychology, emerge as the key to the comprehension of world-views, for the regularities in the structure and development of world-views is more properly analogous to the sphere of language than that of nature."[92]

Dilthey claimed he had discovered the property of mind which saved skepticism from self-destruction. Ermarth suggests Dilthey had discovered the property of modern language which let skeptics avoid the truth about Western history. Language was Dilthey's first line of covert defence against knowing the truth about imperial politics and class conflict. The ethical, economic, and social criticism of nineteenth-century society was taboo. Dilthey's theory of historical "understanding" was the birth of newspeak and political correctness. Controlling the language of historical representation remains the modern Maginot line of class politics, civic religion, and cultural chauvinisms down to the present day.

Dilthey thought he was developing a 'science' which would penetrate down to the level of basic assumptions and uncover the psychological well-spring of history and the Fine Arts. He stressed the difference between a science of strictly causal laws and the historical 'science' of vital relations and structures. Dilthey understood history as the science having "the highest power to make conscious" the thought structures behind human social behaviour. History was the science of "bringing to highest consciousness, founding, judging critically, and relating in the broadest coherence" all empirical questions dealing with culture and politics.[93] History revealed the coherent structures in which empirical events could be understood.

Dilthey could only make these extended claims because he trusted implicitly that words in themselves have a meaning. He depended on an already formed language to sustain and nurture his already formed ideas. He knew the educated elites of his era worshipped the same fallacy. His aesthetic theory of historical "verstehen" was a political marriage of middle-class minds at the deepest level of the new industrial culture. The "psychic lawfulness" of language guaranteed an ordered correspondence between the outer and the inner life. Universal mental structures guaranteed clear narrative language transcended the gap between the spirit and its politics. Nineteenth-century social studies assumed the mental structures of educated readers were sufficiently interchangeable for word worlds to leap from head to head like the goddess of love at Plato's symposium. The empirical language of factual events edified mind and ordered politics at the same time. The honesty of Enlightenment was reduced to the pabulum of sentimentality. More than any other intellectual of the times, Dilthey made nineteenth-century historical studies a moral disaster. His interpretive system did not awaken conscience to the defence of others; it awoke cunning to the service of personal advantage.

Dilthey coined the phrase "lived experience" to describe the structural homology between inner and outer experience in his historical system. In Dilthey's secular homiletics "lived experience" was as dualistic as the old pieties. "Lived experience" retained the inner duality of the old spiritual life. Ideas and events; spirit and world; ethics and politics were parallel structures. Unfortunately for the new fundamentalists, they lacked a Messiah. The new secular politics of the spirit, i.e., "objective mind," had to maintain a level of critical introspection analogous to the guilty conscience of the old religions. The new secular dispensation had no word for sin. "Objective mind" understood the need for inner and outer integrity without having any prescriptive format or categorical obligations by which to orient its behaviour. Dilthey's psychological theory of inner balance let him make thought the moral equivalent of an act. It let him have an immoral history without also having to admit to an immoral mind. "Verstehen" was the historical equivalent of Victorian pornography. The viewer forced himself to look at history in order to understand what an evil old place the lower class had become.

Dilthey "understood" history by seeing the *absence* of the spirit mirrored in the "lived experience" of the other. History provided a double "presence" by which the material world sees its moral poverty or, alternatively, the mental world sees its cognitive inadequacies. Each side of the composite historical experience ratchets itself up by seeing itself in the *presence* of the other. Theological structures implicitly criticized philosophical ones. Social structures implicitly criticized economic ones. Economic structures implicitly criticized cultural ones. Cultural ones implicitly criticized political ones. And so the grand hermeneutical cycle of world historical paper/scissors/rock goes on. These narrative games of cognitive one-upmanship are still being played. Objective scholars in great research institutes faithfully transcribe the ideas and events of history. They make no value judgments and they offer no advice. The facts of history provide the minimum daily adult food for thought a balanced life requires. The study of history brings out the best from good news and bad news, alike.

Historical events were the old Adam seeking salvation and acting out many of his least attractive inclinations. The new, nineteenth-century hermeneutical Adam, "surprised by sin" observes from a distance the evidence of history's misbehaviour. Seeing history triggers a moral response. Those who have developed the requisite "understanding" react morally to the evidence of what "history" has done. "The best that has been written and thought" plays like a giant invisible hand on the heartstrings of humankind. History provides stories we "should" live by. Knowledge of the facts builds up an emotional repertoire of moral empathy for others. This hopeful perspective showed an enthusiastic disregard for empirical confirmation.

Historical events in the twentieth century indicate Dilthey's hermeneutics did not perform as advertised. Unfortunately, the disappointment with events is inversely proportional to the scholarly attention theorists like Dilthey have received. There are many reasons for the comparative inattention of contemporary scholarship to the close relation between history, language, and modern ethics. One reason has been examined in this and the previous chapter. Hegel won and Kant lost the great moral debate for the hearts and minds of Europe's "businesspeople." Sentimental rhetoric defeated the critique of judgment. Hegel had help. The political history of empire- and nation-building has not been distinguished by the quality of its moral judgment. Hegel won because his naïve 'joy' over words, in themselves, was compatible with the treasons, stratagems, and spoils of state-building, imperialism, and the global economy.

The Hegelian intellectual heritage influenced twentieth-century politics. Big men, generals, and religious leaders who claim they "understand" history are a world problem. Dilthey's secular faith in the ameliorative power of word pictures gave extraordinary power to the glib, rich and unscrupulous. Nationalist movements were easily co-opted by the remembrance of martyrs and heroic events. Emotional language has been especially popular in fascist and communist political movements in Europe and Latin America. The religious right in the United States and the Middle East use descriptive language to promote their agenda and consolidate the faithful. A spontaneous understanding of history without critical commentary and philosophical reflection supports their political cause. Late modern media society is, if anything, more susceptible to the blandishments of a spontaneous emotional understanding than the Romantics were. The loyal and faithful will "understand" the words and images without complex debate. The pictures speak for themselves. A viewer/auditor who does not "get it" is outside the fold. They are by definition alien to the moral consensus spontaneously provoked by the images of history. Those who understand the truth and revere the right automatically know what the leader, mullah, party boss, or political talking head is pointing at. This sentimental system of spectator ethics is one of the most powerful components in the haphazard historical rise of the Western religious right. It has its correlate in other conservative societies. Sentiment is an excellent political educator because spontaneous understanding is the countersign and secret handshake of a cultural loyalty oath.

To be fair to Hegel and Dilthey would require a philosophical investment in re-thinking history. Philosophy and history have grown apart over the last two hundred years. Hegel, Dilthey, and a literary system of structural hermeneutics are a great thicket between us and the early promises of moral Enlightenment. Marx's brave effort to combine empirical history with a critical moral philosophy was shot down by an unholy alliance between Cold War capitalists and a well-meaning, but uneducated, religious right in the United States after World War II. The distance between modern philosophy and the practice of historical research and writing is so great they hardly speak the same language. To put Hegel and Dilthey into a non-pejorative context would require a return to Kant's "lower faculty" and it would mean, in practice, generating a dialogue between traditional philosophy of history and modern philosophy. Some essential terms would have to be common to both sides of the disciplinary divide between the two faculties. The disciplinary faculties of academic philosophy and narrative history are well established. To be fair to Hegel and Dilthey requires a hypothetical bending of the two discourses for purposes of possible collaboration.

Philosophy and history have specific disciplinary definitions of the real going back to their foundations in the Enlightenment and the Romantic eras. Philosophy of history was founded in the nineteenth century by Hegel. Modern philosophy was founded in the eighteenth century by Kant. The dialogue between philosophy and history Habermas has attempted amounts to a truce between Hegel and Kant. A permanent truce between the two founding idealists of the modern tradition has been beyond Habermas. It is certainly beyond the scope of anything that could be done here. Goodwill toward Hegel, Ranke, and Dilthey requires an armistice for purposes of discussion. A discursive summit between philosophy and history is the first step toward a tranquil talking cure for Hegel's epochal grief. A relatively large blockade of unexamined assumptions now prevents democratic access to the larger issues. The prose style of intellectual historians and critical philosophers testifies to the complexity, but it also betrays the symptomology of an old and largely ignored problem.

History and philosophy view human life from two contrasting perspectives which each calls "real." Michael Dummett is one of the leaders of a critical perspective in modern analytical philosophy called "anti-realism." From his perspective Hegel, Ranke, and Dilthey are realists. Dummett explains his position in the following way:

> Realism I characterize as the belief that statements of the disputed class [e.g., truth, wisdom, law, spirit] possess an objective truth-value, independently of our means of knowing it: they are true or false in virtue of a reality existing independently of us. The anti-realist opposes to this the view that statements of the disputed class are to be understood only by reference to the sort of thing which we count as evidence for a statement of that class.[94]

By Dummett's definition, philosophers as disparate as Hobbes, Marx, and William James are "anti-realist." Realists believe some ideas are immune to time. Anti-realists believe experience is the only teacher and there are no truths outside of time and place. The higher values (if one may name them so) are the emotional analogue of empirical experience. For anti-realists, history and philosophy are ways of presenting sensory experience and discussing their effects. History and philosophy are just ways time and place can be understood. They each have their strengths and weaknesses. Neither philosophical inquiry nor historical narrative is the appropriate venue for all questions.

Hegel, Ranke, and Dilthey can be appreciated from Dummett's definition of the real. They remained true to their religious heritage at a fundamental philosophical level. The believed certain basic ideas were immune to time. History was a way of re-calling the attention of the great and small to the basic ideas of the civilization. Let us mention, *en passant*, the appropriateness of their secular faith in a culture which still sheltered underneath the memory of Christian charity, human brotherhood, and traditional moral obligation. Even as the ground moved underneath their feet the whiplash of history had not yet turned their heads. Hegel, Ranke, and Dilthey's world still had a vestige of grief. It remembered the old language of moral conviction and it could still be surprised by sin. The Victorian mind Gertrude Himmelfarb defended ardently in the 1980s and 1990s was moved by Burke's appeals to charity. Victorians were not at all points overcome by class advantage. In some cases, their kindnesses were penances for a guilty conscience of which they were well aware. Hegel, Ranke and Dilthey spoke to the conscience of their era in a language it could still understand.

The criticisms of Hegel, Ranke, and Dilthey in this extended essay are militant. I have trotted out my anti-realism in the plain language of an old realist. I have pulled no punches in the attempt to criticize the realist philosophy of history. The prose of this narrative owes debt or blame (as you may see it) to the same people it criticizes. Under these circumstances candour is only fair. Dummett speaks for the goodwill of it. Modern politics of the right have retained Hegel's language and lost Hegel's grief. Hegel's system inspired a class of statements which were true for his time. The late modern anti-realist can accept that class of statements as long as the evidence for them is also explicit. That is, Hegel's faith in history and the faith in narrative historical description which it inspired works for a grieving public intellectual who remembers his or her childhood faith and is concerned about the loss of it. The class of statements Hegel inspired is not intelligible for defenders of the faith Hegel had lost. Dialectics are not truth statements for a pre-Enlightenment fundamentalism (anywhere in the world) or a post-Marxist authoritarianism (anywhere in the world). Dialectics are the language of anti-realism drafted for a last ditch defence of the old ethics. They require a memory of traditional religious faith. Time forces skeptics to be anti-realists in Dummett's sense. We can revere the realism of the past as long as we insist on a significant relation between any class of statements about the past (history) and the system of coherence (philosophy) according to which those statements are understood. The mindset of the modern era moved away from Hegel's grief, but it did not move away from his historical realism. The tectonic movement of only one of the two great plates underpinning discourse has left modern language in a crisis. Institutional conservatism and intellectual anti-realism have combined to render the ethics of modern discourse something of an anachronism.

Inadvertently, Hegel, Ranke, and Dilthey were the bridge which carried Hume's theory of language from the Enlightenment into the twentieth century. An oversight in their system carried a significant impact. The Hegelians were happy to seize upon Hume's theory of language, but they ignored Hume's minor treatise on morality. Ethical theory had profound difficulties with the passions aroused by historical events. Kant's theoretical objection to Hume was ignored. Necessity was the enemy of freedom. The freedom to conform was the freedom of the turnspit. After Hegel, Ranke, and Dilthey, global empire, gender double standards, Social Darwinism, and class struggle could be studied with pornographic accuracy. History had moral impunity. Kierkegaard and Nietzsche were the only major thinkers of the nineteenth century who realized what had been done. The expansion of the social virtues to include consensus politics and the global economy altered the connotation of words like progress, democracy, freedom, truth, and reason. Many of the old words remained in public use; but their motivational drive had been changed. The changes were morally indifferent; the cover up was a crime. Hume's practical faith in noble words sanctioned by time proved wrong. Nineteenth century Romantic idealists spent the century hiding from the truth.

Few noticed the slippery process of political resignification slowing shifting the traditional meaning of heritage words like good, noble, honourable, and true. Kant's rebuke to Garvé in *On The Old Saw* went unheeded. The "motivational drive" behind the rules of daily life and common decency had changed and hardly anyone noticed. By the turn of the twentieth century, public moral conscience was dead, dulled, or pitifully confused. Brooding over the chaos they had caused, the modern middle class, their political representatives in government, and their corporate leaders in business and education looked on what they had done and called it good.

CHAPTER THREE
# *THE LINGUISTIC TURN*

> We are so befuddled by language that we cannot think straight.[1]
>
> — GREGORY BATESON

**THE PHRASE "LINGUISTIC TURN"** was coined by Gustav Bergmann in 1953 and popularized by Richard Rorty (1967).[2] Rorty broke down the turn into three major variants: logical positivism (Carnap and Ayer); pure contextual nominalism (Heidegger and Wittgenstein) and narrative criticism (J.L. Austin and P.F. Strawson). The current literature has turned logical positivism into the "anti-realist" debate represented most prominently by Michael Dummett. Willard Van Orman Quine has been joined to Wittgenstein and Heidegger in what is called "holism." The "holists" are concerned with the problem of justified belief. Hilary Putnam and Nelson Goodman have joined Austin and P.F. Strawson in search of a "plain language philosophy" that expresses classical problems in examples from everyday life.

Rorty sees no connection between the linguistic turn and "the traditional problems of modern philosophy."[3] He popularized the turn with the intention of avoiding theology and ethics.[4] In Rorty's view, the old metaphysical debates were an academic debate appropriate for a by-gone era. The demythologized modern has been able to dispense with these issues. The contemporary public world shares a general structure of cognitive and linguistic skills oriented toward mutual understanding. The accumulated language skills of government, civil administration, and the university have replaced the need for moral introspection in public life. The semantic potential of the modern debate carries the same effect as the old metaphysics without the cumbersome intellectual baggage of belief. Continuing the modern debate in its present form is all that is required of modern philosophy. Rorty attributes his unqualified solidarity with the modern to a "small epiphany" he experienced in graduate school.

Rorty's "encounter between Darwin and Hegel" freed him from the traditional dilemmas of moral philosophy, logical philosophy, and critical theory.[5] "Granted," he writes:

> ... that philosophy is just a matter of out-redescribing the last philosopher, the cunning of reason can make use even of this sort of competition. It can use it to weave the conceptual fabric of a freer, better, more just society.[6]

The current consensus on the linguistic turn follows Richard Rorty. The turn was a transition from metaphysics to modernity. It facilitated the peaceful transition from ideological polemics to identity politics. It has trimmed away the metaphysical half of the modern "conversation of the West" and made the other half safe for democracy.

From Rorty's perspective the linguistic turn ended ideology and ushered in the publishing game. Publish or perish is much preferable to the old moral idealisms of church and state upon whose fatal altars so many lives have been sacrificed. Rorty agrees with Hans-Georg Gadamer, the most noted Diltheyian in the twentieth century. They agree on "substituting the notion of *Bildung* (formal, classical self-cultivation of the liberal arts) for that of 'knowledge' as the goal of thinking."[7] "Gadamer develops his notion," Rorty explains:

> ... to characterize an attitude interested not so much in what is out there in the world, or in what happened in history, as in what we can get out of nature and history for our own uses. Getting the facts right is merely propaedutic to finding a new and more interesting way of expressing ourselves, and thus of coping with the world.[8]

The prudent, personal turn to fulfillment is a practical turn without the horizon of moral duty. Gadamer inspired Rorty's best-selling idea of "a philosophy without mirrors."[9] In the professional pursuit of personal fulfillment, "the concepts of 'art' and 'history' emerge from the universal mode of hermeneutical being."[10] The discursive survival of the fittest unites Romantic hermeneutics with lynx-eyed professionalism.

Rorty's linguistic turn is a turn in solidarity with Hume, Hegel, and Dilthey. Rorty has turned away from the skeptical moral predicament. His turn is the nineteenth century linguistic turn. He takes the turn at the point where skeptics like Hegel believed words in themselves could protect them from the skeptic's moral predicament. There has been another turn since the one Rorty describes. The second turn is the turn against the first one. The second turn is the admission by honest skeptics that modern language has been part of a moral cover-up. The takers of the second turn have tried to face a difficult fact about modern history. They concede the likelihood Western thought, including the heritage it borrowed from the world's religious faiths, has been severely attenuated.

From the perspective of the late modern turn, the "conversation" Rorty wants to continue never really worked. The "conversation of the West" is not able to discuss the moral challenges of late modern life. The history of ideas has been hedged to hide the political economy. The "cunning" of market reason has trickled down into modern life at all levels. Hume's philosophical predicament has been taught to a trusting public without critical commentary. His confidence in heritage words is like a virus in the body politic. It adapts to suit the organism. It mutates without conscience for the sole purpose of gorging itself on whatever is the case. The language practices of pundits who compete at "out-redescribing" each other are not altogether productive of wisdom. The language-games of late-modern public life are an open invitation to bad faith, anti-intellectuality, moral cynicism, and soul murder. The small and still shrinking public world requires a higher standard of public discourse than the language fundamentalism tacitly inherited from Hume, Hegel, Dilthey, and (since Rorty) Darwin.

### *FRIEDRICH NIETZSCHE (1844–1900)*

Friedrich Nietzsche abhorred modern culture. His barbed wit still lacerates the hubris of our era. His most famous polemic, lifted from Hegel who took it from Luther, declared the "death of God." Brian Ingraffia writes, "Nietzsche has the madman in *The Gay Science* proclaim: 'I seek God!' because, the loss of God means the loss of all truth to this culture."[11] Nietzsche was a *philologist*, as linguists were called then. In his frame of reference the "death of God" meant the death of language, the death of meaning, the death of collective conscience and moral empathy in a culture of personal will to power. The death of God meant the end of a philosophical debate going back to the nominalism of Scotus and Abelard, the humanist *consuetudo loquendi* of Petrarch, Valla, and Ramus and the Cartesian recogitation of the world by Leibniz, Mersenne, and Berkeley. For over two millennia, a God had guaranteed the plausibility of law and the dignity of life. The sudden, unnatural exclusion of God from history was, for Nietzsche, the moral abortion of public life. It was a psychic rape of the modern soul. The disconnection of words and things was the heart of Nietzsche's Gothic anguish and the moral burden he dramatized. Nietzsche heaped verbal coals of fire on the theocides whose arrogance had built a wall of silence around the grave of a great civilization.

The notoriety of Nietzsche's madman is equalled by contemporary indifference to his predicament. Everyone knows the passage:

> "Whither is God?" the madman cried. "I shall tell you. We have killed him – you and I. All of us are his murderers. But how have we done this? How were we able to drink up the sea? Who gave us the sponge to wipe away the entire horizon?"[12]

The madman's question is the last philological word in classical philosophy. It marks the chasm of nothingness between theoretical philosophy and political history. For two thousand years Hume's devastating fork had been filled by the knowledge of God. The curious metaphor of God's "death" expresses the modern depths of an ancient problem. Nietzsche's night of the soul was the classical terror of pre-Christian ethics now resurrected in the full light of a modern day. Religious faith is not the issue behind the madman's primal scream. Nietzsche's emotional predicament is the loss of all transcendental guarantees that ideas and events have a moral connection. God's 'death' meant, "All the means by which one has so far attempted to make humanity moral are through and through immoral," he exclaimed.[13] Without God there was no public language of right and wrong and the madman knew his bewildered bystanders did not even realize it.

The madman denounced his audience because the implausibility of the old verities did not bother them. A vicious illusion let a mindless public continue to speak of right and wrong. Nietzsche was Weber's first pariah intellectual, that rare modern person: a colonial in his own culture. His was a heart born elsewhere and a head educated in Europe. He refused to become a comprador and give up what he knew. Nietzsche's dissent now comes to us from the Caribbean, Africa, the Middle East, and South Asia. Its spokespersons try to remind the West we are ethically challenged. Sometimes their moral indignation drives them over the edge.

Nietzsche's father and grandfather had been Lutheran pastors. Nietzsche's mother was the daughter of a Lutheran pastor. When Nietzsche lost his traditional faith he shifted his career from theology to philology. Nietzsche knew the death of faith meant the death of the traditional language of care, compassion, and pastoral concern. The pious pastor's son carried on the wisdom of his fathers with a mad and mighty heart. Love, compassion, care, and concern were rendered speechless by the death of God. Nietzsche had to replace direct reference to the Christian virtues with satire, irony, and wit. He had to use paradox and anomaly to indicate what had been lost. He had to paint the virtues in negative relief. The traditional moral sense of reference and reference to the traditional moral sense had been split apart. Nietzsche experienced the split viscerally, imagining himself as the God, Dionysius, being torn apart and devoured. He finally went completely mad while trying to save an old draft horse from being beaten to death by its driver.

Nietzsche's discursive dilemma affects all who engage in public service occupations like teaching, medicine, social work, and religious ministries. In a democracy, it is possibly the most serious of all ethical predicaments. A people without a plausible language of concern have been morally lobotomized. They are ethical schizophrenics, emotional privateers in a public world of tooth and fang, sad parodies in public of the rich spiritual life stolen off the tip of their tongue. The madman's cry is now only an echo of a repressed sorrow, a grief too blatant to name, too embarrassing to discuss. The madman is indiscrete and his insane grief is politically incorrect. To discuss it we have to admit to a public problem which polite political consensus has long ago laid to rest.

Nietzsche was "sick unto death" with ineffable existential pain. Kierkegaard described its effects on himself as "demonical despair." Modern history had made him absurd. Kierkegaard captured the gritty self-torture of the madman's defiance. "It is as if a clerical error would revolt against the author, out of hatred for him; and were to forbid him to correct it; and were to say, 'No, I will not be erased, I will stand as a witness against thee, that thou art a very poor writer.'"[14] The language that was left to these sensitive souls has been a very poor writer. It left their noblest thoughts in tatters and held their highest ideals up to ridicule.

They wore their pain as an indictment against the monstrous indifference of their age.

Karl Jaspers thought Nietzsche's basic thesis held "uncanny urgency" for us:

> Nietzsche's basic theses remove any basis for repose in this world and offer a challenge of irresistible existential earnestness.

But, Jaspers warned:

> He who allows himself to be enchanted aesthetically by their dramatic magnificence does not even begin to be touched by them.... He who derives from this the determining principle: There is no God, sinks away into a banal Godlessness that is not at all what Nietzsche intended[15]

Nietzsche's madman meant God was dead to history. God need not have died in the heart of the faithful to be dead in public life. The madman meant the coherent public profession of faith had died. God need not be absent from one's personal life for him to be dead discursively to the public world of politics and the professions. The madman's cry means faith has become politically discrete and God's old law is now counted by a show of hands and traded for power and status.

Nietzsche blamed the slave morality of the Christians for the death of God. "God died of pity for men. He beheld man's depths and abysses, his hidden shame and ugliness. His pity knew no moderation.... [Bourgeois, modern, contemporary] Man cannot bear to have such a witness live," he proclaimed.[16] The ulterior intentions of the Christians killed God. Envy, resentment, and will to power were the real intentions behind their moral philosophy. "By way of explanation of how the most remote metaphysical assertions of a philosophy really came to exist, first always ask oneself this: At what morality (or immorality) does it aim?"[17] The Christians whom the Madman lampooned had aimed at a morality of resentment, jealousy, and petty acts of personal will. Their reduction of God to a mean spirit no bigger than their petty wills had killed God in history. "Their faith in something simple, a brute datum, underivable, and intelligible by itself is the basic faith that thoughtless persons apply wherever anything happens." he explained.[18] The modern murderers of all that was holy "have faith in magically effective forces.... It is an atavism of the most ancient origin," he exclaimed. Nietzsche called it "cause and effect."[19]

In his unpublished lectures on rhetoric, Nietzsche described how will to power had destroyed theology and philosophy:

> The intellect, this master of deceit, feels itself freed from its habitual servitude.... Then it celebrates its own Saturnalia.... It juggles metaphors and tears out the bordermarks of abstractions.... It imitates human existence as if it were a fine thing and declares itself entirely pleased with it.[20]

God's killers are entirely pleased to imitate nature. Their world excuses cruelty and aggression by juggling a culture of metaphors, abstractions, concepts, and science. Paul de Man calls Nietzsche's ontological pathos "an inevitable trap." Nietzsche fell to his intellectual death in it.[21] The linguistic turn begins with this great, sad victim of language whose mad Saturnalia lights up the sick solipsism of the bourgeois age. Nietzsche's pain is the psychological anguish of an identified patient whose family is humanity and whose breakdown is symptomatic of an age.

Richard E. Palmer (1969) covers the history of hermeneutics from Schleiermacher (who coined the word) to E.D. Hirsch (1967), who wrote the first full treatise in English on interpretation. Modern hermeneutics began with the historical criticism of the Bible. Historical interpretation was to be "the medium through which God confronts man with the possibility of a radically new self-understanding," Palmer explains. This progression makes Bible criticism "the father of the modern conception of historicality," Palmer concluded.[22] As the modern world grew more secular, history took over the "natural-historic" quest for moral certainty, Palmer observes. The cooptation of the critical method without a God to guarantee it left a huge loophole in the method. With Jehovah dead and Satan buried, the stories we live by had no moral power. Palmer says despite a predilection for the word 'objectivity':

> The centre from which our bearings are taken is subjectivity. But if everything goes back to subjectivity and there is no reference point outside it, human will to power becomes the mainspring of human activity.[23]

When faith in history replaced faith in reason, personal will to power began to impel modern history like a Greek fate. Nietzsche's tortured word "God is dead" articulates the anomaly which drove modern thought to the linguistic turn.[24] In a world where God, himself, has died; ideas and events *do not move in tandem*. They do not correlate in traditional patterns. The truth about history may not have a behavioural effect which a less skeptical society would have called ethical and moral. Nietzsche's preternatural sensitivity to language translated a crisis of faith into a critical suspicion of the way words correspond to things in the modern public world. His anguish is symptomatic of our times.

## FERDINAND DE SAUSSURE (1857–1913)

The Swiss linguist Ferdinand de Saussure carried Nietzsche's pain into scholarship. He confided to his friend Antoine Meillet in 1894 that:

> The utter ineptness of current terminology, the need for reform, and to show what kind of an object language is in general
> – these things over and over again spoil whatever pleasure I can take in historical studies, even though I have no greater wish than not to have to bother myself with these general linguistic considerations.[25]

Saussure's concerns led him to a revolutionary study of language. Subsequent to his letter to Meillet he came to the conclusion that:

> When we speak of particular, tangible facts, there is no panchronic viewpoint.... By himself the individual is incapable of fixing a single value.[26]

The Romantic weasel word around the panchronic problem was *structure*. No one person had an overall view, but the mind is structured to intuit it in history and literature. Saussure criticized the language of modern history. He gave scholarship a rational approach to Nietzsche's pain. He debunked Dilthey's mental structures of intuitive understanding and founded modern linguistics.

In his *Course in General Linguistics* (1916) Saussure criticized "the inner duality of all sciences concerned with values."[27] Saussure's "inner duality" is Hume's fork. The inner duality of all values was not determined by any predictable structure. It was irrational and free-floating. Its conjunctions could not be predicted. Saussure stripped away the hermeneutical veil and invented a plain language for the non-correlation of ideas and matters of fact. He called ideas "the axis of simultaneities". Our idea of things creates a world. He called the world, *synchronic*. Matters of fact were "the axis of successions." He called them *diachronic*.[28] Information flows in only one direction in the system. Synchronic facts "signify" diachronic events, but "a diachronic fact is an independent event; the particular synchronic consequences that may stem from it are wholly unrelated to it," he concluded.[29] So great was the influence of Hegel and Dilthey on the scholarly reading of Saussure that nearly everyone assumed the synchronic sphere was rational. An historical cunning benevolently oriented by nature objectively structured the diachronic arrow of time. It was only natural to believe history passed through synchronous fields of science and criticism en route to being understood. Modern reason was gradually clearing the language and culture of the West of pseudo-science, prejudice, and superstition. The misunderstanding of Saussure's "structuralism" has contributed to the misunderstanding of the late modern linguistic turn. Saussure was the annihilator of Hegel's short-lived joy for language. In Saussure, neither artistic nor linguistic "structures" have anything whatever to do with reason, truth, or the spirit realizing itself in history.

Saussure was a great teacher whose work stimulated tremendous intellectual activity long after he was gone. Saussure's *Cours Linguistique* was a compilation by three students of his Geneva lectures from 1906 to 1911. A world hero to all introverts, Saussure never wrote a book, never sought fame, and never represented his teaching as a new school of thought. Saussure's *Course in General Linguistics* was first published in French in 1916. It is now generally considered that Saussure caused as fundamental a change in modern thought as Copernicus, Galileo, Newton, and Einstein.[30]

Jonathan Culler's *Saussure* (1976) remains the best introduction to Saussure's linguistic revolution. Culler summarizes "the Saussurian legacy" in these words:

> In simply assigning meaning we should have no other resources than ourselves, no other resources than all the notions we had already been living with.... To study man is essentially to study the various systems by which he and his cultures organize and give meaning to the world.[31]

David Holdcroft takes it for granted that "Saussure's impact on the development of structuralist thought and methodologies is unquestionable.... Saussure treated linguistics as a species of something more general, namely a semiological system."[32] Language was the deep structure of human life. It conjoins ideas and events and makes their connection seem natural.

Vincent Leitch's approach to *Cultural Criticism, Literary Theory, Poststructuralism* builds a "sociohistorical locus" for "cultural criticism" out of Saussure's concept of language: Texts are a form of *parole* [sociohistorical language practice] which:

> Emerge out of *langue* [deep structure of symbolic language use]. The author is a scriptor, typically with a name – a specific sociohistorical locus for the intertext ... the private author undergoes an operation of epical and epochal transcription, emerging as a spokesperson for certain values, interests, classes, races groups ... the 'intention' of the author is construed at once as willed purpose, unconscious drive, and epochal utterance. The creation of discourse is both a private and communal event whose production, circulation, and consumption are open to cultural critique.[33]

Robert de Beaugrande agrees. In summarizing the modern linguistics of Bloomfield, Pike, Sapir, Chomsky, Firth, Halliday, Teun van Dijk, and Walter Kintsch, Beaugrande puts Saussure at the foundation of modern textual criticism.[34]

Saussure set in train a series of cultural shocks which extended far beyond linguistics. Saussurian linguistics destroyed the possibility that intellectual documents could ever display the inherent "psychic lawfulness" of an objective mind. Saussure taught:

> The value of any term is accordingly determined by its environment; it is impossible to fix even the value of the word signifying "sun" without first considering its surroundings.[35]

The "relative position" of a sign in its signifying chain gives it value. "Signs function, then, not through their intrinsic value but through their relative position."[36] Saussure boiled down everything he had said to the fact that "in language there are only differences," and even more importantly, "there are only differences without positive terms."[37] Saussure's linguistic turn was the antipodean blood enemy of Dilthey's theory of historical "verstehen." "What is said of journalism applies to diachrony," Saussure quipped. "It leads everywhere if one departs from it."[38] When, in effect, Jacques Derrida realized that Saussure's quip was a critique of the modern social sciences, the postmodern word-world war was on.

Jacques Derrida describes the fallacy Saussure exposed as, "the being beside itself of consciousness." Before Saussure "words were an absolutely central form of Being," i.e., an "origin, *arche, telos, ousia, parousia*" in the expressive language available to us, Derrida writes. History explained being in what was considered transcendental terms. After Saussure, the myth of historical transcendence was turned on its head. The old Romantic idea of absolutes in history became the mythology which *prevented* history from being understood. In Hegel's and Dilthey's view, modern historical consciousness stood outside itself "as if" it could view its world from a platform outside history. Saussure identified the fallacy in their view. He concluded a critical consciousness cannot stand outside history, because it cannot stand outside language. Criticism inspects the performance of language. It confesses its complicity with the history of which it is a part. After Saussure, language is a confessional, not a pulpit. Modern philosophy of history has hidden a scene of moral complicity with the events to which it claims to be opposed. "The word, *history*, in and of itself conveys the motif of a final repression of difference. Were it not for history, one could say that differences can only be 'historical' from the outset," Derrida admonishes.[39] Since the word, history, has been colonized by events, we have difficulty clearly expressing our moral complicity with it. The circularity of a pre-formed language makes guilty conscience hard to even admit; much less describe.

The Saussurian "framework" did not deny history, but it denied the ability of history to know itself "ekstatically" as Hegel and Dilthey claimed. Saussure's theory of language reopened the moral question Dilthey tried to close. Saussure connected the perception of value and the expression of value in a new way. The question: "What does consciousness mean?" involves what it means to develop as a people and a civilization through the use of language.[40] Saussure's "structural criticism" meant consciousness is conservative. It teaches the social in the stories it tells. Language is the "deep play" of modern social life. Social consciousness does not reflect a divinity in which the human partakes or from which the human receives timeless lessons. Cryptically, Derrida concludes, "Consciousness after Saussure signifies the privilege granted to the present."[41] The covert privileging of the present is the core of the language problem in Saussure's new structuralist critique. History is the self-destructing contradictions of a status quo made to appear "natural," "good," "inevitable," "necessary," "unavoidable," etc.

Saussure's "critical framework" permits questions about the covert and reactionary form of historical "self-presence":

> The privilege granted to consciousness therefore signifies the privilege granted to the present and even if one describes the transcendental temporality of consciousness ... one grants to the 'living present' the power of synthesizing traces, and of incessantly reassembling them.[42]

Saussure's "framework" recognizes the language problem of the "living present." Croce's famous dictum that all history is the history of the present has been given a deep critical spin.

Terence Hawkes points out that, in spite of Saussure's careful qualification of the importance of the social, most readers still thought of the language of history as itself being outside of history. They were conditioned to Hegelian dialectic and Romantic hermeneutics. Their Romantic cultural conditioning stood between them and a fair discussion of Saussure's radical new proposals. Twentieth-century structuralists indoctrinated in Hegel and Dilthey used Saussure's terminology to show language was "self-defining and so whole and complete."[43] Hawkes clarifies Saussure's contribution:

> Saussure's insistence on the importance of the *synchronic* as distinct from the *diachronic* study of language was momentous because it involved recognition of language's current *structural* properties as well as its *historical* dimensions [emphasis added].[44]

Before Saussure, the structure of language had been considered *pure*. After Saussure the "structural properties" of language had a history just like any other event. Saussure's work began a line of inquiry which added a political history to the structure of language. The politics of research, writing, and marketing ideas became a part of critical theory.

Since language is involved in *both* motivation and explanation, any ethical slippage between the structure of language (i.e., its formal logic) and the meaning of specific words can be a drastic event. The possibility history might cause the moral debilitation of heritage words devastated the skeptic's secular faith in heritage language. Nietzsche had noticed the same slippage in the general culture of the late nineteenth century. Saussure's advantage over Nietzsche was his emotional stability. Saussure's "non-paranoid style"[45] was a scholarly extension of classical philology into a completely new study. The old realist assumption of edifying analogies between political and historical experience was so naive, Saussure wrote it off. "To try to unite such dissimilar facts [as diachronic and synchronic] in the same discipline would certainly be a fanciful undertaking," he remarked.[46]

Saussure began the resistance to "the tyranny of language over those who propose to inquire into its workings."[47] Nineteenth-century historical idealism fell before the empirical evidence that, as Saussure put it:

> Language is not a mechanism created and arranged with a view to the concepts to be expressed. We see on the contrary that the states which resulted from the changes [in language] were not destined to signal the meaning with which it was impregnated.[48]

Changes in language are fortuitous, and not purposeful. "Fortuitous," does not imply "lawful." The truth about the social studies after Saussure is that history is still a fact, but the language of history is "fortuitous." A distortion of meaning occurs when a language of "fortuitous objectivity" is used as if it were a "natural" language of essential objectivity.

Saussure laid the foundations for a system of inquiry which Jeffrey Alexander calls, "the postpositivist mode." Alexander summarizes the revolution Saussure initiated as the realization that the structure of explanation is as important as the explanation. Saussure transposed historical dialectic into a new critical key. "Discourse becomes as important a disciplinary activity as explanation," Alexander concludes.[49] Language is the natural habitat of social being. To study "us" we have to look at "us" in our natural habitat. John B. Thompson explains that, "habitus," Pierre Bourdieu's key concept, is a Saussurian term. The human habitus is the categories of perception which incline agents to act and react in certain ways. Language always reflects the group's categories of perception. It collates and organizes matters of fact in pre-cognitive ways. Language is the aesthetic domain of Kant's synthetic judgment a priori. It maximizes practices, perceptions, and attitudes prior to the conscious definition of a "rule."[50] Language bridges Hume's fork between ideas and matters of fact. Inappropriate language has, potentially, such devastating force, Jacques Lacan warned, "The unconscious is structured like a language."[51] He based a school of psychoanalysis on the unconscious significance of language as a motivating force. Saussure's revolution affected all areas of the modern humanities. Modern intellectual history was forced toward radical questions of a very different sort from the ones the nineteenth century had asked. Modern intellectual history is about language and, specifically, how and what words mean in an historical context from which all essential (ontological) guarantees had been torn.

Saussure revolutionized the meaning of the word "structure." "Structure" had meant expressive structure in the nineteenth century. The old nineteenth-century aesthetes, Coleridge, Pater and Arnold, Bosanquet and Croce were structuralists. The nineteenth-century "understanding" of literature, history, and culture was a structural psychology of independent mind protected by sensitivity and feeling from the vulgar world of ordinary life. Saussure used linguistics to call this tradition into question. After Saussure, linguistics, philosophy, and anthropology, jointly declared "structures of mind," were a social construction. The new critical direction was unpleasant for defenders of the old tradition. T.S. Eliot, I.A. Richards, Ernst Cassirer, Lionel Trilling, Suzanne Langer, and Hans-Georg Gadamer defended the old structural regime. They fought the new critical structuralism tooth and nail.

The confrontation between the two structuralisms was exacerbated by the impatience of the critics who defended Saussure. Critical structuralists like Luckmann (1967), Berger (1966), Schutz (1973), Ryle (1949), and Lévi-Strauss (1966) did not explain their revision of the term "structure" very patiently. The social structure of language was so evident to them; they were harsh to those who might be confused by the terminology. Confusion over the meaning of the word "structure" has contributed to the persistence of many unnecessary misunderstandings. Critical structuralism does not doubt the existence of reality; it doubts that we are discussing it very well. It uses the phrase "social construction" to indicate certain alleged timeless truths were made up in time and need to be reviewed accordingly. Critical structuralism and structuralism are as different as night and day. Hegel, Dilthey and Ranke are "structuralists". Ferdinand de Saussure, Thomas Luckmann, Peter Berger, and Alfred Schutz are "critical structuralists". The persistence of the Hegelian tradition in the taxonomy of modern thought has led many casual observers of the fray to conflate the two.

After Saussure, there were two structuralisms in modern thought. One was the old structuralism of "objective mind" Dilthey had used to justify Hegel's philosophy of history. The other was the critical structuralism which rejected the cultural and psychological assumptions of the old one. Robert Maxwell Young (1990) explains the difference. Young compares the old "objective" structuralism to the map of London's underground transportation system. The obscurity of the London underground is world-famous. Often the name of a stop is not the nearest stop to the famous site of the same name. Young explains the ambiguous correlation is a ploy to control the tourist traffic. Stops with easy access, larger square footage, and nearby security services are given famous names. The cunning nomenclature "establishes subject-positions which are instrumental as forms of control," Young concludes.[52]

The traditional "structuralism" of Hegel and Dilthey establishes subject-positions for a similar political purpose. Young believes they let "nominally radical or oppositional historians unknowingly, or even knowingly, perpetuate the structures and presuppositions of the very systems they oppose."[53] Young's clever analogy captures the new critical structuralism with admirable accuracy. The scholars who took Saussure's linguistic turn decided (in effect) modern culture was structured like London's underground. Nineteenth-century ideas of history, art, and culture were crowd control devices and systems of surveillance. Their discrete silences and rhetorical flourishes were an emotional mass transit system. They let the problems of modern life be managed under the surface of things as far as possible from the big-name historical events. Romantic culture and politics provided an artful dodge around the sites of peoples' real problems. The nineteenth-century idea of art, history, and literature derailed the discussion of a host of modern problems and still prevents large groups of people from reaching the same destination all at the same time. The subjective 'map' to which Young's clever subway analogy has reference is still displayed prominently in all major bookstores and disseminated avidly by every university in the Western world.

## LUDWIG WITTGENSTEIN (1889–1951)

In *Philosophical Investigations* (1953), Ludwig Wittgenstein identified the "language-game" as the fundamental problem in modern philosophy.⁵⁴ "The modern language-game defines a whole culture." To imagine it is "to imagine a whole way of life," he advised.⁵⁵ He began his philosophical investigation of the language-game with a confession by St. Augustine:

> I gradually learnt to understand what objects' sounds signified; and after I had trained my mouth to form these signs, I used them to express my own desires.⁵⁶

Although Wittgenstein was not religious, he was, like Kant, a man of faith. The trajectory of his painfully private thoughts traces out one of the most important moral odysseys in the modern period.

Wittgenstein was not a professing member of any orthodox creed. His father was a converted Jew and his mother was Catholic. Their religious affiliations played little role in Wittgenstein's intellectual development. He had studied with G.E. Moore before World War I. Moore's criticism of Hegel's language pointed him in the direction of his mature work. Moore also convinced him Kant's theory of aesthetic judgment resolved some of the central paradoxes in modern philosophy. Wittgenstein is the Renaissance man of modern moral introspection. He was a brilliant engineer who loved music and the cinema. An affinity for Kant's aesthetics and a deep suspicion of modern historical idealism came naturally to his personality.

Wittgenstein had concluded the *Tractatus logico-philosophicus* (1922), the only work published during his lifetime, with the cryptic admonition, "Whereof one cannot speak, thereof one must be silent." His later "investigations" indicate he changed his mind. Hilary Putnam, the American pragmatist whose work is most often associated with the tradition of Pierce, James, and C.I. Lewis, says Wittgenstein never counselled silence. He only meant one must be silent until he or she has seen through the game. One must be silent until speaking does not increase the damage. Putnam reads the final counsel of the *Tractatus* as a warning about the moral and psychological dangers of the language-game.⁵⁷ The circularity of modern language, its self-defining, viral regularities; its discursive tautology and self-replicating tectonics; its historical hubris, ethnocentrism, and pious chauvinisms; its indolent formalism, its performative structures, and strange illocutionary force are properties of modern culture. Seeing the world "rightly" requires "surmounting" the behavioural paradoxes enshrined in the game.[58]

The least controversial statement one can make about Wittgenstein's philosophy, and, perhaps, his life, is that he was deeply sensitive to the circularity of language. The final admonition of the *Tractatus* and the unifying theme of his posthumous *Investigations* develop the same point. They are about a tautology in the logic of modern language to which Wittgenstein was painfully sensitive. Explaining the tautology was easier for him than exposing his pain to the baleful scrutiny of a world of strangers. To explain the tautology of modern language he turned, once again, to Augustine:

> And now, I think, we can say: Augustine describes the learning of human language as if the child came into a strange country and did not understand the language of the country; that is, as if it already had a language, only not this one. Or again: as if the child could already *think*, only not yet speak. And "think" would here mean something like "talk to itself."

God gave Augustine an internal soul-mate. He was thrown into the strange world of sin and suffering with an internal moral compass. Augustine realized the moral compass depended on what we would call an *internal dialogue*. The way a child learns to "talk to himself" determines the direction of the child's social development. We *think* using language. When we act as if we already have access to an innate knowledge of the good, we are acting as if we already possess a language of the good; we just do not know how to use it yet.

Christian conscience involved a problem with language. Wittgenstein believed the language problem with moral conscience was one of the oldest problems in Western civilization. Augustine had seen it, but his concern about the close relation between language and conscience had never been systematically explored. Wittgenstein intended to do just that. He continued:

> Someone coming into a strange country will sometimes learn the language of the inhabitants from ostensive definitions that they give him; and he will often have to *guess* the meaning of these definitions; and will guess sometimes right and sometimes wrong.[59]

By "talking to others" a stranger in a strange land learns the new sounds of objects which he already recognizes. Does moral conscience develop the same way? Do we already recognize the good and use language only as a sign to others? If the good is an object that is already in us, then pointing to good and evil in the external world merely lets us signify the existence of these objects to others. Do words point out objects we already understand or are they something much more complicated? This question seemed to Wittgenstein to be the biggest philosophical problem of the era.

The logical difficulty illustrated in Augustine's paradox is that objects in the real world are not Godly. They are what Kant called "phenomena." They are not universals, absolute objects, or "things-in-themselves." Their existence combines many facets (*qualia*, in current terminology) evident in other objects. Objects in the world are related through physical attributes inherent in the world. We know them by knowing the world. We know what another person is "talking about" because we have a prior knowledge of the world and how it works. We have not taken that fact seriously, nor have we inquired whether our prior knowledge is altogether benevolent. For some reason, we act as if "all you need – of course! – is to know or guess what the person giving the explanation is pointing to," Wittgenstein says.[60] We act as if we have an internal guide-book to what pointing at objects actually means. Wittgenstein is not convinced the ostensive process of learning by "pointing to" works very well. After World War I, when Wittgenstein looked at what history and philosophy "point to" in the contemporary world, he wondered whether the pointing process might not be actively malevolent.

Our guide points to a dog and says, "hoont." The viewer usually understands her guide means the composite entity called a "dog" in English and not the qualities hairy, noisy, and fawning. How are these kinds of communication accomplished? Kant had recognized the problem by the mid-1770s. The earliest extant lecture notes from his classes in metaphysics contain a reference to ostensive understanding. Ostensive definition requires an "intuitive" understanding of "things such as they are." "There can be such an understanding, but the human understanding is not it," the note-taker recorded. Human understanding is "logical and discursive," not "ostensive and intuitive," Kant explained.[61]

Wittgenstein carried Kant's critique of ostension and intuition back to the language paradox pointed out by Augustine. Wittgenstein's language philosophy is a unique synthesis of Augustine's moral faith and Kantian logical critique. He blends one of the deepest expressions of religious concern from the Middle Ages with one of the profoundest critiques of human understanding from the Enlightenment. Wittgenstein's philosophy bridges skeptical Enlightenment with the foundations of Christian moral philosophy. He had a monk's grief for others and Kant's faith in reason. Using both, he tried with considerable success to encompass the age.

Augustine and Kant convinced Wittgenstein that communication requires a prior, tacit knowledge which is only understood through moral introspection. He concluded that, prior to having an object pointed out to us, we understand a large number of tacit rules involving the use of language. The efficacy of pointing to something depends on a shared structure of internalized rules. Pointing guides our internal dialogue along a gradient path closely resembling the internal dialogue of the person doing the pointing. Prior to the pointing (if it works) the perceptions of pointer and pointee have already been synchronized. The shared *a priori* structure of experience which guides our eye down the other's line of sight is not a psychological law for Wittgenstein. On this point he breaks with Hegel and Dilthey. The shared structure of experience that lets pointing and naming guide mutual perception is a moral problem for Wittgenstein. The moral problem of pointing out the world to each other is the philosophical problem with which Wittgenstein began.

A pointing-game which is not at all understood is the foundation for the language-game. The language-game cannot be discussed until the pointing-game is understood better. The problem with both games is the circularity of the rules. Their enigma cannot be discussed without using words which are already part of the game of pointing and naming. The enigmas of ostension and intuition cannot be described without using a lexicon of words built up under the regime of uncritical ostension and intuition. Thus the criticism of language is inextricably caught up in the same objectivities one might wish to criticize. This peculiarity of language is not evident until we begin to ask how language works at simple levels of experience. At that point, the ordinary way we learn about objects in our world breaks down. Although this is a complicated problem of the sort philosophers often enjoy, Wittgenstein went one step further. He declared the abstruse logical problem of language to be a deep and personal moral problem in modern life. Why was he convinced so abstruse a logical problem was also a deep moral problem?

Because, "words are deeds," Wittgenstein lamented.[62] And the deeds of the modern world were frequently harmful, destructive, and immoral. "My whole tendency," he wrote:

> And I believe the tendency of all men who ever tried to write or talk Ethics or Religion was to run against the boundaries of language. This running against the walls of our cage is perfectly, absolutely hopeless.[63]

The moving finger of time points, the head turns; but the conscience does not follow. An adventurous and self-reliant reason, habituated to the monkey-see, monkey do world of economics, self-promotion, and power politics, stubbornly extends the language practices of daily life into ethics and religion. In the most personally important domains of daily life, the language of being together in the world fails us for precisely this reason. *It is a language of the world. It is the world's language.* We are caught in the trap of trying to understand the good by using the same language we use when we undertake the bad. We reason and moralize in the same terms we use to make money and make war.

Wittgenstein's discomfiture should be seen against the background of the modern language fallacy that was outlined in the first two chapters. Modern language escaped moral reflection in the modern tradition for almost two hundred years. Both Enlightenment skepticism and the alleged Romantic "reaction" to it had developed reasons why language could be exempted from philosophical reflection and skeptical criticism. Hume's common sense had trusted "mutual dependency among men" to preserve the moral meaning of "an already formed language." Hegel had trusted historical events to force "the cunning of reason" upon otherwise egotistical and amoral "world historical" personalities. Hume and Hegel both thought history assured the integrity of words. It was a "joy" to them "to discover words," which, for all practical purposes, "had meaning, in themselves." Wittgenstein's discomfort takes on an added dimension when placed against the modern tradition of silence about language as an historical system.

At the grassroots of experience, Hume saw the necessities of everyday existence as the inseverable link between words and virtue. At the highest levels of political and economic experience, Hegel saw the sheer complexity of events as a sobering experience that must compel human beings to be "rational." These two positive theories of language linked behavioural norms in early modern Europe with the moral and civil law. They performed for Western culture a role analogous to beliefs we call "superstition" in non-Western cultures. Hume's realism and Hegel's idealism share a common moment when viewed as part of a cultural anthropology of the West. The process is natural and involves real events, real needs, and real people. The moral problem with language is the one Augustine pointed out. How do we know we are pointing to the "good" when we speak of an object? How do we know we are learning the "good" just because we apply the word to real objects in our sensory world? Hume and Hegel contain a metaphysical fallacy about language which does not stand up to Christian or Kantian scrutiny. The "good" is a category of experience beyond nature and before history. The "good" is beyond *physei*, beyond the natural world of primary experience. The theory of language Wittgenstein confronts takes illegitimate credit for sustaining a philosophical position it did not originate and cannot plausibly explain. The provenance of the qualities inherited from traditional theology and classical philosophy to which natural language refers is obscure in late modern culture.

Wittgenstein was troubled because the conservation of pre-Enlightenment metaphysics did not rest on a logical foundation. The world's confidence in a mere language of the "good," appeared to him to have a negative effect on its practice. The natural systems of meaning in which ideas, events, and large theories of value now had to be construed were inadequate to sustain the tradition. How should one speak in a fair, reasonable, and non-polemical way about such a disturbing situation? Wittgenstein had difficulty speaking of these matters. His temperament was not combative. He faced institutional resistance to self-criticism, and systematic or "structural" irregularities to which large numbers of normally adjusted people have become accustomed are always difficult to describe. In addition, Wittgenstein's intellectual tradition *had been trimmed to suit the times*. The functional narrowing of intellectual focus which had slowly excluded the moral argument from modern public life was two hundred years old. It had begun with Hume and continued during the Romantic era. The world wars (hot and cold) of the twentieth century had just about knocked it stone, cold dead.

Kant's theory of aesthetic judgment gave Wittgenstein a way to explain his problem. Kant was favoured in Austrian universities over Hegel's heroically extroverted philosophy of history. Kant's critique of the power of aesthetic judgment had been a basic text in Wittgenstein's academic study of philosophy. He applied the Kantian critique of judgment to his mature considerations of the modern language problem. The moral problem with modern language was the "practical" problem of how schemas or "categories" of understanding shape perception and motivate behaviour. When Wittgenstein decided that the structure of language was a categorical moral structure in the Kantian sense, his emotional pain found a critical voice.

J. Alberto Coffa (1991) has connected the dots linking Kant to Frege's symbolic logic and the Vienna Circle at the turn of the century. Kant's critique of pure reason had included mathematics. Kant criticized Hume for not including mathematical propositions in his explanation of the famous fork between matters of fact and the relation of ideas. Kant thought science was about matters of fact and its logic should not be treated as the unalterable relation of abstract ideas. Beginning with the Czech logician Bernard Bolzano in the 1940s, Austrian mathematicians began to construct a refutation of Kant's critique. They wanted science to be an impregnable fortress of logical ideas. These arguments led to Frege's work on symbolic logic which, in turn, led to the Vienna Circle at the turn of the century. Wittgenstein developed many of his early ideas from these debates.

The Kantian foundations of modern symbolic logic are part of an obscured research area in which a great deal more work needs to be done. Until the development of this topic, many areas of modern intellectual history, including the antecedents of American pragmatism and plain language philosophers like J.L. Austin will remain obscure. The "refutation" of Kant by the Vienna Circle was more like a special theory of logic than a refutation of Kant's whole project. The circle tried to make scientific logic a category of pure reason. They wanted to cleanse modern thought of its covert appeals to metaphysics. If the internal logic of science and numbers was established beyond question, then Kant's ethical project could be completed. Ethics could be placed on a logical foundation.

As Wittgenstein's thought matured, he encountered the perennial Kantian problem of practical [i.e., ethical] philosophy in daily life. Neither the logic of science nor the stories of history seemed adequate for the practical needs of daily living. Science was cold, aloof, and unconcerned. History was an amoral story of power politics which by example and tenet was destructive to ordinary decencies. The plain language history and the complex logic of science left most people out in the cold. It appealed to the comfortable pew of self-satisfied Horatio Algers, the complacent Western leaders of a world-dominant industrial bourgeoisie.

Wittgenstein instigated a linguistic investigation of the power of aesthetic judgment. His philosophy is a return to Kant in one important way. He takes Kant's formal aesthetic and applies it to language. Kant believed human beings have the strange ability to recognize complex patterns. This ability is innate and exists prior to science. All human beings in all cultures recognize and remember formal structures of experience. The satisfaction or discomfort they give us is, for Kant, a basic "motivational drive" in all human life. Wittgenstein realized Kant's critical aesthetic was a therapy for sensitive souls like himself. It could help them survive the regimen of hunkered down genuflections to power and wealth that was the true church of the modern middle class. Wittgenstein was convinced public life, including the modern university, was a shallow and ulterior experience. It was permeated by personal ambition, egotism, and self-interest which it hid behind a heritage language now voided of its moral content. He freely announced his abhorrence of academic life on many occasions.[64]

Wittgenstein takes the logic of his investigations from Kant, but he takes the tone of humility and the solemn mood of deep moral introspection from Augustine. Wittgenstein thought like Kant, but he felt like Augustine. He and Augustine were kindred spirits. In Augustine's honesty, he recognized a moral epistemologist whose systematic coherence inspired him. Augustine lived in one, whole, unified, and emotionally integrated world. His early Christian world was one world in God. Wittgenstein was attracted by the emotional unity of Augustine's world.

In its unity, Augustine's world was structurally analogous to the logical world of Kant. The integrity of these two perspectives inspired Wittgenstein to attempt their synthesis. He saw in them the two forms of logical integrity which the modern world lacked. Theology played the same role for Augustine that science played for Kant. *Mutatis mutandis*, theology and science had congruent effects on the intellectual life of two different eras, i.e., early Christian and late modern. In going back to Augustine and linking Augustine's theology to Kant's aesthetics, Wittgenstein undertook a vast philosophical initiative which has not been widely understood.

Wittgenstein's approach to Augustine follows the method for deducing judgments of taste Kant outlined in section 31 of *Critique of Judgment*.

He is initially detaching himself from the "content of judgment, i.e., from the feeling of pleasure it gives us and merely comparing the aesthetic *form* [i.e., its expression] with the *form* of [its] objective judgments as logic prescribes it."[65] Kant's two uses of the word "form" hold the key to understanding what Wittgenstein is trying to do.

Kant taught Wittgenstein two cooperative, but psychologically distinct meanings for the word "form." One meaning is "aesthetic form" by which Kant meant any expression constructed according to a system of rules. Kant apparently believed the logics of science and religion were similar to fine art. They were representational systems for classifying and correlating experience. Kant had no brief for "truth" in the absolute sense. He was a relativist. Kant's attempt to reduce all representation to the aesthetic was the point against which Frege and the Vienna Circle rebelled.

Kant's larger point was not anti-science and that aspect is important for dealing with Wittgenstein. Wittgenstein is neither mystical nor anti-science, either. Kant's "deduction of taste" only wanted to show that the representation of an object, idea, or event always proceeds according to rules. Unobjectionable as that axiom might seem, Kant drew a second conclusion from it that is quite controversial. Kant believed the power of aesthetic judgment rests on the human ability to "know" the rules of the representation without having to articulate them. The second, controversial aspect of Kant's deduction is the other meaning of the word "form." "Form" is an expressive form *and* a system of rules. Form, in one sense, is a painting, a poem or a law. In another sense it is the system of rules which defines a painting, a poem or a law. Human beings routinely pass back and forth between these two meanings of the word without realizing it. Kant's two-fold definition of "form" provided Wittgenstein with an answer to Augustine's questions about language. Human beings have inner objects they "know" before someone points them out in the external world. The "strange ability" we have to understand the logical form (the second meaning of the word) acts like the old Christian and Platonic theory of intuition. Without a language to articulate what we know, we still "know" what many things mean and how many things fit together in the world merely by having them pointed out to us in context.

Good judgment is a matter of fit between the two forms. It is a matter of correspondence between the two meanings of the word. We construct a judgment by describing how, in our opinion, the expressive "form" of an idea, event, work of art, play, drama, disease, law, etc., corresponds to some logical "category" of experience [the other meaning of "form"]. Remember, without an absolute source of truth beyond nature and prior to history, a theory of general correspondences is the only theory of truth a skeptic has. Wittgenstein accepts the finitude of skeptical judgment and re-reads Augustine with a theory of skeptical judgment in mind. He wants skeptics to live in one, harmonious world like Augustine without the dogmatism to which intuitive judgment is often vulnerable. Kant's aesthetic plus Augustine's monism give Wittgenstein a unified theory of the skeptical moral life.

Kant believed objects of experience were infinite, but categories of experience were finite and could be "scientifically" established by philosophy. The Vienna Circle applied this Kantian dictum even in their attempt to refute him. Thus, the second meaning of "form" is the system of rules on which an expressive form is grounded. Kant believed this second, foundational level of formal experience was not immediately available to consciousness and had to be deduced. The deduction of this level of formal experience was the purpose of metaphysics in a skeptical, science-based society. When Kant used the word, "metaphysics," he meant the formal, organizing principle behind an act of perception.

Wittgenstein accepted much of this Kantian background into his philosophy without spelling it out. Sensory forms like art and science reflect rational templates of human understanding. Sensory objects are "predicates" of the way reason selects and sorts stimuli for our conscious use. We are not usually aware of the formative operations our brain imposes on the raw stimuli which constantly bombard us. For this reason, we are easily seduced into congratulating ourselves for "insight" and "understanding" that do not belong to us at all. We are easily seduced by the formal categories of business as usual in the all-too-skeptical and materialistic world. The shunning of moral introspection at this deepest level leads to much misunderstanding and violence in history. Otherwise well-meaning people defend the forces of "necessity" apparently outside us in the social and historical world. They are unable to see, or refuse to see, that many "necessities" are categories of perception which we ourselves have created. The unconsciousness of the formal aesthetic system is the essence of modern advertising and the essential language problem for Wittgenstein. The formal structure of modern language motivates us in ways we do not acknowledge and leads us into conformist attitudes which are destructive of the higher good.

Wittgenstein realized the "aesthetic form" of the language world resembles any other judgment of taste. In one important way, relativity of language is its own saviour. The process which besets us also provides a way to control it. The unique feature of the aesthetic which fascinated Kant was its purity. The ego temporarily loses interest in the purpose of the experience. It loves the world of perfect order, unity, and coherence which a pure judgment of taste always gives. God was the ultimate aesthetic experience of Augustine. Augustine was happy in God's world, whole and entire, and he needed no other presence than the presence of God. His world of faith is not emotionally fragmented, logically broken up, nor academically vivisected into disciplinary sub-sections.

When Wittgenstein compared Augustine's aesthetic experience with "the form of [his] objective judgments," i.e., with what Augustine said, he discovered an interesting difference. Even though Augustine feels the power of God in every part of the world and this feeling holds his world together for him, Augustine admits he thinks [objectively] of his world as fragmented. Augustine cannot give his unified world of faith a logical representation that would compel universal assent to it. The unified aesthetic world of faith appears to be a broken world of separate and incommensurate parts when viewed logically.

Wittgenstein is intrigued because Augustine's aesthetic view of the world appears to contradict Kant's theory of judgment. Kant believed the categories of judgment were logical *au fond*. Pressed to their maxim, aesthetic judgment and logical judgment could always be reconciled. Augustine is not able to reconcile his aesthetic world of faith with his understanding of history. With this fact in mind, Wittgenstein is on the scent. For him, an epochal game is afoot.

The paradox Augustine poses sets the neo-Kantian view of modern culture in G.E. Moore, Ernst Cassirer and T.S. Eliot at odds with itself. It is also a painful paradox, by all indications, to Wittgenstein, personally. The issue is joined over the written testimony of St. Augustine, obviously a sensitive and refined man. If the Kantian categories of perception are grounded in the human mind, they would appear in the confessions of Augustine. Wittgenstein probes deeper, using Augustine's own words. Augustine felt his mind and heart were at war. He blamed this "peculiarity" in his understanding of the world on his limited perception of time.

"What then is time," he asks? Augustine prayed for God to explain to him how the one world of mercy, truth, and love appeared to have a past, a present, and a future. He continued:

> It is not properly said, "There be three times, past, present and to come." Perchance it might be properly said, "There be three times; a present of things past, a present of things present, and a present of things future."[66]

Augustine wondered if there was not a constant present which grounded the logical perception of three different times. Augustine's idea of a unifying "present" hiding itself in history becomes a decisive idea in Continental philosophy. Wittgenstein seized it to fill the missing link in Kantian aesthetics. Aesthetic form is an act of the present. Its logic is taken from the present. We recognize what it means without having to articulate how we know because the structural regularities we see in its expression are analogous to the regularities around us in our time.

The "aesthetic form" of Augustine's world is the one eternal and timeless presence of God. Augustine's "objective judgment" displays puzzlement over how God's one, universal world can have different "times." Wittgenstein believes he knew why. Augustine's problem with time was the moral problem with the modern era which Kant and neo-Kantians like Moore had overlooked. He notes:

> It is of the essence of our investigation that we do not seek to learn anything *new* by it. We want to *understand* something that is already in plain view. For *this* is what we seem in some sense not to understand.[67]

Sophisticated Western intellectuals were overlooking something that was staring them in the face. It was there in modern history all along. The modern world shares Augustine's puzzlement. It is bewildered by the times.

We moderns also experience our world as a unified whole. We speak of "the world." We discuss civilization and progress just like Augustine discussed faith and redemption. We speak in our scientific world in very much the same formal categories of aesthetics and history (faith and redemption) as Augustine. How can this be? Wittgenstein does not consider for a nanosecond the modern world is better. In many ways, the modern world understands even less about its feelings and its relations with others than Augustine. By this measure alone the times have got us. They hold us in thrall and hide from us the keys to building together a better world. The absence of the qualities which moved Augustine is a large part of Wittgenstein's point. *Absent the love of God*, where does the modern aesthetic sense of "a world" come from? How is an aesthetic perception of "a world" possible in a world that acknowledges no essential foundation for one universal structure of organized experience?

Augustine's confessions indicated to Wittgenstein that the moral life must soldier on even when it faces insuperable paradoxes and overwhelming sorrow. Augustine's example comforted him, for he endured many of the same agonies of guilt, doubt, and concern for the world which had affected Augustine. Wittgenstein's quiet introspections also afforded him another durable comfort. Augustine's confession indicated Kant and Moore were not entirely wrong. Augustine's confessions indicated that people who were interested in traditional "spiritual" issues did, at the same time, make the effort to reconcile the aesthetic and the logical modes of experience. That is, they were troubled when both forms of experience could not be represented as a unified whole.

If you read the relevant passages in the *Philosophical Investigations* carefully, it is pretty clear Wittgenstein agrees with Kant and Moore about the way a judgment of taste is constructed. But the disappointing fact is, in usual practice, people do not undertake critiques of their own aesthetic judgment. If the two forms of aesthetic experience [object and rule-system] are split apart, they go into denial. They blame the turmoil of their inner life on each other. They declare one side or the other of their mixed perception of world to be God's will or the verdict of history. They blame "human nature" for impasses, antinomies, and contradictions which, they allege, are as old as Adam. They alter, distort, and misinform their feelings to cover up self-induced schisms in their view of the world. They undertake every possible socially accepted subterfuge to avoid categorical reflection on the integrity of their moral judgment. The modern world has evolved numerous labour-saving devices to flee from moral introspection and duty. At this point in his investigations Wittgenstein makes a brilliant intuitive leap. He skips several intermediate steps in his historical argument. He jumps from early Christian theology to a trenchant critique of modern philosophy without discussing the career of the idea. He accepts the probable fact that he and Augustine are not representative thinkers in the modern tradition. What is painful and very difficult for Augustine and himself is very nearly impossible for most people.

On reaching this stage, Wittgenstein's philosophical investigations lurch suddenly up out of the circularities of modern thought like a critical Excalibur from a sea of troubles. Wittgenstein rescues Augustine's paradox from its morganatic prison in seven simple words. These words cut open a new horizon for modern philosophy with a subtle dignity rarely seen since Augustine, himself. They evoke such a world of misfortune that the simple declarative sentence dwarfs the act of reading it. He writes:

Our investigation is therefore a grammatical one.[68]

These words define the tragedy of the skeptical moral life for Wittgenstein. Its historical dimension makes the tragedy accessible. Wittgenstein's "grammatical" investigation of the moral life blames modern language for obscuring the essential foundations of ethical theory and moral responsibility. The structure of modern language has nullified the traditional meaning of the heritage words for good, true, moral and noble. The expressive form and the logical system are in mortal conflict in late modern life. This conflict negates the cumulative effect of traditional theology and classical philosophy in the modern world.

"Grammatical" is "the form of objective judgment as logic prescribes it" in modern language. "Grammatical" is the second meaning of Kantian form. It is the deeper, foundational level of the system which we, human beings, have the strange ability to appreciate *a priori*. Our modern dilemma is painful almost past enduring because the structure of modern language is taken from political history. Augustine's timeless present has been replaced by political consensus. We, like Augustine, live in one timeless present which makes past, present, and future appear to cohere. Language is the aesthetic plenum which answers Augustine on history. Sounding out the various extempory "presents" hidden in the grammar of daily life becomes the moral task of the modern individual. We cannot resist the world until we learn to resist the "grammar" of public life in the industrialized world.

The "grammatical" level of aesthetic form is the last metaphysics. It is Augustine's love for the world fortified by Kant's skeptical critique. In the late modern world its focus is language. The competition, individualism, and violence of the late modern world are inscribed on the structure of modern public speech. The grammar of modern language is a structure of violence. Politics, business, and the university subscribes to its codes. Without realizing it, we speak to each other in a language of violence. The way we speak to each other in public on a day-to-day basis confirms the codes that are constantly at work undermining the integrity, consistency, care, and concern characteristic of the moral life.

Like Kant, Wittgenstein believes "we predicate of the thing what lies in the method of representing it."[69] Unlike Kant, he does not believe the predications of "our adventurous and self-reliant reason" are grounded in fundamental categories of reason. Like Hegel, Wittgenstein believes the fundamental categories of reason are historical. They reflect world-historical experiences that have been synthesized by history and registered in the language of public life. Unlike Hegel, Wittgenstein does not believe the world-historical synthesis forces human beings to be rational.

Wittgenstein's Austrian up-bringing, sensitive temperament, and mechanical genius are beautifully blended in the *Investigations*. He was a "practical" thinker in the Kantian sense. He loved the world of tolerance, art, and Viennese *gemütlichkeit* of his youth. World War I had defeated Hegel's progressive faith in historical dialectic. In Austria, Freud proved to the satisfaction of many that even the subjective categories of mind are not, in all cases, reasonable. Wittgenstein is the intellectual heir of two secular cosmologies that had in certain ways stood the test of time, but in others had decomposed under its acid tests. The culture and society he loved had cracked apart. Wittgenstein understood those points of non-confirmation, but he also understood aspects of the older systems which had retained their validity.

In Kant he found a "method" for representing some of these painful and deeply personal paradoxes. Most importantly, he found an approach he could adapt to the discussion of the modern moral life. For Kant, the power of aesthetic judgment is the power to give human purposes to natural processes. Nature has no human purposes, but human beings construct systems of knowledge based on natural processes and these systems of knowledge not only have human purposes, but the purpose is embedded in the logic of the system. The logical integrity of the system is also the emotional foundation for its practical application. In the world of human purposes, judgment is driven by an emotional orientation taken from the logical "grammar" of the system.

In nineteenth-century aesthetics, sweetness and light set a tone, a mood, an orientation, and a higher attitude. Dilthey and Hegel thought aesthetic edification brought a higher tone to society, politics, and professional duties. This gentle perspective is the Marburg Kantianism of the 1860s. It still dominates Kant studies. Wittgenstein recovered Kant's original moral project. After Wittgenstein the aesthetic means this: We are loyal to formal systems that explain our world. We feel "good" when the world conforms to our aesthetic judgments about it. The better, higher, more inclusive the logical judgment, the better higher, more inclusive our feelings toward the world and others becomes. Wittgenstein accepts the Kantian paralogisms of subliminal experience. In philosophical terms, he and G.E. Moore accept Kant's proof for synthetic judgment *a priori*. The brilliance of Wittgenstein's redeployment of this old argument lay in the way Wittgenstein applied the aesthetic idea to the moral tragedies of twentieth-century life.

The logical forms with which we understand the world and to which we are emotionally loyal *are historically acquired.* Individuals are reluctant to admit how much and to what degree social constructions shape spontaneous judgment. Language norms govern the process. We learn to feel "good" in the same way as others around us by talking to each other. We are socialized to the norm by the way we represent the world. Wittgenstein accepted Kant's idea of a "transcendental" dialectic between conscious concept and reflexive judgment. He accepted the Kantian *a priori*, but he was deeply concerned over its origins. He did not think the power of aesthetic judgment was a primary power of reason. He became convinced the historical world of wars, the economy, and petty bourgeois individualism was inscribed upon the aesthetics of modern life. The old Kantian *a priori* was not a form of objective reason. It was the cunning of reason gone mad.

Kant did not think rule systems were a game. He believed reason defined the fundamental rules of normal human perception and these rules were fundamentally logical. Aesthetic judgment was judgment according to a rule and the rules provided a rational basis for all human life. They "promoted life," he often said in his lectures on metaphysics. Being free to promote life was, for a human being, the highest pleasure. Art, science, and ethics met in this world of highest life satisfactions. In a purely rule-governed world, no material stimuli "necessitated" human action. Understanding the "rules" would free human beings from mundane compulsions and lead, inevitably, to moral and political progress. The modern era appeared to have evolved somewhat differently to Wittgenstein than it did to Kant in one critical respect. Wittgenstein agreed that formal categories of conceptual "understanding" were also aesthetic categories. The area of his disagreement concerned the reasonableness of the modern world as a "system." The conceptual structure of modern reason looked to Wittgenstein to be fragmented, incoherent, and humanly ineffective. Modern life was morally impaired. It did not appear to Wittgenstein to "promote life" with much consistency or logic aforethought.

Here in the winter of a deep discontent, the leaves have to be put back on the trees. The cold and hot wars of the twentieth century, the competitive cherry-picking of the publishing game, and the ethnocentrism of classical European culture have obscured modern intellectual history. Wittgenstein disagreed with Kant, Hegel, Dilthey, and Moore over the systematic properties that informed reflexive judgment. He did not disagree with their reasoning processes, or with the intelligibility of the world as a logical system. He disagreed with the aspects of their logical systems which confirmed the aesthetic values of modernity. He had no quarrel with science and democracy. He loved mechanical engineering and could have had a distinguished career in the new science of aeronautics. He was tolerant of others to the point of idealizing everyday life. His investigations try to save everything they can of the modern tradition. His central point concerns history and human nature. He rejected the secular mythology latent in Kant and explicit in Hegel that a system of "right" reason was active in history. The plain sensory evidence from ordinary life contradicted Kant's optimism and made Hegel's enthusiasm dangerous.

The world caused Augustine distress; but Augustine had a *method* for representing his distress. The modern world, Wittgenstein thought, was also distressed but unable to articulate it. The modern language-game had not evolved a method for expressing its pain. The secularization of language foreclosed the old metaphysical debates without replacing their psychological and emotional function. Of all the functions accruing to metaphysics, the issues of right, wrong, interpersonal concern, and social virtue had been foremost. Modern language had failed the task of representing these concepts. I hope I am able to convey with sufficient clarity the crux of Wittgenstein's concern. He is not complaining that ethical questions remain unanswered and moral dilemmas remain unresolved. He is lamenting that the experience of a moral dilemma can no longer even be represented in the present. Augustine's unified world had a moral dimension. God's presence in Augustine's life balanced the dysfunctions of history. Wittgenstein thought the modern era had lost all memory of Augustine's unified world. It knew the language, but it has lost the experience.

Wittgenstein doubted Augustine's sense of moral balance could even be represented in modern terms. So, he approached the issue of re-creating Augustine's world for the modern viewer as if it were a classical problem in Kantian phenomenology. The world, in itself, cannot be known to us. All we can know is our representation of it. Since the cohesion, intelligibility and moral integrity of the world depends upon our representation of it; understanding Augustine's world depends on the method we use in our representation of it. We must be careful. We face the first and perhaps greatest of our ethical challenges in the method we choose to undertake this task. The method we use to organize the representation of experience will drive judgment. The quality of our judgement depends on the coherence of our system of representation. We may hate an experience. We may reject an event. We may be stirred to resist, fight, protest, and change the world; but our striving will be in vain if *we resist the world in its own terms*. If our method of representation is conceptually complicit with the world, then the judgment which follows also will be complicit. Our best efforts will change nothing. To recreate the moral world of Augustine, we have to follow the logical advice of Kant. We must first see the world differently and describe it in logical terms which are not compatible with the logic of this present world.

Wittgenstein begins a new logic by discussing "Two uses of the word, 'see':

> The one: "What do you see there?" – "I see *this*" (and then a description, a drawing, a copy). The other: "I see a likeness between these two faces."[70]

Modern language has drifted into some bad habits. In the simple example of "seeing" something; an objective, spatial, and ostensive use of the word is often conflated with a judgment of what the thing is like. We have borrowed this habit from science and made it a bad habit in the language arts. With numbers likenesses work; with discursive language likeness is misleading. To "see" in the above example also implies a judgment in regards to what is seen. In this case, the second viewer "sees" a thing and sees a likeness without quite knowing the difference. Wittgenstein uses a Kantian concept to try to explain why this simple example has portent. "The importance of this is the difference of *category* between the two 'objects' of sight," he explained.[71]

The *categorical* difference between seeing "what" and seeing "like" should be a sacred difference in a skeptical society. In a public world for which God, himself, has died, the whole issue of what something is "like" is up for grabs. What something is "like" is a judgment of taste. The objective similarities between objects which might be quantified or measured by science do not embrace the conceptual system of a self-legislating viewer who sees according to his or her own tastes. Contrary to the aphorism, skeptics have to account for their judgments of taste. As a rule, they are not very good at it. Judgments of taste are the cross-over experience between law and life. We live according to laws, but we experience the law in the same way we experience a judgment of taste. We judge the law according to concepts that comport with our pre-established habits of thought. What Wittgenstein is getting at, tactfully, is a subtle question of organized perception. Who, or what, does the organizing of our thoughts when large groups agree what the law is "like"?

A skeptical society which practices political democracy and personal freedom should have a language which observes classical philosophical distinctions to a far greater degree and with far greater sophistication than the one we have. Describing the simple act of seeing reveals a fundamental intellectual dysfunction frequently encountered in modern life. We "see" in the university, politics, and the economy in a manner analogous to "seeing" a police line-up or an album of mug-shots. Most of the time, "seeing" is a test of our ability to give the authorities the "right" answer. We "see" the world the way we "should" see it and we practice seeing in the same way others do. We compete at seeing the same things quicker and more accurately than our peers, colleagues, and fellow citizens. We want to see the same similarities as others and then, like Rorty, we compete at describing them. The whole issue of seeing differently is lost in a Procrustean epistemology of perception. What we really have here is "two different language-games and complicated relations between them," Wittgenstein added. "If you try to reduce their relations to a *simple* formula you go wrong."[72]

Simple examples like the little "seeing" story above are Wittgenstein's idea of a polemic. You may imagine from his tone of sensitive understatement and preternatural conflict-avoidance why he published so little in his lifetime. The simple example of "seeing" represents the major obstacle to ethical theory and moral action in the late modern world from Wittgenstein's perspective. The modern auditor, speaker, and writer (educated to Hume's common sense and Hegel's "joy") collapse the categorical difference between seeing objects and seeing likenesses. The offence is widespread in the social studies. "The present hath no space," Augustine lamented.[73] The aesthetic fallacies of "an already formed language" left Wittgenstein without a moral space in any of Augustine's hypothetical present worlds. There was no moral past, no moral present, and no moral future. The one ordering "present" underneath the illusion of time had foreclosed the moral space required for ethical judgment and moral development.

The modern language-game gives aesthetic force to a fragmented world. Augustine's three functions of the soul – memory, sight, and expectation – become the one, uncoordinated function of the modern present. A continual presence (modernity) decides what everything is "like." It determines memory and arouses reasonable expectations based on policy considerations vetted among one's colleagues and peers. The past, present, and future are part of one continuous perspective against which there can be no rational dissent. No alternative concept of order, unity, and coherence balances the unscrupulous cunning of reason. The modern way of "seeing" is a simple indicative mode which leaves the modern world without a moral likeness. The language of daily living confirms the common moral predicament.

Wittgenstein illustrated how his language predicament "felt." "I shall call the following figure, derived from Jastrow, the duck-rabbit," he explained.[74]

The "duck-rabbit" is probably the most famous optical illusion in the history of Western philosophy. The reference is typical of Wittgenstein's dissatisfaction with the ambiguous structure of modern language. One picture is, in practice, two pictures. The image dances before your eyes. It morphs and changes spontaneously while one is viewing it. Wittgenstein used the illusion to illustrate what modern language was like. The duck-rabbit carries the bottomless arguments Kant spun in *Critique of Pure Reason* over the existence of God, immortality, freedom, and infinity down into ordinary, everyday perception. The effect of world-class abstractions on everyday life is Wittgenstein's philosophical forte.

The duck-rabbit plays the role of a "text" in Wittgenstein's idea of language. Statements dance and change shape in ways analogous to the duck-rabbit. When I say, "I see a rabbit," Wittgenstein explains, "I am describing the perception quite as if the object had altered before my eyes." Reporting the alteration in my perception as if I have seen the thing again or seen it in a new way is not an accurate account of the experience. "In any relevant text something different is in question every time we see it now as one thing now as another." The problem is not what we "see." The problem which requires clarification is the connection between "seeing" as a factual, empirical experience and interpretation as a theoretical and subjective experience. "Seeing" and "interpreting" are closely linked, but routinely in statements of fact the difficult and problematic relation is ignored in the reporting of experience. "How is it possible to *see* an object according to an *interpretation*," Wittgenstein asks? He suspects "what is in question every time" is not expressed well in the language of seeing. Saying "I see" does not communicate the combined act of seeing and interpreting very well. "Seeing" is ostensively useful, but not logically correct.[75]

Skeptical, Western, science-based society does not deal with duck-rabbits very well. Science does not like ambiguity and the modern orientation toward science, objectivity, and matters of fact, influences the general culture. The objective way to resolve the paradox of the duck-rabbit explains it as "a visual impression." The impression is analyzed "on a level with colours and shapes." At the level of its constituent parts, the duck-rabbit can be classified and the experience of ambiguity resolved. The image is declared incomplete, inconclusive, a work in progress, more a duck than a rabbit, less a rabbit than a duck, a joke, etc. An analysis of the constituent elements in the image provides a method of classification. The contemporary Western point of view, traditionally, explains ambiguity by classifying and organizing the details very much like Aristotle did. A rational view of the world cannot be expected to tolerate a world of chronic ambiguity so objectivity is used to explain the ambiguity away.

The moral life cannot proceed in this fashion. The moral life requires a higher quality of judgment.

It is natural for us to "see an object as we interpret it," Wittgenstein notes. All human beings "see" the world in terms of the interpretive systems normal to their culture. One must "see" reflexively in normative terms to live in a group. You have to get the jokes, revere the totems, and fear the same juju. To "see" the world reductively is only natural in a skeptical society that does science. Of course, the paradox is obvious. Intellectual and political developments in the twentieth century prove that science offers no protection against atavism. Modern science can enable barbarism just as effectively as any other composite way of "seeing" ever used by any other human group anywhere and any time in the world. Science, in itself, lacks moral judgment. Wittgenstein's generation was preoccupied with that point.

Wittgenstein approaches his moral disenchantment with modern science from a visual perspective. His basic charge against the modern interpretation is the way it "sees" things. He says, "Seeing proceeds from the idea of a visual impression as an inner object." Science does not teach this fallacy. Hume never accepted such a notion. Kant scorned such an idea. The moral crisis of modern life is not science. The moral crisis of modern life is the pseudo-science of the modern liberal arts. "Inner objects" were the explanation of perception favoured by Locke and Berkeley. It was the basic fact that made language possible for Augustine. The Enlightenment shifted the source of inner objects from God to experience. Experience left a cognitive impression which subsequent experiences gathered around like bees to the honeycomb. The intensity of an original impression left a groove into which subsequent experiences fell. Consciousness is a swarm of experiences held together by a primitive life force. Mandeville's "fable of the bees" was the metaphor for consciousness favoured by Diderot, D'Alembert, and Voltaire. We remember objects and ideas which caused our primitive attention to "swarm" around them. The shape of the hive leaves behind the shape of the object of experience. Classical "inner object" theory is an idea from the age of Deism, phlogiston, and chemical affinities. It is a psychological anachronism that has persisted in the arts long after its abandonment by medical science.

The idea of a structural congruence between the inner and outer life is a classical idea. It was a workable notion, as notions go, until God was retired from public life sometime around 1750. God had kept the balance between inner and outer, public and private. An omnipotent power of infinite love and grace had seen to the synchronization of experience. As skeptical science took charge of history and the economy, the old scalene notion of a geometric order *sub species aeternam* broke down. The liberal arts community did not want to admit it. They refused to face the interpretive crisis created by the death of god. In practice, the assumption of a structural correlation between inner and outer objects of experience was left where Augustine left it. God was killed, history was enthroned, the people and the economy were invented, but re-thinking the old inner object idea did not happen. A rational, skeptical correlation between inner and outer forms of experience has not been re-established in modern Western life. Modern culture battens on the language of a correlation it cannot prove. It lives a lie using the language of a prior historical experience it has neither the courage to believe nor the wit to sustain.

The duck-rabbit now appears in its true shape in Wittgenstein's investigation. We can now "see" the duck-rabbit as he saw it. The logical form of modern language is absurdly ambiguous. It prevents us from seeing each other and understanding "that which is the case." "Seeing" as if we are comparing inner and outer objects is a categorical ambiguity in our primary perception of the world. It makes a moral world impossible under current conditions. Modern language "makes the object into a chimera, a queerly shifting construction. The similarity to a picture is impaired," Wittgenstein concludes.[76] His point attacks (gently) the reflexive form of aesthetic judgment which is common to modern culture. He is saying the way we view the world is queer, shifting, and impaired. The formal logic of the liberal pseudo-sciences has created a world of word-pictures divided against itself. The modern humanities deny the social construction of our inner world and that primary form of denial lets us avoid moral responsibility for the outer world we have created. The primary symptom of a cleverly ambiguous view of the world is endless language-games which degrade our personal, political, and moral development.

In the most unobjectionable way he could find, Wittgenstein has returned to the basic Kantian critique of judgment. The biggest and most dangerous disagreements between us concern judgments of taste. The danger arises from two "logical peculiarities" of a judgment of taste which we all share and never talk about. We construct judgments of taste logically as if they were universal and we defend them emotionally as if they were a fact of nature. In fact, they resemble neither. We make them up ourselves. Ethics are not demeaned by the comparison with judgments of taste. The admission does not dismiss the moral life. It simply makes us responsible for it.

Wittgenstein's reticence involves him in a premeditated obscurity no commentator can completely relieve. Any approach to his work is involved in a debate that will continue for a long time. But at least one point about Wittgenstein's logical investigation of the language-game should be clear. To "see" the duck-rabbit rightly is not as important as "seeing" the language-game in which the duck-rabbit appears. The final counsel from Wittgenstein returns to Augustine. St. Augustine, as best he could after his conversion, lived a moral life. His confessions revealed to Wittgenstein a fundamental aspect of the moral life that the modern world cannot even represent.

Ethical philosophy does not begin with a system of axioms and logical postulates. The moral life is not the application of aesthetic judgment to situations by a person who has developed an ability to think critically. We are not moral to the maximum extent we can be because we have internalized the complex logical processes of an advanced civilization. Ethical theory and moral practice begin at a more fundamental level than concept and criticism. The moral life begins with the simple act of perception. Here Wittgenstein departs from Moore and Kant. Augustine's world was like the modern world in the only way that mattered to Wittgenstein. Augustine's whole world was a duck-rabbit, too. Augustine did not know, nor could he understand, whether the world was a timeless world of love or an historical world of reason. He prayed that God would tell him *why the world appeared this way*. God never answered his prayer.

Augustine did not pray for God to kill the duck-rabbit. He prayed for God to tell him why the creature existed. Wittgenstein accepted the duck-rabbits in modern philosophy in what he conceived to be the spirit of St. Augustine. He did not counsel overcoming them. He advised being aware of them. A duck-rabbit is a red flag signalling the immediate need for moral reflection. The duck-rabbits of history and high culture are perceptual moments of shock and awe. They are the zero point on a biographical lifeline where moral decency meets human interests. Duck-rabbits are an emotional moment of rational stasis embedded in the antinomies of pure reason. The duck-rabbits of discourse tie our tongue and open our heart. They are not to be explained by "proving" what they really are or "showing" what they are likely to become. Wittgenstein decided duck-rabbits are a discursive phenomenon often encountered in transitional situations where traditional ways of life are adapting to social change.

Wittgenstein thought modern society resembled late Roman society to a surprising degree. Augustine was his case in point. Augustine had little knowledge of the world, by our standards, but his faith was great. We have great knowledge of the world, by historical standards, but our faith is small. The weighting is opposite but the imbalance is similar. They teetered one way, we teeter the opposite way. The danger is the same. When the tightrope walker falls, no one worries about which side of the rope he fell over. Faith and knowledge define an historical balance in the life of individuals and groups. Moderns have an ancient problem with their historical sense of balance.

Wittgenstein believed certain discursive ambiguities in modern philosophy resembled, in effect, philosophical enigmas which had puzzled Christian philosophers like St. Augustine. He thought both situations indicated a world that was spinning out of control. The 20/20 hindsight of history gave Wittgenstein faith in Augustine's approach to the problem. Obviously, the religious synthesis which replaced classical civilization had "promoted life" to an amazing degree. The wars of the twentieth century could not be laid at its feet. The civilization Augustine had helped begin culminated in applied science and social democracy. From Wittgenstein's historical perspective, the modern era had thwarted the promise of the traditional religious synthesis the Augustinian age had begun.

To refocus the attention of the modern world on issues that were of durable and pervasive value to it, Wittgenstein believed we should follow the intellectual example of St. Augustine. The perceived ambiguities in our philosophical first principles should be our guide. They are valuable to us if they are viewed in a constructive way. They warn us about the coherence of our lives and the integrity of our relationships with others. Now, as then, discursive duck-rabbits are a call to moral reflection. They should awaken us to the well-being of others. Their appearance means that our personal world is narrow. If we face them honestly, they will force us to change the way we "see" the world.

CHAPTER FOUR
# *THE MODERN PREDICAMENT*

> *Our historians, the most discerning in the world, have invented a method.... It is well known that the operations of this method are (in general) trustworthy; although, naturally, they are not divulged without a measure of deceit.*[1]
>
> —JORGE LUIS BORGES

**HUME'S CAVALIER SKEWERING** of ethical theory achieved methodological status in the modern arts curriculum after the Napoleonic wars. Aided by the movement loosely called German historical 'idealism,' historical "understanding" filled the breach between the tines of Hume's disastrous fork. What "is" could be evaluated by the 20/20 hindsight of history. Those who were edified by exposure to the best that had been written and thought could receive similar benefits from an exposure to history. Hegel's and Dilthey's Romantic hubris was not the last word in hermeneutics and philosophy of history. The anomalies in their system provoked a remarkable series of cogent reflections most of them having to do with language and ethics. The Hegelian interpretive system was a moral problem for Nietzsche, a logical problem for Saussure and a psychological problem for Wittgenstein. It became a scholarly problem after World War I.

In 1931 an unheralded Cambridge Don named Herbert Butterfield wrote an inspired meditation on the history of ideas called *The Whig Interpretation of History*. "The Whig interpretation" referred to British politicians and academics who saw history like Hegel. The modern world was an uninterrupted path of progress from the Magna Carta to modern parliamentary government. The word "Whig" caught on. It came to include capitalists who justify the global economy, Americans who defend U.S. military power, liberals who celebrate the rise of the middle classes, and evangelicals who claim direct descent from the saints and martyrs. Butterfield shared the disillusionment of his generation with World War I. Butterfield addressed the mind and heart of his era with the sophisticated voice of a political skeptic with traditional religious faith. His book revisited the philosophy of history on behalf of a generation traumatized by war.

Recent events had proven to him that political history was not benign. Its temporal lessons could not be trusted as a guide to long-range values and moral behaviour. He advised caution in regards to the lessons of the past because:

> History is all things to all men. She is at the service of good causes and bad. In other words she is harlot and a hireling and for this reason she best serves those who suspect her most.[2]

Recent historical experience had been violent and destructive so Butterfield warned against "what is really a gigantic optical illusion.... We cannot organize our history by reference to the present.... The true historical fervour is the love of the past for the sake of the past."[3] The nineteenth-century illusion of great men had been destroyed by the defectiveness of the civil and military administration of the recent world war. "History has never proven any man right in the long run," Butterfield advised. That fact plus recent events indicated, "History records the result of a clash of wills, a result which often neither party wanted or even dreamed of," he added.[4] The disappointments of history leave us "more open for an intensive study of the motions and interactions that underlie historical change," he concluded.[5]

Near the end of his life, Butterfield credited his Christian faith for giving him "flexibility of mind." It was an aptitude clearly in evidence in the earnest young man in 1931. Butterfield's realism is complex, far deeper than the surface remarks most closely associated with his most famous work. C.T. McIntire has shown how Butterfield's lifelong devotion to his Methodist faith animated his historical work. Michael Bentley calls Butterfield's philosophy of history an "unconventional style of Augustinianism." In *The Whig Interpretation* Butterfield defined a fundamental ethical issue in the study and writing of modern history.[6] History's lessons were not object lessons for Herbert Butterfield. History taught important lessons of a deeper sort. History sustained ethics, civilization, and culture at a deeper level than the mere study of yesterday's current events. "In the long run," he wrote, "there are only two views about life or history. Either you trace everything back to sheer blind chance, or you trace everything back to God."[7] Butterfield turned the face of honest faith backwards to the past with confidence that the deep structure of historical events was a moral educator even though the events themselves might often be discouraging.

After reading Butterfield's essay "The Christian and Historical Study," Louis Halle concluded Butterfield's historiographical perspective:

> ... was based upon his acceptance of what the Bible presents as history, his belief in the personal God who created man in his image, his belief in the centrality of man in the universe, and finally his conviction that "God is love."[8]

In 1931, Herbert Butterfield was facing a difficult philosophical and moral issue. He believed:

> Nothing is more important for the cause of religion at the present day than that we should recover the sense and consciousness of the Providence of God.[9]

Butterfield was embarking on a new, Christian humanism updated for the traumas of the time. He was baptizing political realism and giving it a moral role in postwar politics. The courage of Butterfield's position, and to an extent its uniqueness, lay in its attempt to unify two disparate philosophies of history in one coherent point of view. Is Butterfield's concept of Christian politics coherent? Does political realism combine logically with the older tradition of philosophical realism in any realm lower than the rarefied stratosphere of theology?

The most effective collegial criticism of Butterfield was published just one year after the *Whig Interpretation*. The American historian Carl Becker, a realist who agreed with Butterfield in principle, criticized Butterfield's use of language. Becker, like a good historian, reminded Butterfield of how it all began. Modern intellectual history "began as if a rumour, started no one knew when, had at last become too insistent to be longer disregarded." Becker's prose is still a joy after all these years:

What we have to realize is that in the Enlightenment God was on trial. The affair was nothing less than the intellectual *cause célèbre* of the age.... God, having departed secretly in the night, was about to cross the frontiers of the known world and leave mankind in the lurch.... The issues raised were, for that century, fundamental.[10]

God's departure created a cruel ambivalence in the history of ideas. It resurrected nominalist difficulties (the correspondence between words and things) which had been held in theoretical abeyance by acts of God for almost two thousand years.

Ah, Becker laments with modest irony, "If Hume had only published his *Dialogues Concerning Natural Religion* when it was written, he might have saved me much trouble." Hume's discretion during his lifetime did not matter. Hume spoke for the age. "In Hume's day no one could read the *Dialogues*, but the issues it raised were so important and so familiar that no one needed to," Becker explained.[11] The discrete silence of modern intellectual history over the death of God also speaks for our age. The silence around it speaks to a moral difference between then and now. It speaks to questions of moral courage and intellectual integrity. In a society which does science and civil law, it speaks to questions of professional and public ethics. It includes the question of whether a skeptical society can discuss ethical standards and moral probity.

Modern intellectual history has not been receptive to the historical importance of these difficulties. The secular avoidance of questions traditionally regarded as "spiritual" is understandable. The old language of faith is not a comfortable format for secular history, so lost faith is not a scholarly problem the modern research community finds accessible. The avoidance of the realist debate in modern history is no longer tenable. Whatever you want to call it, the breakdown of the essential, cosmological guarantee between words and things is the first and fundamental fact required for an understanding of late modern intellectual history.

Becker was pointing out a new problem which made the old debates more difficult to carry on than at any time since the fall of Rome. The skeptical, modern citizens who house-sat God's heavenly city faced an extraordinary problem. Uncomfortable as it was to consider, the problem was there at the foundations of the new society and it was not going to go away. Beneath the brouhaha over Heaven and Hell there was a deeper human factor. The Western tribe of allegedly sapient human beings had killed its old God. Non-Western societies were doomed to receive this dubious benefit of Enlightenment self-mortification in the next century. There is no reason to be sanguine about the shoddy manner in which the murder of God was done. It was a cruel and unusual punishment.

After God no fundamental and compelling reason existed why the "truth" had to be true for all time. In a skeptical public sphere, there was no essential reason why words like truth, justice, good, and evil meant the same thing to all people at all times and places. At least Becker and Butterfield were willing to talk about it. The historians who continued the "new history" after World War II were not willing to continue the realist debate. The fact was (and is) that the radical empiricism which cured smallpox, tamed steam, and invented the people had a moral problem. *Philosophe et frères* were in the secular redemption business and they needed moral capital fast. Redemption and transfiguration had always required a heavy investment in principle and the new secular redemption business suffered from the lack of it. Fundamental principle was exactly, by its nature, what all-consuming doubt had to lack. Science cannot be done without a fundamental suspicion of first principles. The fundamental contradiction here was disquieting and it has grown no less disquieting over the intervening years.

The leaders of Enlightenment had a queasy feeling:

> Reason is incompetent to answer any fundamental question about God, or morality, or the meaning of life.

In short, *philosophe et frères* discovered pure reason could not cover all of God's old obligations. "The Philosophers could not afford to accept this conclusion," Becker says. They needed "a little intellectual collateral."[12] History was their intellectual loan shark. Little did they know the rate of interest they were going to be paying on that account. Becker, again:

> For the successful conduct of this eighteenth-century search for the Holy Grail, the light of abstract reason had to be supplemented by the light of experience. "Without history," said Priestley, "the advantages of our rational nature must have been rated very low."

History was the Bible for the retooled redemption business. History let the Philosophers "go up and down it with the lamp of enlightenment looking, as Montaigne did before them, for 'man in general.'"[13] The redemption business has always needed a host of good men, in general, to make it work.

Becker summarized the temporal solution *les philosophes* thought they had found:

> Thus, the innate ideas which Locke had so politely dismissed by way of the hall door had to be surreptitiously brought back again through the kitchen window: the soul that Cartesian logic had eliminated from the individual had to be rediscovered in humanity. The soul of the individual might be evil, it might be temporary, it might even be an illusion. But the soul of humanity, this something "essential to" human nature, this "common model of ourselves" was surely immortal because permanent and universal.[14]

Enlightened rationalists were whistling in the dark. The secular redemption business was in trouble from the beginning. *Les philosophes* hired history to turn the redemption business around. History could smuggle metaphysical contraband back into Enlightenment through its literary backdoor. A literary subterfuge was invoked on an emergency basis. History replaced God as a way of discussing right and wrong. God still lived in the hearts of the faithful, but history had taken over politics. God may have made the animals, but history was running the zoo.

In a society where "God, himself, has died" man's inhumanity to man need not necessarily cause even a qualm much less make anyone mourn. Becker cited the moral optimism of the Enlightenment to prove the skeptical philosophers were still thinking in terms of the old faiths. The irony of his title in 1932 reflects a concern for the elementary forms of religious life. The earthly philosophers praised public duty, moral probity, and interpersonal concern in words directly borrowed from the old theological debates. Becker's point rested on an insight future historians did not develop. It may be they did not even pay any attention to it. In Becker's view, the earthly philosophers who took over Augustine's *City of God* still knew an historical fact modern intellectual history appears to have forgotten. That fact was: God had been a practical concept in the lives of ordinary people. Freeing the people from prejudice, dogma, and religious superstition was not an unmixed blessing.

Enlightenment moral philosophy had a double task. Even as it dug a grave for the old religions, it set out to save the empirical gift of grace in Mr. Everyman's life. "The *philosophes* demolished the Heavenly City of St. Augustine only to rebuild it with more up-to-date materials," Becker reminded his readers. Hume's argument for necessity, Kant's categorical imperative, Rousseau's social contract, Lessing's aesthetics, and Mendelssohn's debates with the Spinozists are rational attempts to ground the old Godly realism in a new, scientific perspective. The Enlightenment builders of the new terrestrial *civitas dei* wanted to overcome credulousness while retaining the behavioural effect of the old creeds. They wanted the old ethics without the old God. Becker believed *philosophes et frères* knew they were in trouble.

Voltaire, that literary scourge of the *ancien régime*, understood the new secular redemption business. He was one of its leaders. His impassioned defence of free speech and fair trials earned him the undying hatred of the *ancien régime*. His house at Ferney was just over the border from Switzerland. He had a permanent watch posted on the road so that he could make a quick get-away at a moment's notice. Voltaire's struggles in defence of civil liberties in France garnered him a healthy realism about how the game had to be played. Voltaire did not spare himself from his own skeptical wit. "History is a pack of tricks we play upon the dead," he said.[15] Becker centred his summary of Enlightenment philosophy on Voltaire's witticism. Rhetorical description and its heteroclite list of events was "a pack of tricks." When he reached this point, he had reached the core of his rebuttal of Butterfield. Butterfield's Tory realism was not informed by a candid reflection on real events. History's "pack of tricks" had never been able to sustain moral conviction and justify self-sacrifice. *It was based on language alone.* The French Revolution dashed any hope language alone could sustain the old moral virtues.

Becker was a farm-boy from Waterloo county, Iowa. He knew tender-minded Christian moralists were not the only group of wordsmiths in possession of history's potentially powerful "pack of tricks." Consensus politics, media, and the marketplace also had mastered them. The language "tricks" of plausible description and motivational rhetoric had become as much a part of the modern world as the ideals of Christian service. The new captains of industry and commerce knew all the tricks, too. There was no moral quality control governing their use. Becker was concerned the old ethics might have been lost while the "tricks" remained in play.

Carl Becker asked Herbert Butterfield a realistic question about language. He took an historical approach to it, and his question was all the more interesting on account of the way he framed it. The problem Becker pointed out to Butterfield concerns the "mode of representation" preferred by the skeptical builders of the terrestrial *civitas dei*. In a skeptical society, the "real" values (i.e., objective values which have an independent existence) are the "pack of tricks." The words are eloquent, but the content is not the old moral values. The content is the techniques used in the representation of traditional ideas. By these means, freedom, democracy, liberty, equality, and brotherhood became clichés." The integrity of modern history requires fewer tricks and better language. Healthy realism in history should include more philosophy and fewer tricks. Becker concluded:

> Once those glamorous words, *liberté, égalité, fraternité* lost their prophetic power ... the eighteenth century religion of humanity ... fell to the level of a conventional and perfunctory creed.[16]

Within one generation, the skeptical builders of the secular *civitas dei* had lapsed into a civil religion as conventional as the old regime. Their secular faith had become a philosophy of cultural convention and elite consensus. Butterfield had not addressed the moral problem of modern historical studies. He wanted to turn history back into a medieval chronicle. He had elegantly given up on Enlightenment and dumped a boxcar load of metaphysics on it right through the front door.

Becker was a student of James Harvey Robinson and a colleague of Charles Beard, who succeeded him as president of the American Historical Association. Their work inspired Crane Brinton, Felix Gilbert, and Leonard Krieger. Robinson, Becker, and Beard created the scholarly environment for Hofstadter's "political ideas" in the 1950s. John Higham and Robert Skotheim described them all as *social* historians of ideas. They combined intellectual history with the social history of attitudes and common practice. Their synthetic view challenged the older view of history for its own sake. Becker explained a practical reason for the "new history" in his presidential address to the American Historical Association in 1931. Robinson and Becker wanted history "to meet the daily needs" of a hypothetical average reader, student, and informed citizen whom Becker called "Mr. Everyman." Mr. Everyman was a skeptic in business and politics. He might harbour pre-Enlightenment faith in his private heart, but in his public affairs he was an empiricist. Mr. Everyman had a practical problem with a very old philosophical dilemma. Becker believed Mr. Everyman should not be encouraged to see history through the eyes of pre-Enlightenment faith. Public life in the West had no option, in Becker's opinion, other than the original Enlightenment project. Mr. Everyman had to learn to discuss the old virtues in a better way. He had to save the tenets of his faith in a language which was appropriate for a shrinking globe and a pluralistic society.

In his presidential address to the American Historical Association, Becker warned his academic audience, "Mr. Everyman is stronger than we are, and sooner or later we must adapt our knowledge to his necessities."[17] The title of his address indicated he meant sharing the tricks of the trade, coming clean with the public, you might say. The title of his address, "Everyman his own Historian" rendered concisely the idea he had in mind. Becker believed the research techniques and language skills of historians were of fundamental importance in ordinary life. The research skills of historians were useful at many different levels of daily life, politics included. The example he gave his professional audience was a private consumer buying his winter's supply of coal. He refers to last year's purchase, orders the same amount, makes a record of the payment, and notes down the day it arrives. He uses this documentation if there is any disagreement or discrepancy arising during the transaction. Becker's homespun approach to historical method did not go down very well with his professional audience. The consensus among his commentators was that Becker "catered to the public,"[18] Becker was accused of risking professional standards and compromising the integrity of the university.[19] His concern for the practical effects of history's "pack of tricks" on the life of ordinary people was not followed up. The majority of Becker's colleagues were not concerned, at the time, with theories of interpretation and the history of ideas.

In 1931 and 1932, Carl Becker and Herbert Butterfield debated a fundamental question about history, ethics, and politics. Butterfield transformed the moral shocks his generation had endured into a dignified defence of a deeper realism. He counselled, in traditional terms, that no one should give way to cynicism, opportunism, and political expediency.

The heritage of modern history was rich in truth and alive with meaning. Becker agreed with Butterfield. He was just as concerned with the ethics of history and the life lessons to be learned from its study. Becker contributed to the debate by adding a constructive warning to Butterfield's Donnish optimism. The modern language arts were not enough to sustain the Western heritage. Heritage ideas like freedom and democracy degenerated when all that sustained them were descriptive rhetoric and political consensus. The fault (if there is one) in the debate is where they left it. Butterfield went on to be a distinguished historian of science and Becker turned to constitutional history. If either man had continued to investigate the history of their debate they would have found another important link in the argument.

Carl Becker's "Mr. Everyman" was not a philosopher and political revolutionary. He did not view the alleged "death of God" with sophisticated aplomb. The news from nowhere is that many people are not happy with the moral enigmas of skeptical enlightenment. The majority of citizens in the great democracies suffer daily from the lack of ethical content in their history, politics, and cultural studies. When the traditional foundation for discussing ethics was removed, the unresolved question turned toward language: how we use it, how we shape it, and the kind of world implied by what is considered to be "true."[20] Becker had opened that issue up. Religious individuals in a skeptical society did not have adequate language tools. They might take great personal comfort from their private faith, but the public discussion of moral probity and public duty was in shambles. The industrial democracies faced the practical effect of one of the oldest philosophical issues in Western history.

The Butterfield/Becker debate had raised a moral question about the meaning of public language. Becker warned Butterfield about the degradation of language by democratic politics. Private faith could not protect public virtue. His example was the citizens of eighteenth-century France. By implication, the citizens of the United States were facing a similar experience. Democracy in the United States was spiralling down into a perfunctory creed. Becker believed the legitimate expectations of private citizens had often been disappointed because language tricks had darkened the bright promise of democracy. Political realists in a culture devoid of ontological warrants were careless in the way they used key words in the modern political vocabulary. They passed back and forth between political realism and philosophical realism without explaining the passage between the two. Becker's concern was warranted. The division of labour in the modern humanities was embedded in a larger political economy. The interaction between the idealism of scholarship and the realities of the marketplace is not a popular area of research. Scholars in the safe house of intellect have tended to assume good words are a moral gold standard. Their value cannot be debased. Becker reminded Butterfield that heritage concepts like "democracy," "freedom," and "human rights" are ambiguous. The ideals which sustain ordinary experience suffer from daily degradation in politics, the marketplace and the political economy of the real. Private faith must be able to express itself in a public language which guards its most precious tenets from becoming a "perfunctory creed."

### MAURICE MANDELBAUM (1908–1987)

Maurice Mandelbaum was a philosopher of history at Johns Hopkins University. His last work, *Purpose and Necessity in Social Theory*, was published in the year of his death. Mandelbaum brought a remarkable level of thematic consistency to a lifetime of productive work. His first interest was traditional historical method. His six major books are carefully crafted expositions of what is now called *critical realism*. The leading current exponents of Mandelbaum's position are Roy Bhaskar and Christopher Lloyd.

Mandelbaum's first book was a refutation of the new "relativism" which he believed had crept into modern historical writing. He targeted Carl Becker as a notable example of the way "sociology of knowledge" had begun to erode traditional standards in modern historical research. Mandelbaum accused Becker of basing his arguments on personal experience. Personal experience is subjective, and subjective experience does not yield objective knowledge. *The Problem of Historical Knowledge: An Answer to Relativism* (1938) proceeds from a methodological issue with Becker to a discussion of general methodological problems. Becker was convinced "historical work, like every other intellectual endeavour, is limited by psychological and sociological conditions." Becker and colleagues like Charles Beard believe the meaning of history "can only be grasped by referring its content to these conditions," Mandelbaum explained.[21]

Mandelbaum's refutation of Becker's alleged relativism is carefully crafted. The limits of what can be known are determined by what can be done. The responsible researcher follows a scientific methodology. Her primary responsibility is to her discipline. She must protect its integrity.

The conclusions which follow from historical research are the result of getting the method right. If the method is right, relative questions of how we know what we know and whether what we know is true do not come up. Mandelbaum advises:

> Methodological investigations are to be distinguished from general epistemology, since they do not concern themselves with problems of perception nor with general formulations of the relation between the knower and the known.[22]

Mandelbaum is a disciplined researcher, but he is not above pressing one of the hot-button topics of the time. "Relativism" was a buzzword in the thirties. The word had gained currency in the new physics. Orthodox religious leaders had adapted it for service in their homilies. Anti-relativism was politically correct.

Mandelbaum's attack on "new historians" like Becker avoided mention of an important point of agreement between Becker and his more traditional colleagues. Mandelbaum also ignored the stated reasons why Becker, along with Beard, James Harvey Robinson, Arthur Schlesinger Sr., and George Boaz were attempting to write history from a new perspective. The "new historians" thought methodology *could not be distinguished from* general questions of truth and knowledge. They believed "problems of perception" and "general formulations of ideas" were closely tied to practical questions of social justice and popular democracy in the United States. Mandelbaum shows little concern for the uses of history in American politics. Mandelbaum did not share Becker's concern for "Mr. Everyman." He was not concerned about the possible misrepresentation of the American constitutional tradition by vested interest groups. In his opinion, the scientific rigour of the discipline protected historians from the fuzzy arts of politics. What knowledge was for and how it was used was not the responsibility of professional historians. Becker's response to the crisis politics of the Depression era had only made matters worse.

After World War I the modern democracies faced several severe challenges. Mandelbaum was aware of these problems, but he was concerned, firstly, with the dilution of scholarly standards. He had a scholar's healthy suspicion of tendentious writing which might inflame popular passions. He thought social history and the new intellectual history were too close to the popular imagination to be objective. He feared the new writing was open to abuse. Becker shared Mandelbaum's concerns with the integrity of their profession, but he shared a concern with Butterfield, Beard, and others which Mandelbaum chose to ignore. The new intellectual historians were afraid of modern relativism, too; but they defined the term in a different way. Becker's "Mr. Everyman" was losing faith in his religion, his country, and his fellowman. The new historians believed secular history needed to address the loss of political and religious conviction in modern life. The 'relativism' they wanted to discuss required a modification of the traditional research methodology in the modern social studies. Mandelbaum's refutation of Becker obscured this considerable point of agreement between Becker, Butterfield, Beard, Schlesinger, and a number of other new voices in the modern field. Many historians in the 1930s felt they were witnessing a sea change in the nature of modern history. They were challenged by events to articulate the nature of these changes. From their perspective, "the motions and interactions which underlie historical change" had, themselves, changed. The daily life of large numbers of people was subject to new political, economic, and cultural pressures. The old objectivist method was not meeting the needs of modern life. The "cunning" of history had disappointed most reasonable expectations during and after World War I.

Mandelbaum, let it be said, was no straw man. He included subjectivity in the "field of reality which possesses significance for human life." He based his discussion of historical subjectivity on the Marburg Kantian philosophers, Rickert, Scheler, and Croce. Heinrich Rickert, he says, "stands at the center of all philosophical discussion concerning the problem of historical knowledge."[23] Rickert called history "Kulturwissenschaft" (cultural science). Mandelbaum agreed with Rickert, if by "culture" we mean "human activities in their societal context with their societal implications," he added.[24] Context and implications are the two active ingredients in Rickert's definition of culture. Mandelbaum leans the angle dividing the two factors in favour of implications. He then limits the implications to their effect on traditional historical method. The social context had adulterated the standards of modern historical research. The first and most important job for modern historians was to protect the standards of the modern university from adulteration by popular culture and populist politics.

Mandelbaum's articulate defence of standards could be called one-sided or narrow. It may not, it seems to me, be called wrong, but it was not inclusive of other approaches. His conservative defence of traditional academic standards was definitive, if historians like Becker were, really, a major problem in the modern social studies. If the preservation of traditional research standards was, actually, a major social problem in the United States in the 1930s, then Mandelbaum is correct. Was Mandelbaum justified in his attempt to defend the Rankean tradition? The answer, obviously, has to do with what one thinks the tradition was for. Becker's fundamental premise was that university research had a moral obligation to the larger community outside and around it. Scholarship should include the ways it was reflected in daily life outside the academy. Scholars were responsible, in Becker's opinion, for the effects of scholarship on public life. Mandelbaum was not prepared to indulge Becker's expanded notion of scholarship. If freedom, community, and democracy were becoming "perfunctory creeds," the scholarly role was to document it. Scholars served society by setting the record straight. A negative "societal context" had to be documented so a literate public could discuss it intelligently. Mandelbaum limited "societal context" to the traditional role of academics as research professionals. They stand aside and describe. They do not enter the fray and they never advocate.

"The temporal framework of an event is always far richer than mere chronological sequence," Mandelbaum explained. The "framework" was recognizable by its reasonableness. History was one of the logical frameworks which showed reason at work in human affairs. The scholar's job always concerned the rescue of reason from the rubble of happenstance. Immersing reason in happenstance was taboo. Reason, consciousness, purpose, and meaning give human history the dimension by which we distinguish it from natural history. Mandelbaum has approached a significant research problem in a language of polite understatement. He is discrete and correct in his approach, but the fundamental issue looms no less large. Between them, Butterfield and Becker had raised a fundamental issue about religion and history. Their loyalty to their traditional craft did not prevent them from addressing religion and culture in an historical way. Mandelbaum wants to lower the tone of their debate *without stipulating the fundamental issue between them.* He wants to retain Hegel's faith in history without addressing ethics and morals. He wants the facts of temporal life to produce transcendental moral convictions without God, Heine's "holde kunst" or a vision of the Madonna. He wants reason and faith in one objective package without explaining how, in the skeptical world of Hume's disastrous fork, this package is possible.

Since Hume history could be a matter of fact or a moral homily. The problem was, how could it be both? What was the relation between matters of fact and ethical responsibility? History may either show how things are or show how things ought to be, but can the same historical method provide both services in the same text? According to Hume, the difference between a natural or a moral perspective lies in the eye of the beholder. If there are lessons from history we put them there. Becker believed modern life had degraded the higher lessons of history down to a perfunctory creed. The words of the creed remained the same, but the meaning of the words had been undermined. Mandelbaum dismisses the possibility of a moral dilemma in the study of history. His keyword is pattern. The pattern behind historical events is not social. If historical patterns were innately social then history would be liable to include popular culture and individual subjectivity in its study. Mandelbaum remains a dedicated objective idealist in the Hegelian tradition. He mobilizes a Romantic ideal of historical objectivity against Becker and the new historians who share his subjectivist point of view. The historical context dominates the social one. The historical context must not, in any case, be reduced to a mere matter of human subjectivity:

> The actual pattern of events in time is that which determines the historical context of phenomena.... Thus the historian never treats an event as a momentary happening in time; he views every event as a product and producer of change.[25]

A logical pattern of causes and effects are observable in the events themselves. Issues affecting large numbers of people show rational patterns in which individual subjectivities cancel each other out. Describing events so that they reveal these larger patterns is the historian's true task. "The historian's whole purpose as historian is to describe, to narrate," Mandelbaum explains.[26] Narrative descriptions of objective events will provide readers and scholars with a philosophical distance from events. The natural pattering of events is guaranteed by human reason. The patterns may not be moral but the rationality of them will lead us on. Reason entices us forward through time. Reason inspires politics, culture, and society and, ultimately, reason and right will converge. The actual dilemma of making moral choices is private and need not directly concern those who study public life as a profession.

"No sociological understanding of the conditions under which statements are made [i.e., interpreted] bears the slightest resemblance to an estimate of truth or falsity," Mandelbaum asserts. The sociology of knowledge can be bracketed and held away from the study of history. Personal theological and philosophical questions need not enter here. Mandelbaum calls his philosophical position "the correspondence theory of truth."[27] The fundamentals of history are similar to the fundamentals of any scientific body of research. Historical knowledge is "a type of 'contemporary verification' which is analogous to the 'verification by repetition' which is to be found in the natural sciences."[28] If historians would stick to the foundations of knowledge established by their original method, the study of history would be as dependable a guide to politics and culture as a natural science. Skeptical historians who challenge the foundations of historical knowledge should limit their skepticism to a criticism of the materials themselves. "The correspondence theory of truth only implies a statement is true when it expresses an actual relation," Mandelbaum continues.[29] The source materials limit one's ability to make general statements. Professional restraint in the making of prophetic, tendentious, or moralistic statements is all that is required for history to be true.

Mandelbaum reaches back to the Enlightenment for an objective theory of mind. In his opinion, the simplicity of the model saves it from the later questions in modern theories of knowledge. Since historical events affect us in objective ways, philosophical questions of perception and meaning do not apply to the study of history. The Enlightenment model of perception still applies to history because the facts of history are not like facts in other areas of human experience. The "correspondence theory of truth" pre-dates modern epistemology and symbolic logic. Mandelbaum concludes it has not been superseded in any substantial way because the study of history has not been superseded in any substantial way. History is an enlightened study of the plain truth. It does not contain perceptual problems dating from a later time. History has the advantage of documenting problems in the older way. It links modern knowledge with the traditional knowledge of the past. History makes no claim against more modern intellectual disciplines. Historians ask only to be left alone with theirs.

Mandelbaum's suspicion of subjectivity led him away from one of the most important subjective facts in modern history. The "correspondence theory of truth" is the model of human understanding which Hume skewered with his notorious fork. Hume's fork is the thought problem which correspondence theory could never answer and cannot answer now. Mandelbaum calls Becker a relativist for calling his attention to it. Becker was wrong to pay attention to Hume and Kant. In Mandelbaum's reading of modern intellectual history, Becker's problem began with Kant and Hume. To avoid the problem, just ignore Kant and Hume.

> Since Hume and Kant it has often been assumed by philosophers that the objective structure of our knowledge must be attributed to the activity of the human mind.... The structure which we find in reality as it is known is attributed to the transformation which data undergo in being made objects of knowledge.[30]

History was the collective record of the data in action. The prior, psychological transformation of sensation into data was the research interest of another field. It need not interest historians one whit. Mandelbaum believed historical study was immune to Hume and Kant. Their debate was irrelevant to history. Subjectivity does not create the patterns of historical events. Historical patterns are objective. A rational mind is disciplined. A disciplined intelligence can see objective patterns. Historical events have been caused by rational minds and other rational minds can detect them. Reason and truth meet in history because the same mind which causes history also perceives it. The social and cultural are relative to the environment, but historical understanding is not relative. Dilthey is correct. History reveals the fundamental structures of the human mind. Morality is subjective and it confuses the issue. Human beings are rational, but not, necessarily good. History has no remit to make judgments regarding this fact.

Mandelbaum's history of ideas prompts two related observations. The first observation concerns Hume and Kant. The other one takes us back to the debate with Becker. Hume's position was subtle and Mandelbaum oversimplified it. Hume called cause and effect a subjective illusion in all cases but one. Hume's exception to his own law is the sticking point in Mandelbaum's defence of methodology. Hume accepted natural necessity as an objective historical cause for events. History was real because history was the natural record of human need and mutual dependency. History showed causes and effects because history taught only one lesson. History had only one story to tell and history repeated that story in many versions over and over again. The one and only real story history illustrated continually was the effect of natural necessity on real physical existence. History had no intellectual life and the lessons of history were banal. A child could understand them.

Hume's materialism was the point Kant attacked. Kant broke with Hume over the very point Mandelbaum used against Becker in 1938. Kant claimed Hume was a relativist. He had made ideas a product of environment. Hume's praise of history was a Trojan Horse inside the citadel of moral freedom. Hume's history was "the freedom of the turnspit." It destroyed the nobility of culture, religion, philosophy and law. Kant argued the moral and political price of studying history with Hume was prohibitive. We must be concerned when a trenchant defender of history like Maurice Mandelbaum is misinformed about the history of his own ideas. Mandelbaum excluded Hume's skepticism from the study of history. In 1955 he was still arguing, "Hume's philosophy had not precluded ethical inquiry from investigating problems which concerned matters of fact."[31] Mandelbaum's position on Hume and Kant is disquieting. He has downplayed the moral debate between them by dismissing them both as relativists. He may dismiss Kant on such grounds, but not Hume. Hume saw objective patterns in history just like Mandelbaum. The difference between Hume and Mandelbaum is that Hume drew the ultimate rational conclusions from the patterns he saw. Hume concluded that the patterns of history indicate human freedom is an illusion. Mandelbaum rejects Kant, but he does not explain how he escapes the turnspit of historical materialism.

He does not have to explain his position on Hume. He does not have to have one. The Humean problem is a practical problem of freedom and faith in the larger world of skeptical science and public affairs. Mandelbaum's role as a professional intellectual protects him from the worst ravages of the Humean problem. Mandelbaum is concerned with standards inside the university and their degradation by the external society at large. His position reflects the politics of the Depression university. His unwillingness to transcend his politics poses a serious problem. General ethical questions were being discarded in favour of hard research in the budget restricted depression era. Specific moral questions, of course, would always be relevant. One must not harass or exploit students. One must not lie, etc. The climate and the weather are two different debates. Morality is a practice, much to be regarded, but ethics are a larger question involving climate of opinion and the largest human purposes. A critical theory of ethical anomaly which includes professional intellectuals is repulsive to Mandelbaum. He refuses to consider it. Professional ethics are the issue for Butterfield and Becker. They see in ethics the link between recondite research and the problems of daily life. Ethics is the general issue which awoke Kant from his slumber. Mandelbaum uses research standards and methodological purity to hide from it.

The ethical question brings us back to Becker. Becker was not worried about research standards at modern universities. He was worried about the practical effect of university research and writing on the everyday life of the workaday world. He had criticized Butterfield because Butterfield's approach required a foundation in traditional religious faith. Becker was a skeptic. He shared Butterfield's concern without sharing his piety. Becker's problem was the discussion of ethics in a secular language. His challenge was to speak to the one world in which he lived in the language of that world and no other. Becker thought he was witnessing firsthand a serious ethical anomaly at a general level of public life in Europe and the United States. The standards Becker defended were language standards in the community outside the University. The research university was not maintaining the language standards of politics and public life. History and ethics met for Becker in the public use of the heritage language. The misuse of keywords in the historical heritage was immoral to Becker. Hyperbole had passed beyond politics and crossed over into the unscrupulous. Words like "liberty," "fraternity," and "equality" had become "perfunctory creeds" which ignored the suffering of millions of people just as they had during the French Revolution. Becker saw a "pattern" in history, too. He agreed with Mandelbaum about that. The pattern he saw was the moral degeneration of the heritage language. Professional historians who ostensibly held the American heritage in high esteem seemed indifferent to the way the grand heritage was being mooted in public. In the public world, genuine care, social responsibility, and political concern were buried under an avalanche of hollow words.

The "relativism" Mandelbaum confronted was not a serious factor affecting the scholarly profession he and Becker shared. The university community was not, then or now, internally threatened by a diminution of standards or a degradation of its mission inside the academic profession. The threat was outside the university. Public life was being threatened by relativism and the diminution of political standards. Democracy was being threatened by a degradation of its mission. By missing the point Mandelbaum had clouded the issue. No reputable scholar, least of all Becker, doubted the importance of scholarly standards. Mandelbaum's defence of disciplinary standards and traditional methodology avoided Becker's point. Becker was afraid the language of modern scholarship had been co-opted. He was afraid of the use to which scholarship was put outside the university. He saw scholarship becoming a tool of social conformity and political obedience. Becker was concerned about his roles as a teacher, a shaper of public opinion, and a commentator on modern life after the words left the lecture hall and took flight off the page. Becker believed the language of university scholarship had been naturalized for uses outside the university in ways very few scholars would have supported.

Mandelbaum did not address Becker's issue. In slighting Becker's issue in preference for his own, he left a gap in the debate and created ground for ambiguity. The issues should have been clearer at the time, even if considerable latitude for disagreement remained. Mandelbaum did not understand modern intellectual history well enough to debate it with Becker. His dismissal of Hume and Kant together is erroneous. He must dismiss each one on different grounds. Hume supports Mandelbaum's objective idealism. Mandelbaum takes his idea of a deep logical framework from a scholarly tradition saturated with Hegel. The Hume-Hegel tag team is one of the most interesting associations in modern intellectual history. They have been made to work together with Hume kept the silent partner in the duo. Kant is the arch-critic of Hume and Hegel. He respected history, but he did not enjoy reading it and he did not think narrative history was very helpful. He was afraid the facts of history were a moral minefield laid by simple-minded materialism. Narrative description had no moral value for Kant. Things fork. We can never know how things are once and for all time. We can only know how things are for us. We know how to use things and what they do to us. We organize things according to our own experience. Simple narrative description does not give us direct access to the categories we use in organizing our understanding of the world. Hume, and, by association, Hegel had omitted the fundamental category of judgment from their understanding of history. They had assumed good judgment was an inevitable by-product of observing history from a safe distance. Becker has returned to Kant. Mandelbaum did not want to know why.

Mandelbaum's workplace was a modern university. The rigours of a discipline, the candour of colleagues, and the spiritual strength of the liberal arts tradition won him a refuge. His life and work were protected from the worst ravages of moral nihilism. Becker's "Mr. Everyman" did not enjoy similar protection. Mr. Everyman did not enjoy the luxury of holding history at arm's length. He lived its vicissitudes far away from the comparatively safe salient of an archive. Becker never forgot the practical difference between his life at Cornell and life in Waterloo, Iowa, where he had been born. Becker tried to get colleagues like Mandelbaum to understand a critical point about modern history he thought they had forgotten. A moral hurricane was blowing around outside the safe houses of modern intellect. The modern world had blown away the traditional meaning of words like "liberty," "brotherhood," "democracy," and "freedom." Working people in a world unprotected by status, tenure, and colleagues were vulnerable to a new problem which scholarship was reluctant to address. Wittgenstein described it to his sister one day when she upbraided him for wasting his genius on books no one could understand. He told her she was safe inside a house so sealed and secure that the hurricane outside was not even audible. She was looking at him through the window and wondering why he was staggering, falling backward, and sometimes clinging to the ground. To her he appeared drunk or out of his mind. She had no idea of the hurricane raging against him. She had no idea how hard it was to walk against the wind.

Mandelbaum is Wittgenstein's sister in a safe house secure from the storm. Becker's *The Heavenly City* was a dignified disgrace to him. Becker's scholarship was shoddy and his ideas were unstructured. Mandelbaum had no idea of the storm raging against Becker. He refused to go outside and see how the lives of ordinary people were affected by his standards, his philosophy, and his detachment from daily life. He refused to relate his scholarly standards to the verbal tumult of the new information age. He was not willing to consider whether the managed consent of perfunctory creeds had now become the mantra of democracy. Becker's discussion of history's pack of tricks was a plain language approach to the moral ambiguity of modern politics. Becker realized the old words had lost their old meaning. They could be read and used with duplicity. Most of Becker's scholarly readers were too concerned with the pattern of their own lives to spare time for the tumult outside their well-organized study. Fortunately, Mandelbaum's refutation of Becker did not escape criticism.

Typically, Mandelbaum's major critic was a philosopher. By the late 1930s modern historians had built a fortress of impregnably conventional attitudes toward the modern history of ideas.

### HEMPEL'S COVERING LAW

Carl Hempel (1905–1997) was a logical positivist. As an undergraduate at the University of Göttingen, he had been impressed by the logic of mathematics. Proving the consistency of mathematics using elementary propositions led him to an interest in truth statements in general. He and Rudolf Carnap met in 1929 and each was favourably impressed with the other. Carnap invited Hempel to Vienna where he took courses under Carnap, Schlick, and Waismann. While in Vienna he took part in the meetings of the Vienna Circle. Carnap helped Hempel immigrate to the United States in 1939. Hempel insisted he was not concerned with prediction but with making general statements that describe the world. For most of his career the logic of mathematics interested him more than discursive logic. The political crises of the period turned Hempel's attention, briefly, to history and theories of historical explanation. While on staff at Queens College, New York, he published a short paper entitled "The Function of General Laws in History" (1942). His conclusions were debated by historians in philosophy and methodology for the next twenty years.[32]

Hempel read Mandelbaum's *The Problem of Historical Knowledge* (1938) and found it a "generally very clarifying analysis." It confirmed a suspicion Hempel had harboured since undergraduate school. Historical narrative looked as if it were logically flawed. Historians did not appear to understand the importance of the philosophical enigmas first articulated clearly by Hume. Mandelbaum claimed to be a realist, but he had not addressed Hume's fork.[33] He had not explained how ideas could exist outside empirical experience. Hume was an extreme anti-realist. He doubted the independent existence of ideas. He claimed Christian ethics, classical moral philosophy, and Deist "natural law" were merely the rationalization of necessity. The brute facts ruled human life. Mutual need forced human beings to invent fancy terms like "noble," "honourable," "faithful," and "true." Civilization was the natural outcome of enlightened self-interest. History was morally indifferent to ideas and no separate spiritual space or higher intellectual function was involved in the production of them. In Hume's world, natural law was a polite term for natural necessity. Mandelbaum had not explained why ideas mattered in human history.

He had not even justified their use in public life. From a philosopher's perspective, Maurice Mandelbaum had missed the point.

Hempel had hit the historical nail on its sometimes obdurate head. All children of Europe's historical Enlightenment face the practical effects of a moral chasm first articulated with world-class cogency by the master-skeptic, David Hume. The way things were, are, and ever more shall be has no rational connection with human values. We live and love by noble fictions concocted in clear and obvious defiance of the way things are. Indispensable though it may be, the quaint word "should" is irrational and indeterminate. Humans care; history does not. Human nature needs others. Physical nature does not. God's law may govern the world of Platonic ideals, but Hume's law rules the world in which we live.

Hume himself had never shown concern over the skeptical moral dilemmas he had provoked. He called the putative moral effects of his devastating fork "a superficial paradox of the skeptics." In ethics and morals Hume did not think he was a skeptic. Hume trusted history. The historical record indicated modern history was making us moral. "Our hearts beat with correspondent movements to those which are described by the historian," he exclaimed.[34] The fixed relation which had saved history from skepticism was, according to Hume, "the very nature of language." The credulous language of previous eras "guides us almost infallibly in forming a judgment ... concerning the general foundation of morals."[35] Hempel's basic position was simple. By 1942, Hume's nonchalant faith in the language of historical study had been rebutted by the horror of historical events. The language of modern politics was based on a sentimental theory of value older than the steam engine. After centuries of service, it had finally exploded.

Hempel wrote that Mandelbaum "seems to hold that there is a difference between 'causal analysis' or 'causal explanation' of an event and the establishment of scientific laws governing it." Hempel could not understand how an analysis or an explanation could take place outside a system of law. Hempel's approach is bedrock logical positivism, the garden variety empiricism usually identified with modern science. "Every 'causal explanation' is an 'explanation by scientific laws,'" Hempel writes, "for in no other way than by reference [explicit or implied] to empirical laws can the assertion of a causal connection between certain events be scientifically substantiated."[36] Data does not cohere according to the sentimental good intentions of the researcher. Data coheres because there is a natural order at work behind it. The natural order may be counter-intuitive like a sunrise. Our senses may deceive us concerning its true nature. It may be implicit or sensual like a work of art. It may also be quite mad.

Hempel was raising a controversial question in a non-polemical way. Hempel had no doubt history, politics, society, and culture are real objects and their study was rational. He did not doubt the study of history, politics, and society was as important as the study of physical nature. He doubted whether the "social" sciences were proceeding in a rational manner. They seemed to be assuming a necessary lawful order between the description of events and the meaning of events. Hempel wanted to know what universal law of history or human nature guaranteed the connection between ideas and events in concrete human experience. Why did historians believe the rational study of events proved the events themselves were also rational?

Hempel was putting the same question to historians the Vienna Circle had put to Kant. How do you know you are not imposing your own mind on the world? What protects your method from solipsism? The logic of numbers protects physical science from solipsism. Numbers are the logic of the physical world. Math crunches the data in natural science. Historians seem to believe the social sciences enjoy a similar certainly. What makes them believe discursive language crunches events with the certainty of a science? What guarantees the universal connection between words and things at a level that comes anywhere near the precision needed to manage public affairs? What internal logic or iron-clad, structural correspondence protects historical explanations from psychosis, mass folly, and murderous abuse?

Mandelbaum's theory of interpretation only stands if there are two different worlds of lawful order at work in the same event. One lawful order dictates how events should be described. The other lawful order dictates how events should be interpreted. The study of interpretation is called "hermeneutics." The word, "hermeneutics" was not even invented until modern Europeans decided they had perfected the art. Along with their confidence went a dismissal of the fundamental paradox Hempel raised again in 1942. How do you know your language of description corresponds to the logic of events?

The Enlightenment answer to questions like Hempel's had been a theory of objective correspondence borrowed from Christianity. Universal reason had instilled "inner objects" in the psyche and external objects "corresponded" to these objects. Romanticism replaced the soul of reason with high culture. Good taste ran the gamut from art to ethics. The best that had been written and thought educated the feelings. Every cultured Westerner had been sensitized to react in ways analogous to the teaching of classical philosophy and traditional theology – or so it goes. The dumbing down of the dialogue between history and philosophy had left a hundred years of history with little idea of what the classical question of interpretation had been all about. The political disasters of the twentieth century brought the old Christian and Enlightenment question of interpretation back to the frontlines of scholarship.

Scientific research and political disasters in the twentieth century challenged the romanticism of the social sciences. Their implicit theory of a parallelism between ideas and events did not have sufficient explanatory force in a society that does science, world wars, and genocide—all on an equally unprecedented scale. Hempel was not an historian, anthropologist, or moral philosopher. He was a philosopher of symbolic logic and he tried to stick to what he knew. He was confident scientists do not use a theory of parallel worlds to validate their research. A skeptical, science-based society lives in one world and that which is true is true for all parts of it. Apparently, historians and "social" scientists have a different perspective. Hempel accuses Mandelbaum of concealing an unwarranted assumption in his theory of interpretation. Without admitting it, Mandelbaum is claiming historical knowledge has unique logical status in an otherwise scientific world.[37]

Mandelbaum, Hempel asserts, wants history, "in contradistinction to the physical sciences," to consist:

> Not in the formulation of laws of which the particular case is an instance, but in the description of the events in their actual determining relationships to each other; in seeing events as the products *and* producers of change [emphasis added].[38]

Historians may accept Mandelbaum's reasoning, but outside Clio's museum, the rest of the world has been living out Hume's major treatise on *Human Understanding*. Hempel writes:

> This is essentially a view whose untenability has been pointed out already by Hume; it is the belief that a careful examination of two

specific events alone, without any reference to similar cases and to general regularities can reveal that one of the events produces or determines the other.[39]

Mandelbaum's theory of explanation stands "outside what may be called the methodological unity of empirical science," Hempel concludes.[40]

Hempel was asking the same formal question astronomy asked astrology, chemistry asked alchemy, and medicine asks shamanism. The general form of the question is about description versus explanation. Does colloquial description explain phenomenon? Hume said it does not in his major treatise on *Human Understanding*. What Hempel did not realize was that Hume had said *it does* in his 'minor' treatise on morals. The logical difference between the major and minor treatises is an historical contradiction built into the intellectual history of the culture. Hume did not build the contradiction in all by himself. He spoke for an era which expected progress to take care of its moral problems without much effort on its part.

Hempel knew that modern science agrees with Hume's major treatise. He felt entitled to stick with the major treatise on *Understanding* without muddying the waters with non-scientific references. Hempel's greatest weakness in the argument was his scanty understanding of his own intellectual history. The water had already been muddied. Hume and a succession of impressive skeptical realists had left behind a pat answer to the difficulty Mandelbaum was being charged with. Hempel had logic on his side, but Mandelbaum had custom, tradition, and an institutionalized discourse on his. The issue was truly joined at a level of complexity that neither interlocutor really understood in full detail.

Hempel's objection points directly to a logical paradox ensconced in humanist scholarship. Mandelbaum had not explained how "a set of statements asserting the occurrence of certain events at certain times and places" can "state the *determining conditions* for the event" and therefore "contain the general laws on which the explanation is based."[41] The key word is, as Hempel said, "explanation." The key problem is a theory of language. Mandelbaum wants the same words to do two jobs at the same time. He wants the same words to be both a description of events and an explanation of their actual determining relationship. His culture and system of logical reference in the humanities disciplines has told him it is possible for one language to do a double duty. Mandelbaum is building on Hume, Hegel, Dilthey, and numerous equally diligent defenders of the tradition. Hempel, without realizing it, is challenging one of the major intellectual fallacies of the age.

Hempel lives in the one-world paradigm of science and empirical experience. He wants his one world to use one logical language in the description and explanation of experience. He takes the process of description and explanation to be cumulative. Description accumulates data until a law governing the data emerges from its study. The language of description reaches a higher order of explanation by means of orderly study and investigation. The difference between science and history concerns the kind of language used at each of the two stages. The explanatory stage requires new words not used in the descriptive stage. The new words are a causal explanation. The study of gravitation, polio, photosynthesis, and other natural events illustrates the way scientific description builds up a language of causal explanation. Mandelbaum has violated the cardinal first premise of scientific description and analysis. He uses the same words for a description *and* an explanation. He has admitted two orders of logic into the one world of observation and understanding. Science has one order of logic and a system of description and which differs from its system of analysis. History has two orders of logic which operate inside one system of description. Hempel wanted his colleagues in the social studies to understand that to be like science discursive scholarship should have only one logical structure. When scholars confuse explanation with different styles of narrative description, they have created fundamental cognitive disorder in the everyday understanding of the real.

The important thing is "structural equality of explanation and prediction,"[42] Hempel emphasizes. His language was too sparse for readers skilled in colloquy. Like many professional researchers, Hempel's pedagogical skills were underfed. The conjunction, "and" put Hempel's interdisciplinary readers on the wrong track. Hempel uses "and" like a mathematician. The word, "and" means "is the equivalent of." The square root of 4 and the number 2 are equivalent. Hempel wants historical explanation to be the *logical* equivalent of science. He wants the form of historical explanation to be as coherent as a scientific explanation. He means historical method and scientific method have to make equivalent logical sense. He does not mean history and science have the same applications nor does he mean to imply that human behaviour can be reduced to mathematical formulas.

Hempel wanted history to have the same intellectual coherence as the physical sciences. The infelicitous couplet "explanation and prediction" meant history should explain past events as logically as science predicts future ones. Hempel does not think Mandelbaum's theory of historical explanation is logical. His emphasis on descriptive language has blurred the logical distinction between description and explanation. The hard sciences have an organized system of induction which lets them move plausibly from "explanation sketch"[43] to "general law" to "universal hypothesis."[44] Does history have anything like the same sort of system? On the basis of reading Mandelbaum, Hempel thinks not. There is a hierarchy of narrative explanation in science, Hempel says, and history does not have anything which corresponds to it. The social studies have not addressed the question of how factual knowledge accumulates into generalizations which appear to be "true."

Hempel describes "the scientific explanation of an event" as consisting of:

1) A set of statements asserting the occurrence of certain events $C_1$, ...... $C_n$ at certain times and places,
2) A set of universal hypotheses, such that,
    a) The statements of both groups [time and place] are reasonably well confirmed by empirical evidence, and
    b) From the two groups of statements the sentence asserting the [likely] occurrence of event $E$ can be logically deduced.[45]

The Hempel debate concerns whether *all* coherent narratives must take this logical form. Hempel believed they must. The only reasons his general theory is disputable in historical narrative, he says, are:

1) The universal hypotheses in question frequently relate to individual or social psychology.
2) It would often be very difficult to formulate the underlying assumptions explicitly.[46]

These two limitations matter greatly if the purpose of narrative explanation is prediction and control. They are not fundamental to the question of logical form. The absence of universal hypotheses or foundational assumptions in history does not preclude discussing ideas and events in the same way skeptics discuss everything else. The historian simply must give up trying to control events. He must be content with subsuming events under general categories of experience.

Hempel contended literacy and numeracy should be formally equivalent. The one should make just as much sense as the other. The two systems of representation might do different things and be applied to different categories of experience, but the same logical structure should govern both. The historians who criticized Hempel did not accept Hempel's basic contention that literacy and numeracy had to have the same logical structure. William Dray concluded that Hempel's "empirical explanation means the use of empirical 'laws' in history." Hempel is saying, Dray replied:

> There is no difference, in this respect, between history and the natural sciences: both can give an account of their subject-matter only in terms of general concepts, and history can 'grasp the unique individuality' of its objects of study no more and no less than can physics or chemistry.[47]

Dray objected because history cannot use empirical laws in the same way as the natural sciences. Scientists can predict the outcome of controlled laboratory experiments. Human life is not a controlled experiment except in the ultimate dystopia of a Stalinist super-state. Hempel shows no understanding of the way the social world really works. The only way we can know with certainty that an explanation is correct is if it is so air-tight that an event *necessarily* occurred. No political and social event was ever absolutely necessary. Hempel and his few defenders do not understand the special status of history as a language art of moral, intellectual, and social evolution.[48]

Hempel responded formally to Dray and his other critics in 1962. His article "Explanation in Science and in History" was not even able to sustain the debate let alone win a new audience for his position. If ever the medium were mistaken for the message, Hempel's 1962 article is an example. Hempel's supercilious tone alienated the profession. "The nature of understanding ... is basically the same in all areas of scientific inquiry," Hempel chided.[49] The historians who were prepared to give up on nineteenth-century historical *verstehen* were not willing to be lectured as if they were undergraduates.

Hempel's covering law model did not exclude agency and individuality, but the language Hempel insisted upon using left him open to that charge. Hempel replied:

> Dray conceives a rational explanation as being based on a standard of appropriateness or of rationality of a special kind which he calls a *"principle of action,* i.e., 'a judgment of the form "When in a situation of type $C_1$, $C_2$, ... $C_n$ the thing to do is X."'[50]

Hempel argued Dray's "rational explanation ... does not explain what it is meant to explain." Just because $X$ is the appropriate thing to do does not mean that $A$ did $X$ for the appropriate reason. Dray's principle of action is "necessary though not sufficient for an adequate explanation," Hempel concludes.[51]

Hempel's riposte amounted to saying the *rationale* for an action is not necessarily *rational*. He pointed out an irrational motivation can always be construed as having been rational after the fact. Historical explanation should protect its narrative theory against this problem. Doing so must include a criterion of rationality. Part of the description of events should be an explicit avowal or disavowal according to disciplinary criteria of the coherence of a selected series of acts. Hempel is not satisfied with the standard historical practice of referring coherence to the context in which the action took place. Hempel's indiscreet concern for the overall coherence of history rests on the point that a series of contextual justifications does not add up to a coherent view of history. Hempel says Dray skipped a step in summarizing the covering law debate. An explanation is only rational if we insert between the situation and the act the intermediate proposition, proof or likelihood that agent "$A$ was disposed to act rationally."[52] Here Hempel, unfairly it seems to me, lost his audience.

Louis O. Mink (1963) accused Hempel of "setting up a kind of *conceptual barrier* to a humanistically oriented historiography."[53] Unless history is exempted from "methodological unity" with the 'other' sciences, its discoveries cannot be used in politics and education. Mink doubts that modern philosophy has anything to offer history. "Historians suspect this," Mink writes "and to them it seems, as one [Leonard Krieger] has said, that 'what philosophers seem to be interested in are the remains rather than the views of historians.'"[54] Mink spoke for the majority of practising historians. Mink rejected the "covering law" idea because "Historians and philosophers are too sophisticated to reveal the deepest concerns and creeds which inform their work."[55]

Mink was indiscreet, but not inaccurate. Coherent explanation in the social studies uses concepts borrowed from what most people believe to be true at the time. The wide world of students, pundits, and the book trade pay the bills. Unfortunately, they may not have the same concerns nor share the same creeds as historians and philosophers. Professional writers in the social sciences must move like a fish in water among the concerns and creeds of the people. Hempel's question opened up an old wound in a society that values science but has devalued belief. Whose concerns and creeds are the most important? Whose deepest concerns have the most significance and whose beliefs should be given the widest scope in modern public life?

Hempel's argument was the logical scalpel which cut the social studies at its most vulnerable point. The "covering laws" of the social studies are everyday ideas about politics, human nature, and society. Historians and "social" scientists use conventional ideas as a rubric for raising consciousness and directing the attention of a wider reading public to deeper questions in public life. Through teaching, writing, and research they hope a deeper appreciation of the basic issues governing modern life will filter down to a busy and often ill-informed laity. Professional intellectuals may not want to admit it, but they play a role in deliberately manipulating public opinion. Leonard Krieger called constructive manipulation of popular opinion, "the politics of discretion." A 'sophisticated' denial of his deepest concerns and creeds was the discreet approach required in public debate. Krieger's positive point was taken from the great Romantics of the nineteenth century. The negative side had been addressed by Hempel. Mink's sophisticated silence over his deepest concerns and creeds closed off candid discussion of what a less skeptical society would have called "spiritual problems." Hempel's "covering law" was the last prominent attempt among the logical philosophers to explore the epistemological foundations of the social sciences from a moral point of view.

In his explanation of *Time's Reasons* (1989), Leonard Krieger wrote that Hempel's covering-law provided him with the "conceivable limit to the externalization of the principle of coherence."[56] Hempel "stands for our century's most decisive effort at reestablishing for the issue of historical coherence a basis in certainty *which is external to history itself*" [emphasis added].[57] Krieger's objection to Hempel is more subtle than Dray's and

Mink's. Its subtlety provides a doorway into the mind of an academic word-world at war. The phrase, "coherence ... which is external to history," is a euphemism. The phrase functions for Krieger as Mink had divulged. It seamlessly conceals his deepest concerns.

Privately, Krieger had complete faith in the "already formed language" of the "social" sciences. He distrusted all "certainty which is external to history." He did not expose his Hegelian biases in his discussion of Hempel. Because he was a prolific author, his deepest concerns can be pieced together from his later work. Krieger was concerned about modern history at two levels and, unlike most of his colleagues, Krieger had read the basic texts. I wrestled for years with Krieger's disparate readings of Hegel and Hume. More than one version of this book contained histrionics against what I considered the moral treason of clerics like Krieger. I now think differently. The problem with Krieger's "political discretion" is the discourse in which he speaks. Krieger has a discursive duck-rabbit in his philosophy of history. His language is morally ambivalent and he has no way to discuss it in the tradition he mastered. Krieger's deepest concerns are complex and relevant, but his idea of the kind of thing language is creates ethical dilemmas for anyone who studies his work. The ethics of texts like Krieger's are the heart of the modern predicament.

Krieger was a realist after Mandelbaum's own heart. The historically "real" was real in two senses. There are "certainties" which are internal to history and "certainties" which are external to history. You discover the latter by being loyal to the former. Krieger took his internal historical realism from Hume and Hegel. He explained it with reference to the life of Jean-Paul Sartre. "History and social solidarity were precisely what the pre-war Sartre needed," Krieger concludes.[58] Sartre's war trilogy, *Les Chemins de la liberté*, "embodies the contemporary expression of his [Sartre's] attitudes for the critical war-time interval."[59] History itself gave Sartre an insight into the study of history.

The practical insights which saved the pre-war Sartre from morbid self-destruction were recorded in the war trilogy. They are contrary to the nihilism of *La Nausée* (1938). This fact about Sartre's literary and philosophical opus is also a fact about Sartre. It confirms the dual status of history as a body of knowledge with its own interpretive laws. Krieger continues:

> In short, what replaced the individualistic temporal paradoxes and failures of his first stage [existentialism] was the conviction,

mediated by contemporary history, that individuals could join with their fellows in an *historical* process in which they could recover their integrity.[60]

"If we do not apply our history to this end we fail both as the historians and as the historical agents of our age," Krieger concludes.[61] The "synthetic role" of history defeats in practice what the existentialists tried to conquer in theory. Krieger read Sartre's existential philosophy the same way Dray and Mink read Hempel. Abstract reason is not able to see what history shows until the heart enters into solidarity with its fellowmen and stands up for the great lessons that only history can be trusted to raise.

Roquentin, Sartre's alter ego in *Nausea*, was an historian, and the working title for *Nausea* was *Melancholia* until just before publication. When Sartre wrote, "Human reality, therefore, is by nature an unhappy consciousness with no possibility of surpassing its unhappy state," we may assume, I believe, Sartre was unhappy.[62] We may also take it as written that his emotional condition did not improve rapidly.

Sartre's pain is the existential torment of a sensitive soul imprisoned in an era of bad faith. It is impossible to be innocent in such a place. Sartre blamed history. Krieger refuses to blame history. He blames Sartre. He makes Sartre's unhappiness Sartre's own fault. Sartre's "integrity" depends upon "joining his fellows in an historical process." History is Krieger's answer to Sartre's unhappiness. Sartre could find the integrity his life lacked in the great issues of history. Sartre's philosophical and moral introspection were misplaced. Sartre's historical experience as recorded in the war trilogy was the human truth he should have followed. Sartre's theoretical head got in the way of his healthy human heart.

Krieger's discussion of Sartre is more candid than his discussion of Hempel. The Sartre essay reveals Krieger has no faith in principles of coherence outside history. The suicidal depression of Roquentin, Sartre's alter-ego, was caused by an emotional refusal to join history. Integrity is an historical experience best achieved from inside an historical perspective. The search for absolute integrity outside historical reality caused Roquentin/Sartre's suicidal depression. Criticizing existentialism to an American audience was politically correct during the 1960s.

With Hempel, Krieger faced a problem similar to one he had faced with Sartre. He needed to debunk theory without giving up on the existence of timeless ideas. Traditional realism requires objective ideas which exist independently of empirical verification. Krieger does not believe the theoretical problem of realism is a real problem. To avoid political difficulties with his larger readership outside the profession, he finds an interdisciplinary phrase which is acceptable to both sides of the realist debate. The phrase "external coherence" is acceptable to moral realists *and* political realists. It means two different things to the two different auditors, but Krieger is not worried about that. Krieger finds a politically correct way to describe Hempel which pleases both moral realists and political realists at the same time. He speaks from a point of view that sounds valid to two different theoretical perspectives. "External" is a political weasel word. It lets Krieger form a temporary political consensus among his auditors at the expense of a larger and more durable mutual understanding.

With Sartre and Hempel, Krieger is saying one thing to moral realists in theology and philosophy and something else to his colleagues in the disciplinary study of history. Few professional historians retained the larger perspective of Butterfield and Becker by the time Krieger was summing up *Time's Reasons* in 1989. Krieger and his colleagues in the 1980s were nearly unanimous in their belief that the Butterfields and Beckers of the profession end up like Roquentin. Writer's block should be the least of their worries. The professional in the field finds her integrity inside history. The real knowledge of history is internal to events. The description of events is a causal explanation because events describe the conditions which determine belief in that time.

The word "external" is a portmanteau term for Krieger. It carries a double meaning. One meaning assuages the doubts of moral realists in philosophy and theology and the other meaning is a warning to political realists in politics and the economy. The "conceivable limit to the externalization of the principle of coherence" was a limit political realists should avoid crossing. Krieger codes a warning to political realists in a language that comforts philosophical realists outside the profession. Krieger's discussion of Hempel is a duck-rabbit. It is a case-study of the language that caused Wittgenstein so much pain. A double image is caused when two contexts cross, confuse, and, finally, short-circuit each other.

Krieger addresses the same explanation to two different readerships. The explanation is appropriate for one or the other, but not both. The two explanations taken together are indeterminate. They are not "equivalent," they are structurally incoherent. The two philosophical positions, philosophical realism and political realism, cannot be addressed together in the same language. They are not coherent inside the same language of historical description and traditional 'causal' explanation in the social studies. The ambiguous analysis is what Kant called an antinomy and Wittgenstein called a duck-rabbit. The feelings it raises causes Roquentins and the arguments it stirs up cause Hempels. Krieger has ignored the need for coherence at the logical level of plausible belief.

Krieger was a prominent historian in a politicized generation of academics. A "hard-headed generation of political historians" thought of ideas as "ex post facto rationalizations of modern politics" Quentin Skinner remarks. Stephen Jay Gould called the post-war research university "the magister's pox." Academic freedom had developed a split personality. It retained the courageous "hedgehog" vitality of the classic researcher, but a new attitude guided the work. The "hedgehogs" of research also became "foxes" in politics. The intellectual honesty of Butterfield, Becker, and Hempel was declared indiscreet. History joined history. The academy went to war. Howard Zinn has strongly denounced "the Cold War bias" that marred his university years.[63] The most entertaining, albeit one-sided, criticism of the modern research university after World War II is *Profscam* by Charles Sykes (1990).[64] Robert Darnton accuses post-war historians in the United States of "cutting American intellectual history free of its moorings in social history and drifting off in pursuit of a disembodied national mind."[65] These criticisms are barbed references to discursive anomalies of the kind Wittgenstein and Hempel addressed.

The way post-war historians rejected Hempel is more important than the negative position taken. The language politics of the debate are as important as the theoretical concerns which lay behind it. The way historians after World War II apologized for intellectual history hid an obvious moral question behind an obscure hermeneutical one. Hempel was warning historians that their principles of coherence and patterns of regularity might be vulnerable to malpractice. Hempel was afraid aficionados of modern historical method had little protection from inadvertent complicity with destructive behaviours a less skeptical society would have called evil. The best of personal intentions could not protect the truth from the moral indeterminacy of modern language. Hempel had sided with Becker.

## *LEONARD KRIEGER (1918–1990)*

Leonard Krieger was the most intellectual historian in the United States during the Cold War. He was a German-language scholar who considered himself a "new historian" in the tradition of Robinson, Becker, and Beard. Krieger's books are the intellectual autobiography of a rigorous scholarly life served in the defence of classical historical ideals. *The German Idea of Freedom* (1957) defined Krieger's field of research. *The Politics of Discretion: Pufendorf and the Acceptance of Natural Law* (1965) was his philosophy of history. *Ranke: The Meaning of History* (1977) was his defence of traditional historical method. *Time's Reasons* (1989) was his last intellectual will and testament. By the end of his life, Leonard Krieger had built a scholarly Thermopylae which he defended as if Western civilization depended upon it. It was his duty and he did it well. The triumph and the tragedy of his perspective is part of the legacy of modern intellectual history.

World War II led Krieger to his field of research. Looking back thirty years later he explained, "For those of us who were raised politically on the vicarious experience of National Socialism, its graduation into an apparently successful and overpowering regime was a cataclysm of unparalleled proportions.... Nazism, in short, was a massive central reality, *sui generis*."[66] The failure of democracy in a country like Germany was a worldwide eye-opener to Krieger. Where Adorno had said no more poetry, Krieger was afraid there could be no more history. Since German idealist philosophy and Fine Arts culture had not prevented fascism, Krieger never doubted a similar cataclysm could happen anywhere. The "Nazi cultural matrix" was a perennial theme in his work.

Carl Schorske called Krieger's *The German Idea of Freedom* (1957) a "pioneering work" which sets out "the moral implication of the limits of history as a mode of comprehension."[67] Schorske used Krieger's analysis of German liberalism in his explanation of Vienna's "nervous splendour." Krieger's defence of Dilthey influenced Michael Ermath's biography of Dilthey at several key points. Otto Pflanze cites Krieger's analysis of German liberalism in the introduction to his biography of Bismarck. Arthur Danto, Louis Mink, and William Dray enlist Krieger in their attempt to refute Hempel's "covering law thesis." Krieger's definition of "historicism" is the most frequently cited definition of the word. Krieger's colleagues at Yale joked that *The German Idea of Freedom* could only be read in a German translation. Krieger's English was German in syntax and American in its ideals. History of ideas to Krieger was the life of the mind being realized in historical events. His instinctive sympathies lay with the events. His language was the language of ideals. The rendezvous of ideas and events was a manifest destiny to Leonard Krieger.

*The German Idea of Freedom* traced German political idealism to Kant. Unlike his intellectual mentors, Lewis White Beck and Ernst Cassirer, Krieger described Kant's aesthetics as noble in form but unworkable in practice. Kant's moral philosophy was not suitable for the give and take of democratic politics. *The German Idea of Freedom* portrays a Kant who, caught on the cusp of historical disillusionment, "perpetuated the traditional German confusion about the relationship between morals and politics," Krieger concluded.[68] Kant's system lacked the "moral motor" of democratic debate. History has shown "politics is the crucial arena which terminates the traditional categorical distinction between the spirit and the flesh," Krieger concluded.[69] Kant's world of freedom only existed in the mind. Kant's critical detachment made possible an austere individual moral life but foreclosed all possibility of political activism. He did not understand politics so, "Kant had not questioned or demonstrated whether his two distinct spheres of pure and practical reason were actually harmonized."[70] The idea that politics plays a transcendental role in the modern moral life was the critical point of departure for Krieger from Beck and Cassirer. It was a point of departure that was typically American and defines in its scope the severe perturbation of classical idealism, particularly Enlightenment idealism, in modern American life.

*Time's Reasons* (1989), published as he lay dying, was a defiant refusal to surrender to forces which, he felt, were threatening civilization. The book is, Malachi Haim Hacohen deduces, "a declaration of war on a host of social and cultural histories of the 1970s" because they represented to Krieger "not merely an intellectual challenge and a moral problem, but intellectual paralysis and moral disease…. *Time's Reasons* is not an innovative work, but an affirmation of faith."[71] Leonard Krieger was a secular man of faith. The foundation of Krieger's faith was politics. Ideas gave politics a noble language for discussion and debate. The intellectual heritage was a rhetorical smithy where consensus and solidarity were forged during the hot and cold wars.

Krieger thought history illustrated the "sinews of wisdom" without which civilization would fail. History, for him, was the place where:

> Conversation with the great dead joins the resurrection of the souls of the mute in common perspective upon the autonomous role of ideas.[72]

Political history resurrected the souls of the mute and the history of ideas was their conversation with the greats of the past. The suffering of the mutes needed the wisdom of the magi. Krieger conceded human nature was not, in all cases, equal to the task. History and human behaviours were often incoherent. Explaining history in ways which fostered progress was a difficult job. He admitted:

> The problem of historical coherence is a genuine problem; humans are simply not satisfied with the individuality, the diversity, the refractoriness of past human things which has been the implication of the historian's use of *the* critical method and which has been the strength of modern historiography [emphasis added].[73]

"*The* critical method" of traditional historical study was the only way to make life's refractory particularities cohere.

The "souls of the mute" were deeply affected by events. The great dead and the mute masses meet in stories about historical events. In narrative history, the mute masses discover the "sinews of wisdom" holding history together. Wisdom is discovered by its virtuous influence or its evil absence. In either case, the concrete particulars of the past point irrefutably to a practical wisdom. Mute souls damaged by time and place can see the wisdom of significant events and practice that wisdom at all levels of their lives. History was philosophy teaching by example a perspective it could not prove. History remained, for Krieger, the indispensable crossroads where political democracy, personal probity, and private faith meet.[74]

Krieger was confident that he and his colleagues would "cautiously and self-consciously separate our assumptions from the reality that we treat and look to the *validity* of our method."[75] He was not disingenuous. He had inherited a civic culture of manifest political and economic destiny. The politics of moral progress were historically self-evident to him. He was confident the dialectical clash of heart and head would sprout world freedom like the abundant fruit of a well-tended orchard. He considered himself a diligent husbandman and shepherd to the flock. He warned that:

> The current disputes about the social relations of ideas ... has too many methods.... This diversity has raised serious doubts about its integrity as a distinct and autonomous field of history.[76]

In a paper he delivered to the American Historical Association in 1971, Krieger put on notice anyone who doubted the purity of the traditional historical method. They were subject to exclusion from the charmed circle. He singled out one group in particular.

"Intellectual historians," Krieger concluded, "have become the cuckoos in the historical nest.... The historical validity of the universal ideas on which historians have traditionally depended ... is now widely denied," he warned.[77] The "cuckoos" he blamed were, in most cases, radical intellectuals with socialist, existentialist, or postmodernist tendencies. "To the consternation of their colleagues they like to think and to talk about method," Krieger grumbled.[78] The difference between Krieger and the "cuckoos" was a matter of loyalty to fundamentals. The "cuckoos" who debated ideas were disrupting the integrity of the method and its systematic approach to truth.

The 1971 paper was developed from an article, "Culture, Cataclysm and Contingency" (1968). Here he pointed for the first time to "Hume's critique of the Enlightenment's standard version of rational coherence." Hume "emphasized the autonomous side of history's unifying function." Krieger called Hume's "deliberate turn from philosophy to history" an "indisputable fact" in modern philosophy, but he concludes "the reason behind this fact remains highly disputable." "Personal cataclysm that he experienced" and "personal cataclysm that he feared" were without doubt factors. Krieger's analysis of Hume resembled his analysis of Sartre. It was historical and autobiographical. He had applied the same analysis to himself and his colleagues after the war. "Time's reasons" were the only reasons you have. "Time" is the determining fact in everyday life.

Hume's answer to cataclysms experienced and feared was also Krieger's answer:

> Hume's distinctive focus on history ... shifted the locus of coherence from the relations of ideas to the relations of facts and showed that history served as the same kind of ordering medium as the logic of abstract reason. For if Hume subscribed neither to a necessary connection between ideas nor to the primacy of reason among the human faculties, he did subscribe to general principles in human nature, and, in his attempt to elicit them and their non-logical relations, he stumbled on history as a vehicle for organizing the varieties of human reality.[79]

Krieger gives Hume credit for inventing the language Becker called a "pack of tricks." Krieger does not think it is a trick. He lays out Hume's solution to the skeptical moral dilemma in positive terms. The mute masses will not get their daily dose of wisdom without the benign narrative devices that living scholarship must adapt to their needs. Krieger's theory of narrative origins was unexceptional in the United States after World War II. His work on methodology explained narrative practice in Europe and the United States. Very few scholars imagined there could be a problem.

Krieger's re-reading of Hume sounds like Butterfield, Becker, and Hempel, but it is not. Krieger has trimmed away the moral debate of the 1930s. Hume's skepticism was a moral problem for Butterfield, Becker, and Hempel. They viewed the skeptical problem from the perspective of the ordinary, everyday reader whom Becker called "Mr. Everyman." Hume's turn to history meant to them Mr. Everyman had no foundation for public probity and personal belief. Hume had politicized a two-thousand-year tradition of philosophical realism. The critical tradition which had stood flint against the expediencies of the prince and the prudence of the businesspeople was reduced to a tactic.

Hume had trusted the healthy lifestyles and good work habits of ordinary people to sustain the moral force of old-fashioned metaphysics in the new, enlightened era. His confidence in the people is the last metaphysics. Hume's faith in the people and their politics is the last, great scholastic school of dialectical debate. It is enshrined in American historiography and spread by American culture around the world. Krieger defends Hume's method and uses Hume's language, but he does not share Hume's faith in ordinary people. Krieger calls ordinary people the "mute masses." Krieger's new faith is in the language of blunt political trauma. History helps keep the masses in line.

Krieger believed Enlightenment philosophy "had been able to divorce the persistent principles of human nature ... from the metaphysics they denied and to orient it toward the actualities of human behaviour in which they were expressed."[80] Hume was his prime example. Hume's use for history was to "infer" the motive of an action. After destroying inference in philosophy, Hume allowed its possibility in history. Human nature gave "the union betwixt motives and actions the same constancy as that in any natural operation," Hume believed.[81] History was the science of human nature in action.

Hume's skepticism in philosophy led to a practical flexibility in politics which Krieger admired. Krieger thought Hume was a "trimmer." He believed Hume's use for history was a storehouse of wisdom artfully "trimmed" to suit the needs of the times. He was not embarrassed to defend the "trimming" of great ideas to suit social and political success. Krieger took up what he thought was Hume's cause in defence of what he thought was the way the modern world must and would continue to make progress. He was not shy about asserting that what Becker called a "trick" was, in fact, the solution to the realist problem in ethics and the challenges facing global democracy. Krieger thought Hume's model of history explained a public process that was inevitable, timely, and necessary.

Krieger wrote a biography of "an indubitably representative figure," who, in his opinion, embodied Hume's pragmatic understanding of history. Samuel Pufendorf (1632–1694) was "the father of natural law" theory in Europe. He wrote a text on civil law which was used in European universities for over one hundred years. After a distinguished academic career, he served as a minister to the King of Sweden. Krieger understood the secret of Pufendorf's success. "He was a trimmer," Krieger explains.[82] Pufendorf, the scholar, succeeded as a prominent public figure because he trimmed the timeless truth to suit the exigencies of his time.

History shows how few of us are given the opportunity to do great deeds. So Krieger explains:

> We inhabit along with a host of others, that second level in the structure of human society whence ideas are transmitted from the study to the forum, and experience is passed back from the forum to the study.[83]

Krieger identified with Pufendorf. He thought of himself and his colleagues as trimmers in the service of the same historical ideal. We serve "as rather humble and obscure mediators," he concluded:

> For a mediator of the Pufendorf type, the canons of life and thought are too flexible to be convulsed by any new experience; they are simply bent by the weight of the experience which they undergo.[84]

Trimmers bend with the times, but they do not break. Their strength lies in their flexibility and their courage is defined by the difficult experiences they are willing to undergo.

Krieger's "trimmer" represents a considerable trimming of the tradition he inherited from Butterfield and Becker. Butterfield believed history should inspire dissent and dedicated acts of Christian conscience. Becker believed Mr. Everyman had to be his own historian. Krieger thought Mr. Everyman needed a "trimmer" to provide him with these services. The people needed "trimmers" like Pufendorf to explain the truth about history in a language they could understand. Time reasons better than any individual so it is better to leave history to the professionals. The people have to learn to work with history and not against it. Pufendorf took "the rational faculty which inheres in every man" to the next level. He was able to explain time's reasons to his times.[85]

The British historian Michael Oakeshott explained the nautical origins of the term "trimmer." "The trimmer is the sailor who disposes his weight so as to keep the ship upon an even keel."[86] Oakeshott praised the trimmer in *The Politics of Faith* (1996), a work published posthumously.

> The trimmer believes that there is a time for everything and that everything has its time – not providentially, but empirically. He will be found facing in whatever direction the occasion seems to require if the boat is to go even.... The 'trimmer,' then ... is a 'time-server.' ... His task ... is, first, to restore the understanding of the complexity of modern politics.[87]

Oakeshott wrote that the 'trimmer' understands "It is our predicament to be able to enjoy a complex manner of government only at the cost of an equivocal political vocabulary.... He accepts what is undeniable and makes the best of it."[88] Oakeshott has a skeptical faith in the political practice now ordinarily known as "spin." One recent reviewer has called the unifying framework of Oakeshott's political philosophy "skeptical idealism."[89] If so, the idealism of the "trimmer" is the true descent into discourse. It represents the historical negation of classical philosophy and traditional theology. Trimming and spin are a kind of civil fideism in modern public discourse. The lack of faith proves the need for it in public life since the Napoleonic wars.

The trimmer has faith in the truth, but not the whole truth. Dark clouds of grey edging toward the pall of misinformation do not, usually, darken his discourse. A stoic citizenry, competently acculturated to painful differences between policy and probity, cunning and candour, principle and practice, try to make the best of slippery practices they have come to regard as a sign of political acumen. What has actually been "trimmed" here? What does the "trimmer" accomplish in addition to his or her personal success? From the older perspectives of Christian theology and classical philosophy, the trimmer has whittled away all solid reference to principle. What have been trimmed away are the fundamental questions of logical and behavioural integrity that nurtured Western civilization for two millennia.

As a "practical" matter, the trimmer sets politics above ethics, prudence above morality, and self-promotion above good will.[90] Malachi Haim Hacohen's gentle critique of Leonard Krieger's method is a generic critique of the trimmer's role. S/he appears in religious robe, business suit as well as the deceptively dishevelled denims of academe:

> Precisely where the appeal of Krieger's scholarship lies ... there also lies its great danger, the muting of protest against history and power.[91]

Krieger offered Samuel Pufendorf's life as an example of how to:

> Make a doctrine porous without sacrificing its essential virtue.[92]

Pufendorf had faced the job of selling the old landed aristocracy on the idea of universal justice and natural law. Pufendorf had faced the career challenges of his moral duty with as much courage and consistency as one could while, at the same time, pleasing his patron, the Swedish king.

Leonard Krieger thought Samuel Pufendorf was a role-model for twentieth-century academics and public service professionals. Krieger uses Pufendorf's life to compose an amazing intellectual *tour de force*. He enlists the natural law argument from the seventeenth century for service during the Cold War. The professional trimmer, the articulate mediator, the public service middle-man, Mr. Everyman's mentor and political advisor had the civic duty and moral responsibility to defend the authority of the state. The authoritative institutions that guarded democracy were under attack. Krieger exhorted his colleagues to resist the tide.

"The Idea of Authority in the West" was Krieger's explanation of "the much-discussed crisis of authority ... which became particularly visible with its spread from the society at large into the groves of academe during the sixties."[93] Great ideas were the rallying ground for the "natural leaders" of American society. History of ideas should confront "the contemporary challenge to authority." The history of ideas showed "the projective tendency and the projectile force of the long-range process in which authority in the West has been involved."[94]

Authoritative life lessons required "a psychologically authoritative debate" at all levels of public life. The foundation of authoritative debate was "the obscure frictions" of academic research.[95] Scholarship was the only defence against "the production of authoritarian personalities and one-dimensional individuals in the very image of a coercive society." Self-integration without the guidance of history was a danger to great ideas and global democracy. "The growing loss of valid authority between individuals was being compensated by a growing belief in a valid authority among the drives *within* the individual," Krieger concluded.[96] Krieger's duty was clear to him. Mr. Everyman had lost contact with the "sinews of wisdom" which were the cornerstone of American democracy. He was falling prey to primary animal drives "within" him. Those with the ability to do so had to teach a trimmed history that would protect Mr. Everyman from the psychological and emotional enemy within. Those who understood the danger had to protect the public from itself. Under current conditions, the risks of an open society were too great to risk having one.

Krieger closes his biography of Pufendorf with the advice, "When all else fails, you can always turn to God."[97] His concluding admonition was neither the counsel of intuition nor irony. On the basis of a venerable but ambivalent heritage, Krieger taught respect for moral philosophy, religious faith, and American democracy without asking whether heritage ideas, traditional faith, and American politics were compatible in all points. He did not entertain the possibility that these ostensibly noble causes could be in conflict with each other. Krieger's idea of authority absolved the sinews of Western wisdom from the treasons, stratagems, and spoils of power politics. Krieger ignored the skeptical difficulty with religious faith and he was not afraid his own intellectual politics might be just as slippery a slope as the inherent lawlessness of the masses.

Krieger's intellectual politics create philosophical issues in history and credibility issues in politics. Krieger offers no reasonable explanation why a "trimmer" should be trusted. He does not explain how a history that has been "trimmed" can still be "authoritative." Shaping history to the perceived needs of Mr. Everyman involves selective attention to the historical details. The tacit priorities which inform Krieger's perspective involve value parameters he did not address. Krieger does not consider the contribution non-Western cultures can make to a less "trimmed," more open, and less inequitable world. He does not examine the tautology of secular faith. His preoccupation with intellectual politics takes moral relativism to a level that is not, on the face of it, warranted in any of the world's great religions. Krieger's secular faith is in moral conflict with the traditional wisdom he said it was his purpose to defend.

### KANT AND MARX

Krieger presented a paper on Karl Marx at Columbia University in 1960.[98] Krieger tried to fit Marx comfortably into the general "principles of action" which he always referred to as "natural law." He advised that taking Marx's "categories as questions and not as canons" automatically made them "valid ... for the purpose of translating historical materials into some kind of rational process."[99] Krieger was in the vanguard of the movement to read Marx as "post-Kant," instead of anti-Hegel.[100] Americans led the charge to Kant because the Kant they read was culture vulture number one. Their Kant was an aesthetic idealist who had proven the intuitive connection between pure reason and the Romantic culture of sweetness and light. The title of the Columbia essay, "The Uses of Marx for History," begins with one of Krieger's portmanteau word games. Does Marx have a use for History or does History have a use for Marx? Krieger's position is that "time reasons." History has a use for Marx which the radical philosopher himself had not understood.

History always has a cunning rationality which transcends the grasp of any one thinker. The class struggle is a theory which has to be rethought by every generation of scholarship. The Russians and the Chinese have taken Marxist theory from the nineteenth century and followed it as if it were true for all times. They are mistaken and the difficulties of their domestic political situations *circa* 1960 are a symptom of it. Krieger jocularly advised against following "the criteria of Marx chosen by the 'enemy.'" "It would be better," he advised, "to 'select our own.'"[101]

Substantively, Krieger thought that Marx provided "little sustenance for historians" because historians proceed on "assumptions of historical discontinuity, plurality of causation, and *merely formal* absolutes when we admit any at all" (emphasis added).[102] Still, Marx was "one of those pivotal thinkers" to whom we apply "the criteria of intellectual greatness." Why? Because:

> The measure of greatness is the illumination of what is fundamental to humanity in all ages ... the immortals are those who, regardless of their partisan solutions and followings, have something to say to everybody because they encompass both sides of eternally vital issues.[103]

Marx was an "immortal" in spite of his "commitment to economic primacy and to political and ideological dependence as absolute principles," Krieger concludes. Krieger is developing a Marx who stands above the Cold War and class conflict. The Marx who "encompasses both sides" of the issues is not the Marx of the Cold War. Marx's politics were local in time and place. What survives of value from Marx is not his politics, but his method. "Marx's method," Krieger wrote, "of integrating man's historical activities in any one period is the most intellectually satisfying means yet devised."[104]

Well, that puts the fox among the pigeons. What, pray tell, is left of Marx's "method" if one excludes "economic primacy" as one of its "absolute principles"? The fine little print which sets Krieger's game afoot is "in any one period." The content of Marx's argument was important for the nineteenth century, but far less important for us. The contemporary world faces a different range of problems and Marx's thought does not directly address these. The importance of Marx for us lies in his, "insistence on wholeness and totality, as the only basis for rational freedom."[105] The Marx who seeks wholeness and totality as a matter of principle is the Kantian Marx, the Marx whose concrete approach to history also offers an historical approach to the first principle of democratic politics. Marx is still relevant to contemporary historians because his method shows "a process of immanent rationalization informs history with a pattern."[106] The largest and most inclusive rational pattern in history is the emergence of self-government and participatory democracy. Political Marxists mistake "economic categories" for "philosophical categories," Krieger advises.

It is the latter which "illuminate the external relations of historical facts and find a common measure for them," he concludes.[107] "We cannot use the substance of Marx [i.e., economic analysis], but we can use the form in which he couched it."[108] Marx's formal approach remains one of the most constructive approaches to history in the Western canon of ideas.

Krieger's discussion of "form" is a duck-rabbit – a Machiavellian moment for anyone subject to the old master's spells. 'Form' works in the paper on Marx the way 'external' worked in the comments on Hempel. 'Form' is a portmanteau term, a pivot term that clues in some and coddles the others. In defending the "form" of Marx's philosophy, Krieger leaves moot the central question that links Marx and Kant. Marx and Kant were moralists. They were repulsed by the apparent moral indifference of their eras. They both tried, using different methods, to raise the moral consciousness of a secular era in which the traditional wisdom of religious realism had little effect on public life. They were both concerned, in different ways, with the same question. Can a science-based, skeptical society do ethics? Can rationalists be taught to act morally? Is philosophical realism sustainable in a culture of materialists? These are the most important philosophical conundrums of the modern age. Krieger deflects the discussion away from practical engagement with these perennial concerns.

Marx "intrigues us," Krieger believes, because he has the:

Capacity to find an essentially ethical rationale running within and across the centuries at the very same time that he perceives the diversity and complexity of historical existence.[109]

So, in spite of Marx's lapse into "the doctrinaire of 1848 who flatly announced that, 'the history of all previous society is the history of class struggles,'" Marx provides us with "something about the principles of synthetic judgment which we so sorely need." Marx's fruitful application of philosophical categories to economic processes is a case in point. Marx shows historians across the ages how history should be done. The researcher, teacher, and writer of history bring formal categories of judgment to bear on the facts. The ability to synthesize the facts of history into large and coherent systems of knowledge is the essential task of the modern researcher. Krieger considered this the essence of the "new history." Marx was the turning point from dry-as-dust historians like Ranke and Acton to the dynamic modern history of great souls and timeless ideals.

Krieger uses Kant to support his reading of Marx. Synthetic judgment is a Kantian concept and Krieger sees the Marxist synthesis as a fulfillment of the Kantian ideal. Kant did, indeed, put the phrase synthetic judgment into the modern philosopher's professional vocabulary. The way Kant used it is different from the way Krieger uses it. Kant's approach to the *formal* problem is subtly different from the tack Krieger has adopted. One has to look carefully at the language of the debate to see the difference. Kant discusses "synthetic judgment *a priori*." His boxcar phrase for a moral judgment included the phenomenal fact they appear to happen intuitively. Human beings appear to have an inner, affective sense of right and wrong. They seem to be able to make complex moral judgments prior to having had the empirical experiences which would seem to be required for making such a judgment. People may reject war without having been to war. They may eschew lascivious behaviours prior to experiencing their negative consequences. They are capable of quitting a job or leaving a scene before the trouble breaks out. They appear to have an intuitive capacity (not always used) to imagine probable consequences which they have, in fact, not experienced.

Kant noted moral behaviours are a gestalt process involving reason and feeling. The moral life was in part calculating, but it was in greater part an emotional orientation reached prior to the concrete experience. Kant was puzzled by this phenomenon. Krieger has trimmed Kant's theory of judgment down to a way of thinking about history. He has lopped off the *a priori* aspect of synthetic judgment. Krieger has trimmed away the most interesting aspect of ethical theory and moral behaviour. He has cut Kant's critique of judgment by one half. He accepts the rational role of judgments *about* history, but he does not discuss how the emotional capacity for judgment is developed *by* history.

According to Krieger, Kant could not have known he was part of:

> The composite movement which would later produce a Hegel and a Marx.... [This new lawful order] was, together with the direct channel which links the witty, tolerant, critical, reasonable, socially concerned minds of all ages, the other main conduit through which the civilization of eighteenth-century Europe passed into the contemporary world.[110]

Kant brought together freedom and art in a new way. Kant's synthesis became one of the main currents in late modern thought. Kant is one of the "immortals" because he showed:

> The primacy of freedom and the role of art in synthesizing the sensual and moral natures of man into the wholly free individual.[111]

Kant was the philosophical coast road running parallel to the superhighway of witty sophistication. He made social sophistication available to those without social advantages.

Those who were not born to leisure and affluence could develop an aesthetic link with the concerned minds of all ages. Romantic culture was the indirect conduit to a sophisticated view of the world. Kant gave art and culture the prominence they now enjoy in late modern life. Kant's synthesis of the sensual and the moral filtered down into popular consciousness as the other "conduit" through which civilization could be passed. Hegel and Marx were interested in the same thing. They wanted to bring wit and sophistication to ordinary people.

Krieger says the first step toward a witty, tolerant, reasonable, and socially concerned populace is the Kantian emphasis on moral feeling. A "composite movement" in modern history builds on Kant's new emphasis. Hegel and then more concretely Marx follow up by finding a political role for Kant's moral aesthetic. "From this angle, Marx's insistence that both history and society were nature for men was a radical confession of what was held more moderately and more covertly elsewhere along the intellectual spectrum," Krieger concludes.[112]

In Krieger's history of the world, elite wit and cosmopolitan sophistication are brought down to earth by Kantian aesthetics, Hegelian 'cunning,' and Marxist dialectic. The people are blessed with an alternative route to the critical superiority that had always linked concerned minds of all ages. Modern individuals are aesthetically "educated" to appreciate higher ideals and finer things. High culture teaches freedom within the law and an elegantly edited sense of moral responsibility to the world around them. Kant started the secular moral curriculum with a theory of aesthetics. Hegel and Marx continued the lesson in political history.

The Promethean progression of culture down from the castle to the keep does not square off with the Kant that Krieger describes to a less general readership in his major opus, *The German Idea of Freedom*. There are inconsistencies between Krieger's account of Kant in *Ideas and Events* and his account in *The German Idea of Freedom*. In *German Idea*, Kant is on the moral cusp between law and art. He embodies the classical liberal problem. Kant's philosophy lacks the "moral motor" of democratic debate.

How does history link Kant to Hegel to Marx? Krieger's answer is the rise of democracy. Krieger wrote:

> After the identifiable Kantian residues of natural law had dropped away their legacy of a universal truth binding upon men's behaviour remained built into their successors.

In *The German Idea of Freedom* Krieger portrays a Kant who "perpetuated the traditional German confusion about the relationship between morals and politics."[113] But to read Kant as drawing "a radical distinction between the world of the spirit and the world of the flesh … is only partially true," Krieger concludes.[114]

"The idea of freedom" became the *leitmotiv* of Kant's political philosophy. Through a unique rethinking of the concept freedom, Kant attempted to save the traditional core of the German intelligentsia from radical disillusionment.

> Kant still thought in terms of two realms, a realm of nature which was the sensible world and a realm of freedom which was the intelligible world.[115]

The intelligible world of freedom was the ideal half of a split world. Hegel and Marx took Kant's split world and showed how it was brought together in history. Hegel and Marx made the sensual side of the "intelligible world" intelligible to ordinary people. Their theory of political dialectic describes the active, historical force which brings together the real and the ideal in modern practice. Kant did not see this far. He never explained how the alleged two worlds of the real and the ideal can coexist.

Kant, Krieger says, pitted the realm of nature against the realm of freedom. Kant had not reconciled these two realms:

> The first of these realms [nature] was organized by the human understanding in accordance with principles of knowledge and

the second of these worlds [freedom] was defined by the human will in accordance with the principles of action.[116]

Hegel and Marx continued the discovery of man's sensual nature in *action*. The German idealists improved Kant's liberalism and gave it a radical thrust. The "composite movement" represented by Kant, Hegel, and Marx is a political movement carried forward by historical events. Theory has never been able to grasp this movement in its entirety until after it has happened. The world of freedom must always be adapted to the sensory world and the only valid test for the sensory world is political action.

Krieger's *German Idea* connects the great ideas of history with historical events much more candidly than his more popular articles and papers. In *German Idea* Kant's philosophy illustrates how subjectivity is always filtered through political history:

> The [French] Revolution insured that when Kant turned in the 90's to integrating freedom into the phenomenal world ... he assumed the primacy of nature in the social and political affairs of men and etherealized freedom to the point where it was compatible with this primacy.[117]

To protect freedom, law, art, and beauty from the violence of the French Revolution, Kant made freedom a pure concept. Events forced him to defend his ideals at a high level of philosophical abstraction where they could not be reached by the violence of his time. Freedom was "natural," so Kant secured it in the Romantic love of fine art and natural beauty. Art kept freedom alive at a time when citizens in the Western nation-states were not free. Aesthetic freedom was Kant's great achievement. It preserved the concept of freedom for later use by Hegel and Marx. Kant was able to pass the concept and experience of freedom on to a later generation in spite of the difficulties of his time.

Marx performed the same crucial function for us. Marx rescued freedom from the bourgeois economy. The "primacy of economics" in his system is not the accomplishment which makes him great. Marx showed us how to discuss freedom in concrete terms. Marx brought freedom down from the sublime and introduced it into daily life. Marx gave freedom a concrete meaning. After Marx, people had a way to discuss freedom in real terms. Marx gives the idea of freedom to Becker's Mr. Everyman. He gives people everywhere a way of describing freedom in sensual terms. Marx's rescue of freedom is a timeless contribution to the study of history.

Krieger's reading of Kant and Marx shines like a flaming sword. Patience with his Hegelian prose cannot fail to leave some favourable impressions. History "shows" great thinkers saving truth, freedom, and the moral life from destruction by historical events. History shows the heritage culture at work in modern scholarship. Seeing how 'immortals' like Kant and Marx protected the heritage should be a source of constant inspiration. Each generation must resolve to follow their example.

Krieger's explanation of Kant and Marx is a job description for the modern intellectual. He has described in theory and by example the general tasks facing concerned scholars in the late twentieth century. He and his colleagues are the guardians of a heritage. They must preserve the best in that which has been written and thought. They have superb role-models before them. Go thou and do likewise, Krieger implies. His impressive position does not forestall a modest objection. One may base the objection on several of the so-called "immortals." Kant, Augustine, Socrates, and Jesus Ben-Joshua come to mind. Krieger presents a satisfying account of the professional responsibilities of a concerned scholar, but I cannot help thinking that one traditional stone has been left unturned.

Krieger has deftly woven two different historical experiences into one critical text. History is synthetic when it comes to Marx's economic categories and Kant's theory of synthetic judgment. That is, history combines the partial insights of 'immortals' like Kant and Marx into a larger insight that is useful for later eras. By Krieger's own admission, the use of history for Kant and Marx is only half the story. The constructive yin of Hegel also requires the destructive yang of Robespierre and the industrial bourgeoisie. In their respective eras, Kant and Marx endured the destructive side of history. They were dissenters who saved great ideas from political destruction amid the violence and tumult of their times. Krieger is no dissenter, nor does he counsel dissent. Leonard Krieger is a joiner. He is a social convenor of the intellectual elites in post-war U.S.A.

Surely, the obvious questions here are not the research equivalent of rocket science. How do I know the nature of my own age? Is *my* era constructive or destructive? Is my life part of a synthesis or a deconstruction? How can I tell? How am I to live? How am I to act in my own time? Can I participate in the politics of my city, region, or nation-state with a sense of moral integrity? How can one, in Kant's words, live an *intelligible* life under circumstances where history is alternatively constructive and destructive and only the verdict of history long after the fact tells us which it was?

Logically, Leonard Krieger's idea of history is a Kantian antinomy. Emotionally, it is Wittgenstein's duck-rabbit. It passes the cunning tests required to do modern politics, but it fails the intelligibility test required by science and ethics. Krieger's explanation of Kant and Marx undermines religious belief and devalues ethical integrity. Hume's hard-working yeoman farmer will find no support for the common sense of daily life in Krieger's idea of history. Personal morality eludes Krieger and it will elude anyone who looks for wisdom in Krieger's history of ideas. In Krieger's reading, history treats human beings as a means to an end. History condones conformity and ulterior behaviour. The life wisdom consecrated in the world's great religious texts is incompatible with this philosophy. Faith and traditional realism find heartbreak here and the young person who teeters on the cusp of conscience will find no guidance.

Krieger's impressive reading of modern intellectual history is ambiguous. There are two ways to describe the ambiguity. One way is polemical and involves the reader in harsh controversies. One might call Krieger a hypocrite. He defends the highest ideals in theory, but in practice he admits to being a "trimmer." His philosophy of history involves the "mediation" of ideals to curry favour with the rich and powerful. His writing often adulterates the moral idealism he wants to defend. This was my original position on Krieger. I have modified it. Krieger is a classic duck-rabbit. He has been seduced by the last metaphysics in late modern life. Krieger's ambivalence is "grammatical." Leonard Krieger is not a hypocrite. He is a devout apostle of Hegelian "joy." Leonard Krieger still believes in "words which, in themselves, have a meaning."

Leonard Krieger believes heritage words like "beauty," "law," "democracy," and "freedom" have meaning in themselves. History realizes facets of their larger meaning and the progress of history brings us closer and closer to the ideal. Krieger's faith in language betrays his unimpeachable good intentions. Words like "beauty," "law," "democracy," and "freedom" are ambiguous in a culture where God, himself, has died. Krieger is a philosophical realist (he believes in objective ideals outside empirical experience), who eats his daily bread with Hume's disastrous fork. Behind the dark tapestries of his Hegelian prose, Dr. Leonard Krieger is Mr. Everyman. He shares with Carl Becker's ordinary citizen the inadvertent lies and unwonted gridlocks of modern life. He is a noble character, but his language betrays his ideals.

Krieger's reading of Kant and Marx bears out Hempel's point in his article on the covering law and it illustrates the source of Sartre's and Wittgenstein's existential pain. Krieger's reading of Kant and Marx is internally coherent for Kant *or* Marx considered individually, but *not for both* considered together. Combined together in one unified perspective, Krieger's reading of Kant and Marx cancels itself out. The internal short-circuit of the combined reading is not a logical quibble without effects on ordinary life. Krieger's idea of history has robbed these men of their moral conviction. In Krieger's reading, Kant and Marx are unconscious playthings of world politics. They float on a consensus which uses them for its purposes without regard for the purposes Kant and Marx set themselves. History has a use for Kant and Marx. Their use for history is secondary. Leonard Krieger's discussion of Kant and Marx neutralizes the concrete moral concerns of the two greatest secular philosophers in modern history.

Krieger takes the most intellectual of all moral realists, Immanuel Kant, reads him as if he were a lake poet, and then notes that his activism is based on an "ethereal" concept of freedom. Krieger takes Karl Marx, the most visceral activist in modern intellectual history, reads him as if he were a moral realist, and apologizes for the weakness of his "philosophical categories." Krieger's interpretations make legitimate use of the available facts and each argument is plausible. The difficulty Krieger's interpretation presents does not concern the facts or the plausibility of each interpretation taken singly. The difficulty with Krieger's interpretation is the cumulative effect of both readings taken together. The difficulty is Krieger's perspective when viewed as a systematic argument. The combined effect of Krieger's interpretation of Kant and Marx is demoralizing. The combined effect of the two explanations leaches moral conviction from intellectual history like the chemical erosion of a fertile soil flowing inexorably down to a dead sea. Krieger's treatment of Kant and Marx lacks internal coherence at the general level usually associated with a discipline or a field. In Krieger's discussion, Kant and Marx are contradictory positions competing for control of his field. A dissonance in the modern interpretation of Western intellectual history is reflected in Krieger's cosmopolitan point of view. Krieger's point of view reflects his politics. His interpretations reflect the radical politicization of Western society over the last two hundred years. Leonard Krieger does not seem to want to distinguish, in his writing, between politics and ethics. The composite crisis of interpretation Krieger displays is a more serious problem than Kant and Marx, themselves. I suggest Krieger's composite crisis is emblematic. It represents a typical difficulty in modern intellectual history. The inability or unwillingness of modern scholarship to discuss ethics as a whole is a significant limitation in modern Western scholarship. It represents a far greater dilemma in modern history than the scholarly debate over particular meanings deriving from Kant, Marx and, indeed, any number of intellectual giants from the past.

Krieger's contradictory position falls somewhere between two ideal limits set out in previous portions of this monograph. His assessment may be considered a confirmation of Hegel's dialectic in action. History has re-evaluated the older idealisms and found them wanting in some important ways. The perceived dissonance between Kant's aesthetic idealism and Marxist materialism define two thetical extremes. Their synthesis is a work in progress and Krieger has done us the scholarly service of identifying the process. The counterthesis is less lovely. The schism in Krieger's treatment of the giants may illustrate the side of the Hempel debate most historians did not want to discuss. Contradiction may be the "covering law" in modern historiography and democratic politics. A radical critique of modern intellectual history could regard Krieger's work as a brilliant synthesis perfectly designed to fulfill the most nefarious purposes of the age. Krieger has put the finishing touches on a Romantic masterpiece. Krieger's static treatment of Kant and Marx empowers politics, market economics, and managed consensus at the fundamental level of modern history of ideas. Krieger's position enables cynical conflict by paralyzing the power of ideas. Krieger's position is a psychological attack on the moral confidence of academics, churchmen, and other civic leaders. His radical position is the core, creative synthesis of political and economic forces which have been brewing in the West since the Enlightenment. Intellectual gridlock secures the marketplace from humanitarian intervention and saves politics from the scourge of social conscience.

Krieger's description of Kant and Marx was the kind of argument Kant called an antinomy. Hempel said it lacked a "covering law." The softer picture of the same difficulty is Wittgenstein's "duck-rabbit." Krieger's intellectual history reflected the politics of the post-war world. Duck-rabbits abounded in politics after World War II. Overall, their moral effect was not positive. Krieger-like figures educated the post-war generation. As a pedagogical practice, he and his colleagues taught the baby-boomers to think and to write about the world as if it were a moral impossibility. Modern post-secondary education in the United States was an incomprehensible lesson in the ways of paradox. The generations who were taught to see history like Krieger had not been tempered by depression and war. They were economically privileged and ethically challenged. The language arts they studied attenuated the principles needed to criticize post-war American politics and the global economy. The avowed preference for moral ambiguity and political discretion in American culture was the "deep play" of a society in chronic distress. I believe the practical effects of a "duck-rabbit" education can be seen in American society since World War II. Over the last sixty years most American civic and political leaders have been unable to discuss with plausibility the importance of ethical theory, moral practice, and simple social justice in the daily life of Becker's Mr. Everyman.

The linguistic turn was occasioned by 'critical' texts like Krieger's. The principle source for the turn is Kant. Kant argued cogently that phenomena do not have to be 'true' to be 'real.' Phenomena are 'real' as long as they make sense within their own frame of reference. Phenomena are 'real' inside the system of knowledge to which they belong. One may reject science and religion, but one may not reject the categorical structure of unified reason they employ, each within its own domain. Leonard Krieger used politics to mix the two domains. He imported faith from religion and facts from history. He trusted politics to combine them. Krieger's discrete political appeal to parallel worlds does not conform to the logical structure of either religious faith or applied science. It violates the moral freedom required by faith and it undermines the logical system required by science. The least abrasive way to describe Krieger's political faith is a metaphor from Wittgenstein. The modern world is a moral duck-rabbit, and it can drive its more sensitive members to moments of near suicidal despair.

CHAPTER FIVE
# *POSTMODERNISM*

> *There is no sharp dividing line between an 'empirical language' and a 'theoretical language.' We are theorizing all the time, even when we make the most trivial singular statement.*[1]
>
> — KARL POPPER

**WHEN HISTORY TURNED MALEVOLENT** during the first half of the twentieth century, it was, for many skeptical scions of Europe's historical Enlightenment, the second death of God. Socialism and the market were equally compromised after World War II. Their most-touted virtues were seen to be equally tainted. While a disillusioned laity lived political lives of stoic discretion, some concerned scholars on both sides of the Cold War divide turned back to the theoretical roots of their secular faith. There, at the end of Europe's historical Enlightenment, they rediscovered the great skeptical debates over reason and faith; history and human nature; knowledge, science, and truth. They discovered that many of the classical dilemmas over authority, freedom, and democracy were still active in the modern world. They discovered that critical theory and "the" historical method had not saved them from the traditional questions of good and evil. In comparison with the vast majority of scholars who had preceded them they discovered a disturbing fact about themselves. The late modern world had damaged their conscience. It had given them a polite, politically correct excuse to avoid the traditional questions of faith and knowledge, ethics, truth, and a coherent life.

The world wars occasioned a level of moral outrage which most skeptics found difficult to express. They could not access their discomfiture in the terms of traditional piety because they were skeptics in the tradition of Kant and Marx. To voice their concern, they invented a number of much-misunderstood neologisms. The most famous neologism of the post-war skeptics was "Postmodernism."[2] Jean-François Lyotard took the word from architecture and applied it to other social constructions like art, literature, and language. He contended most modern systems of knowledge were like most modern buildings. They were hard to inhabit, difficult to enjoy, and often dangerous to use.

Some of the most radical neo-Kantians were also the most voluble in expressing their disillusionment. They blamed the modern era and claimed it had eliminated moral responsibility from its vocabulary. It had made the traditional challenges of human spiritual development difficult even to represent in plausible terms. The totalizing presence of the West in the world had made simple decency almost unpresentable in the language of daily life. Their ultra-radicalism led them to: "Wage war on totality and be witnesses to the unpresentable." For them:

> The postmodern would be that which in the modern puts forward the *unpresentable in presentation itself*; that which denies itself the solace of good forms, the consensus of a taste which would make it possible to share collectively the nostalgia for the unattainable.[3]

From their perspective, the modern era was a "metanarrative" which had thwarted the last, best hopes of all humankind. They blamed the West for the plights of the world's peoples and the violence of the world wars. The way the modern West saw, pointed to, and talked about the world had failed. To do better would require a new theory of ethics and a new language of responsibility, care, and concern.

## MARTIN HEIDEGGER (1889–1976)

"Martin Heidegger's thought ... embodies the powerful disillusionment of the German tradition at the death of God and its pessimism about the Western project of humanism and modernization," David Luft explains.[4] David Krell believes "the death of God was that one experience on the basis of which *Being and Time* (1927) was thought."[5] Modern intellectual history led Heidegger into nihilism, Nazism, and existential nothingness. The words of Nietzsche's Madman fell on Martin Heidegger like a dead dove crashing down on a stone-age Pentecost.

Heidegger said he wanted a "historicity" in which "Conscience summons Self from its lostness in the 'they.'"[6] Heidegger had been shocked at the callousness of Europe during and after World War I. The "cunning of reason" did not have a conscience. The way the call of conscience "gets interpreted is for the most part *inauthentically* oriented and does not reach the essence," he lamented.[7] Modern war was the secular Golgotha of a tortured world spirit. "Being there" during the wars taught Heidegger a new philosophy. After World War I he saw the Western world trapped in time, caught philosophically between authentic and inauthentic concepts of history.[8]

Heidegger wrote his student, Karl Löwith, in 1920 that "The old one" [Husserl] regarded him as "still really a theologian."[9] Jeffrey Barash records this small reminiscence Heidegger wrote at the age of 65:

> The secret juncture in which the church festivals, the devotional days, and the course of the seasons fused together; the joining of morning, afternoon, and evening hours of each day, so that one peal of the bell went continually through young hearts, dreams, prayers, and games – this is indeed what, with one of the most magical, blessed, and lasting secrets, was sheltered in the belltower; it was offered, ever transformed and unrepeatable, until the last peal into the mountain of Being.[10]

John Caputo explains Heidegger's dismay at what he calls our "throwness" into the "everyday world." Moderns live a life in which "the silent peal of Being remains unheard, in oblivion."[11] The existential peal of traditional ecclesiastical piety rings through Heidegger's life from childhood down to the last *Der Spiegel* interview.

The debate Heidegger continued in the twentieth century is, as Anthony Carty casually observes "in fact reconstructing a place for quite traditional metaphysics." Otto Pöggeler concurs. Turning away from the Catholic Church did not close down Heidegger's loyalty to "the life experience of Christian faith." Heidegger wanted to rescue a religious hermeneutic for secular philosophy of history. His *habilitation* address *The Concept of Time in the Historical Sciences* used Dilthey's theory of historical "understanding" to posit the practical possibility of an historical ethic that retains a moral conscience. Heidegger based his argument on the fundamental, structural difference between natural and historical "science" that

Dilthey had defended in his work. In Heidegger's interpretation, neither "science" offered a moral imperative to the modern soul, but the difference between them did. An "ontological difference" in the foundations of modern life was the cornerstone of a new historical approach to modern secular ethics. His masterpiece, *Being and Time* (1927), resulted directly from his theory of the fundamental historical difference between two equally "objective" perceptions modern life.[12] Modern life, for Heidegger, is a continuous experience of essential and inescapable difference at the deepest and most fundamental levels of experience.

Martin Heidegger was a shy, devoutly Catholic boy who, in addition to these qualities, also lacked interpersonal skills. He launched his career just after World War I at a time when academic positions were hard to find in Germany. The competitive environment into which he was thrust was foreign to his sensitive nature. His chronic poor heath was exacerbated by political and economic stresses as well as by a devastating erosion of personal faith. Heidegger was trained, initially, in a philosophical curriculum, which had been trimmed to suit the Biedermeier culture of the nineteenth-century German middle class. The bookish boy who loved poetry was educated in an aesthetic doctrine of personal edification. The doctrine suited Heidegger, but it did not suit the changing times into which he felt he had been thrown.

In 1909, after completing high school, Heidegger became a Jesuit novice, but was discharged within a month for reasons of health. He then entered Freiburg University where he studied theology. The deterioration of his health was connected to his personal crisis of faith. The combination of these two factors led Heidegger in 1911 to leave the seminary and break off his training for the priesthood. He took up studies in philosophy, mathematics, and natural sciences. At that time he discovered Edmund Husserl's *Logical Investigations*. In 1913 he completed a doctorate in philosophy with a dissertation on Husserl under the direction of the neo-Kantian philosopher Heinrich Rickert.

The outbreak of the First World War in 1914 interrupted briefly Heidegger's academic career. He was enlisted in the army, but after two months released because of poor health. Hoping to take over the chair of Catholic philosophy at Freiburg, Heidegger began work on his habilitation thesis on *Duns Scotus's Doctrine of Categories and Meaning*, the second qualifying dissertation that would win him a licence to teach at the university. The dissertation was completed in 1915 and in the same year

Heidegger became a Privatdozent or unsalaried lecturer. He taught mostly courses in Aristotelian and scholastic philosophy. He regarded himself as defending a Catholic world-view. His success as a lecturer masked his loss of personal faith. Like Kant and Husserl, he felt compelled to provide an alternative foundation for the system of belief in which he had been raised. In 1916 Edmund Husserl joined the Freiburg faculty and Heidegger was able to make his acquaintance first as a mentor and then as a friend. In 1919, he announced his break with the "system of Catholicism" (January 9, 1919) and was appointed Husserl's assistant (January 21, 1919).

Heidegger was deeply influenced by the same reading of Kant that had prompted Husserl's phenomenological investigations. Although critical in some respects of Husserl's neo-Kantian turn towards transcendental subjectivity, Heidegger accepted the dominant Marburg interpretation of Kant's aesthetics that set the tone for Kant studies down to the present time. The triumph of the "inner" Kant of aesthetic sensibility over the critical Kant whom Hume had "awakened" influenced Heidegger's thought. Language was an aesthetic dimension for Heidegger. Through language, fundamental categories of human experience were revealed. The search for a transcendental language of authentic experience dominated Heidegger's thought for the rest of his life. Heidegger, in spite of what he knew, said, and objected to in theory was always fascinated by the traditional idea of Kantian aesthetic intuition. The traditional, aesthetic Kant of Biedermeier sensitivity, betrayed Heidegger and he became, for a time, the enemy he opposed. His life and work are instructive for this fact alone.

In 1923 Heidegger moved to Marburg University, the inner sanctum of traditional Kant studies, where with the help of Paul Natorp he obtained a position of associate professor. At Marburg, between 1923 and 1928 he enjoyed his best years as a lecturer. It was there he met Hannah Arendt and had an affair with her. His vigour during these years did not affect his work. Arendt remained his friend and defender for life. Many other students testified to the originality of his insight and the intensity of his work. Hans-Georg Gadamer studied with Heidegger and never hid his admiration for Heidegger's "well integrated spiritual energy.... Who among those who then followed him," Gadamer wrote:

> ... can forget the breathtaking swirl of questions that he developed in the introductory hours of the semester ... and then,

in the final hours of the semester, to roll up deep-dark clouds of sentences from which the lightning flashed to leave us half stunned?[13]

Heidegger extended the scope of his lectures and taught courses on history of philosophy, time, logic, phenomenology, Plato, Aristotle, Aquinas, Kant, and Leibniz. But since 1916 he had published nothing and the lack of publications stood in the way of his advancement. Finally, in February 1927, partly because of administrative pressure, his fundamental, but also unfinished treatise, *Being and Time*, appeared. Heidegger used the unpolished manuscript to jump the queue in line to replace Husserl who had retired. Early publication of the profound, but poorly edited work was not an unqualified success. Thomas Sheehan, one of Heidegger's most balanced commentators, believes *Being and Time*, while groundbreaking, was poorly thought out. "Heidegger published *and* perished," he quips.[14]

The problem, which defeats *Being and Time*, is the Marburg reading of Kant. Heidegger said as much on a number of occasions. One of the big debates in late century Heidegger studies was the so-called "turn" in Heidegger's thought after *Being and Time*. The "turn" was portrayed as a "turn" against Kant. The debate over Heidegger's "turn" has died down, because it was not accurate. Heidegger stayed with the aesthetic Kant of Dilthey and Hegel. He never reformulated Kant's core critique of moral judgment in light of Bismarck, modern Germany, modern culture, and the world wars.

Conceptually, Heidegger's ethics are tenable. Heidegger knew Hegel's political head and Kant's moral heart were at war in the German psyche. Husserl's failure to achieve a middle way between the two giants convinced Heidegger the Kant/Hegel debate was coterminous with the history of Western thought. Kant and Hegel were Heidegger's philosophical duck-rabbit. They were the two irreconcilable perspectives at war in his head and his heart. His respect for Husserl was one of the guiding forces leading him toward a phenomenological synthesis of Hegel's history and Kant's ethics. Heidegger was the first major philosopher to realize the Kant/Hegel problem was a stalemate. He saw Kant and Hegel did not represent the progress of an idea. They represented a contradiction. The difference between them was a roadblock in Western culture. His study of Hegel and Kant convinced him modern intellectual history had stalled. Heidegger was determined to kick start it.

Heidegger decided the split life of modern thought extended into the language we speak. It had a behavioural dimension that influenced the most basic facets of the modern experience. Healing a badly fractured life world required a new way of discussing the problem. Before the problem could be discussed in a new way, a critical "destruction" (*Abbau*) of the old language had to be undertaken. Heidegger was nothing if not thorough. The language problem in Western thought gave Heidegger's general disillusionment a specific research focus. Heidegger's claim that modern language "conceals" modern history gives him first rank philosophical status along with Kant, Hegel, Nietzsche, and Marx. His work is controversial, but his contribution to the modern intellectual debate is undeniable.

Kant erred, Heidegger believed when he failed to distinguish between a "phenomenon" and an "appearance." What Kant called phenomenal is only the physical relationship between phenomena. A *phenomenon* "shows itself, in-itself," Heidegger writes. It "signifies a distinctive way in which something can be encountered. *Appearance*, on the other hand, means a reference-relationship." Kant misunderstood the phenomenology of "appearances" and Heidegger was going to set him straight.[15] Heidegger bases his separation of phenomenon and appearance on language. Language is an appearance. It is a living phenomenon and it plays a role in the world. Language is a secular epiphany. The word bubbles up from phenomena and defines our relationships to it. Kant's phenomenology is shallow because, he excludes language. Language acts in a way Kant did not understand. Words are the true "in-itself," the transcendental noumenal glimpse of absolute value, which Kant denied we could ever know. In a skeptical, science-based society where God himself has died, words have noumenal force. The word is a thing in itself. It is the one thing, which can be known as it really is. Words are the last remaining mirror of the mind of God. A phenomenology of modern language was required to complete the Kantian moral project.

According to Heidegger, the Greek word for word, "logos" derives from the Greek, *legein* meaning "to gather." The etymology of the word explains the importance of language in history. When we see how language "gathers" history, we will penetrate the veil of appearances and understand what modern history means.[16] The first sentence of Aristotle's first treatise on ontology is: "*Pantes anthropoi tou eidenai oregontai physei.*" It is usually translated, "All men by nature desire to know." A more literal translation would be, "All men seek knowledge naturally" (or, "by natural means").

Whether *physei* means "natural" or "natural means," the passage, in the context of Aristotle's opus, leaves little doubt he believed human beings were part of nature and could only know those things that were available there. Heidegger assumes that all men seek knowledge by the most natural means available to them. A phenomenal translation of the passage has to do justice to the means mankind uses in his search for knowledge. A set of relationships is implied by the passage. Elucidating the historic depths of human relationships is the search for Being. A translation from pre-classical to late modern time must invoke the concrete experience of the search for authentic Being. The search for Being has been lost in the modern world, because the modern world does not understand what language is.

Heidegger did not translate the famous passage in the normal way. Heidegger translates "All men seek knowledge naturally" as "The care for seeing is essential to man's Being."[17] He traces the root of *eidenai* to the word for "to see," not the word for "idea." Heidegger's translation implies seeing is a form of knowing. He wants to "see" history with a moral knowledge of what history "should" be. Seeing history means seeing that which is most essential. Seeing puts a "lumen naturale" on the facts of history. "Seeing" in this sense, creates the "clearings" for moral ideas and authenticity in everyday being-there [*Dasein*]. Heidegger says his "conception of 'sight' has been gained by looking at the basic kind of disclosure which is characteristic of being-there." Modern language prevents us from "seeing" history. Destructing the false history gathered in the language is basic to the moral project of historical disclosure. The history gathered in words discloses the nature of history. Seeing the meaning "hidden" in the history of words tells us what is most important in history and warns us how easily we can be deceived. History can be "seen" in the evolution of words and their meaning. Lavish etymological liberties are the direction of Heidegger's philosophy for the rest of his life. As scholarship they fail, as a genre of moral poetry unique to Heidegger and his time, they succeed admirably. Heidegger's etymologies are a case study in the Nietzschean pain which drove the late modern linguistic turn.

The meaning of "Words in themselves" was not a joy for Heidegger. Heidegger believed the modern moral life was betrayed by modern language. His moral criticism of modern language makes him the father of postmodernism and the language criticism associated with it. The history "gathered" in and projected by the language of late modern public life was hateful to Heidegger. He thought modern history had destroyed modern ethics and all sense of human community. To defend his radical critique of modern history, Heidegger set out on a life-long search for an authentic language. His search was compromised by a combination of factors. Under the circumstances, some allowances should be made for Heidegger's susceptibility to them.

Heidegger takes the position the modern world has forgotten what the great keywords like "state," "community," "the people," "care," "concern," "duty," and "love" mean. Through a phenomenal study of language, the authentic meaning of key words can be recovered. The way he puts it, history has to be "unforgotten" through uncovering the *original* language of civil law and political philosophy. "The Greek words for 'truth,'" he writes, *he aletheia, to alethes* are compounded of the privative prefix *a-* (not) and the verbal stem *-lath* (to escape notice). The truth may be thus looked upon as that which is unconcealed, that which gets discovered or uncovered (*'entdect'*).[18] "Seeing" history uncovers our being as it really was and ought to be.

Robert Bernasconi explains, "What *gathering* means in Heidegger is reflected in his dictum that Parmenides cannot be interpreted in terms of Kant, whereas the reverse is both possible and necessary."[19] Kant's philosophy has "gathered" the history of modern thought since Parmenides. History conglomerates around us, in us, and through us, without our wishing or willing the process. Kant, for instance, cannot be understood without an understanding of the history that is collected in the structure, organization, and focus of his prose. Parmenides, on the other hand, is free from the corruptions of Western history. His writing has a purity and original focus that later work cannot have.

Heidegger's historical poetics are premised on a negation. He reads Hegel backwards using the "cunning of reason" as an enemy not an ally. Adorno's "negative dialectic" was taken from Heidegger's historical perspective in *Being and Time*. Heidegger accepts Hegel's transcending historical "cunning," but Heidegger argues the "cunning of reason" plays us false. Historical dialectic exists, but it flows backwards and the progress of right reason through conflict and synthesis is moral delusion. By this line of argument, Heidegger concludes the modern historical project is morally flawed. He sees Western civilization being expelled from the political garden of a classical Greek Eden when Pericles and the Socratic idealists turned the language of community into demagoguery. Heidegger wants to use the allegedly "pure" language of pre-imperial classical politics as the model for a new, resolute, and community-minded contemporary *polis*.

The world wars would not permit Heidegger to share Hegel's historical optimism, so he took Hegel's dialectic and logic and he read them in reverse. He read the shifting meaning of words like "physics," "nature," "language," "spirit," and "truth" as a negative dialectic of the human spirit. The ur-myth of a code of original meanings wrought in words by the first Greek *polis* was Heidegger's Garden of Eden. He sought the original language of pre-modern Greek politics. There, he believed, was the lost purity of a spirit, which had once stood naked before God. Modern history had cloaked civic virtue in an exoskeleton as hard as ice and as hideous as a spider. Heidegger set out on a phantasmagorical mission to save the lost language of original community from the babble of modern history.

The pre-modern nature of being together in the world can be seen in the language of pre-Socratic philosophy. The authentic nature of Being (capital $B$) is revealed in the structure of the original political argument and the examples that carried the argument forward. Heidegger notes how Pre-Socratic philosophy is rigorously empirical. It avoids historical references and does not employ political symbols for rhetorical effect. Its examples are taken from everyday life in the great Greek out-of-doors. Earth, air, fire, and water are the foundations for exposition and reference. The logic of early Greek science and early Greek humanism *is the same*. As science departs from common sense and ordinary experience so does the language of public reference depart from its fundamental emotional grounding in the daily experiences of ordinary life. This negative fact, for Heidegger, makes language the most fundamental event in history. The study of language as a meta-historical mirror of moral decay lets Heidegger have a quasi-religious metaphysic without having to seek sanction and solace for his faith outside the secular world of historical events. Heidegger clings to language, the last tenet of his lost childhood faith, as a drowning man clutching a spar. The last metaphysical truth left in human history lies hidden in modern language. Heidegger, in his opinion, has discovered it.

Modern theories of interpretation assumed language consisted of a one-to-one correspondence between words and things. Heidegger finds this oversimplification in Dilthey and Count Yorck, but he does not investigate the history of modern hermeneutics in any systematic way. His interest is the structure of language and the way it works on the mood, behaviour, and concerns of those thrown together in time. "Structure" for Heidegger is a Kantian schema. Words directly point to objects, but they also organize objects in hierarchies of value. Hierarchies of value are embedded in the structures of discourse (logos) for Heidegger. Human beings have the ability to understand the value orientation connoted by discursive systems as a whole. Heidegger condemns the limitations of modern discourse. He sees language use in scholarship, philosophy, politics, and business as a schema organized around the denial of ethics, care, compassion, and concern. Modern discourse tacitly points away from the most important things in everyday life.[20]

The true history of Being is found in the most fundamental phenomenon of human life. Language lets the truth about Being "shine through" it. Language is a window on the nature of the human world. Language is the area where the Kantian aesthetic still works as Heidegger learned it should work while a student at Freiburg. Remember, he accepts an arguably flawed reading of Kant. *Noesis* [knowing] contains an aesthetic truth greater than the logic of scientific rationalism. When aesthetic knowing turns to the study of language, it let us know intuitively about higher things. The transcendental level of knowledge aesthetics provides shows us "*logos* as *dianoiein*" [word as power]. Word power is world power. The aesthetics of word power fracture Heidegger's methodology and corrupt his moral voice. Heidegger contemplates the history of language like a little bird fascinated by the penetrating stare of a snake.

"Aristotle," Heidegger writes, "has explicated this function more precisely as *apophainesthai*, literally the apex of shining though."[21] Nineteen years after *Being and Time*, in his "Letter on Humanism" (1946), Heidegger dubs this fundamental object, immortally: *logos*, "discourse" – for Heidegger, "the house of being."[22] The ultimate reasons for Being in the world shine through the original language or "discourse" of civic virtue practised by the pre-Socratic Greeks. Western history since Plato and Paul has hidden the truth about language and the real function of the spirit from philosophical investigation. Since the modern "house of being" is corrupt, it must be "destructed." Heidegger calls the historical razing of modern philosophical discourse "the destruction of the history of ontology."[23] When the modern is destroyed, the original, historical essence of being will shine through. History and the moral imperative will once again be as one.

"Logos has the structural form of a *synthesis* ... because the function of the *logos* as *apophainosis* lies in letting something be seen by pointing it out," Heidegger explains.[24] A pure language, which had not accumulated so much modern history, would theoretically, perform the same perfectly transparent function for the ordering of society which mathematics provides for the ordering of nature. "*Logos*," he writes, "acquires the signification of *relation* and *relationship*." Language "gathers" the truth. "*Logos* can signify reason," because of the history it gathers. The language of history is the poetry of the modern soul. The history modern language has "gathered" has made the soul sick. He continues:

> *Logos* is used not only with the signification of *legein* but also with that of *legomenon* (that which is exhibited, as such), and ... which, as present-at-hand, already lies at the bottom of any procedure ... *logos qua legomenon* means the ground, the *ratio*.[25]

Language shows the ground of being. Language shows the ground and one's emotional reaction to the ground of being provides the basis for resistance or consent.

Logically, in the spirit world of an Hegelian protestant like Heidegger, the nearer one gets to the origin of language, the purer one's reaction to history will be.

> Thus "phenomenology" means *apophainesthai ta phainomena* – to let that which shows itself be seen.... This is the formal meaning of [Husserl's] "phenomenology." We are expressing nothing else than the maxim: "To the things themselves."[26]

Language is an object with a transcendental function. All other objects are mute tools lying at hand. Language is the tool which uses us. Language is a spiritual sponge. The history it soaks up lies hidden inside it waiting to be released by the pressures of daily life. "We encounter the 'thing' phenomenally" in the everyday world.[27] A dangerous methodological anomaly lurks in Heidegger's phenomenal encounter with language. Heidegger trusts the same history, which corrupted language to be pure at its source. History, which has betrayed him, will in the end reveal to him a pure language that is uncorrupted.

Jane Rubin and Hubert Dreyfus call *Being and Time* "Heidegger's secularization of Kierkegaard." Heidegger uses Hegel's method but he is inspired by the same "sickness unto death" that impelled Kierkegaard.

Heidegger accepts Kierkegaard's account of the present age as an anxiety-motivated cover-up, they explain. Kierkegaard's speculations indicate, "If a human being chooses to face up to her anxiety rather than to cover it up, her first leap will be the leap into the aesthetic sphere of existence."[28] Heidegger's use of the aesthetic sphere is a frightfully two-edged sword. One edge cuts through the idealistic pathos of absolute knowledge, which underwrites the chauvinisms of states and class culture. The other edge cuts open the psychological nether-worlds of misanthropy, fascism, and primitive fear. A "sense" for the phenomenology of language is the old Romantic *Bildung* in late modern linguistic form. Heidegger has not left the classical culture of Plato's cave behind. He has in one dangerous sense merely reinvested the old Hegel in a classical search for a pure time before history was dialectic.

Heidegger has to ground the possibility of a pure time on a theory of pure discourse. Heidegger has felt Hegel's infinite grief. He cannot ground his search for a pure time on the existence of God. The surreptitious hold of Romantic absolutes on Heidegger opens a dangerous ambiguity. Kierkegaard's defence of the absurd, his call to be educated by dread, and his praise of despair disappear in Heidegger. Heidegger wanted Romantic confidence without the moral compromises their confidence required. In rejecting fear and dread, he left himself vulnerable to a different form of the same Romantic double standard. He trusts noble feelings to build a new politics, culture, and economy. His faith in language is Romantic, and is open to the same moral compromises as the era in which it was conceived. Heidegger has not rescued moral theory from Dilthey and Hegel. He has taken their theory of language and carried it back to classical times. Karen de Boer doubts Heidegger has invented a new philosophy. Heidegger's logic is Hegelian and the spirit he is trying to rescue is the Hegelian "world spirit" in history. Heidegger puts the "world spirit" in the distant past rather than the dramatic present. De Boer believes Heidegger's language philosophy attempts "to overcome Hegel from within.... Heidegger's thought is infinitely problematized by this decision," she concludes.[29]

Heidegger binds himself, inadvertently, to the happy spirit of the Hegelian state which defeated the Persians in the fifth century B.C.E. He turns Hegelian dialectic backwards, but he retains the keystone of the Hegelian logic. Heidegger and Hegel are morally bound to the iron law of modern language. History has given us words, which have a meaning in themselves. History has keywords and key concepts that are hallowed by time and sanctified in the lives of ordinary citizens. Great historical events live in emotional memory through the language of public life. There is no higher logic, no greater political cunning, and no deeper philosophical position than to understand and use the great God-given language of events. Language plays the same role for Hegel and Heidegger. Public language is the pre-formed fulcrum between head and heart, body and mind, spirit and the flesh. The bifocal treatment of language as both historical and spiritual involves Heidegger in the same historicist fallacy as Hegel. In his attempt to rescue history, Heidegger "deconstructs the projective preconception of history on which the Hegelian phenomenology is based," de Boer explains.[30] He does not, however, deconstruct the Hegelian dialectic on which Hegel's "happy consciousness" is based. He destroys projective history without revisiting Hegel's conformist theory of joining history and fitting in with the spirit of the age. Conformity pumps Hegel's system. It fills the word with the world spirit of progress. Conformity is the engine of historical cunning by which the world spirit becomes word and the world and I are at-oned. Mindless conformity at any time, to any time is still the same invitation to ethical indifference and moral moronism.

Hegel had rejected morality "of the ethical reflective kind." In his *Philosophy of History* he had argued duty to the state transcended mere morality. Heidegger does not appear to see any trap here. He follows Hegel's hopes backwards instead of forwards. Heidegger uses classical language skills to carry Hegelian philosophy back into classical studies, and there conduct the search for the perfect political language. The classical ur-text of civic virtue spoken in the *polis* before Plato can still redeem the modern age. Heidegger hopes philosophy of language can bring ethical reflection back into what Hegel called "the antique morality based on the principle of abiding by one's duty to the state."[31]

Heidegger apparently did not realize he had saved Hegel's lack of ethics along with Hegel's theory of reason. The moral outcome to be expected is the same whether history ends in the distant past or the distant future. A world, which learns ethics from history, will be a world where the state makes the moral law. With an obtuseness that would be unbelievable were it not a common practice, Heidegger leaves the moral dimension of ordinary being open to re-definition by the state. After rejecting Hegel's idea of progress, Heidegger tries to save Hegel's idealization of history. History can still provide a skeptical people with a language of moral reason and social progress. Modern history has failed, but the modern philosophy of history has not. History still holds the answer to moral politics and a positive cunning of reason. The past has a model upon which a new community can be founded. The people who can re-establish the original political state in which the modern ideal of politics is rooted will be the state that can resolutely face its own destiny and revitalize the whole history of the West.

Heidegger's reactionary defence of history has saved Hegel at grave risk to every landmark in Western civilization since Plato. Christianity, Renaissance humanism, the common law, the classical Fine Arts, and common sense are all rejected. Heidegger's "Greek way of seeing" language overthrows the accumulated processes of forbearance, tolerance, mutuality, and due process that a muddled history had, by the sheer force of blunt trauma, crammed down the gullet of a reluctant but sometime sobered historical reason, during wars of superstitious violence over the course of two and one-half thousand years.

Heidegger's philosophy of history is two-sided. One side is potentially positive, but the other is atavistically negative. The negative side is aesthetic politics. A putatively authentic language is not a language disencumbered of historical experience, modern jurisprudence, and the rise of democracy. Heidegger looks for authenticity in the primary, not the proximal. He sees what is nearest as corrupt and then leaps, in faith, to the conclusion that history once was uncorrupted. "Seeing" in this reactionary sense holds the object lessons of modern history in abeyance. It holds history and one's fellow human beings at arms' length. It precludes the most important reality check available to any knowledge system. Kant called it the "kingdom of ends." This simple measure is how knowledge functions in the lives of others – 'real' others, other human beings just like ourselves. Under the auspices of any given system, do we treat others as an end in themselves? Do we show respect for other people's individuality and overall well-being? Both Heidegger and Hegel fail this elementary moral test.

History is the last god for Hegel and Heidegger. Heidegger believes history offers an answer to the moral problems of the modern world:

> Above all, the Greek conception of truth has been misunderstood. *Aisthesis*, the sheer sensory perception of something, is "true" in the Greek sense, and indeed more primordially than the *logos*,

which we have been discussing. Just as seeing aims at colours, any *aisthesis* aims at its *idia*.... Both realism and idealism have – with equal thoroughness – missed the meaning of the Greek conception of truth.[32]

Those who "see" the truths "gathered" in the classical Greek language are permitted to attach themselves to popular opinion and the "ordinary way of taking things." The "Greek way of seeing" protects the seer from moral responsibility for phenomena ordinary people might call evil. Those who understand the direction of the spirit have the obligation and the right to pull the world by its ear. Those who "see" have the power and the right to coerce the actions of others.

Heidegger explains the ethic of "*noein* – 'beholding' in the widest sense" quite openly as if it were of little consequence:

In controversy over principles, one must not only attach oneself to theses which can be grasped doxographically [i.e., 'graphed' or 'illustrated' by opinion]; one must also derive one's orientation from the objective tendency of the problematic, even if it does not go beyond a rather ordinary way of taking things.[33]

"Greek seeing" lets Heidegger participate in Nazi politics from a position of higher knowledge. He is renewing the language of civic virtue, which the West has lost. He considers himself one of the privileged few, who understand the aesthetics of historical memory. He can "see" how the Nazis are restoring the memory of values, which have been forgotten. Victor Farias is the most strident critic of Heidegger's complicity with the Nazis. "Heidegger is not able to see or sort out the greatness or misery of actual particular historical occurrences," he observes.[34] Heidegger has no moral position outside the language of his profession, his life-work, and his interactions with colleagues. In spite of his noble intentions and high ideals, he remains a confirmed trimmer. He is dependent on an already formed language and he will trim his politics to suit the things his ideal language lets him say.

Heidegger believed when one "sees" history rightly one can suspend ordinary moral judgment and participate in the great historical project of re-inventing the *polis*. Rhetoric, which rekindles the lost language of civic virtue, will bring about a new political community. In substance,

Heidegger still believed Hegel's ethics after he turned Hegel's "cunning of reason" inside out. The conceptual ingenuity he brought to his task is impressive, but the use to which he put his critical insights never broke away from the elite self-satisfactions of the nineteenth-century middle-class. Gayatri Chakravorty Spivak accuses Heidegger of entrapping himself in the same "idealistic pathos of absolute knowledge," which he ostensibly condemns. She remarks, "Heidegger's method finally excuses everything."[35]

Heidegger is a magnificent case of an academic disease often spread by word of mouth from scholars to media and politics and back again. Heidegger forgot to ask whether he was hurting others. He failed to see the effect of "seeing" in any sense, Greek or otherwise, on the lived experience of those around him. He was indifferent to suffering because of the grandeur of his quest. Heidegger's linguistic turn to "seeing" the history words "gather" carried the social context of interwar Germany, not the "sinews of wisdom" in Western history as a whole. His magnificent abilities flowed into reinforcing an unusually volatile political situation. Heidegger's critical method could not resist the political vortex into which his secular faith was being drawn. Pierre Bourdieu is the most trenchant critic of Heidegger's polemical moral turn:

> This bastard language embraces perfectly the purpose of the elitism which is within reach of the masses and which offers the most 'ordinary' people the promise of philosophical salvation provided they are capable of hearing, above the corrupt messages of wicked pastors, the 'authentic' thoughts of a philosophical Führer."[36]

In the end, Heidegger's "Greek way of seeing" connived at the reproduction of evil.

Heidegger's complicity with the Nazis is doubly ironic because history without a conscience was, for Heidegger, the major problem of modern being in time. Robert Denoon Cumming observes in Heidegger "a *Dummheit* which can apparently be elevated to the philosophical level."[37] "Dummheit" is the only admission Heidegger was ever known to make about his membership in the Nazi party. He never apologized or offered any explanation for how he was taken in and why his philosophy of Being did not protect him from political seduction. Jacques Derrida calls

Heidegger's philosophical opus, "none other than a *Weltpolitik* of spirit."[38] Derrida traces Heidegger's moral complicity to Hegel.

Hegel's philosophy of history did not understand the function of language in Western culture after the death of God. Derrida criticizes Heidegger for ignoring the meaning of one word in particular. He picks out the word, "spirit," to criticize Heidegger in a style similar to Heidegger's own. He uses the style of Heidegger's language to show Heidegger does not understanding keywords in the history he claims to be deconstructing. "Without *Geist* it is impossible to think Evil," Derrida reminds us.[39] The modern world had stripped away the concept of evil from the leftover language of faith after Europe's skeptical Enlightenment. Neither Hegel's nor Heidegger's philosophy has a substitute concept for it.

Heidegger was a passive spectator to the holocaust and the world war. He did not commit or condone hate crimes. He lectured publicly in 1934–35 in the style of a Nazi and he refused to recommend a colleague for promotion because he was a Jew. On the other hand, he insisted the dedication of *Being and Time* to Husserl be retained. He never hid or renounced his appreciation for Husserl at any time before or during the war. Heidegger was a bitter man who had difficult relations with all of his colleagues. He used worse language against Catholic colleagues than he ever used against Jews. Heidegger was never a Nazi racist. The biographical evidence of his racist behaviour indicates Heidegger's fascism never sank any lower than vicious careerism.

Heidegger's reputation suffers because his philosophy of Being was an uncompromising indictment of just "being-there." Heidegger denounced the loss of authentic being in a mindless conformity he called the "they-self." He defined the goal of philosophy and the last task of modern metaphysics as true concern and an authentic life. His petty careerism undermines the credibility of his self-appointed task. Heidegger's hypocrisy stands out in much starker relief than the hypocrisy of many others whose careers were just as complicit and cowardly as Heidegger's. Sluga (1993) discovered that by 1940 half of the German philosophical community was Nazi. Frege, Russell's old teacher, became a Nazi in 1924.[40]

Heidegger could not "see" the potential for evil in his own work. He could not criticize the history "gathered" in his own research and writing. He was indifferent to evil as a real historical problem. He was detached from the plight of his fellow human beings by his commitment to his work. The history of a deep and distant past and the futuristic illusions of a better life to come excluded the middle earth in which daily life is ineluctably carried on. The world of the "they-self," the "in between world" of beings in contemporary time has no dignity for Martin Heidegger. To deplore this denouement without compassion for Heidegger would make Heidegger a special case. It would separate me from the humanity, angst, anger, and disillusion that Heidegger embodied for everyone who has felt Hegel's "infinite grief."

Without minimizing the political vulnerability of Heidegger's position, it is only fair to note one fruitful aspect of it. Heidegger's reverted dialectic serves the invaluable purpose of reopening the secular moral question in modern intellectual history. Heidegger's theoretical position is no more extreme than a number of similar positions, equally unworkable in practice, which broadened conscious awareness during the modern era. The solipsism of Leibniz and Berkeley; Hume's disastrous Fork, Kant's radical subjectivism, Nietzsche's will to power, Marx's materialism and Freudian libido were radical positions which provided the essential service of expanding the legitimate range of acceptable intellectual debate. The one-sidedness of these positions was fruitful in context. As a counterweight to the conventional culture, these arguments bore abundant fruit.

Heidegger is able to argue, cogently, in my opinion, that Kant, Kierkegaard, Hegel, and Nietzsche were each correct in their own way. Kant was correct to say a disinterested reason reflexively creates moral duties for itself without even being aware of what it is doing. Kierkegaard was correct to claim this overpowering sense of emotional involvement with the world can make you sick. Hegel was correct to say reason and feeling evolve by opposition and synthesis. Nietzsche was correct to call the psychological need to have power over others the prime mover of the age. Heidegger's grim perspective powerfully articulates selected aspects of all these great positions.

Heidegger added Nietzsche to his critical philosophy of Being after World War II. Will to power was the reason for the chaos of modern existence. The moral individual was thrown into a world governed by the happenstances of arbitrary power enacted daily at every level of life. Nietzsche was the first to realize this important historical fact. In Heidegger's opinion, the "throwness" of modern life, i.e., its chaotic unintelligibility, is the meaning of the 'nihilism' Nietzsche described. Heidegger wants to know why the self-evident truth of Nietzsche's critique is not universally accepted. The answer, he says, is Christian and classical philosophy. Plato and Christ are to blame for the collective unconsciousness of contemporary life. "It is a precondition for nihilism that we seek a 'meaning' in 'all events' that is, in being as a whole," Heidegger asserts.[41] The classical view of meaning is used by the contemporary world to hide the meaninglessness of modern existence.

The link Heidegger offers between four influential philosophers and two contrasting eras is a theory of language. Words are a synthetic laboratory where the great debates of the ages are mingled. Heidegger's investigations of the history "gathered" in language turned the public/private dichotomy of bourgeois experience inside out. His theoretical conclusions rescued Romantic aesthetics from the morganatic prison of bourgeois self-satisfaction. From a personal nightmare of resentment, angst, and infinite grief, Heidegger sleepwalked boldly into the central issue of late modern thought.

Manifestly, for Heidegger, language is something that for the most part does not show itself at all: it is something that lies hidden. An enormous burden of inarticulate anxiety is hidden by the history of our being together in a language world that defeats our moral sense – the most fundamental of all abstract human needs. History has accumulated a gross weight of moral and emotional misunderstanding which, in common practice, betrays our hopes and defeats our highest ideals. The spirit of humankind is weighed down by this accumulated history. Hegel's "joy" is a great sorrow and the comforts of "an already formed language" are a snare and delusion in their current form.

Heidegger believed "language had been debased to a means of commerce and organization. Thought rooted in language was a mere philosophy of words no longer adequate to the pressing realities of life," he lamented. Building on this insight, he contended, "We no longer have the power to trust that the word is the essential foundation of all relations to [other human] beings as such."[42] Modern language had failed. The lost language of authentic human community became Heidegger's Holy Grail. In no small way, the moral ambiguity of Heidegger's quest defines the modern dilemma for all skeptics in a society in which "God, himself, has died."

Heidegger had witnessed the emotional miracles of pulpit rhetoric and traditional faith in his youth. He knew in the body of his being that faith was possible and faith could change worlds. The last spiritual spar for an existentially drowning man was the same "joy" which had comforted Hegel. Those who have felt Hegel's "infinite grief" are susceptible to Hegel's joy. Heidegger was such a person. Many academics have felt the same pain and taken refuge in an analogous joy. Disillusionment (pervasive, current, and inescapable) drives them to the solipsistic solace of an already formed language. "Hegel's conception of time presents the most radical way in which the ordinary understanding of time has been given form conceptually, and one which has received too little attention," Heidegger explained.[43] Heidegger took from Hegel the hermeneutical secret of a skeptical faith. His work was the critical decoding of Hegel's "joy" over "words which in themselves have a meaning." Heidegger simply undertook the re-reading of Hegelian "joy" backwards.

In his solemn quest, Heidegger missed one of the most elementary facts in modern history. He was so wrapped up in his linguistic method, he never checked to see if history had any other lessons for him. He developed his linguistic turn to the "Greek way of seeing" at the beginning of the radio and television era. Even in the 1920s it was evident "Greek seeing" was not social. If it had been, it was not social in the early twentieth century. In Europe before the war, millions of anxious Romantics had shared the same classical music, poetry, literature, and art. They "saw" the same events around the world from the same imperial point of view. They heard the same political debates and they knew they were members of the same social world. "Seeing" did not bring them together. If anything, the act of seeing detached them from each other. "Seeing" taught bourgeois Europe a sense of privacy and detachment. We see ourselves attached to the place we are, not the images we share. In the modern world we are alone with our thoughts. Just "seeing" history is not sufficient to recover the magnificent transformational grammar that was lost with the old religious sense of community. Just seeing, Karl Jaspers remarked, "Is only the freedom to watch."[44]

Heidegger's "Greek way of seeing" is not unique to Heidegger. It is a moral epidemic in the public and professional culture of the economically developed countries. Journalists, politicians, businessmen, and academics are susceptible to its effects. Heidegger was the physician who could not save himself. Although he is biographically compromised, he coined the missing term in this modern form of secular piety and personal devotion. The critical missing term is "discourse." To understand the limits and liabilities of "seeing," we have to be willing to criticize the way words create worlds. Language stores and teaches the schemas, categories, *episteme*, manifold of perception, phenomenology, future anthropology, and deep play of what is 'seen' as a 'world.' In a world in which "God, himself, is dead," words are given their structure and "grammar" by the social schema in which they are practised. The self-replicating correspondences between language system and social being are a discourse. Language is the abstract shape of society. It is the social form of our being alone together in the world. Human beings cannot use words without implying a value statement about what appears to be the case.

Heidegger pointed out the moral relation between history and modern language. He will, likely, always have a prominent place in modern intellectual history on account of this fundamental insight. After Heidegger, what was implicit in Kant's ethics becomes explicit in a mainstream debate over history, politics, and culture. The debate is critical of the way nineteenth-century value assumptions were engrained in the language of daily life. After Heidegger, it is possible to argue 'language' is social. The language we use creates a society, history, politics and culture. Those who suffer and those who could and should ameliorate the suffering are not brought together by merely 'seeing' things as they really are. Heidegger drew the controversial conclusion that seeing is a social construction learned from language. The syncretic debate he began draws together the most influential philosophical positions of the last two centuries.

Heidegger's life and work come together in a positive moment of insight and a negative moment of biographical example. What he brought together in theory he suffered in composite form in his personal relationships with others. The difference between his practice and his preaching is part of the significant legacy of the man and his work. The great difference in Heidegger's life makes him human, all too human. What Heidegger realized in theory is proven out in the man's biographical experience. To see Heidegger— life and work—is to see a composite of theory and practice that have come together in a surprising, even shocking way. Michael Allen Gillespie has summarized the composite legacy well. Heidegger takes the radical theoretical position that history is not just what has occurred. History is the discursive objectification of what has occurred. The objectification of events can be seen in the language of daily life. The hinge between the theory and the man swings for Gillespie on the pivotal idea: "Insofar as it is an objectification, however, history is severed from history itself." Heidegger, the man, severed himself from the history he had to live. His life was a victim of the philosophical dilemma he had to live.

Heidegger illustrates this epochal duality in two contrasting ways. He theorized it in a dramatic and extensive opus, which still invites a serious and informed commentary. He also lived the problem against which he struggled. His own life is a biographical example of his own worst fears. Gillespie continues:

> History thus serves only as an apologetic and polemic for ... unlimited objectification and exploitation. History, thereby, becomes entangled in this conflict itself.... History (as a study, as a way of seeing the world and relating to others) thus becomes ideology and replaces philosophy, politics, art etc. ... as the determinative explanation of human life.[45]

Heidegger developed this theoretical position and waged a Pyrrhic struggle against it in his own life. For him, the theory and the practice suffered from striking instances of ordinary human frailty, but the combined lesson is a robust confirmation of the moral challenges of late modern life. He won in theory and lost in life.

Jeffrey Barash has come to a similar conclusion. Heidegger's philosophy of history rests on a distinction that was traditionally considered metaphysical. His problem is how to find a moral stance in a skeptical, science-based world. His answer, Barash explains, is the famous "ontological difference." Barash's explanation of the great, governing "differences" in our lives is the best I have found:

> We have noted Heidegger's thought concerning history reposes on the presupposition that the epochal distinction between [ideal] Being and beings [human beings in the world] ... is not predisposed by a determinate human character [Dilthey] or mode of existence [Marx], but that inversely, the human essence changes in relation to epochal ways of drawing this distinction [ brackets added].[46]

To save a moral world from skeptical destruction Heidegger posed the most radical challenge to the modern liberal arts in the history of modern thought. He charged all modern theories of interpretation: biblical, aesthetic, historical, and literary with complicity in a cover-up. He claimed that what has been taken as evidence for becoming better is, really, an excuse for staying the same. The modern world's systematic apologies for not living up to its ideals are not explanations. They are excuses. The whole cultural and intellectual teleology of becoming in the hermeneutical tradition since Plato is a lie. Western becoming is merely a process of avoiding what we have become. The modern personality and its culture are determined by this lie. Grand strategies of moral avoidance are the historical content of what purports to be our highest ideals.

In an interview given for posthumous publication he declared he had returned to a cynical version of his lost faith. "Only a God can save us," he lamented.[47] Hegel's "infinite grief" left Heidegger with half the truth. Words "gather" meaning from history, but they do not "gather" moral integrity and interpersonal concern. Their meaning is limited to the social contexts from which they gathered their significance. Heidegger's life and work are a morbid commentary on just "seeing" history without everyday moral concern for others. His insight that language "gathers" history was a significant moment in Western thought. Understanding the imperial violence and sublimated egotism "gathered" in language becomes the great task of Continental philosophy after the war.

On November 10, 1946, Jean Beaufret had put a number of public questions to Heidegger regarding Marx and Sartre. Heidegger responded publicly in 1947 with his "Letter on Humanism." Heidegger's "Letter" strongly criticized the Marburg Kant whose alleged idealism was the framework for modern humanities scholarship. Heidegger's "Letter" hurled the *Panzerprinzip* of postmodern thought across the Rhine: "Language is the house of Being," he intoned.[48] Modern history had destroyed the innate human capacity for culture, conscience, and moral concern. Its weapon was language. Heidegger's mordant nihilism was resonant with the mood of the era. The spectres of de Gaullism, the nuclear sword, existential melancholia, mass culture, and consumerism melded with Heidegger's critical rejection of the Western intellectual tradition. Young French intellectuals immersed in Sartre's melancholy faced a new enemy: the pessimistic denial of all classical values since Plato. Some of them determined to champion a new humanism. Their task was formidable because there was no denying the wars.

With the Cold War settling over Europe and the reactionary reoccupation of the old empires under way, the mood was ripe for moral defeatism. Scholars and serious readers who are impatient with the late modern linguistic turn on the Continent need to remember the fiery Braille alphabet from which it was lifted. The turn in France grew out of passionate disgust with murderous betrayals and bad faith. A horrible complicity between traditional values and the worst imaginable crimes against humanity screamed out for justice. The modern "house of being" was implicated in the most unspeakable horrors. Shriving history and cleansing it of complicity with the horror was the highest priority of French intellectuals after the war. The pandemic of murder and bad faith had to be stopped. The complicity between history and the horror of the wars seemed clear to a young Algerian *colon* raised in the interspaces between North and South, French and Arab, Jew and Muslim, colonial and colonizer. His name was Jacques Derrida. He understood Heidegger's method and he knew about Heidegger's life. He was determined to save the first and avoid the path of the other.

## *JACQUES DERRIDA (1930–2004)*

A "tension with history, first of all" was the reason Jacques Derrida gave for a "deconstruction" within the Western heritage itself.[49] "History," he wrote, "has always been in complicity with a teleological and eschatological metaphysics, in other words, paradoxically, in complicity with that philosophy of presence to which it was believed history could be opposed."[50] The "tension" he described was not with history itself but with the language of history. The "complicity" Derrida described is the moral complicity between the conventional language of modern historical narrative and bourgeois politics. "It is as if a virus were introduced into the matrix of language, the way such things are today introduced into computer software, the difference being that we are – and for a very good reason – very far from having at our disposal any of these diagnostic and remedial antiviral programs that are available on the market," he explained.[51]

Derrida introduced the concept of a deconstruction at Johns Hopkins University in 1966. The controversial neologism tapped into a broad base of inarticulate disgust with academic politics and media sensationalism.[52] Nauseated at academic complicity with the fascists, Gaullists, and superpower politics, Derrida's neologism gave French existentialism a new focus. Derrida's famous paper, "Structure, Sign and Play in the Discourse of the Human Sciences," denounced the methodological assumption of "objectivity" in the social sciences. The modern idea of "objective mind" was full of ulterior motives, Derrida announced. The hidden motives were structured into the language. At a prestigious international conference on structuralism, Derrida placidly read the august establishment there assembled its intellectual obituary. It was a fairy tale moment for a scholar. Derrida claimed the logic of the traditional humanities implied European civilization was the top of a hierarchy of human cultural development. Derrida was convinced no one could assume the cultural superiority of the West after Auschwitz. His attack on the alleged ethnocentrism of the old humanism gave it a blow from which it has never fully recovered.

Derrida objected to any humanist study formed according to a concept of objectivity borrowed from modern science. He denounced as "ethnocentric" the illusion of structural analogies between the humanities disciplines and the primary, "natural" order of the physical sciences. The infamous neologism, deconstruction, is taken from Heidegger's *abbau*, a term he uses synonymously with *destruktion* in *Being and Time* (1927) and *The Basic Problems of Phenomenology* (1927).[53] Derrida had not just taken over a term. His critique of concept-structuralism faced the moral problem Heidegger had avoided. Derrida's attack on "the status of a discourse" lay bare what Thomas Flynn calls "the Achilles' heel of Marxism and structuralism alike: the moral implications of their theories of history and society."[54]

He was misunderstood from the outset. Derrida's attack on structuralism sounded to most readers like a nihilistic attack on scholarly standards and moral idealism. They failed to notice the scholarly point of Derrida's attack. Derrida attacked the ethnocentric notion that Western art and science were advanced stages in the evolution of language. He attacked the illusion of moral evolution in modern history. He did not attack the possibility of moral evolution. He attacked the dubious idea Western culture had an Archimedean perspective on truth. The West claims it "borrows" from its own "heritage the resources necessary for the *deconstruction* of that heritage itself." It claims it can find principles of moral transcendence at work in secular history. The dual claim that Western history is objective and self-transcending is not a coherent proposition in a culture which does with science and does without gods. The historical anthropology of the West is logically arrogant and conceptually detached. It makes *others* the object of history. It uses history in a dual mode that camouflages a painful moral ambiguity. History is both real and ideal. The difference between the real and the ideal is Heidegger's "ontological difference" in practice. Heidegger took it from Hume whose great philosophical fork defines the primal moment of original secular expulsion from the garden of Romantic sentiment. The history of modern moral development worships the general and denies the particular. The language games of the modern social studies are political games of moral avoidance and emotional indifference to others.

Derrida's anti-structuralism marks a return to some of the oldest questions in Western history. His purpose was simple and consequential, if not altogether clear. It was Derrida's intention to free language studies from the binds, traps, and tricks of traditional history of ideas. Derrida's attack on structuralism was a criticism of the moral hubris of the West. It was an attempt to reaffirm the moral and ethical values which Hegelian dialectic had paralyzed. Derrida derided the "readers-consumers of Fukuyama" in 1993 for identifying him with the end of history:

> In the '50s, that is, forty years ago, the eschatological themes of the "end of history," of the "end of Marxism," of the "end of philosophy," of the "end of man," of the "last man" and so forth were our daily bread.[55]

The existential crises of the war years were understandable. The world wars had seared a permanent question mark on the Western moral and political tradition and it had become unintelligible. Young French intellectuals had the "bread of apocalypse" in their mouths. The Romantic dyad of "infinite grief" and boundless hubris had come roaring back to haunt, daunt, and terrify modern history. A political discourse in fundamental self-contradiction had bankrupted the moral credibility of the West. Derrida's extremism is no less intelligible than the stubborn defence of political progress through dialectical thuggery that has been the hallmark of modern history for almost two hundred years.

The neologisms, witticisms, polyglot puns, and intellectual improvisation of his approach are not always appreciated. Derrida was skilled at ad hoc-ery and tweaking the nose of tradition. He practised an impious mischief which, no doubt, he enjoyed. Behind his witty iconoclasms are serious issues. The modern cultural narrative has a language problem. Derrida's wordplay is an attempt to describe the double binds of modern language without reproducing the conditions which caused them. He coined the neologism, *différance* to dramatize the self-destructive cycle of abstract dissent and concrete complicity that, in his opinion, had compromised the thought of Lévi-Strauss, Sartre, and Heidegger. *Deconstruction* describes the moral impact of inadvertent language practices which a less skeptical society would have called evil.

Jacques Derrida spent his life arguing the modern West lives in moral and emotional denial over what its economy, culture and politics have done to the world. Derrida's world includes the psychological and emotional life of Carl Becker's "Mr. Everyman." There are moral termites in modern language. Modern critical theory has, in most cases, created differences of opinion which serve, in practice, to defer the great moral issues of our time. "Deconstruction" is the buzzword which captured media attention in the 80s and 90s, but it is not the keyword which most closely defines Derrida's work. A less widely known neologism must be given that honour. The modern determination to avoid the immorality of modern language is the source of a paralyzing *différance* in modern life. *Différance* is Derrida's most complex piece of polemical wordplay. The disproportionate inattention *différance* received in comparison with "deconstruction" illustrates Derrida's central critical contention. *Différance* is the preferred tactic of moral avoidance in the modern West. It means to *differentiate* and at the same time to *defer*. He described it as: "A confusion of value and existence ... sheltered beneath the equivocal category of the historical."[56]

"*Différance* produces what it forbids, makes possible the very thing that it makes impossible," Derrida muses.[57] The *a* in Jacques Derrida's concept of *différance* is Jacques Lacan's *"petite a"* in *The Four Fundamental Concepts of Psychoanalysis*. Lacan called the *petit a*, "the Cartesian term" in his therapeutic model.[58]

*Différance* is the subliminal residue of professional, political, and economic desire. It writes texts without ethical knowledge and makes meanings without a moral purpose.[59] The language "gathered" in history evokes meaning without understanding its effect on behaviour, promotes ideals without a coherent frame of reference, and teaches moral standards that conform to the status behaviours of the times. In Lacan's therapeutic model, the *a* in *différance* is an open function [(A+1)] that corresponds to bourgeois economics. It is the infinite additive which can never be satisfied. It is the subjective formula for the compulsive dissatisfactions of modern culture and eternal return of desire. Like the history which made it, its maxim is itself. Its goal can never be determined and its restless spirit can never be at peace. It is a system of knowledge at war with itself.

The in-different watcher who is the superior odd-man-out summed up Derrida's colonial experience in Algeria. The colonial experience developed in him a peculiar tactile genius for language unrivalled except, perhaps, by Roland Barthes. Derrida could sculpt images from the shape of words as if language were a visual Braille in three dimensions for the eyes. The *petite a* was a neo-Freudian concept familiar to French intellectual circles after the war. Derrida appropriated it to dramatize the sadism of the modern watcher. "Watchers" like Heidegger have a psychological problem. Their language of so-called objective discovery reproduces the structures of violence to which they claim to be opposed. Derrida's work calls attention to the tug of war inside the modern cultural narrative.

In 1988, in an article significantly titled, "Afterword: Toward an Ethic of Discussion," Derrida called the historical effect of *différance* on ideas and events by the name: "deconstruction." The convenient differences between politics, art, philosophy, and culture are an undoing, a deconstruction of the moral life:

> "Deconstruction" is firstly this destabilization on the move in, if one could speak thus, "the things themselves." ... before becoming a discourse, an organized practice that *resembles* a philosophy, a theory, a method – which it is *not*.[60]

The famous postmodern buzzword, "deconstruction," is not a method, a research strategy, a system of knowledge, or a new form of criticism. The deconstruction (destructive self-contradiction) of modern history describes an alleged moral paralysis in traditional scholarship. The source of the paralysis is language. An internal short-circuit in modern language undoes the value dimension scholarship might contribute to contemporary social experience.

In *Psyché*, Derrida explains:

> Deconstruction does not return [*ne revient pas*] to a *subject*, whether individual or collective, which exercises the initiative in carrying out the deconstruction.... The deconstruction takes place; it is an event which does not wait upon deliberation, consciousness, or the organization of the subject.... It

> *deconstructs itself....* And the "itself" or "deconstructs itself" is not the reflexivity of a self or of a consciousness.[61]

A grammatical pun is the darkest secret of the Hegelian boudoir. Deep in the genetic code of modern language, deep in the transcription of modern being is a flaw, an error in scriptase, a phenomenological typo of such gravity that the whole intellectual history of the West misreplicates.

The old language can be used to describe its own deconstruction, but the adventure is a winding road. Derrida traces the road back to Hegel. He calls the modern text Hegelian *Aufhebung*, i.e., a transformative carrying over of the past.[62] Jürgen Habermas defines *Aufhebung* as "transcending incorporation." It is Hegel's key word for the dynamic process of progress through dialectical confrontation.[63] Derrida deflects the Hegelian meaning back upon itself. Hegelian transcendence is the negative dialectic which undoes the ideal effects which theory has tutored the competently adjusted European to expect. "The *Aufhebung* **is** history," Derrida complains and he means a general history, Hegel's old "world history" that showed all things becoming whole as if by an act of God.

The quasi-theology of historical progress is dysfunctional in a skeptical society without God, grief, or moral introspection. Its logic is circular. Its language "is subject to the same law as what it is the law of: it first gives ***itself*** as immediate, then mediatizes itself by denying itself, and so on," Derrida muses [author's emphasis].[64] Hegel's language is the historical code for a social cancer. It reproduces itself, for itself, without any responsibility for the whole. "That it is subject to the law of what it is the law of, this is what gives to the structure of the Hegelian system a very twisted form so difficult to grasp," Derrida explains.[65] Derrida was rather a prude and his secular ethic contains residual Levitical overtones. "The effect of ideality that always ensues also belongs to the structure of animal desire in general," Derrida concludes.[66]

Derrida's dictum, "There is nothing outside of the text" (*il n'y a pas hors-texte*) is his way of explaining the skeptical problem with Hegelian history.[67] In a skeptical world, "reading" "doubles" the world. Texts refer to this one present world and there is no other, exterior referent. The secular reader cannot explain how this world "refers" to significances that are outside of it. The modern world lacks the capacity to refer to any other significance than those that exist historically and materially for it. Conscience and culture move inside a social history. They seek the transcendental virtue of the vicarious experience mediated by texts. The inspiration of a spiritual sphere outside history to which history refers is a literary illusion.

In *Glas* Derrida psychoanalyzes the exculpatory flight of secular faith into the language of history. *Glas* (death knell) is the jarring clash of Heidegger's church bell, still a "secret juncture … ever transformed and unrepeatable, until the last peal into the mountain of being"[68] – now a jangle of broken metal and arrhythmic dissonance, drowning speech and breaking over the spirit like a death in life from which we reawaken minute by minute with no rest and no final return. The sexual re-reading of Hegel's *Philosophy of Nature* in *Glas* is Derrida's prurient reaction to the loss of this most sacred of vessels – modern language – to an historical return of animal passion without grief, fear, or even the memory of what has been lost.

Derrida's prudish poetry is a moral language of last resort. History has been taken captive by its own word pictures. The binding tactic of Hegel's language – the artifice whereby good intentions are the captive of their history – drives Derrida toward the moral criticism of modern scholarship. No plain language of moral dissent is available in the common history of the modern era. Derrida compares Hegelian language to sadistic sexuality. Hegel screws us – screws us up – with his language. Hegelian transcendence is the Sadean philosophy of copulation [synthesis]. "Copulation relieves the difference [between the sexes]," he writes. "*Aufhebung* is very precisely the relation of copulation to sexual difference."[69]

"What are the conditions of this relieving copulation," Derrida asks?[70] Sadistic, mean, disappointing, brutal, and selfish, he answers himself. The Hegelian return to itself "idealizes nature in denying it, produces itself *through* what it denies."[71] And how is the denial accomplished? How, according to the chaste lips of this postmodern Jerome, does denial of life penetrate life? The clincher – predictable, fated, classic Derrida:

> In language, the invisible sonorous, evanescent milieu, theoretical consciousness effaces itself, denies itself, reduces itself to the punctual instant…. This freedom [in language] converts itself into its contrary. Its universality becomes pure singularity, its freedom caprice or hard-headedness. The *proper sense* of this hard-headed freedom is death [author's emphasis].[72]

Language against life is the "practical consciousness" of Hegel's 'copulation' [i.e., synthesis] with the spirit. "This is played out in the passage from desire to labour," Derrida laments.[73] All labour, including that most beautiful of natural conceptions – the labour of language – is negated by the secret, salacious Hegelian phenomenology of desire. To Jacques Derrida, the body of being in the world is defiled by the linguistic brothel of Hegelian 'joy.'[74]

Hegel nauseates Derrida. The Hegelian "cunning of reason" is as offensive to him as temple prostitution to a rabbi. Hegel is a sin. The Hegelian "cunning of reason" has seduced the spirit of the law. The sovereign unity of historical method with the idea of historicity, itself, made the language of history and the history of language subject to the same political economy. The idea that the tradition is *one* – "*the one* history itself ... *the one* tradition" needs to be "contested at its root," Derrida says.[75] A new skepticism has returned to Enlightenment questions in a late modern context. It wants "to be the Enlightenment of our time," Derrida declared.[76] Contesting this linguistically determined totality is "what is best about Enlightenment," John Caputo proclaims.

Derrida describes Hegelian unity as the movement of modern politics "from restricted to General economy."[77] The Hegelian investment in language moves modern politics from the political economy into the economics of desire. Hegel's prostitution of the political economy defers an ethical accounting of what the political economy has done. The unity of history and understanding is disclosed in a way which sells essential differences solely for pleasure. The pimped language of personal pleasure never encounters *an other*. A bourgeois political economy of the sign sates dialectic in a compulsive autoerotic haze. *Grammatology* is the Boy Scout manual of the postmodern linguistic turn. One notes there the warning "that most dangerous supplement" can even make one go blind.[78]

Until words are made aware of the supplement that they receive from the political context, they cannot account for the violence of history. Modern language produces a dysfunctional populace like Merleau-Ponty's Schneider. It cannot remember what it intended. It cannot keep a purpose in mind.[79] The dystopian language of internal historical transcendence is a program for going through the motions which an anonymous, but ubiquitous authority, outside, other, and indifferent to our well-being tells us to do. The language Derrida hates is shell-shocked by moral indifference. Our sensual seduction by language is "the historical and epochal *unfolding* of Being" for us.⁸⁰ This new difference – a new sovereign difference that rapes the spirit – is the sensual masochism which Derrida calls "*différance*." "The *a* in *différance* marks the movement of this unfolding" of the sovereign differences over which the disciplinary languages of late modern culture show hardly any concern.⁸¹

A language "supplemented" by Hegelian *différance* degenerates into semantic quibbles – "obscure frictions" – more vexing than illuminating and shedding little understanding on politics, ethics, and art. The cathartic circle of simple, representative language consoles the victim of Hume's disastrous dualism with the appearance of intellectual progress. In point of fact, s/he is circling within a linguistic labyrinth of a self-imposed avoidance of others. S/he is confirming her/his imprisonment within Lacanian desire without having ever made one bit of difference at all. Much contemporary debate illustrates the desire to avoid the truths about modern history rather than to try to discover them. A psychology of avoidance and ethical silence represents a refusal to overcome our supplementary myths and reflect rationally on the behavioural effects of the cognitive style of modern scholarship.

Traditional liberal arts studies have created differences which have as their greatest effect the political deferring of common decency and a discussion of the good. "This is why," Peggy Kamuf explains, "Derrida wishes to constrain the *Aufhebung* to write itself otherwise, or simply to write itself, to take into account its consumption of writing.... there is always an effect of *différance* when the same word has two contradictory meanings."⁸² A lifeworld flatly mapped as a linear chain of "dialectical" progress can permit, in practice, a convenient repression of foundational issues. "Thus," Irene Harvey writes:

> The two movements which Derrida claims produce the operation of textuality itself seem to (a) contradict one another; (b) paralyze one another; and thus (c) produce the conditions of the impossibility of each other at the same instant.⁸³

The "operation of textuality" which is organized around *différance*, not difference; suppresses moral reflection. The centred, but repressed *différance* between me and the world text may encode unscrupulous or even unconscious behaviour, legitimated between the lines of disciplinary disputes.

To liberate political, cultural, and personal relations from the phenomenology of Hegelian *différance* requires a moral history of Hegelian cunning. Derrida concludes:

> How on the stage of history, can writing ... be put into communication with what is said in *Numbers* about the parched woman drinking the inky dust of the law; or what is said in *Ezekiel* about the son of man who fills his entrails with the scroll of the law which has become sweet as honey in his mouth?[84]

One might wonder why such dramatic language has not been widely recognized and named again for what, in essence, it is – ethics. It is an ethical criticism of bourgeois language. It exposes the dark professional strategies of personal and professional desire behind the aesthetic politics of a putatively professional humanism. The postmodernists believe the obscurity of their language has been forced on them by the complicity of plain language history with the bourgeois political economy. The neologisms, impressionism and obscurity of their puns, are not a warrant to dismiss the hard core of humanitarian concerns evident at every turn.

The rejection of Derrida and postmodernism has been simple and relatively effective. The existence of a deconstruction is denied by denying the influence of Hegel, German *historismus* and the dialectical tradition in late modern thought. The conditioning of politics by dialectical thuggery, the whole illocutionary force of a commodity fetish for texts, a Biblical sanctimony for ordinary words – a whole complex of discursive values affecting the moral life are simply denied. Derrida claims modern history has denied the cultural violence and interpersonal aggression carried inside the modern text. His work denounces a condition of subjective imprisonment inside the discourse strategies of late modern life. He claims the Hegelian predicament defines the modern text and it is one of the biggest theoretical stonewalls facing ethical theory and moral action in late modern life.

### MICHEL FOUCAULT (1926–1984)

To Leonard Krieger, Michel Foucault was "the poor man's cultural historian."[85] In place of real research, Foucault did "mere linguistic inference." As usual, Krieger was a perfectly competent "trimmer." He was right about the facts and completely missed their significance for Mr.

and Ms. Everyperson. What may or may not be inferred from language use is of pressing importance in a media culture where the information economy directly affects history. Linguistic inferences motivate a society which discovers "truth" by cooperative consensus and informed discussion. Foucault's signal achievement was to carry Kant's project in *Critique of Judgment* into the study of history. Foucault's "histories" contend that discursive principles in science and history are "mediating concepts" for conventional politics. Mr. and Ms. Everyperson learn the structure of their world from the "grammar" of its description. Language use links "is" with "ought" for most moderns. What is licit in language is licensed for behaviour. As in Derrida, the presumption of objective research in history, politics, and culture is a potentially devastating contradiction in the lives of people who believe it.

"My essential task," Foucault wrote, "was to free the history of thought from its subjection to transcendence." Foucault's "histories" are studies of sign-systems he called "epistemes." Modern medicine, penology, the military, visual art, and biology were examples of "the grammar of a discourse." "Looking at the grammar of a discourse was a way of avoiding transcendental questions," Foucault explained. He said he wanted:

> To establish a system of signs that would be transparent to the continuity of being. What modern thought is to throw fundamentally into question is the relation of meaning with the form of truth and the form of being.[86]

The times were formally out of joint. Foucault's emphasis on "form" is the key to his work. It is an old emphasis which connects Foucault to the critical Kantian idea of form.

Good form was a classical illusion of the Romantic middle class. Schiller, Hegel, Coleridge, Pater, Arnold, Burckhardt, Bosanquet, Dilthey, Croce, in fact, a full century of Romantic formalists preached self-transcendence of the political economy through cultural self-edification. Foucault realized the daily life of ordinary people had been left out of the formula. He found himself in league with a large silent majority who were doubly discriminated against. The cultural project of Romantic self-edification was a false promise to workers, women, gender and sexual minorities, as well as the great anonymous majority of the non-Western world's working poor. Foucault was an honest skeptic and an avowed homosexual. Neither orientation is convenient. It seemed to Foucault that the social issue of homosexuality was embedded in a larger issue of bourgeois status and political conformity. He called the system of muted intolerance which oppressed him a "grammar of transcendence." The bourgeois idea of personal, self-motivated emotional and intellectual "transcendence" was a seedbed of social intolerance and political misunderstanding for Foucault.

For Foucault, whose lifestyle was progressive in a number of controversial ways, the social structures of bourgeois culture were a penal discipline which punished individuality and held its members in aesthetic prisons of guilt and conformity.[87] Foucault wrote "histories" that "opened" or "cleared" pathways through the deep structure of bourgeois feelings and values. He took Heidegger's language and method seriously, but he added a Kantian critique of form to the method. Foucault's method is a Kantian critique (i.e., behavioural and 'practical') of bourgeois language. He believed the political economy and social conformity are linked by the public language of modern life. He called the language link between conformity and economy a "discourse." The biggest obstacle Foucault faced was the Romantic effacement of the old Kantian project. With Foucault the heart of the Kantian moral critique returns, united with Marx, in a constant and unrelenting diatribe against all things bourgeois.

The possibility that forms of practical knowledge like medicine, penology, botany, and history might also communicate bourgeois norms was an outrageous idea in the 1970s. The intellectual history behind Foucault's "archaeologies" is the Kantian critique of form. Foucault carried Kant into a moral anthropology of bourgeois life. Gilles Deleuze praises Foucault for redefining "the point of Kant's decisive break with Descartes."[88] Kant was the first Western philosopher to realize that the "spontaneity of the 'I think' ... acted on receptive beings who necessarily represented this spontaneity to themselves as something other than social and historical."[89] And Deleuze credits Foucault with seeing something which Kant did not. Kant did not realize that the ethical inquiry which he began requires "coadaptation of the two forms [space and time] or two sorts of conditions, which differ in nature," Deleuze says.[90] The "coadaptation" which Kant did not foresee was accomplished perniciously in modern language. Foucault draws Kantian ethics into the study of language. He added to Heidegger the ethical dimension of the Kantian critique of form.

The French Ph.D. requires two manuscripts: a main thesis and a complementary one. Michel Foucault's secondary thesis was an essay on Kant's

*Anthropology from a Pragmatic Point of View* [accepted: May 20, 1961]. There for the first time Foucault explained what he called "archaeology." He proceeded from Kant's *Anthropology* backwards to a discussion of Descartes and Aristotle. Instead of building toward Kant in a conventional historical sequence, he "deconstructed" Kant in terms of the major influences on him. [91] Foucault's "thése complementaire" on Kant began his idea of a spatial dispersal of thought which classical history hides. In Foucault's thinking, the idea of "mankind" is a spatial accident which a particular history has given a temporary plausibility. The references to "archaeologies of the text" which dominate Foucault's thought appear here for the first time. Foucault recognized Kant's critical method as a forensic laboratory in which to diagnose the ethical pathology that had infected language after God himself has died.

Deleuze described Michel Foucault's "archaeologies" and histories of "words and things," as "a sort of neo-Kantianism unique to Foucault."[92] Consciousness is a "receptive form," susceptible to the structures of language.[93] The "Neo-Kantianism" toward which Foucault directs our attention is a critique of pure language in which a whole culture shares Hegel's "speculative joy" without any memory of his "infinite grief." Deleuze calls the possibility of an historical *a priori* which has forgotten its social history, "the paradox of intimate meaning" in Kant's *Critique of Pure Reason*.[94] Foucault saw the specialized languages of modern "discourse" as the social maxims behind gender and sexual politics. The expansion of elite discourses until they become a controlling maxim was the process Foucault placed at the foundation of modern history. His "archaeologies" interpreted the structures of traditional narrative as secular moral maxims extended and elaborated for purposes of social and political control.

"Rationality cannot be understood," Foucault wrote, "except in relation to the establishing of a power exercised on the body itself." On one occasion he described his work in the following way:

> What I want to show is how power relations can materially penetrate the body in depth, without depending even on the mediation of the subject's own representations.[95]

In Foucault's perspective, a certain historically specific form of reason (*episteme*) holds together the culture and thinking of an era. The ethos of an era is internalized through 'rational' debates (what Kant called "schematism" or "maxims") over science, religion, art, and politics. Individuals absorb the 'rationality' of their culture by mastering the professional and political jargon of their time. Foucault's work inspired a number of "insurgent" histories. His historical descriptions of a power/knowledge axis have encouraged political dissent at the cultural level. The first accomplishment of "insurgent" historiography is the shedding of all panoptic reference points. The god's-eye view is also dead and to understand our situation we must see knowledge as a linguistic network of socially constructed values.[96]

Hubert Dreyfus and Paul Rabinow divided Foucault's work into four stages:

1) early Heideggerian stage
2) proto-structuralist or archaeological stage
3) genealogical stage
4) ethical stage[97]

Foucault's "ethical stage" is the return of a deep debate in the history of modern thought. Foucault understood Kant's critique of Hume. Human beings give themselves a social order, law, culture, and philosophy. Foucault added an unconscious history to the creative process. Human beings let history have an autonomous role in the construction of the world. History plays back the structure of its basic bargains in politics and with nature. People learn power-games along with the knowledge-games of the modern era in the spatial dispersions of knowledge that seem 'normal.' Modern knowledge is taught, learned, and practised in a "discourse." The modern age has reached the point where its self-replicating cultural mechanisms must become conscious. The history which confronts people as alien, other, and threatening is a social construction they have perpetrated on themselves.

Heidegger was Foucault's "essential philosopher," Simon During concludes.[98] In theory – no, Foucault's essential theorist was Kant – but, in method – yes, Heidegger set the stage for Foucault's mature work. Foucault saw in Heidegger's etymological method a way of investigating and naming the linguistic strategies by which the bourgeois political economy proliferates. Heidegger helped Foucault reach the point where he "had no difficulty in accepting that man's languages, his unconscious, and his imagination are governed by laws of structure," During understands

Foucault as saying: Language is the way "transcendental questions" are "interiorized" without ever having to be made conscious.[99] Foucault accepts Heidegger's critique of individual being and collective Being in the world, but he moved the modern way of "seeing" from Plato up to Kant. He began the modern era with Descartes and then added a critical dimension to Descartes' detached observer which he learned from Kant. Foucault calls Descartes' way of seeing "classical" and adds a Kantian critique of form to it.[100] Cartesian consciousness views the world "as if" it were a solitary observer, but the view is conditioned by history. The solitary observer "sees" with eyes developed by looking at history in a pre-inscribed way.

The "inauthenticity" of modern life began with "classical" detachment and skeptical doubt. The problem, to Foucault, is not detachment and doubt, but the erroneous notion that detachment and doubt are objective conditions of universal mind. The Cartesian problem begins when detachment and doubt are framed as universal traits and not culturally specific ones. Since Descartes the social world has appeared to rational skeptics as an 'other,' outside, alien, doubtful, and threatening. The integrity of their individuality is defined by doubting all these 'other' things. In the declension of the modern from Descartes to Freud, the experience of radical doubting has hidden logical antinomies which nearly drove Foucault mad. These antinomies have left us vulnerable to horrible accidents that are misread as acts of self-improvement and social progress. Radical doubt has left us emotional solipsists who can easily be duped into doubting our senses. The Cartesian project of radical doubt is still required, but a competent critique of form has to be added to it. Otherwise, radical doubt paralyzes moral action.

Foucault takes Heidegger's portmanteau term, being, and translates it as the 'other.' Our being is defined by the way we see "others." Sometimes he uses, "the other" to mean "the one over whom power is exercised;" but the classical "other" in Foucault's work is usually the way normative acculturation teaches us to "see" others.[101] Gilles Deleuze defines Foucault's "Other" as:

*The structure which conditions the entire field* [of sense] *and its functioning, by rendering possible the constitution and application of categories* [like] *... form-background; depth-length;*

theme-potentiality; profiles-unity of the object; fringe-centre, text-context; thetic-nonthetic; etc.... The concept of the "Other" = an expression of a possible world [brackets added].[102]

The significant "Other" to which Foucault is opposed is the mad modernist project known as bourgeois man. Born in Descartes' *Discourses* and taught to speak by the Jesuits at Port Royal, bourgeois man works as a guard in Bentham's ideal prison. He has declared all who challenge his authority clinically insane. This mature monster of mediocre, middle-class modernism bestrides the world. He thinks he is timeless and arrogates all recorded history unto himself and his selfish project of personal becoming. In fact, his majority is less than two hundred years old and he will likely die a neurotic death by his own hand.

The "Other" is a semiotic code which carries with it all the power of "common sense" to those whose lives have been inscribed within it. Deleuze writes:

>...not at all a particular "form" inside a perceptual field, but rather a system which conditions the functioning of the entire perceptual field in general.[103]

"Others," in the moral sense, are not what generates meaning for bourgeois man. The example, suffering, and objective condition of "others" are not the tokens from which the bourgeoisie take their understanding of the world. The action-orientations of daily life are epistemological. They are "read" from the current field of organized knowledge. They are not "others" as people, but other ways of organizing the experiences people have.

> The Other-structure [other *as* structure] conditions the entire perceptual field, the application to this field of the categories of the perceived object and the dimensions of the perceiving subject, and finally, the distribution of concrete Others in each field [brackets added].[104]

History, society, and culture could not exist for us without the structuring effect of a generalized "Other-structure" which determines the appropriate expression of political consciousness in a given era:

> I am nothing other than my past [semiotic] objects, and my self is made up of a past world, the passing away of which was brought about precisely by the Other.... I am a past world.[105]

The "other" is *our* history in *me*. My "other" is the way my history has taught me to define myself and "see" other people. The "other" is the embodiment of what I "see" in them. Modern history is not embedded in me like a wart on my finger. It is a tumour near my heart. Modern history is systemic in me. It is part of my social, political, and cultural DNA. I carry it like a fingerprint and I leave it on everything I touch. I hallmark all that I do with this systemic other that engorges me.

The secular incarnation of social history is the crisis point in modern philosophy David Copp has called it "a subject-specific *moral* epistemology."[106] Foucault extends the crisis of epistemology in philosophy to the study of history. I do not, "think, therefore I am;" I am "an impulse of thought," I am "an intentional act of thinking, therefore I am," Merleau-Ponty warned.[107] The detached cogitations of the critical spectator are no longer enough. The classical "I think" is now saturated with history:

> I am an intersubjective field, not despite my body and historical situation, but, on the contrary, by being this body and this situation, and through them, all the rest.[108]

Descartes' solitary doubter is immersed with everyone else in the same daily life. Her experience is driven by the history we all share. Her life is emotionally spliced, politically interfaced, and psychologically twinned to the secular order of things. Until the history of the spatial dispersion of bourgeois thought is written, modern perception remains ineffectively fragmented. Foucault gave historical depth to the embodiment problem in late modern life.

The *cogitanes* of history, a being thought by events, is the "other-structure" embodied in me. It is Ridley Scott's alien bursting out of the modern body politic. The meaning of the past consumes me from within. Yet what should we do? To share the world with real "others," we must share the history that gives us institutions, law, and language. The liminal boundary between my self and real "others" is language. Modern language is the cask of Amontillado. It lets us bury alive the thousand, million insults of Fortunato on our lives. The difference between us and Poe's horror story is that we seal up ourselves. We lose each other in a language which isolates us from the human condition. We bury our own spiritual selves alive. "To renounce the other [real, human other]," Derrida admonished, "is to enclose oneself within solitude (the bad solitude of solidity and self-identity) and to repress ethical transcendence."[109] To accept the "Other" [structural, epistemological Other] is to enclose oneself within consensus. The structural, epistemological "Other" is a postmodern pivot chord. It is the postmodern word which corresponds to the word, "real," in formal philosophy. "Other" is paradoxical, the essence of ambiguity. Its formal meaning is the exact and precise opposite of its colloquial one. The formal, structural "Other" is the most dedicated and decisive enemy of freedom and community. "Other" bespeaks the cruel ambiguity of a world which refuses to define its basic values and face up to its basic moral responsibilities. The word acts out in neurotic silence a mute gesture of protest against bourgeois life.

In presenting these ideas, Foucault dismisses the possibility of reasonable dialogue in language of pure otherness, a language which has no memory of the kind of thing language is:

> As for a common language, there is no such thing; or rather, there is no such thing any longer; the constitution of madness as a mental illness, at the end of the eighteenth century, affords the evidence of a knowledge of a broken dialogue.[110]

Foucault uses a Heideggerian etymology to illustrate the course of modern language. "Madness is indeed *delirium*," he wrote. "This word is derived from *lira*, a furrow; so that *deliro* actually means to move out of the furrow, away from the proper path of reason."[111] An historically specific definition of "reason" excludes from consideration alternative paths to community, truth, meaning, and value.

"History," Foucault wrote, "is one way in which a society recognizes and develops a mass of documentation with which it is inextricably linked."[112] But the link remains a secret acted out by the research and writing. Narrative history can remain a "secret presence to itself in the interplay of a constantly recurring absence," Foucault warns.[113] In Foucault's format, historical narrative "acts out" its relation to the present like a disruptive child. It piles up nervous trauma in an unforgiving cycle of repetition and return. "Let us say," Foucault continued, "that history, in its traditional form, undertook to 'memorize' the *monuments* of the past.... History is that which transforms *documents* into *monuments*."[114] Just as Freud's neurotic transforms the "truth" of an unbearable fear into an indecipherable mimetic display, so, according to Foucault, traditional narrative history "presents" and "acts out" a negative relation between present and past which its refusal to understand condemns it to repeat.

Foucault contended that each historical era had its own "specific *discursive* apparatus."[115] Discourse fetishes in history were the methodological foundation for Foucault's "archaeologies of knowledge." State and corporate power was historically elaborated in "techniques of discursive rendition of daily life," Foucault argued.[116] The language of the confessional, the parade ground, natural science, and empire penetrated into the language of vernacular and corrupted the concept of many other things. The discursive apparatus of each era is a hypoverbic needle of normalization. We have daily life under our skin. It is introjected through language. The language of modern public life is the deep play for all those painful norms which wrongly assimilate us.

Language is the naturalistic foundation for a principled paradox of the cruellest dimensions. In the deep play of its grammatical structure, modern language teaches the ethical acceptance of an unethical world. Foundational contradictions in the modern way of "seeing" the world are reproduced in the conventional language of politics, the economy, and the Fine Arts. An authentic culture of moral dissent means "pulling back from the metaphysical and moral prejudices generated by naturalistic origins," Foucault wrote. Foucault re-read Kant and found there the cornerstone of a rational moral project. A potentially liberating critique had been the promise of Enlightenment. An incarcerating logic of empire and personal gratification had been the outcome. What happened, Foucault asked?

Foucault's voluble dissertations on the broken promise of Europe's historical Enlightenment have garnered ridicule from Hegelian scholars of the old Romantic school. His over-the-top prose has been accused of nihilism and misanthropy. Foucault said:

> Before the end of the eighteenth century, man did not exist....
> He is a quite recent creature, which the demiurge of knowledge
> fabricated with its own hands less than two hundred years ago;
> but he has grown old so quickly that it has been only too easy
> to imagine that he had been waiting for thousands of years in

the darkness for that moment of illumination in which he would finally be known.[117]

In Foucault's opinion, modern language has succumbed to the language of empire. It is unable to articulate the liberating ideas of Europe's historical Enlightenment. Even the modern definition of "humankind, "mankind," *homo sapiens*, and the like are constructed ambiguously in the politically opportune euphemisms of exploitation, empire, and sexual chauvinism.

"Man," to Foucault, is an imperial ostension. "Man" is the shrivelled being to which the bourgeois world points with malicious pride. Modern "man" is a metafiction, the unhappy by-product of a middle-class "metanarrative." "Man" is a pejorative term bound on all sides by fetish limitations on what the truly human could really mean. The modern limited liability concept of mankind binds us to recent history and blinds us to each other. The narrative fictions of the modern era include the historical illusion that human nature is the aggressive, white, middle-class, masculine conquerors of the British Empire and the American frontier. Deprived of a world history which includes all humankind, we are slaves to an imperial definition of what it means to be human. In our ignorance, we blame the internal contradictions of Western culture on "man." The modern West has defined human nature as the nature of white, middle-class, male imperialists and then imposed this fetish definition on the rest of the world.

Foucault called the nineteenth-century system of history, culture, and politics a "grand normalization." It gave the modern world "its language of calculation," he wrote.[118] Its totalizing perspective was epitomized by the utilitarian prison. The nineteenth century was a utilitarian prison with the mundane goals, purposes, and pleasures of the middle-class defining the way to see everything. The bourgeois ontology of the nineteenth century required an ideology which did not look like an ideology. Foucault continues:

> It was therefore necessary that the Classical theory of the sign should provide itself with an "ideology" to serve as its foundation and philosophical justification, that is, a general analysis of all forms of representation from elementary sensation to the abstract and complex idea.[119]

The nineteenth century attached a middle-class metaphysic of meaning to their idea of the world. The intellectual history of the modern era was turned into an ideological apology for the era. Modern intellectual history became a formal system of reproducing middle-class culture, politics, and political economy. The genius of the mock synthesis was as deep, incisive, and foundational as any determining structure in natural science.

The nineteenth century had done for culture and politics what Smith had done for economics. The bourgeois cultural economy rationalized its mean spirit and transformed philosophy and theology into monuments of bad faith. With conviction, Foucault wrote:

> It's not a matter of emancipating truth ... but of ascertaining the possibility of constituting a new politics of truth. The problem is not changing people's consciousnesses, but changing the political, economic, institutional regime of the production of truth.[120]

The rationality of the whole system has to be brought into question. "Rationality isn't considered an anthropological invariant in my work," he explained.[121] "Rationality," to beings in time, "is the over-all discursive fact that cannot be understood except in relation to the establishing of a power exercised on the body, itself."

> What I want to show is how power takes hold on the body ... [without] its having first to be interiorised in people's consciousness.[122]

The 'power' which penetrates the body is the power of aesthetic judgment Kant described in the last great critique. The "schemas" of everyday life perform a pleasant and indispensable double duty for normatively well-adjusted, adult human beings coexisting in the society of others. The "schemas" of daily life coordinate the inner and outer worlds of "rational" experience. Individuals accept the knowledge/power axis of their culture because the putatively "disinterested" categories of reason are also the "practical" categories of civil law and the economy.

Foucault, not Krieger, is the real reader of Marx in the tradition of Kant. The link from Kant to Marx is the moral link a disjointed duck-rabbit reading of the modern tradition effectively has suppressed. The debt to Marx is so obvious in Foucault's critique; he could not believe the connection was not self-evident. He was incredulous anyone could doubt his appreciation for the work of Marx:

> It is impossible at the present time to write history without using a whole range of concepts directly or indirectly linked to Marx's thought and situating oneself within a horizon of thought which has been defined and described by Marx.[123]

Late modern language and the "grammar" which governs it are the proletariats' chains for Foucault. What troubled him about Marxism in postwar France was the simple concept of ideology. He explained:

> What troubles me with these analyses which prioritize ideology is that there is always presupposed a human subject on the lines of the model provided by classical [i.e., age of reason] philosophy, endowed with a consciousness which power is then thought to seize on.[124]

Late modern historical experience has called into question the idea of "seeing history" as if the knower/viewer stands outside the fray. The role of the knowing subject is not independent of the power complexes of late modern life. History creates the consciousness from which it requires an act of logical detachment.

In Foucault's unorthodox opinion, history has lied about modern historical experience. The lie creates a bind, knot, and gridlock in consciousness from which the normalized individual cannot detach. Well-socialized self-immiseration is an unspeakable psychological burden in late modern life. "The exercise of power perpetually creates knowledge and, conversely, knowledge constantly induces effects of power. The university hierarchy is only the most visible, the most sclerotic and least dangerous form of this phenomenon," Foucault believed. Radical, liberating knowledge poses the question of power across the whole range of modern experience. It reaches from the most practical technical procedure to the most abstract philosophical idea. The intimate and indissoluble connection of power/knowledge is prior to the traditional Marxist questions of economic determination, false consciousness, and immiseration. The reason the modern university cannot apply critical consciousness to the university environment, the marketplace of ideas, and the bourgeois cultural economy is connected to the prior question of how consciousness is created by historically specific discourses.

The apriority of discourse does not preclude or in any way transcend the Marxist critique. In a manner of speaking, it fulfils it for Foucault. The body is the most basic material in history. The bourgeois political economy has shaped, tortured, and distorted the five senses. Foucault's Marxism is a materialism of the human body, its senses, its needs, and its desires. "Indeed," Foucault asked:

> I wonder whether, before one poses the question of ideology, it wouldn't be more materialist to study first the question of the body and the effects of power on it.[125]

The history of modern knowledge is properly understood as "a field of regularity for various positions of subjectivity."[126] Even modern sexuality is penetrated and defined by various historical "subjectivities." Victorian empire and the imperial duties of the ruling class broke sexuality away from pleasure in nineteenth-century England. In Foucault's opinion, the infamous Victorian double standard owed as much to the British Empire as to the Christian church.[127]

Foucault's "strategical model" requires a critical willingness to investigate the structural connection between language and modern history. Modern language has been filled with physical violence and emotional intimidation. The language of modern life has injected world-historical violence into the most intimate corners of private life. The grammatical connection between history and language provides a strategic model for breaking the hold of empire, militarism, chauvinism, and, for Foucault, sexual prudery, on daily life. Foucault's 'strategical model' of language is the ally of democracy and the friend of Mr. Everyman.

Language and history form the epistemological bedrock of postmodern ethics. Foucault is the poster child for the connection. His life and opus are the personal record of a definitive modern identity crisis. He moved from "suffering in rhythm" with Roquentin to wondering why, *for some reason*, his misery was synchronized with the misery of others. He decided the structures of language at every grammatical level – definition, grammar, syntax, and style – organize human experience prior to consciousness. Although controversial in many of its details, one aspect of Foucault's critique is undoubtedly correct. The politics of language require discursive analysis of a kind for which traditional theology and classical philosophy were unprepared.

## UNDERSTANDING POSTMODERNISM

In Paris in 1981 Diane Michelfelder and Richard Palmer organized a conference featuring Hans-Georg Gadamer and Jacques Derrida. Gadamer's *Truth and Method* (1960) is a definitive explanation of Dilthey's theory of language. Derrida was the most famous critic of traditional structuralism, the general theory on which Dilthey's position was based. The participants at the conference expected a memorable encounter between the two thinkers. "This was not how it went," Michelfelder and Palmer reported.[128] The two likely adversaries talked past each other. Neither appeared willing to grapple with the other's position. Derrida was reticent. He asked one question and offered no rebuttal to an answer he obviously thought unsatisfactory. Gadamer was indifferent to the postmodern movement and made no mention of Derrida's general contention structuralism was dead.

"Man in history is wholly defined by the relation between individuality and objective spirit," Gadamer explained.[129] The language arts are the catch-basin for lived experience. Historical study congeals human experience into a concrete record. The human moral compass responds instinctively to the record. History "touches us in enigmatic fashion," Gadamer explained. "It shatters and demolishes the familiar: It is not only a 'This art thou!' disclosed in a joyous and frightening shock: It also says to us: 'Thou must alter thy life.'"[130]

The "thou must" of history is the holiest hope of the old structuralist tradition. History supposedly transforms base political cunning into high moral imagination. The facts of history paint a moral world in negative relief. They awaken the inner eye of conscience. They jangle the moral cochlea of the human sprit. They lift politics to a higher level of ethical awareness. Gadamer was the last high priest of historical *verstehen*. Skeptics who mourn the death of traditional ontology have been turning to history for moral guidance for over two hundred years. Gadamer's paean to the old structuralism was beautifully tuned to the tenor of modern times.

When his turn came Derrida skipped the high hermeneutics and went for a more mundane point. Gadamer had mentioned mutual understanding. History promotes mutual understanding. It makes "the partners in a conversation more open to what the other has to say."[131] Derrida did not connect "partners in a conversation" with mutual understanding. He connected Gadamer's "partners" with moral understanding. There is a difference. We may presume Hitler and Mussolini had a mutual understanding after 1935. Stalin and Mao certainly understood each other when they met in Moscow in 1950. Khrushchev and Castro were quite open to what each other had to say in the early sixties. When Roosevelt declared, "He's *our* son-of-a-bitch," Rafael Trujillo, likely, was completely open to what Roosevelt had to say. The quality of being "open to what the other has to say," sometimes leaves a very great deal unsaid.

Derrida found a simple way to say it. He asked Gadamer whether his ideal "conversations" were conducted with *good will*. Gadamer took the bait. "Nothing at all about philosophical hermeneutics depends on good will," he retorted. Open conversations depend on the Socratic Method. History asks universal questions. It raises the issues which link politics and philosophy. History is the empirical horizon of human experience. History is self-discovery on a global scale. When individuals see themselves mirrored in history, they see themselves from the perspective of others. Good will is an inevitable by-product.

Gadamer's answer was not as important for what he said as for what he did not say. Derrida had asked Gadamer a question from Kant. Is the "thou must" of mutual understanding a moral imperative? Does the "joyous and frightening shock" of self-discovery change our attitudes toward others? Is the "this art thou" to which Gadamer alluded categorical or politically correct? Does historical understanding promote a spirit of moral responsibility? Does it promote compassion and concern for other people who are outside the conversation? Does history educate a kinder, gentler, and more loving people? Does history include ethics?

"Good will" was Kant's highest moral category. Kant believed, "Nothing in the world – indeed nothing even beyond the world – can possibly be conceived which could be called good without qualification except a good will." Kant thought a good will required us to treat others as an end in themselves and never a means to an end.[132] Beyond the shadow of a doubt, Gadamer knew the source of Derrida's question. He also knew he did not need to respond to it. He knew the general intellectual orientation of his audience. Most of the participants at the conference were traditional disciplinary scholars. They would not readily connect history and ethics. Most of them would not be curious about the ethics of traditional historical understanding. They would not be as sensitive to the modern language issue as Derrida. Gadamer knew modern theory of interpretation is not compelled to address ethical questions. The modern intellectual is part of a grand division of labour in all things – even the traditional labours of the spirit. The ethics of history are not a disciplinary topic inside the conventional academic frame of reference.

Derrida's question touched on a workplace enigma in the concrete practice of Gadamer's philosophical hermeneutics. It returned to the site of an obedient absence in late modern writing, teaching, and lawmaking. Derrida's simple reference to Kant's *Groundwork of the Metaphysics of Morals* exposed one of the most murderous plots in modern history. Gadamer stood there, mute before it, the fully modern man, the last man, the confidence man of the bourgeois political economy. With eloquent passion he embraced the politically correct paradoxes of ethical conflict, selfish spirituality, and the moral marketplace. He did not need to discuss good will. The study of modern history guaranteed it. Good will was inevitable among people who had learned the lessons of history. Patently violent events in a history reeking with ego, ambition, and soft-core solipsisms must, by some incomprehensible alchemy of the soul, guarantee good will. The invisible hand of historical *verstehen* will defeat the social pathologies, the will to power, and the personal ambitions of public life. An understanding of history assures it. History was the new god of Gadamer's secular spirit. Its power guaranteed the old ontology. Its constructive force would prevail, in time, over the sins of the world.

Derrida's charge against Gadamer was loaded with a history Gadamer did not want to discuss. Gadamer had studied with Martin Heidegger. He had heard Heidegger explain that language "gathers" history. Heidegger had called language the "house of being." He did not like the house modern language had built. He did not like the being modern language had gathered into its bosom. Heidegger compared the modern world to a black forest of the spirit. Philosophy had to create clearings inside the modern forest of the spirit where community, care, and concern could dwell. Heidegger rejected structural *verstehen* – the spontaneous emergence of moral experience from history. He called it the language of a 'they-self' and he criticized it as insincere and shallow. Derrida wanted to know how Gadamer answered his old teacher. Heidegger said modern historical understanding had lost its moral senses. It had lost the indispensable traditions of community, compassion, and concern without which human life is incomprehensible. The way history and philosophy were represented in modern times precluded a recovery of the oldest and most important human values. "Only a god could save us, now," Heidegger had concluded.

Derrida had asked Gadamer about his intellectual roots, his education, and the source of his ideas. Since he had broken with Heidegger, let him show his old teacher wrong. Let him produce evidence modern history cares. Let him produce evidence the professional cultures of academics, politicians, and media pundits care. Derrida's simple Kantian question had raised the most ancient question in all the world's holy writs. Derrida had asked tersely whether care, compassion, and brotherly love were still the practical measure of a philosophy.

A history Gadamer could ignore was packed into every syllable and silence in Derrida's simple question. Did Gadamer's philosophical hermeneutics bear any moral fruit? Gadamer answered in the classic style of the Pharisees of every age. He deliberately misunderstood the question. Every era develops its own way of missing the point. Derrida's simple question was irrelevant. Democratic due process packages it in bulk at every election. Undergraduate philosophy classes pedal it like a periodic fire-sale from the closets of antiquity. Ethics were a private matter. Politics had replaced them in global affairs. Modern history was a moral algorithm vastly superior to the old philosophy. History was the higher math, a general function, the irrefutable felicific calculus of souls so far from others they only knew the abstract word, man.

Derrida did not blame history for its ethical absences, silences, and moral black holes. He separated the facts of history from the way modern history had been studied and taught. History has never looked kindly on moral values. History has never worn a human face. The facts of history inspired Derrida's question. Given the violence of modern history, how could Gadamer take good will for granted? How could anyone suppose a history of violence could teach ethical norms? How could examples of moral indifference be expected to generate moral understanding? How could a history of ill will inspire its polar opposite? Derrida's question raised the central question in postmodernism and the late modern linguistic turn. The structure, grammar, and philosophy of history are organized to do politics. Politics are violent. Derrida believed the study of modern politics reflects the moral void within it. Gadamer's position illustrated the problem. Modern philosophy of history confuses good will with ill will, or, even, no will at all.

Derrida refused to recapitulate his lifework in his meeting with Gadamer, but his specific contribution to scholarship since 1967 had been to show the cruel limits of Gadamer's position. The narrative tradition Gadamer defended was not, in Derrida's opinion, transparent to great ideas or conducive to moral progress. Gadamer's narrative tradition was infested with politics. It was a labour-saving device for short-term coalitions with no long-term memory. Gadamer's language was a Platonic pharmacy of metaphysical prescriptions which could not bear the objective scrutiny of its own test cases. When tested for probity and integrity, Gadamer's tradition had failed. The history "gathered" in the politics of late modern life was the wrong kind of history. Its metaphors, imagery and system of reference could not sustain the values, attitudes, and mutuality required by ordinary citizens in the conduct of their daily lives. Derrida did not denounce Gadamer. He raised a seemingly obscure point and let it speak for itself to those who were willing to hear. Derrida's reticence acted out the political vulnerability of the postmodern position. Postmodernism was vulnerable to the pack of tricks it tried to expose. The language of modern structural theory precluded the discussion of modern structural theory. Challenges to Gadamer's position had to use Gadamer's language. To end run around Gadamer's position required breaking the rules of the game. One had to invent a new language and suggest a new system of interpretation. Ironically, the modern language difficulty left historical research the weak point in the postmodern position. The general rejection of historical *verstehen* carried over into the scholarship and research methodology of the movement.

Derrida's encounter with Gadamer is a microcosm of the postmodern encounter with Hegel, Dilthey, structuralism, and bourgeois politics. The weak point in Gadamer's philosophical hermeneutics was his overt faith that politics were a moral force for good. Derrida would not buy it. He believed Western democratic politics were morally compromised. They were complicit with many of the greatest problems in the twentieth century. The postmodernists criticized the "spirit" of modern life. They claimed the mean spirit of modern life was mirrored in the modern language tradition. In the twentieth century, the language of the liberal arts tradition had become destructive to its own ideals.

The liberal arts of the nineteenth century were developed during a period of global double standards. The language of modern politics and the liberal arts was conceived in the time of empire, racism, and gender chauvinism. Modern language was a victim of the "objective spirit" of the age of military empires and social Darwinism. The language arts were the political unconscious of a racist and imperial culture. Here the issue stood. Does modern politics and scholarship value good will? Do politics, public service, media, and modern business even recognize the need for good will? If sometimes not – perchance – how can one discuss the absence of good will in modern life?

Gadamer was able to avoid the question. The most striking feature of the history of postmodernism is the ease with which it was ignored. Whether it was right, partially right, right in principle, or totally wrong is not the first issue. The first issue is how cleverly mainstream academic politics was able to ghettoize the movement. Academics took the brunt of the postmodernist critique. They did not relish facing a late modern conflict of the faculties in their backyard. Most academics rejected the implication they supported in practice what they denied in theory. Gadamer typecast himself as the archetypical affronted intellectual during the encounter in Paris. He does not answer Derrida. He ignores the charge his structural aesthetics could be the crisis it claims to cure. He disdains to speculate about the bind, knot, antinomy, or contradiction which might be involved in his form of secular moral faith.

Gadamer's theory of ethics is the purloined letter in Poe's famous mystery story. Modern politics have hidden ethics in plain sight, right on top of the historical record. The horrors of modern history are obvious. The obviousness of history was the perfect place to hide a theory of ethics. No one would expect so complex and important a topic to be simple and obvious, plain to see, right on the surface of things. Intellectually simple conditions like good will, brotherly love, and mutual respect could not possibly hold a key to modern world problems. No leader in his field could be expected to jeopardize his prestige by admitting to so simple a proposition. Gadamer refused to look in the obvious place for the great moral problems of late modern life. He was, in this, an adroitly well-adjusted citizen of the world.

Derrida claimed modern history had "deconstructed." The claim was distorted by the critics of postmodernism. The distortion was part of the refusal to consider what the postmodernists were saying. Detractors claimed postmodernists doubted history. Postmodernists were said to claim history was not true and the facts in history could not be proven. The detractors misrepresented the debate in order to avoid the question. Postmodernism was not about the facts of history. It was about the ethics of history, the social studies and the Fine Arts. The postmodernists believed the language practices of modern public life work against ethical philosophy and moral action. Derrida did not doubt the veracity of modern historical events. He doubted the moral efficacy of the traditional *narrative description* of historical events. He believed traditional narrative was morally implicated in the events themselves. The moral failure of modern historical study was the deconstruction at work in the material itself. Derrida's criticisms applied to the language arts and they spread further than historical study. His central contention was that the modern language arts do not promote moral reflection. The encounter with history was forced on Derrida and the whole movement by the massive dramas of world historical events.

The central critical focus of postmodernism is the relation between narrative theory and moral development. Skeptics who do not otherwise acknowledge metaphysical entities celebrated the narrative arts for their spiritual beauty and their moral value. Words were very important in the Romantic trinity of politics, art, and commerce. Words were the music of the soul. They provided the secular spirit with an objective system of traditional values. The postmodernists demurred. Modern history was medieval dialectics without the Christian God. It was Abelard's "this and not" with no God to moderate the conversation. Under such anomalous conditions, the word world wars of scholarship and politics could not automatically point to great ideals, the great dead, and a separate spiritual space. Modern dialectics were ludicrous to the postmodernists. For them, the word wars of the nineteenth and twentieth century pointed to a political practice very far from the ideal. In practice, the word wars favour ambition, self-promotion, and aggrandizement. Modern language practice teaches emotional indifference to others in the name of higher values which are often discussed but rarely seen. The postmodernists called the moral aphasia of the modern language arts the internal deconstruction of the text. They believed scholarship and politics used a language in structural contradiction with itself. The internal contradiction between the general and the specific levels of the text degraded the integrity of the culture. It negatively affected how a literate people feel, act, study, and vote.

Postmodernism did not reject history. It rejected Hegel's heterotopias of "objective spirit." It rejected the idea of history as an external god whose invisible hand promoted the general good over the heads and behind the backs of the people. Its intellectual ground was Kant. Kant thought Western intellectual history contained sources of pernicious error which, left uncorrected, would lead modern judgment astray. The "ancients" had invented a "logic of illusion" which still tempted general logic with its "specious art," he warned. "It is an art unfortunately very commonly practiced by metaphysical jugglers." "General logic," he advised, "when thus treated is called *dialectic*." Kant called the "dialectical illusions" of the schools mere "cobwebs" of words. "The schools," as he put it, have made rhetoric into a "canon of judgment." They take mere words to be "an organon for the actual production of objective assertions," he advised. "Any attempt to use logic as an instrument that professes to extend and enlarge our knowledge," Kant wrote, "can end in nothing but mere talk."[133]

Postmodernists rejected the "cobwebs" of Hegel's historical idealism. They rejected all talk of higher insights growing out of gross and aggressive behaviours. Postmodernists never doubted history. They never doubted the facts. They doubted the categories of judgment which informed allegedly coherent modern interpretations of historical facts. Postmodernism was the guilty conscience of classical aesthetics. It was the return of a repressed knowledge, a tactile sense of painful loss which had haunted modern thought since the Enlightenment. Its exponents had returned to the central question of Kant and Marx – a fundamental question left over from Europe's historical Enlightenment. Can skeptics do ethics? Can those this-worldly citizens of the one world of science and materiality transcend their mundane condition and practice the traditional higher values of religion and moral philosophy?

Skeptics who were old-fashioned enough to mourn with Hegel found few sources of comfort in world political history. The grief they shared with Hegel led them back to Kant and forward again to Marx. Postmodernism was Kant's philosophy and Marx's politics held together by Hegel's infinite grief. Skeptics who mourn the death of traditional ontology turned to Kant for theory and to Marx for a guide to political practice. Kant insisted pure reason was not pure. Marx insisted free enterprise was not free. The postmodern synthesis of Kant and Marx insisted modern reason had become a form of free enterprise. It was neither pure nor free. Kant is the brain, but Marx is the heart of postmodernism. The postmodernists re-established the relevance of Marx after the Cold War. Their work made Marx the foundation of personal practice and a healthy heart test against moral complicity with the slogans of the age. Section 4, Chapter One, of *Capital* is the heart of postmodernism. Marx called it, "The Fetishism of Commodities and the Secret thereof."

Marx credited Locke, the "philosopher *categorein*" and "the celebrated Franklin" along with medical men like Petty, Barbon, and Mandeville for inventing the labour theory of value. "Their discovery marks, indeed, an epoch in the history of the development of the human race, but, by no means, dissipates the mist through which the social character of labour appears to us," he advised.[134] Marx said he had advanced the labour theory of value from the point where bourgeois economists had left it. He said he "was the first to point out and to examine critically the two-fold nature of the labour contained in commodities."[135] Marx's two-fold theory of commodities is the critical foundation of *Capital* and the first premise in Marx's critical philosophy. The postmodernists understood it.

"A commodity is a very queer thing abounding in metaphysical subtleties and theological niceties.... [In the commodity fetish of the bourgeois marketplace] a definite social relation between men assumes the fantastic form of a relation between things," Marx observed. The confusion of a social relation with a material object was what Marx called "fetishism."[136] The bourgeois economists believe "value stalks about with a label describing what it is. On the contrary, it is value that converts every product into a social hieroglyphic," he warned. What does the capitalist value? Why, commodities, of course. He values commodities more than his fellow man. The result is a confusion that penetrates every level of society and contaminates every human relationship within it. Bourgeois man is not just confused about the way the world is. He does not even see the way the world is. Under the fetish of commodities, "Man's reflections on the forms of social life take a course directly opposed to that of their actual historical development.... The world of commodities actually conceals, rather than disclosing, the social character of labour and the social relations between the individual producers," Marx concluded.[137]

Postmodernism connected the "commodity fetish" in *Capital* to the late modern linguistic turn. Words in late modern culture have become commodities. They destroy the moral capacity for independent judgment in all who fall under their power. The language of modern intellectual enterprise conceals the social character of the labour required to produce them and the anti-social values of the producers themselves. Words, with meanings in themselves, are intellectual commodities in the marketplace of ideas. Heritage words taken from the history of Western civilization have been confused with real social relations. A language of intelligible events and ostensible moral concern is traded as a commodity on the open market. The commodity fetish is the secret heart of the old structuralism. The social relations concealed within it have paralyzed the power of ideas. The intellectual capitalism of commercial writing is as destructive of moral values as consumer capitalism on the material side of the commodity experience. It is as if the material base and classical superstructure of nineteenth-century Marxism have been pushed over onto their sides. Like a giant geological stratum pushed up and over by a volcano, intellectual labour has joined commodity labour as a capital foundation of the bourgeois age. The two-fold nature of commodities affects intellectual and material life equally. Both mind and body are buried under its destructive upheavals.

When language is treated as a commodity it mirrors social relations just like any other commodity. It becomes part of the general "reflex of the age." Postmodernism was a political critique of language as a commodity. The idea came directly from Marx. A mystified commodity language creates the same political illusions as a mystified system of material production. Bourgeois history becomes the only plausible history. Industrial society is the only plausible society. The language fetish hides the human relationships characteristic of the political economy it serves. It denies the possibility of any plausible alternative. The cruelty of the system is camouflaged by quasi-religious appeals to unworkable worlds of sentimental values. Postmodernism attempted to rip away the mystical veil and expose the capitalist system of intellectual production.

For Marx, Hegel's abstract dialectic was a philosophy without content. Hegel was the prophet of nothing, the maestro of irrelevance. "Hegel has no problems to formulate," Marx complained. The bourgeois philosophers do not realize the emptiness of their abstract dialectics. Their philosophy hides their moral poverty. The bourgeois philosophers confuse description with explanation. Proudhon, Feuerbach, and Bruno Bauer used Hegel's language to describe history. They have described nothing, Marx declared. Marx's materialism gave him a moral insight the bourgeois philosophers tried to ignore. Marx understood Hume's fork. In a skeptical world, error does not imply obligation. Descriptive narrative is only the freedom to watch the world process. The bourgeois philosophers expected eloquent description to accomplish moral wonders. Marx called their history the political equivalent of their religion. It was just another opiate. "The bourgeois philosophers have only dialectics without any understanding."[138] They are happy to have cunning without moral obligation. They use history to prove the inevitability of bourgeois life. Their history is part of the general commodity fetish. Marx was explicit: "Their language hides their idea of value," he declared. Hegel's logic has given them "the absolute method which explains all things and the movement of things."[139]

The fetishes of bourgeois life have corrupted everything of higher value that might be called good:

> This is the time when the very things which till now had been communicated, but never exchanged; given, but never sold, acquired, but never bought – virtue, love, conviction, knowledge conscience, etc. – when everything, in worth, passed into commerce. It is the time for general corruption, of universal venality, or to speak in terms of political economy, the time when everything moral or physical, having become a marketable value, is bought to the market to be assessed.... Contradiction is the basis of this existence. Its life, its philosophy and its politics are nothing but social contradiction in action.[140]

The postmodernists declared language structurally analogous to the commodity fetish Marx described in *Capital*. The language of high culture, history, and art is a contradiction in action. It mystifies the real social relationships in the culture.

The effect of the language fetish in modern developed economies is the same as the material fetish in the developing economies of the nineteenth century. The contradictions of the system paralyze conscience and destroy integrity. The contradictions of the system are excused as inevitabilities. Dissent against them is logically impossible. Science – the pseudo-science of bourgeois social life – proves the modern world to be the best of all possible ones. The contradictions in the system show the world dialectic in action and, at the same time, put traditional moral questions out of bounds. Common decency does not have to be discussed. Moral consistency is outside the parameters of modern progress. The traditional language for what the system lacks is not even in play. It is illegitimate to even bring it up.

Marx's motto for the bourgeois philosophers was: "Where concepts are missing, a word will come to you at the right time."[141] The bourgeoisie have no concept of what they are doing, but they have infinite faith the right word will magically appear at just the right time to cover their lethal deficiencies. They rely on words and avoid understanding. The words they use sustain the contradictions of the bourgeois system. "What appears paradoxical as a result is already contained in their presuppositions."[142] They have just the right words to paralyze action, destroy discussion, and deny social responsibility. They excel at tying good intentions in knots and undermining good will. The postmodernists claimed the old factory system was inherent in the language of the modern system. The moral logic of the capitalist system is reproduced in modern art, literature, and bourgeois political history. The language of the system is the lethal enemy of world peace, sustainable development, and cross-cultural dialogue.

Christian Comeliau has identified the "logic of modernity" as "resting upon private appropriation and competition." He adds:

> It entails individualist rivalry far more than mutual support as the basis for relations among the members of a society. It thus has a destructive impact upon the 'social fabric' itself.[143]

The theologian Richard Roberts has suggested:

> A responsible postmodern theology of integrity must recognise and own new affinities and new allegiances if it is to grapple in effective ways with the contemporary orgies of collective tribal power.

Roberts' answer is "postmodern saints" who "will be able to extinguish themselves in seeking to enter this dialectical complex. There is no easy way forward," he concludes.[144] The pathfinders will be men and women without the qualities conventionally associated with achievement and success.

Roberts adumbrates a possible shady connection between the human sciences and the modern economy:

The realisation that the human sciences should be employed in inner-directed and emancipatory, rather than outer-directed and hegemonic terms occurs at core points within management theory and practice where it [theory] critically differentiates itself from its shadow side, managerialism.[145]

Roberts is a theologian who uses secular language. Skeptics who mourn the loss of the old ontology are entitled, *mutates mutandis*, to the same dispensation. Skeptics who mourn have an equivalent right to speak of spirit, brotherhood, honour, and truth. The history of inner-directed moral autonomy includes traditional problems of the spirit. The postmodernists were skeptics who admitted to traditional problems of the "spirit." Their project was an open admission of the need for new ways to discuss traditional ethical theory and moral practice.

Kant advised the skeptics of the Enlightenment to find new ways to transcend their self-tutored imprisonment in the mundane.[146] History, art, and culture were not adequate vehicles of spiritual Enlightenment in Kant's opinion. For those who lack the intuitive gifts normally associated with traditional faith, there are no extrinsic modes of self-transcendence. Derrida's question to Gadamer illustrates the general direction of the articulate dismay felt by skeptics who mourn the plight of traditional ethics in late modern life. The postmodernists championed Kant and Marx as the founders of their method. They read Kant and Marx in a diametrically opposite way from the deconstructive reading of modern intellectual historians like Randall, Barzun, and Krieger. They believed Kant and Marx together had broken through the bourgeois mystic veil. Language was the centerpiece. Every malicious two-fold contradiction to be found in the economy was replicated in modern language. Postmodernists made skeptical ethics into a material etymology of the power of words. The colloquial power of the mundane in human life preoccupies skeptics who mourn.

Recent social history has added ethnicity, sexuality, and physicality to the older social topics of culture, work, and gender. The current direction of political debate in the modern democracies gives reason for optimism. Disciplinary attention to the invisible minorities of history is a promising area of study. The older topics are not compromised by recognizing new areas of invisibility in late modern life. Postmodernism spoke for one of the minority experiences of late modern life. The experience is no less important than any other. Since postmodernism, skeptics who feel Hegel's grief are no longer an invisible minority. They have a voice and a contribution to make to the diversity of the modern consensus.

Social history indicates minorities have always had to push their own cause. History has never shaken the cataracts from its eyes without dramatic provocation. Postmodernism was a dramatic provocation. It pushed the plight and right of another invisible minority before the bar of history. It said, simply, skeptics are language challenged. They are pedestrians in what seems to them an exceedingly slippery world. Their closet is pernicious because the traditional language is not adequate or even available to them in the important areas of ethics, morality, social responsibility, care, nurture, and interpersonal concern. Their significant area of challenge affects their politics, jobs, families, and friendships. Humankind is the animal who uses language and the skeptical language problem affects everything s/he does.

Professional intellectuals, many of whom are avowed religious skeptics, have been slow to recognize the disabling effects of the modern language tradition. Many modern intellectuals have not felt Hegel's infinite grief. They are, in most cases, adequately protected from nihilism by the disciplinary traditions of their research. Outside the university, skeptics have fewer disciplinary protections from the disabilities of language and the loss of moral direction which often attends it. Carl Becker's "Mr. Everyman" is, figuratively, an abused adult. He is molested everyday by incoherent figures of speech. He has been taught Hegelian history without being taught how to mourn. He has been dosing on doubt for two hundred years and no one has shown him the warning label. Mr. Everyman has been taught to believe in words which, in themselves, have a meaning. His secular faith in an unworkable hermeneutical tradition victimizes him. He throws words like freedom, democracy, development, duty, and beauty around like Queequeg's harpoon. He is hooked by heart, head, and body to the vocabulary of a traditional past which cannot be recovered in its traditional form. His sense of decency is affronted by events which seem incomprehensible. He is led about the world by his unprotected ears.

Postmodernism was a recondite academic protest against an arguably dishonest interpretive tradition. Postmodernism attracted the attention of academics, but it failed to reach Mr. Everyman. Mr. Everyman needed postmodernism, but no one told him what it was about. In the late twentieth century, Mr. Everyman presented symptoms of political illness. His basic decency was often threatened by political mood swings. He was alternatively cynical and idealistic. Global cooperation competed with patriotic fervour, and moral idealism played Dr. Jekyll to the profit motive. Chronic indifference toward politics was interrupted by bouts of militarism several times during the century. Mr. Everyman had few protections from the raw cunning of national politics. The inconsistency of his indelicate condition has been hard to discuss. Mr. Everyman showed a distinct inability to hold intellectuals, pundits, military generals, and national politicians accountable for what they said. He was, often, confused.

The violence of the dialectic in history knows no class barrier. In modern adversarial culture, Everyman is everyone. Postmodernists argued Mr. Everyman had to unlearn the Hegelian lessons of head-on dialectical thuggery taught him by bourgeois political history. Unlearning the romance of violence on which modern history was weaned begins with the simplest and most inclusive proposition in twentieth-century philosophy. Words *do not* have a meaning in themselves. Keywords from the great heritage of Western civilization do not carry the world spirit on horseback. Mr. Everyman has to recover the great lessons of history in a language he can trust. The academic responsibility to assist the citizens of the great democracies in the quest for political integrity would seem self-evident.

Metaphysical generalities like freedom, democracy, development, duty, and beauty have no meaning outside the doing, the feeling, and the concrete physical being which, in fact, are consummated in their name. Words, Derrida reminded Gadamer, *should* imply a moral obligation. The right words, at the right time, are expected to command moral compliance. In the modern world, just the opposite has been the case. Words, in themselves, have been opportune. They command little more than the moment. They cannot be trusted to protect the integrity of politics or promote the moral development of a people. The truth about war, global development, and the clash of cultures is not measured in the words bourgeois politicians, pundits, and global economists use with effulgent skill.

Words with a meaning in themselves promote ill will. They foster a climate of moralism, competition, and violence. They intensify factual misunderstandings and degrade the quality of compromise. They make "the partners in a conversation more open to" management and control. The history gathered in talismanic words is not and cannot be the measure of a culture and a people. Until the late twentieth century, fabled words, cynosure words, magical motivational words of hideous strength had been the prison house of mirrors for skeptics who mourned the loss of the traditional ontologies. The mourners were comforted by the linguistic turn. Postmodernism gave them a political identity. Since postmodernism, Hegel's grief has been outed. Skeptics who mourn are a visible presence in the late modern world.

# NOTES

## INTRODUCTION

1. In John Caputo, *Deconstruction in a Nutshell: A Conversation with Jacques Derrida* (New York: Fordham University Press, 1997), 8, 20 and 3. The frontispiece quotation is from Georges Canguilhem, *The Normal and the Pathological*, 282. "Already and before all relations between it and the environment, [a name] contains collective norms for evaluating the quality of these relations," he advised. Names treated as facts of nature make life "an already constituted fact and not a fact to be constituted" (282).
2. J.G.A. Pocock, *The Machiavellian Moment: Florentine Political Thought and the Atlantic Republican Tradition* (Princeton, NJ: Princeton University Press, 1975).
3. Jürgen Habermas, *Postmetaphysical Thinking* (Cambridge, MA: MIT Press, 1992), 142.
4. Habermas, *Postmetaphysical Thinking*, 15–17.
5. Immanuel Kant, *Concerning the Ultimate Ground of the Differentiation of Directions in Space*, trans. David Walford and Ralph Meerbote (London: Cambridge University Press, 1992), 361–73.
6. Immanuel Kant, *On the Form and the Principles of the Sensible and the Intelligible World*, trans. David Walford and Ralph Meerbote (London: Cambridge University Press, 1992), 277.
7. Immanuel Kant, *Critique of Pure Reason*, trans. Norman Kemp Smith (London: Macmillan, 1927), 41–42.
8. Kant, *On the Form and the Principles*, 277.
9. George Dennis O'Brien notes that Pierce said he learned philosophy by reading Kant's *Critique of Pure Reason* every day for four hours, for ten years: O'Brien, *All the Essential Half-truths about Higher Education* (Chicago: University of Chicago Press, 1977), 196.
10. C.I. Lewis, *Mind and the World Order* (New York: Dover, 1929), 130.
11. C.I. Lewis, *The Ground and Nature of the Right* (New York: Columbia University Press, 1955), 4.
12. Lewis, *The Ground and Nature of the Right*, 4.
13. Lewis, *Mind and the World Order* (New York: Dover, 1929), 116.
14. Hilary Putnam, *Meaning and the Moral Sciences* (London: Routledge & Kegan Paul, 1978), 15.
15. Putnam, *Meaning and the Moral Sciences*, 15.
16. Putnam, *Meaning and the Moral Sciences*, 37.
17. Jean-Paul Sartre, "Introduction," in Frantz Fanon, *The Wretched of the Earth*, trans. Constance Farrington, 24–25 (New York: Grove Press, 1963).
18. Sartre, *Being and Nothingnes*, trans. Hazel E. Barnes (London: Methuen, 1957), 615.
19. Jean-Paul Sartre, *Nausea*, trans. Lloyd Alexander (New York: New Directions Publishing, 1938), 134–35.
20. Immanuel Kant, *Critique of Pure Reason*, trans. Norman Kemp Smith (London: MacMillan, 1929), 29.

## CHAPTER ONE: HUME'S PREDICAMENT

1. Ernest Gellner, *Language and Solitude: Wittgenstein, Malinowski and the Habsburg Dilemma* (Cambridge: Cambridge University Press, 1998), 47.
2. Scholastic theologians noted the problem of language in the twelfth century. They trusted God's providence to maintain the integrity of the connection between words and things in ordinary use. Renaissance humanists developed the psychological and emotional properties of language. In the sixteenth century, Descartes, Leibniz, and Mersenne began the modern study of epistemology. From their point of view, language showed how the mind worked and the human mind was created in the likeness of God. Words constituted a natural covenant between a rational God and physical nature. Words performed a double duty

in conscious life. They were objective windows on the world and the mind of God. Late Enlightenment philosophers like Hume, Rousseau, Condorcet, and Kant ejected God from the picture. They replaced the mind of God with 'human nature.' They revisited Renaissance humanism from the psychological perspective of Hartley and Locke. Human nature proved to be less impervious to the political environment than the mind of old Jehovah God.

3  Ian Hacking, *Why Does Language Matter to Philosophy?* (Cambridge: Cambridge University Press, 1975), 52.
4  Willard Van Orman Quine, "Epistemology Naturalized," in *Naturalizing Epistemology*, ed. Hilary Kornblith (Cambridge, MA: MIT Press, 1985), 17; J.L. Austin, *How to Do Things with Words*, ed. J.O. Urmson and Marina Shisa (Oxford: Clarendon Press, 1975), 101; A.J. Ayer, *The Central Questions of Philosophy* (London: Penguin, 1973), 147; Michael Dummett, "The Justification of Deduction," in *Proceedings of the British Academy* 59 (1973) (London: Oxford University Press, 1975), 201.
5  David Hume, *An Enquiry Concerning Human Understanding*, Introduction, notes, and editorial arrangement by Antony Flew (Chicago: Open Court, 1988), 71.
6  Hume, *Human Understanding*, 103.
7  Hume, *Human Understanding*, 75.
8  Richard H. Popkin, *The History of Scepticism from Erasmus to Spinoza* (Berkeley: University of California Press, 1979), 248.
9  Hume, *Human Understanding*, 86 and 30.
10 Hume, *Human Understanding*, 92–93.
11 Hume, *Human Understanding*, 121.
12 Stephen Darwall, *Philosophical Ethics* (Boulder, CO: Westview Press, 1998), 22. The quotation is from David Hume, *A Treatise of Human Nature*, ed. L.A. Selby-Bigge (Oxford: Clarendon Press, 1978), 468–69.
13 Hume, *Human Understanding*, 91.
14 Hume, *Human Understanding*, 97n.
15 Hume, *Human Understanding*, 91.
16 Hume, *Human Understanding*, 54.
17 Hume, *Human Understanding*, 74.
18 Hume, *Human Understanding*, 82.
19 Hume, *Human Understanding*, 96.
20 Hume, *Human Understanding*, 99.
21 Hume, *Human Understanding*, 54.
22 Hume, *Human Understanding*, 56.
23 Hume, *Human Understanding*, 53.
24 V.C. Chappell, ed., "Introduction," in *The Philosophy of David Hume* (New York: Modern Library, 1963), viii.
25 The English edition contained a special proposal to the English for raising a supplemental provision for the poor.
26 David Fate Norton and Richard Popkin, eds., *David Hume: Philosophical Historian* (Indianapolis: Bobbs-Merrill, 1965), 35.
27 Cited in Norton and Popkin, eds., *David Hume*, 35.
28 Cited in Norton and Popkin, eds., *David Hume*, 45.
29 Hume, *Human Understanding*, 32, 44, 45.
30 Hume, *Human Understanding*, 40.
31 David Hume, *An Enquiry Concerning the Principles of Morals*, ed. Tom Beauchamp (Oxford: Oxford University Press, 1998), 160–63. "But though reason, when fully assisted and improved, be sufficient to instruct us.... It is requisite a sentiment should here display itself, in order to give a preference to the useful above the pernicious tendencies. This sentiment can be no other than a feeling for the happiness of mankind, and a resentment of their misery; since these are the different ends, which virtue and vice have tendency to promote (158).... Why do philosophers infer, with the greatest certainty, that the moon is kept in its orbit by the same force of gravity, that makes bodies fall near the surface of the earth, but because these effects are, upon computation, found similar and equal? And must not the argument bring as strong conviction in moral as in natural disquisition?" (121).

32  Hume, *Principles of Morals*, 116 and 112.
33  Hume, *Principles of Morals*, 73–76.
34  Hume, *Principles of Morals*, 105.
35  David Hume, "Abstract of a Treatise of Human Nature," in *Human Understanding*, 41.
36  Hume, *Human Understanding*, 72 and 86.
37  Knud Haakonssen, *Natural Law and Moral Philosophy: From Grotius to the Scottish Enlightenment* (Cambridge: Cambridge University Press, 1996). Haakonssen calls natural law, "the 'core curriculum' in practical philosophy" (p. 62).
38  Antony Flew, *Philosophy, An Introduction* (Buffalo: Prometheus, 1980), 38.
39  Flew, *Philosophy*, 37.
40  Flew, *Philosophy*, 112.
41  Flew, *Philosophy*, 132.
42  See Ayer, *Central Questions of Philosophy*: "For the most part, when we speak of the causes of human behaviour, we use the word 'cause' in the sense of 'necessary conditions'" (180).
43  Flew, *Philosophy*, 132.
44  Kant, *Prolegomena to any Future Metaphysics* (1783), ed. Lewis White Beck (Indianapolis: Bobbs-Merrill, 1950), 8.
45  Kant, *Prolegomena*, 8.
46  Kant, *Prolegomena*, 6. See Manfred Kuehn, *Scottish Common Sense in Germany, 1768–1800: A Contribution to the History of Critical Philosophy* (Montreal and Kingston: McGill-Queen's University Press, 1987), 4 and 171.
47  Kant, *Critique of Judgment*, trans. Werner S. Pluhar (Indianapolis: Hackett, 1987), 319.
48  Kant, *Critique of Pure Reason*, trans. Norman Kemp Smith (London: Macmillan, 1927), 635.
49  Immanuel Kant, *Theoretical Philosophy after 1781*, ed. Henry Allison and Peter Heath (Cambridge: Cambridge University Press, 2002), 464n. "Elsewhere he adds a fourth question, What is man?," which he claims pertains to anthropology and encompasses the first three (See *Jäsche Logic* in the Academy Edition, 9:25).
50  P.F. Strawson, *Individuals: An Essay in Descriptive Metaphysics* (London: Methuen, 1959), 100.
51  Kant, *Critique of Practical Reason*, trans. Lewis White Beck (New York: Macmillan, 1993), 101.
52  Strawson, *Individuals*, 100.
53  *Critique of Practical Reason* contains a table of the categories "with reference to the concepts of good and evil" (p. 67 of the Beck translation). Kant calls the categories "the categories of freedom." Freedom is first an idea and then an event. The prerequisite for freedom is an orderly and intelligible understanding of the world. The measure of order and intelligibility is whether the categories into which sensation are sorted are universally applicable by all human beings, in all times and all places in the world. Sorted sensation into universally recognized categories of experience is our only freedom. It is the only area of experience over which we have complete control. The categorical understanding of the world is a psychological imperative for the individual and a moral imperative for the group.
54  Strawson, *Individuals*, 100.
55  Paul Abela, *Kant's Empirical Realism* (Oxford: Clarendon Press, 2002), 174. See Crispin Wright, "Realism, Antirealism, Irrealism, Quasi-Realism," in *Midwest Studies in Philosophy* 12 (1988): 25–49. One may also note Ian Hacking, *Historical Ontology* (Cambridge, MA: Harvard University Press, 2002): "Discourse is, then, to be analyzed not in terms of who says what but in terms of the conditions under which those sentences will have a definite truth value, and hence are capable of being uttered." Such conditions will be in the "depth knowledge of the time" (79).
56  Kant, *Theoretical Philosophy after 1781*, 8.
57  Kant, *Critique of Judgment*, 21. Hereafter the three critiques are noted as *Pure Reason, Practical Reason* and *Judgment*.
58  Kant, *Pure Reason*, 633.
59  Kant, *Pure Reason*, 175.
60  Kant, *Judgment*, 165. In *"Religion within the Limits of Reason Alone,"* Kant declares, "And we shall have enough of the vices of culture and civilization (which are the most offensive of all)

to make us rather turn away our eyes from the conduct of men lest we ourselves contract another vice, misanthropy" (29).

61 In *Practical Reason*, Kant says, "I do not know why the educators of youth have not long since made use of this propensity of reason to enter with pleasure upon the most subtle examination of practical questions put to the young.... By the mere habit of frequently looking upon actions as praiseworthy or blameworthy, a good foundation would be laid for righteousness in the future course of life" (160).

62 Kant, *Judgment*, 173.

63 Kant, *Judgment*, 144.

64 G. Felicitas Munzel, *Kant's Conception of Moral Character* (Chicago: University of Chicago Press, 1999), 298. Munzel takes the position that the aesthetic is "reason's partner" in the development of character (305). "The cultivation of our capacity to take pleasure in purposive form ... ultimately is in fact required from a moral point of view for the complete realization and exercise of moral character" (307). For related positions see Reinhardt Brandt, "Kants Anthropologie: Die Idee des Werks und die Bestimmung des Menschen," paper presented at the Central Division meeting of the American Philosophical Association, Pittsburgh, April 1997; Paul Guyer, *Kant and the Experience of Freedom: Essays on Aesthetics and Morality* (Cambridge: Cambridge University Press, 1993) and Birgit Recki, "Das Gute am Schönen: Über einen Grundgedanken in Kants Ästhetik," *Zeitschrift für Ästhetik und allgemeine Kunstwissenschaft* 37 (1994): 15–31. The Romantic emphasis on aesthetic intuition does not account for Kant's puritanical rejection of pleasure in favour of satisfaction in *Critique of Practical Reason*. Kant disdains personal outcomes as a reason for morality. The law is not a source of personal gratification. Kant thought secular law and traditional morality should have the same rational foundation.

65 Peter Gay, *The Science of Freedom: The Enlightenment: An Interpretation*, Vol II (New York: Alfred Knopf, 1969), 217.

66 Kant, *Judgment*, 321.

67 Kant, *Judgment*, 79 and 66.

68 Kant, *Pure Reason*, 637.

69 Kant, *Pure Reason*, 614.

70 Kant, *Practical Reason*, 66.

71 Kant, *Pure Reason*, 89.

72 See Immanuel Kant, *On the Old Saw: That May Be Right in Theory but it Won't Work in Practice*, trans. E.B. Ashton (Philadelphia: University of Pennsylvania Press, 1974), 55. Christian Garvé was an ethical philosopher and literary critic who goaded his friend, Immanuel Kant, into writing a "popular" explanation of the relation between action and the will. Garvé was the greatest translator and conveyor of British moral and political thought to Germany in the eighteenth century. Their collegial debate is worth a few moments to recover. Kant's "On the Old Saw" was published in 1793 in the *Berlinische Monatsschrift*, one of the major journals of the German Enlightenment. Garvé's position was that Kant's idealistic "niceties ... evaporate altogether when it comes to action" (53). Kant asked Garvé how the human law was to be determined in the age of science and accused him of paternalistic maxims that would lead to "the worst conceivable despotism" (59). The first and fundamental freedom is how the world is thought. Ideas precede events and until the way we explain the world changes, nothing in the world can ever change.

73 Kant, *Pure Reason*, 535.

74 Robert Bellah, Richard Madsen, William Sullivan, Ann Swidler, and Steven M. Tipton, *Habits of the Heart* (Los Angeles: University of California Press, 1985); George Lakoff and Mark Johnson, *Metaphors We Live By* (Chicago: University of Chicago Press, 1980); Dan P. McAdams, *The Stories We Live By* (New York: Guilford Press, 1997), and J.G.A. Pocock, *The Machiavellian Moment: Florentine Political Thought and the Atlantic Republican Tradition* (Princeton, NJ: Princeton University Press, 1975).

75 Kant, *Judgment*, 149n.

76 Kant, *Judgment*, 149.

77 Kant, *Judgment*, 295–96.

78 Kant, *Judgment*, 15.

79  Kant, *Judgment*, 288.
80  Kant, *Practical Reason*, 14.
81  Kant, *Pure Reason*, 50–51.
82  Kant, *Pure Reason*, 589.
83  Of the second edition, Kant wrote, "In this edition I have sought to make improvements which should help in removing, first, the misunderstanding in regard to the Aesthetic, especially concerning the concept of time" (*CPR*, 34). The aesthetic concept of time is, of course, history. From a Kantian perspective, the Hegelian study of history is the most conflicted and morally challenged area of modern aesthetic philosophy.
84  Kant, *Pure Reason*, 575.
85  Kant, *Judgment*, 23.
86  Kant, *Judgment*, 21.
87  Richard Popkin, ed. *The Columbia History of Western Philosophy* (New York: Columbia University Press, 1999), 521. The author of this section is Frederick Beiser.
88  Kant, *On the Old Saw*, 54.
89  Kant, *On the Old Saw*, 60.
90  Kant, *On the Old Saw*, 55.
91  Lewis White Beck, ed., "Introduction" to *Critique of Practical Reason and Other Writings in Moral Philosophy* (Chicago: University of Chicago Press, 1949). The phrase was canonized by Lewis White Beck in a Romantic sense he took from Ernst Cassirer. Our feelings are a moral compass which art teaches to point true north.
92  Immanuel Kant, "Perpetual Peace. A Philosophical Sketch," in Beck, ed., *Critique of Practical Reason and Other Writings in Moral Philosophy* (Chicago: University of Chicago Press, 1949), 327. The essay on "Perpetual Peace" was the former Secretary of State, Henry Kissinger's introduction to Kant. William Yandell Eliot used to drive his undergraduate honor students away by assigning them an independent Kant study in their first year at Harvard. Kissinger completed the assignment and returned to Eliot with a well documented argument for the unworkability of Kant's ethics in politics. The problem of ethical judgment among a race of devils never came up for Kissinger again. See Walter Isaacson, *Kissinger: A Biography* (New York: Simon & Schuster, 1992), 62–67.
93  Kant, *Pure Reason*, 384.
94  Immanuel Kant, *The Metaphysics of Morals* (1798), trans. Mary Gregor (Cambridge: Cambridge University Press, 1991) "Nothing in the world – indeed nothing even beyond the world – can possibly be conceived which could be called good without qualification except a good will" (9).
95  Kant, *Practical Reason*, 30.
96  Eckart Förster, *Kant's Final Synthesis* (Cambridge, MA: Harvard University Press, 2000), 168.
97  Kant, *Practical Reason*, 66.
98  Immanuel Kant, *Groundwork of the Metaphysics of Morals*, trans. Mary J. Gregor (Cambridge: Cambridge University Press, 1996) "It is impossible to think of anything at all in the world, or indeed even beyond it, that could be considered good without limitation except a good will" (49). "There is therefore, only a single categorical imperative and it is this: act only in accordance with that maxim through which you can at the same time will that it become a universal law" (73), and the kingdom of ends: "So act that you use humanity, whether in your own person or in the person of any other, always at the same time as an end, never merely as a means" (80). The *Groundwork* (1785) is often confused with *Metaphysics of Morals* (1798). It is a separate and earlier work. *Groundwork* lays the foundations for a concrete discussion of the metaphysics of the moral law. The objections of Garvé and Kissinger are addressed in *Metaphysics* (1798). It took Kant a long time to realize many people – particularly the "businesspeople" – prefer to act before they think.
99  Immanuel Kant, *Groundwork of the Metaphysics of Morals*, trans. Mary Gregor (Cambridge: Cambridge University Press, 1996), 76.
100 The *Lectures on Metaphysics* are students' notes from Kant's lectures on Baumgarten. The notes range from the mid-1770s to 1795 and two sets are anonymous. What we get there is a general agreement that metaphysics is a "psychological" dimension of human life and

concerns the unity of cognition. See *Lectures on Metaphysics*, trans and ed. Karl Ameriks and Steve Naragon (Cambridge: Cambridge University Press, 1997). "Metaphysics is thus the science of the first principles of the entirety of human cognition" (111). "Metaphysics distinguishes itself from physics and all doctrine of experience through this, that it is a science of pure reason" (43). "Metaphysics is the system of pure cognitions of reason through concepts" (418). The last definition from the Vigilantius notes of 1794–5 mentions that Aristotle founded metaphysics but did not separate them from physics. He "tacked them on" just beyond physics without really knowing how they operate. These student notes, read in conjunction with the *Groundwork*, indicate Kant believed the foundations of the motivational drives at work in human life are not directly available to experience. Kant's fundamental contention does not seem without relevance in questions of ideology, nationalism, and political idealism.

101 Kant, *Judgment*, 21.
102 Kant, *Groundwork*, 78.
103 Kant, *Judgment*, 144.
104 Immanuel Kant, "The Conflict of the Faculties," in *Kant: Religion and Natural Theology*, trans. and ed. Allen W. Wood and George Di Giovanni (Cambridge: Cambridge University Press, 1996), 257–58, 281n, and 261.

## CHAPTER TWO: HEGEL'S PREDICAMENT

1 Max Horkheimer and Theodor Adorno, *Dialectic of Enlightenment*, trans. John Cumming (New York: Seabury, 1972).
2 G.W.F. Hegel, *Faith and Knowledge*, trans. by Walter Cerf (Albany: SUNY Press, 1977), 190. Martin Luther had used the phrase, "God's death," to refute the Nestorian heresy that only the physical man, Jesus, was crucified and God did not suffer. "God's martyrdom, God's blood, and God's death" proved to Luther that Nestorius was a "crude, unlearned man" who "lacked the intelligence to express his thought properly.... Thus Nestorius's error was not that he believed Christ to be a pure man, or that he made two persons of him.... Nestorius will not admit a *communicatio idiomatum* between the two natures of Christ." Martin Luther, "On the Councils and the Church," *Luther's Works*, American edition, Vol. 41, ed. Eric W. Gritsch (Philadelphia: Fortress, 1966), 102–103. I am indebted to Dr. Barry Rasmussen for pointing out the background in Lutheran theology of Hegel's word, "God is dead."
3 G.W.F. Hegel, *Faith and Knowledge*, trans. Walter Cerf (Albany: SUNY Press, 1977), 190.
4 Hegel, *Faith and Knowledge*, 190. By which Hegel means Kant.
5 Hegel, *Faith and Knowledge*, 77.
6 Hegel, *The Philosophy of History*, 50.
7 Hegel, *The Philosophy of History*, 51.
8 G.W.F. Hegel, *Lectures on the Philosophy of Religion*, ed. P. Hodgson (Berkeley: University of California Press, 1984), III: 323.
9 C.K. Ogden and I.A. Richards, *The Meaning of Meaning* (London: Routledge, 1985), 29n and 31.
10 Peter A.M. Seuren, *Western Linguistics: An Historical Introduction* (Malden, MA: Blackwell, 1998), 467.
11 G.E. Moore, *Principia Ethica*, ed. Thomas Baldwin (Cambridge: Cambridge University Press, 1993), 2nd ed., 170.
12 Moore, *Principia Ethica*, 85.
13 Moore, *Principia Ethica*, Moore believed the highest ideals are "goods or ends in themselves" (233). They bring about "certain states of consciousness" in us which are fundamental for the moral life. The experiences which produce the ideal states of consciousness most conducive to the moral life "may be roughly described as the pleasure of human intercourse and the enjoyment of beautiful objects (237).... Personal affection and aesthetic enjoyments include *all* the greatest, and *by far* the greatest, goods we can imagine," Moore concludes (238). These sentiments were the Bible of the Bloomsbury Group of whom Lytton Strachey, Leonard Woolf, and J.M. Keynes were prominent members.

Strachey thought *Principia Ethica* had "wrecked and shattered all writers on Ethics from Aristotle and Christ to Herbert Spencer and Bradley" (Introduction, xi). Keynes called Moore's discussion of "The Ideal" (Chapter Six), "a religion – the opening of a new heaven on earth." Writing in 1938, Keynes could still say, "The New Testament is a handbook for politicians compared with the unworldliness of Moore's chapter on 'The Ideal.' I know no equal to it in literature since Plato. And it is better than Plato because it is quite free from *fancy*" (Introduction, xxxiii). Thomas Baldwin calls Moore, "the definitive starting point for twentieth-century ethical theory" (Frontispiece).

14 Margaret Urban Walker, "Naturalizing, Normativity, and Using What 'We' Know in Ethics," in Richard Campbell and Bruce Hunter, ed., *Moral Epistemology Naturalized, Canadian Journal of Philosophy*, Supplementary vol. 26 (Calgary: University of Calgary Press, 2000), 101.
15 Paul de Man, "Sign and Symbol in Hegel's *Aesthetics*," in *Critical Inquiry* 8 (Summer 1982): 763.
16 Georg Wilhelm Friedrich Hegel, *Philosophy of History*, trans. J. Sibree (Buffalo: Prometheus, 1991), 15.
17 Hegel, *Philosophy of History*, 14 and 8.
18 Hegel, *Philosophy of History*, 33.
19 Stephen Priest, ed. "Introduction," *Hegel's Critique of Kant* (Oxford: Clarendon Press, 1987), 7.
20 Laurence Bonjour, *Epistemology: Classic Problems and Contemporary Responses* (New York: Rowman & Littlefield, 2002), 51n13 and 237.
21 William Dray, *Philosophy of History*, 2nd ed. (Englewood Cliffs, NJ: Prentice-Hall, 1993), 120.
22 Charles Taylor, *Human Agency and Language* (Cambridge: Cambridge University Press, 1985), 223, 88, and 77.
23 Charles Taylor, *Sources of the Self: The Making of the Modern Identity* (Cambridge, MA: Harvard University Press, 1989), 205–7.
24 Glenn Alexander Magee, *Hegel and the Hermetic Tradition* (Ithaca, NY: Cornell University Press, 2001), 61–62.
25 Hegel, *The Philosophy of History*, 1.
26 Hegel, *The Philosophy of History*, 7.
27 Hegel, *The Philosophy of History*, 1.
28 Hegel, *The Philosophy of History*, 1.
29 Georg Ephraim Lessing, *Laocöon*, trans. Robert Phillimore (London: George Routledge and Sons, 1874), 131–32 and 322.
30 G.W.F. Hegel, cited in Jean-Michel Rey, "Commentary," in *Nietzsche's New Seas: Explorations in Philosophy Aesthetics and Politics*, ed. Michael Allen Gillespie and Tracy B. Strong (Chicago: University of Chicago Press, 1988), 75–96. From Hegel's *Logic* I: 119–20. The language of state-building is inherently logical to Hegel. See also G.W.F. Hegel, *The Philosophy of History*: "Speech is the act of theoretic intelligence in a special sense; it is its *external* manifestation.... The rapid growth of language, and the progress and dispersion of Nations, assume importance and interest for concrete Reason, only when they have come in contact with States, or begin to form political constitutions themselves.... This development implies a gradation – a series of increasingly adequate expressions or manifestations of Freedom (63).... But it is the State which first presents subject-matter that is not only *adapted* to the prose of History, but involves the production of such history in the very progress of its own being.... A State ... thus produces a record as well as an interest concerned with intelligent, definite – and, in their results – lasting transactions and occurrences (61).... The logical ... by this very process of transcending its earlier stages, gains an affirmative, and, in fact, a richer and more concrete shape" (63).
31 Cited in Paul Gorner, *Twentieth-Century German Philosophy* (Oxford: Oxford University Press, 2000), 9.
32 Cited in Magee, *Hegel and the Hermetic Tradition*, 12.
33 Magee, *Hegel and the Hermetic Tradition*, 84–85 and 93. Hegel scholars call the fragment "*eine Ethik*" because of the first words of the fragment. Otto Pöggeler calls this fragment "The Earliest System-Program of German Idealism," in *Hegel-Studien* 4 (1969): 17–32. It is "Hegel's first attempt to reconcile philosophy and religion.... Philosophy for Hegel will

have as its task the recovery and perfection of these pre-reflective thought forms granted to mankind from time immemorial.... This wisdom belongs not to the consciousness of a people, but to its *unconscious*" (85). Pöggeler traces the fragment to Hegel's Berne period, in late 1796 or early 1797.

34  G.W.F. Hegel, *The Phenomenology of Mind*, trans. J.B. Baille (New York: Harper and Row, 1931), 660–61 & 670. Hegel goes on to stipulate: "When any one says he acts towards others from a law and conscience of his own, he is saying, in point of fact, that he is abusing and wronging them" (670).

35  Hegel, *The Philosophy of History*, 27.

36  Hegel, *The Philosophy of History*, 33.

37  Hegel, *The Philosophy of History*, 6.

38  Cf. Hegel, *The Philosophy of History*: "The French, on the other hand, display great genius in reanimating bygone times, and in bringing the past to bear upon the present condition of things" (7).

39  Hegel, *The Philosophy of History*, 7.

40  Hegel, *The Philosophy of History*, 9.

41  Seuren, *Western Linguistics*, 466. "Formalism" is the "scandal" Chomsky exposes in the language Newton used to "explain" gravity. From a linguist's point of view, "Newton demonstrated that the world is not a machine. Rather, it has occult forces after all. Contact mechanics simply does not work for terrestrial and planetary motion. Some mystical concept of 'action at a distance' is required. That was the great scandal of Newtonian physics.... [In physics] Newton exorcised the machine, leaving the ghost intact" (Noam Chomsky, *Powers and Prospects: Reflections on Human Nature and the Social Order* [Boston: South End Press, 1996], 5 and 42). Karl Popper blamed Nazism on formalist fallacies in the language of modern social studies. See Karl R. Popper, *The Poverty of Historicism* (London: Routledge & Kegan Paul, 1957). Physical scientists "regard *words* merely as *useful instruments of description*," Popper advised. Oddly, social scientists do not. The difference between the languages of science and history is that "[w]hile the methods of the natural sciences are fundamentally nominalistic, social science must adopt a methodological essentialism," 30.

42  Surprisingly to me, many current readers do not recognize the phrase:
Take up the White Man's burden –
Send forth the best ye breed –
Go bind your sons to exile
To serve your captives' need.
To wait in heavy harness
On fluttered folk and wild –
Your new-caught, sullen peoples,
Half devil and half child.
*Rudyard Kipling: Selected Verse*, ed. James Cochrane (New York: Penguin, 1977), 128.

43  G.W.F. Hegel, *The Phenomenology of Mind*, trans. by J.B. Baillie (1910), 808.

44  Schlomo Barer, *Doctors of Revolution* (New York: Thames and Hudson, 2000). "Kant was our Robespierre. Then came Fichte with his 'transcendental ego,' the Napoleon of philosophy.... The earth trembled ... until Hegel, the Orleans of philosophy, finally founded, or rather systematized, an eclectic form of government with room for the Jacobins, the Bonapartists, aristocratic peers and minions of his own as well" (cited, 320). Heine coined the famous phrase, "German philosophy has been nothing but the dream of the French Revolution" (320).

45  Paul de Man, *Allegories of Reading: Figural Language in Rousseau, Nietzsche, Rilke, and Proust* (New Haven, CT: Yale University Press, 1979): "This is precisely how Nietzsche also defines the rhetorical figure, the paradigm of all language. In the 'Course on Rhetoric,' metonymy is characterized as what rhetoricians also call metalepsis, 'the exchange or substitution of cause and effect'" (108).

46  Hegel, *The Philosophy of History*, 66.

47  Cf. Hegel, *The Philosophy of History*: "That intellectual position ... presents a vast field for ingenious questions, erudite views, and striking comparisons; for profound seeming

reflections and declamations, which may be rendered so much the more brilliant in proportion as the subject they refer to is indefinite, and are susceptible of new and varied forms in inverse proportion to the importance of the results that can be gained from them and the certainty and rationality of the issues" (66).

48  Hegel, *The Philosophy of History*, 66.
49  Hegel, *The Philosophy of History*, 66.
50  Hegel, *The Philosophy of History*, 66.
51  Hegel, *Phenomenology of Mind*, 547.
52  Hegel, *Phenomenology of Mind*, 547–48.
53  Hegel, *Phenomenology of Mind*, 5.
54  Hegel, *Phenomenology of Mind*, 5.
55  Hegel, *Faith and Knowledge*, 560 & 190.
56  Hegel, *Philosophy of History*, 60.
57  Hegel, *Philosophy of History*, 60.
58  Cf. Hegel, *Philosophy of History*: "It is, moreover, a fact, that with advancing social and political civilization, this systematic completeness of intelligence suffers attrition, and language thereupon becomes poorer and ruder; a singular phenomenon – that the progress towards a more highly intellectual condition, while expanding and cultivating rationality, should disregard that intelligent amplitude and expressiveness – should find it an obstruction and contrive to do without it.... The rapid growth of language, and the progress and dispersion of Nations, assume importance and interest for concrete Reason, only when they have come in contact with States, or begin to form political constitutions themselves" (62–63).
59  See Richard Bodéüs, "Aristotle," in Richard H. Popkin, ed., *The Columbia History of Western Philosophy* (New York: Columbia University Press, 1999), 64.
60  Priest, ed., "Introduction," 31.
61  Priest, "Introduction," 3.
62  Barer, *Doctors of Revolution*, 539.
63  Leonard Krieger, *Ranke: The Meaning of History* (Chicago: University of Chicago Press, 1977), 76 and 135.
64  Krieger, *Ranke*, 132.
65  Krieger, *Ranke*, 81.
66  Krieger, *Ranke*, 292.
67  Krieger, *Ranke*, 293.
68  Krieger, *Ranke*, quoted 76.
69  Krieger, *Ranke*, 77.
70  Krieger, *Ranke*, quoted 142. Krieger quotes Ranke from Leopold von Ranke, *Aus Werk und Nachlass*, Vol. 4: *Vorlesungseinleitung*, ed. Volker Dotterweich and Walther Peter Fuchs (Munich, 1964–75), 133–35, 177.
71  Krieger, *Ranke*, 69.
72  David K. Naugle, *Worldview: The History of a Concept* (Grand Rapids: Eerdmans, 2002), 82. For Gasset, see, *Concord and Liberty*, trans. Helene Weyl (New York: Norton, 1946), 131.
73  Robert Chia and Ian King, "The Language of Organization Theory," in *The Language of Organization*, ed. by Robert Westwood and Stephen Linstead (London: Sage, 2001), 311 and 314. The Cooper reference is from Robin Cooper, "Modernism, postmodernism and organizational analysis 3: The contribution of Jacques Derrida," *Organizational Studies* 10, no. 4 (1989): 479–502.
74  Cited in Ramon J. Betanzos, "Wilhelm Dilthey: An Introduction," in *Introduction to the Human Sciences: An Attempt to Lay a Foundation for the Study of Society and History*, by Wilhelm Dilthey, trans. Ramon J. Betanzos (Detroit: Wayne State University Press, 1988), 17. Betanzos cites Ortega y Gasset (1946): "As Dilthey has no true religious belief, study of religion turns for him into study of history" (p. 143).
75  Quoted in Otto Pöggeler, *Martin Heidegger's Path of Thinking*, trans. Daniel Magurshak and Sigmund Barber (Atlantic Highlands, NJ: Humanities Press International, 1987), 23.
76  Pöggeler, *Martin Heidegger's Path*, 33.
77  Betanzos, "Wilhelm Dilthey: An Introduction," 61n.

78 Wilhelm Dilthey, *Dilthey's Philosophy of Existence: Introduction to Weltanschauungslehre*, trans. with Intro. by William Kluback and Martin Weinbaum (London: Vision Press, 1957), 23 and 17.
79 Dilthey, *Philosophy of Existence*, 67.
80 Dilthey, *Philosophy of Existence*, 104, 126, 138, 127, and 67.
81 Rudolf Makkreel, *Dilthey: Philosopher of the Human Studies* (Princeton, NJ: Princeton University Press, 1975), ix.
82 Makkreel, *Dilthey*, 36.
83 Makkreel, *Dilthey*, 38.
84 Makkreel, *Dilthey*, 54.
85 Dilthey, *Philosophy of Existence*, 46.
86 Dilthey, *Philosophy of Existence*, 111 and 150. See also Wilhelm Dilthey, *Pattern and Meaning in History*, H.P. Rickman, ed. (New York: Harper & Row, 1961): "I have shown how significant the objective mind is for the possibility of knowledge in the human studies. By this I mean the manifold forms in which what individuals hold in common have objectified themselves in the world of the senses (120).... The placing of the individual expressions of life into a common context is facilitated by the articulated order in the objective mind.... In this sphere the relation between expressions of life and mental content is fixed everywhere by a common order" (121).
87 Cited in Russell Jacoby, "A New Intellectual History?" *American Historical Review* 97 (1992): 407–8. The quotation is from Carlo Antoni, *From History to Sociology: The Transition in German Historical Thinking*, trans. Hayden V. White (Detroit, MI, 1959), 38.
88 Karl Marx, *The Poverty of Philosophy* (New York: International Publishers, 1903), 112 and 189–90.
89 Quentin Skinner's *Reason and Rhetoric in the Philosophy of Thomas Hobbes* (1996) "may be said to exemplify the approach I have used here." Skinner explains, "The essence of his method consists in trying to place texts within such contexts as enable us in turn to identify what their authors were *doing* in writing them" (7). Skinner calls this approach "contextualism ... the study of the range of things that speakers are capable of doing in (and by) their use of words and sentences." Skinner takes "seriously the implications of Wittgenstein's motto, 'Words are also deeds'" (Ludwig Wittgenstein, *Philosophical Investigations*. trans. G.E.M. Ascombe (Oxford: Oxford UP, 1958) ¶ 546, p. 146e). The "deed" is the behavioural world which the narrative text implies. All words imply worlds. The historical fact that texts are contexts is fundamental to the way skeptics do ethics. Human beings communicate the foundations of their politics and culture through apparently 'innocent' and 'neutral' texts. Skinner learned the approach from John Pocock who took it from Whitehead and the Vienna Circle. They, in turn, had found it in Kant.
90 Dilthey, *Meaning in History*, 73.
91 Cited in Michael Ermarth, *Wilhelm Dilthey: The Critique of Historical Reason* (Chicago: University of Chicago Press, 1978), 15.
92 Ermarth, *Wilhelm Dilthey*, 328.
93 Ermarth, *Wilhelm Dilthey*, 328. Dilthey source is *GS* V: 407, 413.
94 Michael Dummett, "Realism," in *Truth and Other Enigmas* (Cambridge, MA: Harvard University Press, 1978), 146.

## CHAPTER THREE: THE LINGUISTIC TURN

1 Gregory Bateson, *Steps to an Ecology of Mind* (New York: Ballantine, 1972), 275.
2 The phrase "linguistic turn" was popularized by Richard Rorty in *The Linguistic Turn* (Chicago: University of Chicago Press, 1967). It was coined in print by Gustav Bergmann, "Logical Positivism, Language, and the Reconstruction of Metaphysics" *Rivista Critica di Storia della Filosofia* 8 (1953): 453–81. Bergmann incorporated the article into his book, *Logic and Reality* (Madison: University of Wisconsin Press, 1964). It was reprinted "in a truncated form" in Rorty, ed. *The Linguistic Turn*, 63–71.
3 Richard Rorty, *Philosophy and the Mirror of Nature* (Princeton, NJ: Princeton University Press, 1979) "The only point on which I would insist is that philosophers' moral concern

should be with continuing the conversation of the West, rather than with insisting upon a place for the traditional problems of modern philosophy within that conversation" (12).

4  "Talk of the will of God or of the rights of man, like talk of the honour of the family or of the fatherland in danger are [sic] not suitable targets for philosophical analysis and criticism. It is fruitless to look behind them" (*Philosophy and the Mirror of Nature*, 394).

5  Habermas writes, "I do not believe that we, as Europeans, can seriously understand concepts like morality and ethical life, person and individuality, or freedom and emancipation without appropriating the substance of the Judeo-Christian understanding of history.... Without the transmission through socialization and the transformation through philosophy of *any one* of the great world religions, this semantic potential could one day become inaccessible" (*Postmetaphysical Thinking*, 15–17). Late modern "postmetaphysical thinking ... frees us from the dilemma of having to choose between Kant and Hegel," Habermas concludes in *Postmetaphysical Thinking* (1992), 12. His work has insisted on variations of this theme going back to *Theory of Communicative Action* (1976). In the modern world, "The ego presents itself to itself as a practical ego in the performance of communicative actions; and in communicative action the participants must reciprocally suppose that the distinguishing-one-self-from-others is recognized by those others. Thus the basis for the assertion of one's own identity is not really self-identification, but intersubjectively recognized self-identification" (107). He takes the "performative attitude" of playing a role from George Herbert Meade. Habermas is a Marxist in the U.S. and a pragmatist in Europe.

6  Richard Rorty, *Philosophy and Social Hope* (New York: Penguin, 1999), 11.
7  Rorty, *Philosophy and the Mirror of Nature*, 358–59.
8  Rorty, *Philosophy and the Mirror of Nature*, 359.
9  Rorty, *Philosophy and the Mirror of Nature*, 358–59.
10 Hans-Georg Gadamer, *Truth and Method* (New York: Seabury, 1975), 433.
11 Brian D. Ingraffia, *Postmodern Theory and Biblical Theology* (Cambridge: Cambridge University Press, 1995), 29.
12 Friedrich Nietzsche, *The Gay Science*, trans. Walter Kaufmann (New York: Random House, 1974), 60.
13 Friedrich Nietzsche, *Twilight of the Idols*, "The Improvers' of Mankind," 5, in *The Portable Nietzsche*, Walter Kaufmann, ed. (New York: Penguin, 1976).
14 Søren Kierkegaard in *The Living Thoughts of Kierkegaard*, collected and edited by W.H. Auden (Bloomington: Indiana University Press, 1966), 154.
15 Karl Jaspers, *Nietzsche: An Introduction to the Understanding of his Philosophical Activity*, trans. Charles F. Wallraff and Frederick J. Schmitz (Chicago: Henry Regnery Co., 1965), 244–45 and 183.
16 Cited in Jaspers, *Nietzsche*, 243.
17 Cited in Michael Davis, *The Autobiography of Philosophy* (Lanham, MD: Rowan & Littlefield, 1999), 31. Davis takes the reference from Nietzsche, *Werke in drei Banden*, ed. Karl Schlechta. V. II, p. 571.
18 Davis, *Autobiography*, 31.
19 Nietzsche, *Gay Science*, 183.
20 Quoted in Paul de Man, *Allegories of Reading*, 114.
21 The last entry in Paul de Man's notes for his seminar on modern rhetoric reads: "la fonction référentielle est un piège, mais inevitable." Andrzej Warminski, "Introduction," to *Aesthetic Ideology*, ed. Andrzej Warminski. Theory and History of Literature, V. 65 (Minneapolis: University of Minnesota Press, 1996), 1. For the alternative perspective, see Christopher Norris, *The Truth about Postmodernism* (Cambridge: Blackwell, 1993), 128.
22 Richard Palmer, *Hermeneutics* (Evanston, IL: Northwestern University Press, 1969), 49 and 117.
23 Palmer, *Hermeneutics*, 225.
24 The best discussions of Nietzsche's language I discovered were Brian Leiter, "The Paradox of Fatalism and Self-Creation in Nietzsche," in *Willing and Nothingness*, Christopher Janaway, ed. (Oxford: Clarendon Press, 1998), and David Couzens Hoy, "Nietzsche, Hume and the Genealogical Method," in *Nietzsche, Genealogy, Morality: Essays on Nietzsche's On the*

*Genealogy of Morals*, ed. Richard Schact (Berkeley: University of California Press, 1994), 251–68.
25 Cited in Fredric Jameson, *The Prison-House of Language* (Princeton, NJ: Princeton University Press, 1972), 13.
26 Ferdinand de Saussure, *Course in General Linguistics*, ed. Charles Bally and Albert Sechehaye, in collaboration with Albert Reidlinger; trans. Wade Baskin (New York: Philosophical Library, 1959), 95 and 113.
27 Saussure, *Course*, 79.
28 Saussure, *Course*, 80–81.
29 Saussure, *Course*, 85.
30 John Carlos Rowe, "Structure," in *Critical Terms for Literary Study*, ed. Frank Lentricchia and Thomas McLaughlin (Chicago: University of Chicago Press, 1995), 26.
31 Jonathan Culler, *Saussure* (London: Harvester Press, 1976), 114 and 117.
32 David Holdcroft, *Saussure: Signs, System, and Arbitrariness* (Cambridge: Cambridge University Press, 1991), 5.
33 Vincent Leitch, *Cultural Criticism, Literary Theory, Poststructuralism* (New York: Columbia University Press, 1992), 36.
34 I have followed Robert de Beaugrande's selection of fundamental contributors to modern linguistic theory in his book, *Linguistic Theory: The Discourse of Fundamental Works* (New York: Longman, 1991).
35 Saussure, *Course*, 116.
36 Saussure, *Course*, 118.
37 Saussure, *Course*, 120.
38 Saussure, *Course*, 90.
39 Jacques Derrida, "*Différance*," in *A Derrida Reader*, ed. Peggy Kamuf (New York: Columbia University Press, 1991), 69 and 62.
40 Derrida, "*Différance*," 68.
41 Derrida, "*Différance*," 68.
42 Derrida, "*Différance*," 68.
43 Terence Hawkes, *Structuralism and Semiotics* (Berkeley: University of California Press, 1977), 26.
44 Hawkes, *Structuralism*, 20.
45 The phrase is from Gordon S. Wood, "Conspiracy and the Paranoid Style: Causality and Deceit in the Eighteenth Century," in *Knowledge and Postmodernism in Historical Perspective*, Joyce Appleby et al. (eds.) (New York: Routledge, 1996), 98. The inclusion of Gordon Wood's famous article on "Conspiracy and the Paranoid Style" is the outstanding feature of the collection. Appleby et al. remind us through Wood that when cause and effect were relativized, moral rhetoric became implausible. "The paranoid style" was the way rhetoric appeared to Enlightenment. After Enlightenment, what Wood has famously called "a mode of causal attribution based on particular assumptions about the nature of social reality and the necessity of moral responsibility in human affairs" (95) sounds "paranoid" to skeptical realists.
46 Saussure, *Course*, 85.
47 Ogden and Richards, *The Meaning of Meaning*, 4.
48 Saussure, *Course*, 85.
49 Jeffrey Alexander, "General Theory in the Postpositivist Mode: The 'Epistemological Dilemma' and the Search for Present Reason," in *Postmodernism and Social Theory*, ed. Steven Seidman and David G. Wagner (Cambridge, MA: Harvard University Press, 1992), 316.
50 Pierre Bourdieu, *Language and Symbolic Power*, ed. John B. Thompson (Cambridge, MA: Harvard University Press, 1991), 12.
51 Jacques Lacan, *The Four Fundamental Concepts of Psycho-analysis*, trans. Alan Sheridan (London: Penguin, 1979): "The unconscious is constituted by the effects of speech on the subject, it is the dimension in which the subject is determined in the development of the effects of speech, consequently the unconscious is structured like a language" (149).

52  Robert Maxwell Young, *White Mythologies: Writing History and the West* (London: Routledge, 1990), 117 and 160–62.
53  Young, *White Mythologies*, 117 and 160–62.
54  Ludwig Wittgenstein, *Philosophical Investigations*, trans. G.E.M. Anscombe (Oxford: Blackwell, 1963) "I shall also call the whole, consisting of language and the actions into which it is woven, the 'language-game'" (5e). Part I was written in 1945. Part II was written in 1947–49. Wittgenstein died in 1951.
55  Wittgenstein, *Philosophical Investigations*, ¶19, and Ludwig Wittgenstein, *Lectures and Conversations on Aesthetics, Psychology, and Religious Belief* (Berkeley: University of California Press, 1966), 8.
56  Wittgenstein, *Philosophical Investigations*, ¶2e.
57  Hilary Putnam, *Words and Life*, ed. James Conant (Cambridge, MA: Harvard University Press, 1994), 269.
58  Ludwig Wittgenstein, *Tractatus Logico-Philosophicus*, in *The Wittgenstein Reader*, ed. Anthony Kenny (London: Blackwell, 1994) ¶6.54, p. 31.
59  Wittgenstein, *Investigations*, ¶32, p. 15e.
60  Wittgenstein, *Investigations*, ¶33, p. 16 e.
61  Immanuel Kant, *Lectures on Metaphysics*, trans. and ed. Karl Ameriks and Steve Naragon (Cambridge: Cambridge University Press, 1997), 58.
62  Wittgenstein, *Investigations*, ¶546, p. 146e.
63  Ludwig Wittgenstein, "A Lecture on Ethics," *The Philosophical Review* 74 (1965): 3–12, quoted in Richard J. Bernstein *Praxis and Action: Contemporary Philosophies of Human Activity* (Philadelphia: University of Pennsylvania Press, 1971), 158.
64  James C. Edwards, *Ethics without Philosophy: Wittgenstein and the Moral Life* (Gainesville: University Presses of Florida, c. 1974) Wittgenstein believed, "A normal human being cannot be a university teacher and also an honest person" (218).
65  Kant, *Judgment*, 144.
66  *The Confessions of St. Augustine*, trans. E.B. Pusey (London: J.M. Dent, 1907), XI/20.
67  Wittgenstein, *Philosophical Investigations*, ¶89.
68  Wittgenstein, *Philosophical Investigations*, ¶90.
69  Wittgenstein, *Philosophical Investigations*, ¶104.
70  Wittgenstein, *Philosophical Investigations*, II/xi, p. 193.
71  Wittgenstein, *Philosophical Investigations*, II/xi, p. 193.
72  Wittgenstein, *Philosophical Investigations*, II/v, p. 180.
73  Augustine of Hippo, *The Confessions*, trans. Maria Boulding (New York: Random House, 1998) X/15, p. 264.
74  Wittgenstein, *Philosophical Investigations*, II/xi, p. 194.
75  Wittgenstein, *Philosophical Investigations*, II/xi, p. 195.
76  Wittgenstein, *Philosophical Investigations*, II/xi, p. 196.

## CHAPTER FOUR: THE MODERN PREDICAMENT

1  Jorge Luis Borges, *Ficciones* (New York: Grove Press, 1956), 71.
2  Herbert Butterfield, *The Whig Interpretation of History* (New York: Norton, 1931), 13.
3  Butterfield, *Whig Interpretation*, 96.
4  Butterfield, *Whig Interpretation*, 75 and 28.
5  Butterfield, *Whig Interpretation*, 46.
6  Michael Bentley, "Herbert Butterfield and the Ethics of Historiography," *History and Theory* 44, no. 1 (Feb. 2005): 55; C.T. McIntire, *Herbert Butterfield: Historian as Dissenter* (New Haven, CT: Yale University Press, 2004).
7  Philip Wiener, "Herbert Butterfield," in *Journal of the History of Ideas* 41, no. 1 (1980): 157–58. The Butterfield quotation is from Herbert Butterfield, *Writings on Christianity and History*, ed. C.T. McIntire (New York: Oxford University Press, 1979), 22.
8  Louis Halle, "The Historian as Philosopher," in *Herbert Butterfield: The Ethics of History and Politics*, ed. Kenneth W. Thompson (Washington: University Press of America, 1980), 24.
9  Herbert Butterfield, "God in History," in *God, History, and Historians: An Anthology of*

*Modern Christian Views of History*, ed. C.T. McIntyre (New York: Oxford University Press, 1977), 193.
10 Carl Becker, *The Heavenly City of the Eighteenth Century Philosophers* (New Haven, CT: Yale University Press, 1960), 73–74.
11 Becker, *The Heavenly City*, 71 and 73.
12 Becker, *The Heavenly City*, 82–83.
13 Becker, *The Heavenly City*, 88 and 86. In *Eloise*, Rousseau advised, "We should distinguish between the variety in human nature and that which is essential to it" (87).
14 Becker, *The Heavenly City*, 87.
15 Becker, *The Heavenly City*, 88.
16 Becker, *The Heavenly City*, 31 and 161.
17 Burleigh Taylor Wilkins, *Carl Becker* (Cambridge, MA: MIT Press, 1961), 207.
18 Wilkins, *Carl Becker*, "If what Becker said about facts and evidence and Mr. Everyman means anything, it means not only that the historian ultimately must cater to Mr. Everyman or perish – this is an existential necessity – but that because he is part of the same 'climate of opinion' as Mr. Everyman he could do nothing else – this is a logical necessity" (207).
19 Carl Becker, *Everyman His Own Historian: Essays on History and Politics* (New York: F.S. Crofts, 1935), 252.
20 See Ian Hacking, *Why Does Language Matter*, "We have displaced mental discourse by public discourse," he complains, "and ideas have become unintelligible" (52).
21 Maurice Mandelbaum, *The Problem of Historical Knowledge: An Answer to Relativism* (New York: Liveright, 1938), 17–18 and 19.
22 Mandelbaum, *Historical Knowledge*, 1.
23 Mandelbaum, *Historical Knowledge*, 119.
24 Mandelbaum, *Historical Knowledge*, 9.
25 Mandelbaum, *Historical Knowledge*, 6.
26 Mandelbaum, *Historical Knowledge*, 5.
27 Mandelbaum, *Historical Knowledge*, 184–85. "It seems clear when we examine actual historical works that they all presuppose a correspondence theory of truth, no matter how relativistic the theories of the historians themselves may be" (p. 185).
28 Mandelbaum, *Historical Knowledge*, 88 "We hold that the order to be found in nature and history as they are known to us may really characterize the events of the world independently of the mind's activity" (p. 204).
29 Mandelbaum, *Historical Knowledge*, 89.
30 Mandelbaum, *Historical Knowledge*, 203.
31 Maurice Mandelbaum, *The Phenomenology of Moral Experience* (Glencoe, IL: The Free Press, 1955), 13.
32 Carl Hempel, "The Function of General Laws in History," *Journal of Philosophy* 39, no. 2 (1942): 35–48. Reprinted in *Theories of History*, ed. Patrick Gardiner (New York: Free Press of Glencoe, 1959), 344–56. Hempel's covering law was an important debate. Louis Mink contended that Hempel's covering-law model was so important that "It could be said without exaggeration that until about 1965 the critical philosophy of history *was* the controversy over the covering-law model." See Louis O. Mink, "The Divergence of History and Sociology in Recent Philosophy of History," in *Historical Understanding*, ed. Brian Fay, Eugene O. Golob, and Richard T. Vann (Ithaca, NY: Cornell University Press, 1987), 169. Karl Popper adapted Hempel's covering law as his "hypothetico-deductive device" in *The Logic of Scientific Discovery* (1959). Krieger, Mink, Donagan, and Dray read Hempel's "covering law" as an attempt to "prove" that history was a science. They constructed the narrowest possible reading of Hempel and then rejected it. See Alan Donagan, "Explanation in History," reprinted in *Theories of History*, ed. Patrick Gardiner (New York: Free Press of Glencoe, 1959), 430, and Richard T. Vann, "Turning Linguistic: History and Theory and *History and Theory*, 1960–1975," in *A New Philosophy of History*, ed. Frank Ankersmit and Hans Kellner (Chicago: University of Chicago Press, 1995), 132–56.
33 Hempel, "Law," 37n and 46n.
34 Hume, *Principles of Morals*, 116 and 112.
35 Hume, *Principles of Morals*, 73–76 and 105.

36 Hempel, "Law," 37n.
37 If Hempel had invested his time in modern philosophy of history and theories of culture, he would have found ample documentation to support his theoretical criticism of Mandelbaum. Hempel knew Hume through the major treatise on *Human Understanding*. No evidence exists that he knew the lesser treatise on *Morals*. He was unaware of Hume's casual answer to "the superficial paradox of the skeptics." Hempel knew Hegel's "Logic" as presented in his *Encyclopedia* (1817). The "Encyclopedia Logic" is a shorter version of a two-volume work intended to function as part of an "outline" of the larger work. Hempel was not familiar with *Phenomenology* or *Philosophy of History*, so he would not have suspected the nonchalant link with language. Dilthey was his historical Mandelbaum, if he had known him. Hempel's theoretical criticisms are impressive given his inattention to the history of the debate.
38 Hempel, "Law," 46n.
39 Hempel, "Law," 46n.
40 Hempel, "Law," 48.
41 Hempel, "Law," 38.
42 Hempel, "Law," 38.
43 Hempel, "Law," 42.
44 Hempel, "Law," 41.
45 Hempel, "Law," 36.
46 Hempel, "Law," 36.
47 Hempel, "Law," 37.
48 William H. Dray, *Philosophy of History* (Englewood Cliffs, NJ: Prentice-Hall, 1993), 10–11. See p. 11, note 5 for an extensive footnote on the Hempel-Dray debate. Dray's original attack on Hempel is in William Dray, *Laws and Explanations in History* (London: Oxford University Press, 1957), 123–26.
49 Carl G. Hempel, "Explanation in Science and in History," in *Explanation*, ed. David-Hillel Ruben (Oxford: Oxford University Press, 1993), 41. First published in R.B. Colodny, ed. *Frontiers of Science and Philosophy* (Pittsburgh: University of Pittsburgh Press, 1962), 7–33.
50 Hempel, "Explanation," 35.
51 Hempel, "Explanation," 35.
52 Hempel, "Explanation," 36.
53 Louis O. Mink, "The Autonomy of Historical Understanding" in *Historical Understanding*, ed. Brian Fay et al., 64.
54 Mink, "The Autonomy of Historical Understanding," 63. The Krieger citation is from Leonard Krieger, "Comments on Historical Explanation," *Philosophy and History*, ed. Sidney Hook (New York: New York University Press, 1963), 136.
55 Mink, "The Autonomy of Historical Understanding," 63.
56 Leonard Krieger, *Time's Reasons* (Chicago: University of Chicago Press, 1989), 140.
57 Krieger, *Time's Reasons*, 141.
58 Krieger, *Ideas and Events*, 118. "Because he saw in their possession of a common time the basis of meaningful relations among individuals, he came to see in the succession of these relations a meaning not only within but through history" (122–23).
59 Krieger, *Ideas and Events*, 119.
60 Krieger, *Ideas and Events*, 123.
61 Krieger, *Ideas and Events*, 125.
62 Jean-Paul Sartre, *Being and Nothingness*, trans. Hazel E. Barnes (London: Methuen, 1957), 90.
63 Quentin Skinner, *Liberty Before Liberalism* (Cambridge: Cambridge University Press, 1998), 104, and Montgomery, ed. *The Cold War and the University*, 40; Howard Zinn, "The Politics of History in the era of the Cold War: Repression and Resistance," in *The Cold War and the University*, ed. David Montgomery (New York: New Press, 1997), and Stephen Jay Gould, *The Hedgehog, the Fox, and the Magister's Pox: Mending the gap between Science and the Humanities* (New York: Harmony, 2003). See also Quentin Skinner, "The idea of negative liberty: philosophical and historical perspectives," in *Philosophy in History: Essays on the historiography of philosophy*, ed. Richard Rorty, J.B. Schneewind, and Quentin Skinner (Cambridge: Cambridge University Press, 1984), 193–221.

64 Sykes, Charles. *ProfScam: Professors and the Demise of Higher Education* (New York: St. Martin's Press, 1990), and Charles Sykes, *The Hollow Men: Politics and Corruption in Higher Education* (Washington: Regnery Gateway, 1990). See also Andrew Abbott, *The System of Professions: An Essay on the Division of Expert Labor* (Chicago: University of Chicago Press, 1988); Burton Bledstein, *The Culture of Professionalism* (New York: W.W. Norton, 1976); Gary Graff, *Professing Literature: An Institutional History* (Chicago: University of Chicago Press, 1987); Martin Anderson, *Imposters in the Temple: The Decline of the American University* (Bellevue, WA: S&S Enterprises, 1992) and Bruce Wilshire, *The Moral Collapse of the University* (Albany: SUNY Press, 1990).

65 Robert Darnton, *The Kiss of Lamourette: Reflections in Cultural History* (New York: W.W. Norton, 1990), 193.

66 Leonard Krieger, "Nazism: Highway or Byway?" *Central European History* 11, no. 1 (March, 1978): 2–22. Reprinted in *Ideas and Events/Professing History*, ed. M.L. Brick with Introduction by Michael Ermarth (Chicago: University of Chicago Press, 1992), 355–73.

67 Carl Schorske, "Leonard Krieger," In *Journal of the History of Ideas* 52 (1991): 340. Krieger wrote six books, co-authored one with John Higham and another with Felix Gilbert and edited two collections of essays. He was series editor, for *Classic European Historians* (Chicago: University of Chicago Press) from 1967 to 1976. From 1949 to 1989 he published thirty-seven articles.

68 Krieger, *German Idea of Freedom*, 85 and 87.
69 Krieger, *German Idea of Freedom*, 125.
70 Krieger, *Ideas and Events*, "Kant and the Crisis of Natural Law," 260.
71 Malachi Haim Hacohen, "Leonard Krieger: Historicization and Political Engagement in Intellectual History," *History and Theory* 35, no. 1 (1996): 84 and 116.
72 Leonard Krieger, *Time's Reasons: Philosophies of History Old and New* (Chicago: University of Chicago Press, 1989), 176, 177, 175, and 177.
73 Leonard Krieger, *Time's Reasons*, 167.
74 Krieger, *Time's Reasons*, 25.
75 Leonard Krieger, *Ideas and Events*, 280.
76 Leonard Krieger, "The Autonomy of Intellectual History," in *Ideas and Events*, 159.
77 Krieger, "The Autonomy of Intellectual History," 159 and 176.
78 Krieger, "The Autonomy of Intellectual History," 159.
79 Leonard Krieger, "Culture, Cataclysm, and Contingency," in *Ideas and Events*, 211–12.
80 Krieger, *Time's Reasons*, 48.
81 Krieger, *Time's Reasons*, 44.
82 Krieger, *The Politics of Discretion: Pufendorf and the Acceptance of Natural Law* (Chicago: University of Chicago Press, 1965), 3.
83 Krieger, *Politics of Discretion*, 18.
84 Krieger, *Politics of Discretion*, 18.
85 Krieger, *Politics of Discretion*, 69.
86 Michael Oakeshott, *The Politics of Faith and the Politics of Scepticism*, ed. Timothy Fuller (New Haven, CT: Yale University Press, 1996), 123.
87 Oakeshott, *Politics of Faith*, 128, 123–24.
88 Oakeshott, *Politics of Faith*, 132–33.
89 Ian Tregenza, "The Sceptical Idealist: Michael Oakeshott as a Critic of the Enlightenment," In *History of Political Thought* 24, no. 4 (Winter 2003): 706.
90 Krieger, *Ranke*, 356.
91 Hacohen, "Leonard Krieger," 127.
92 Krieger, *Politics of Discretion*, 16 and 38.
93 Leonard Krieger, *Ideas and Events*, 26. "The Idea of Authority in the West" appeared in the AHR in April 1977.
94 Krieger, *Ideas and Events*, 27.
95 Krieger, *Ideas and Events*, 32.
96 Krieger, *Ideas and Events*, 51.
97 Krieger, *Politics of Discretion*, 269.

98  Krieger, *Ideas and Events*, 273–95. First published in *Political Science Quarterly* 75 (Sept. 1960): 355–78.
99  Krieger, *Ideas and Events*, 293.
100  See Robert C. Tucker, ed. *The Marx /Engels Reader* (New York: Norton, 1972), vii.
101  Krieger, *Ideas and Events*, 273.
102  Krieger, *Ideas and Events*, 274.
103  Krieger, *Ideas and Events*, 275.
104  Krieger, *Ideas and Events*, 277.
105  Krieger, *Ideas and Events*, 290.
106  Krieger, *Ideas and Events*, 291.
107  Krieger, *Ideas and Events*, 294.
108  Krieger, *Ideas and Events*, 293.
109  Krieger, *Ideas and Events*, 280.
110  Krieger, *Ideas and Events*, 237.
111  Krieger, *Ideas and Events*, 236.
112  Krieger, *Ideas and Events*, 269.
113  Krieger, *German Idea*, 87. "During the postwar period of disillusionment, disappointment with the monarchical states' exercise of their monopoly for the establishment of secular liberty helped spawn the third type [Kant's type] of liberal politics" (85).
114  Krieger, *German Idea*, 87.
115  Krieger, *German Idea*, 88. See Ernst Cassirer. *Kants Leben und Lehre* (Berlin, 1918), 435.
116  Krieger, *German Idea*, 88 John Herman Randall accepted Krieger's reading of Kant in his *The Career of Philosophy* (1965). Randall wrote, "Reason cannot 'know' anything beyond experience – the 'actual'"; but reason is sovereign in the realm of action – in the 'ideal.' I encountered Randall at the University of Indiana in 1969. Randall's romanticism perplexed me for twenty-five years. The discovery of this passage in Krieger sometime in the winter of 1993–94 provided the key to a career puzzle and the occasion for writing this book. Krieger showed me what Randall's ambiguous voluntarism meant in practice. The research for this book led me to conclude my education in the United States in the 1960s was a "duck-rabbit."
117  Krieger, *German Idea*, 89 and 94.

## CHAPTER FIVE: POSTMODERNISM

1  Karl Popper, *The Logic of Scientific Discovery* (London: Hutchinson, 1971), 423.
2  Jean-François Lyotard popularized the word, "postmodernism" in *The Postmodern Condition* (1984). Lyotard took the term from the architectural historian Charles Jencks (1977). Lyotard used the term to evoke a critical predisposition against the perceived narrowness, literalness, and lack of moral imagination in modern culture. Sartrean existentialism played a formative role in Lyotard's rejection of the modern. Jencks had taken the term, "postmodern" from Robert Venturi, Denise S. Brown, and Steven Izenour, *Learning from Las Vegas* (1972). Irving Howe had used "postmodernism" in *The Idea of the Modern* (1967) and Harry Levin's "What Was Modernism?" appeared in 1966. The first critical use of the word "post-modern" may have been by Arnold Toynbee in Vol. V of *A Study of History* (1939). The "post-Modern" represented the last phase of the breakdown of Western civilization. According to Toynbee, "Human beings in the modern world have lost control over their own destinies," a consequence of extreme "moral aberration," Toynbee interjected. See Richard Appignanesi and Chris Garratt, *Introducing Postmodernism* (New York: Totem, 1995), 10–11.
3  Jean-François Lyotard, *The Postmodern Condition: Towards a Postmodern Philosophy* (Cambridge: Polity Press, 1998), 81–82.
4  See David S. Luft, "Being and German History: Historiographical Notes on the Heidegger Controversy," *Central European History* 27, no. 4 (1994): 499 and 494.
5  David Krell, *Intimations of Mortality* (University Park: Pennsylvania State University Press, 1986), 111.
6  Martin Heidegger, *Being and Time*, trans. John Macquarrie and Edward Robinson (New York: Harper & Row, 1962), 319. Hereafter referred to as *B & T*.

7. *B & T*, 326.
8. "*As care, Dasein* is the 'between,'" (*B & T*, 427).
9. Theodore Kisiel, (1993) *The Genesis of Heidegger's Being and Time* (Berkeley: University of California Press, 1993), 150.
10. Jeffrey Barash, *Martin Heidegger and the Problem of Historical Meaning* (Dordrecht: Martinus Nijhoff, 1988), 90.
11. John Caputo, *Heidegger and Aquinas: An Essay on Overcoming Metaphysics* (New York: Fordham University Press, 1987), 165.
12. Anthony Carty, "Editor's Introduction," in *Post-Modern Law: Enlightenment, Revolution and the Death of Man*, ed. Anthony Carty (Edinburgh: Edinburgh University Press, 1990), 38n. See Pöggeler, *Heidegger's Path*, 19–20.
13. Hans-Georg Gadamer, *Philosophical Apprenticeships*, trans. R.R. Sullivan (Cambridge, MA: MIT Press, 1985), 19.
14. Cited in Herman Rapaport, *Heidegger & Derrida: Reflections on Time and Language* (Lincoln: University of Nebraska Press, 1989), 80. The Sheehan quip is in Thomas Sheehan, "Time and Being, 1925–1927," *Thinking about Being*, ed. R.W. Shahan and H.N. Mohanty (Norman: University of Oklahoma Press, 1984).
15. *B & T*, 54.
16. *B & T*, 58–59.
17. *B & T*, 215.
18. *B & T*, 262.
19. Robert Bernasconi, *The Question of Language in Heidegger's History of Being* (Atlantic Highlands, NJ: Humanities Press International, 1985), 7.
20. *B & T*, 56.
21. *B & T*, 56.
22. Martin Heidegger, "Letter on Humanism," in *Martin Heidegger, Basic Writings*, ed. David Farrell Krell (New York: Harper & Row, 1977), 193.
23. *B & T*, 44.
24. *B & T*, 56. See Herman Rapaport, *Heidegger & Derrida: Reflections on Time and Language* (Lincoln: University of Nebraska Press, 1989). Heidegger writes, "Hence *logos* gives rise to the word *legein*, which means saying aloud. '*Legein*,' or in Latin, '*legere*,' is the same as our word, '*Lesen*,' ... Lesen is to be understood in the broader and more original sense of *die Aehren auf dem Acker lesen* or *das Holz lesen im Wald*, that is, picking ears up from the fields or taking up wood in the forest." Rapaport says Heidegger views "man" as a collection of closely related attributes that in their proximity to one another have achieved both nearness and distance. These attributes occur together according to the way in which *logos* is gathered or collected over time (105). See also William J. Richardson, *Heidegger, Through Phenomenology to Thought* (The Hague: Martinus Nijhoff, 1967), 631 and 249.
25. *B & T*, 58.
26. *B & T*, 58.
27. *B & T*, 59.
28. Hubert Dreyfus and Jane Rubin, "Kierkegaard, Division II, and the later Heidegger," in *Being-in-the-World: A Commentary on Heidegger's Being and Time* (Cambridge, MA: MIT Press, 1992), 299.
29. Karin de Boer, *Thinking in the Light of Time: Heidegger's Encounter with Hegel* (Albany, NY: SUNY Press, 2000), 4.
30. De Boer, *Heidegger's Encounter*, 281.
31. Hegel, *Philosophy of History*, 39.
32. *B & T*, 57.
33. *B & T*, 131.
34. Victor Farias, *Heidegger and Nazism* (Philadelphia: Temple University Press, 1989), 62.
35. Gayatri Chakravorty Spivak, *A Critique of Postcolonial Reason: Towards a History of the Vanishing Present* (Cambridge, MA: Harvard University Press, 1999), 418 and 39.
36. Pierre Bourdieu, *Language and Symbolic Power*, ed. John B. Thompson (Cambridge, MA: Harvard University Press, 1991), 151. "The role of this kind of expression is to mask the primitive experiences of the social world and the social phantasms which are its source ...

to allow them to speak, while using a mode of expression which suggests that they are not being said (142–43).... It is this which frustrates the attempts of Heidegger's critics to find blatantly Nazi theses in his works and political writings.... The imposition of form is in itself a warning. By its elevated nature it indicates its sovereign distance from all determinations, even from those 'isms' which reduce the irreducible unity of a thought system to the uniformity of a logical class (144).... He, who is more than a Fürsprecher, [is] a humble advocate serving the sacred word and thereby [himself] made sacred" (151).

37 Robert Denoon Cumming, *The Dream is Over* (Chicago: University of Chicago Press, 1991), 78.
38 Jacques Derrida, *Of Spirit*, trans. Geoffrey Bennington and Rachel Bowlby (Chicago: University of Chicago Press, 1989), 46.
39 Derrida, *Of Spirit*, 32.
40 Hans Sluga, *Heidegger's Crisis: Philosophy and Politics in Nazi Germany* (Cambridge, MA: Harvard University Press, 1993), 4 and 250.
41 Martin Heidegger, *Nietzsche: Nihilism* (1961), trans. Frank A. Capuzzi (New York: Harper & Row, 1982), I: 30.
42 Martin Heidegger, "On the Essence of φυσισ" in *Pathmarks* (Cambridge: Cambridge University Press, 1998), 214.
43 *B & T*, 480.
44 Karl Jaspers, *Philosophy*, II: 113.
45 Michael Allen Gillespie, *Hegel, Heidegger and the Ground of History* (Chicago: University of Chicago Press, 1984), 129.
46 Jeffrey Andrew Barash, *Martin Heidegger and the Problem of Historical Meaning* (Dordrecht: Martinus Nijhoff, 1988), 276.
47 Martin Heidegger, "Only a God can Save Us: The Spiegel Interview," in *Heidegger the Man and the Thinker*, ed. Thomas Sheehan and trans. William J. Richardson, S.J. (Chicago: Precedent, 1976).
48 Martin Heidegger, "Letter on Humanism," in *Basic Writings*, ed. David Farrell Krell (New York: Harper & Row, 1977), 193.
49 Jacques Derrida, "Structure, Sign and Play," 290. The article is the one presented at the famous Johns Hopkins seminar on structuralism, October 21, 1966. It appeared in English in the proceedings of the Johns Hopkins conference: *The Structuralist Controversy*, eds. Richard Macksey and Eugenio Donato (Baltimore: Johns Hopkins University Press, 1971).
50 Derrida, "Structure, Sign and Play," 291.
51 Jacques Derrida, "'To Do Justice to Freud': The History of Madness in the Age of Psychoanalysis," in *Foucault and his Interlocutors*, ed. Arnold I. Davidson (Chicago: University of Chicago Press, 1997), 81.
52 The paper is the famous, "Structure, Sign and Play in the Discourse of the Human Sciences," reprinted in *Writing and Difference* (1978).
53 In *Basic Problems*, Heidegger calls for "a critical process in which the traditional concepts, which at first must necessarily be employed, are *de-constructed* down to the sources from which they are drawn" (21). Cited in Richard Polt, *Heidegger: An Introduction* (Ithaca, NY: Cornell University Press, 1991), 37.
54 Thomas Flynn, "Foucault as Parrhesiast: his last course at the college de france," In *The Final Foucault*, ed. Manes Bernauer and David Rasmussen (Cambridge, MA: MIT Press, 1988), 114.
55 Jacques Derrida, *Specters of Marx*, trans. Peggy Kamuf (New York: Routledge, 1994), 14.
56 Derrida, *Writing and Difference*, 161; and Derrida, *Grammatology*, "... That Dangerous Supplement ...," 143; See also Christopher Norris, *What's Wrong with Postmodernism* (Baltimore: Johns Hopkins University Press, 1990), 205; Leonard Orr, "The Post-Turn: Derrida, Gadamer and the Remystification of Language," in *Deconstruction: A Critique*, ed. Rajnath. (New York: Macmillan, 1989), 199; and J. Mehlman, "Introduction" to "Freud and the Scene of Writing," in *Yale French Studies* 48 (1972): 74.
57 Derrida, *Writing and Difference*, 161.
58 Jacques Lacan, *The Four Fundamental Concepts of Psycho-analysis*, trans. Alan Sheridan (New York: Penguin, 1977), 62.

59  Cf. Lacan, *Four Fundamental Concepts*, 33 and 63.
60  Quoted in Nicholas Royle, *After Derrida* (Manchester: Manchester University Press, 1995), 128 from *Limited Inc.*, trans. Samuel Weber (Evanston, IL: Northwestern University Press, 1988).
61  Quoted in Cumming, *The Dream is Over*, 166, from J. Derrida, *Psyché*, 391.
62  Derrida, *Writing and Difference*, 114. '*Aufhebung*' has in the German language a double sense: that of preserving, *maintaining*; and that of leaving off, bringing *to an end*. To preserve, moreover, has a negative sense (from Hegel, *Wissenschaft der Logik*, I, pp. 124–25). All nineteenth-century philosophers were aware of the plagal cadence in music (the "Ah-Men" ending to a hymn) and the standard II, V, I cadence in which the tonic note is suspended throughout as a home drone awaiting final resolution. The Hegelian "*Aufhebung*" is easily heard as an interdisciplinary metaphor which Hegel borrowed from the classical theory of nineteenth-century musical harmony. The hometone or tonic drone of an essential relation is sounded through the changing harmony until all dissonance is resolved. See Yirmiahu Yovel, *Kant and the Philosophy of History* (Princeton, NJ: Princeton University Press, 1980) "Hegel can develop the Kantian themes on history more comprehensively and more coherently because he overcame the Kantian dualism – and thereby the historical antinomy – within a new *Aufhebung*, using his own view of rationality" (302). On Heidegger's use of the word, see Bernasconi, *Question of Language*, 15.
63  Jürgen Habermas, *Moral Consciousness and Communicative Action*, trans. Shierry Weber Nicholsen (Cambridge, MA: MIT Press, 1990). Habermas waxes rhapsodic over the modern parallels "between moral stages on the one hand and stages of [historical] interaction on the other"(168).
64  Derrida, *Writing and Difference*, 331.
65  Derrida, *Writing and Difference*, 331.
66  Derrida, *Writing and Difference*, 330.
67  Jacques Derrida, *Of Grammatology*, trans. Gayatri Chakravorty Spivak (Baltimore: Johns Hopkins University Press, 1974), 158.
68  John Caputo, *Heidegger and Aquinas: An Essay on Overcoming Metaphysics* (New York: Fordham University Press, 1987), 111.
69  Jacques Derrida, *Glas*, in *A Derrida Reader*, ed. Peggy Kamuf (New York: Columbia University Press, 1991), 323.
70  Derrida, *Glas*, 323.
71  Derrida, *Glas*, 328.
72  Derrida, *Glas*, 329.
73  Derrida, *Glas*, 329.
74  Derrida, *Glas*, "So practical consciousness is at once the negation and the posit[ion]ing of theoretical consciousness.... Desire is theoretical, but as such is tortured by a contradiction that makes it practical (p. 329).... Desire perforce implies just what it denies: theoretical consciousness, memory and language" (330).
75  Caputo, *Deconstruction in a Nutshell*, 37. Cf. Derrida, *On the Name*, 71.
76  Caputo, *Deconstruction in a Nutshell*, 54. Cf. Derrida, *Points*, 428.
77  Derrida, *Writing and Difference*, 251–77.
78  See "... That Dangerous Supplement ... " in Derrida, *Grammatology*: "Blindness to the supplement is the law (149).... It is from a certain determined representation of 'cohabitation with women' that Rousseau had to have recourse throughout his life to that type of dangerous supplement that is called masturbation and that cannot be separated from his activity as a writer.... In other words, between auto-eroticism and hetero-eroticism, there is not a frontier but an economic distribution.... This is Rousseau's general rule (155).... This perversion consists of preferring the sign and protects me from moral expenditure. To be sure. But his apparently egotistical economy also functions within an entire system of moral representation (156).... Through this sequence of [masturbatory] supplements a necessity is announced: that of an infinite chain, ineluctably multiplying the supplementary mediations that produce the sense of the very thing they defer: the mirage of the thing itself, of immediate presence, of originary perception. Immediacy is derived (substitute: ersatz)" (157).

See "The Essay on the Origins of Languages," in *Grammatology*: "In as much as it *puts into play* the presence of the present and the life of the living, the movement of language does not, one suspects, have only an analogical relationship with 'sexual' auto-affection. It is totally indistinguishable from it.... In the same way that the 'fatal advantage' of sexual auto-affection begins well before what is thought to be circumscribed by the name of masturbation (organization of so-called wrong and pathological gestures, confined to some children or adolescents), the supplementary menace of writing is older than what some think to exalt by the name of 'speech.'

From then on, metaphysics consists of excluding non-presence by determining the supplement as *simple exteriority*, pure addition or pure absence. The work of exclusion [of real relationships] operates within the structure of supplementarity [masturbation] ... *What is added* [to the world] *is nothing because it is added to a full presence to which it is exterior* [it inseminates nothing, it is just more stuff in the world]. Speech comes to be added to intuitive presence (of the entity, of *essence*, of the *eidos*, of *ousia*, and so forth); writing comes to be added to living self-present speech; masturbation comes to be added to so-called normal sexual experience; culture to nature, evil to innocence, history to origin, and so on.

The concept of origin or nature is nothing but the myth of addition, of supplementarity annulled by being purely additive. It [myths of origin] is an originary différance that is neither absence nor presence, neither negative nor positive. Originary difference [full exteriority to which nothing can be added] ... is the myth of the effacement of the trace.... Originary différance is supplementarity as *structure*. Here structure means the irreducible complexity within which one can only shape or shift the play of presence or absence: that within which metaphysics can be produced but which metaphysics cannot think" (167; my brackets).

79  Maurice Merleau-Ponty, *Phenomenology as Perception*, trans. Colin Smith (London: Routledge & Kegan Paul, 1962) Merleau-Ponty's Schneider had a sex, but no sexuality. Though physically and mentally capable of every normal human function, he could not string behaviours together and hence was socially helpless. He could not keep in mind an organizing intentionality under which a sequence of normal behaviours "made sense." "The world no longer has any physiognomy for Schneider," Merleau-Ponty concluded (p. 132). Merleau-Ponty was of two minds about modern culture. One side, the bright side, he represented with modern art. He represented the other half of the modern body with the case of a World War I veteran who had suffered a shrapnel wound to the back of the head. Gelb and Goldstein, the two German psychiatrists who studied him, called the man Schneider. Schneider was the broken half of modern experience. If the aesthetic condition of modernity was positive like Cezanne, the political condition of modernity was apraxic like Schneider. Schneider's apraxia is not unknown in modern bureaucracies, the university, corporations, and government. The existential issue is whether we are Cezannes of modern, multi-media technology or Schneiders of aimless, apraxic literality.

80  Derrida, "Difference," in Kamuf, *A Derrida Reader*, 74.
81  Derrida, "Difference," in Kamuf, *A Derrida Reader*, 75.
82  Kamuf, *A Derrida Reader*, 78n.
83  Irene Harvey, *Derrida and the Economy of Différance* (Bloomington: Indiana University Press, 1986), 218.
84  Derrida, *Writing and Difference*, 231.
85  Krieger, *Ideas and Events*, "He seems to provide access to social history for those who are not social historians and access to structural history for those who are not structuralists. Foucault, in short, has become the poor man's cultural historian" (190).
86  Michel Foucault, *Order of Things* (London: Tavistock, 1970), 208. See *Archaeology of Knowledge*, 203 and 55 and *Power/Knowledge*, 197.
87  Simon During, *Foucault and Literature* (New York: Routledge, 1992), 22.
88  Gilles Deleuze, *Foucault*, trans. Sean Hand (London: The Athlone Press, 1988), 61.
89  Deleuze, *Foucault*, 60.
90  Deleuze, *Foucault*, 60.
91  Foucault was inspired by Heidegger's reverse chronological order in *The Basic Problems of*

*Phenomenology* (1927). The backward chronology which is also a "deconstruction" of the chronology appeared to Foucault as an "archaeology" of knowledge. See Polt, *Heidegger*, 37.
92  Gilles Deleuze, *Foucault*, trans. by Sean Hand (London: The Athlone Press, 1988), 60.
93  Deleuze, *Foucault*, 60.
94  Deleuze, *Foucault*, 140n.
95  Foucault, *Power/Knowledge*, 186.
96  I take the word, "insurgent" from James Holston, "Spaces of Insurgent Citizenship," in *Making the Invisible Visible*, ed. Leonie Sandercock (Berkeley: University of California Press, 1998): "By insurgent I mean to emphasize the opposition of these spaces of citizenship to the modernist spaces that physically dominate so many cities today. I use it to emphasize an opposition to the modernist political project that absorbs citizenship into a plan of state building and that, in the process, generates a certain concept and practice of planning itself.... I use the notion of insurgent to refer to new and other sources of legitimacy" (39).
97  During, *Foucault and Literature*, 7. See Hubert L. Dreyfus and Paul Rabinow, *Michel Foucault: Beyond Structuralism and Hermeneutics*, 2nd ed., with an Afterword by and an Interview with Michel Foucault (Chicago: University of Chicago Press, 1983).
98  During, *Foucault and Literature*, 19–20.
99  Foucault, *Power/Knowledge*, 197, 183 and 201.
100  David Macey, *The Lives of Michel Foucault* (New York: Pantheon, 1993) "The problem facing contemporary psychology is its ability, or otherwise, to abandon its 'naturalistic objectivity'" (62).
101  Michel Foucault, "The Subject and Power," *Critical Inquiry* 8 (1982): 789. The Foucault article follows Paul de Man's article on "Sign and Symbol in Hegel's *Aesthetics*." Together the two articles form a kind of *locus classicus* on the postmodern.
102  Gilles Deleuze, *The Logic of Sense*, trans. Mark Lester (New York: Columbia University Press, 1990), 209 and 310.
103  Deleuze, *The Logic of Sense*, 318.
104  Deleuze, *The Logic of Sense*, 318.
105  Deleuze, *The Logic of Sense*, 310.
106  David Copp, "Normativity and the Very Idea of Moral Epistemology," *Southern Journal of Philosophy*, ed. Mark Timmons, XXIX (1990), Supplement (*Proceedings of the Spindel Conference* at Memphis State University, 1990). After clarifying the two normative assumptions required for morality and moral claims, Copp explains the additional assumption required for a subject-specific *moral* epistemology. "A subject-specific *moral* epistemology requires at least the additional assumption (3) that certain special problems stand in the way of explaining the justification of our moral beliefs, which are different from and additional to the problem that afflict explanations of the justification of our non-moral beliefs" (189). Copp is the only contributor to both the Spindel Conference and the Campbell and Hunter (eds.) reader *Moral Epistemology Naturalized* (2000).
107  Merleau-Ponty, *Phenomenology of Perception*, xii–xiii. "I rediscover [the world] 'in me' as the permanent horizon of all my *cogitationes* and as a dimension n relation to which I am constantly situating myself" (xiii).
108  Merleau-Ponty, *Phenomenology of Perception*, 452.
109  Derrida, *Writing and Difference*, 91.
110  Michel Foucault, *Madness and Civilization: A History of Insanity in the Age of Reason* (New York: Pantheon, 1965), x.
111  Foucault, *Madness and Civilization*, 99.
112  Michel Foucault, *The Archaeology of Knowledge*, trans. A.M. Sheridan Smith (New York: Pantheon, 1972), 7.
113  Foucault, *Archaeology of Knowledge*, 25.
114  Foucault, *Archaeology of Knowledge*, 7.
115  Foucault, *Power/Knowledge*, 197.
116  Foucault, *Power/Knowledge*, 200.
117  Foucault, *Order of Things*, 308.
118  Foucault, *Order of Things*, 63.
119  Foucault, *Order of Things*, 67.

120 Foucault, *Power/Knowledge*, 133.
121 Michel Foucault, "Questions of Method," *I & C* (Spring, 1981): 8.
122 Foucault, *Power/Knowledge*, 133.
123 Foucault, *Power/Knowledge*, 53.
124 Foucault, *Power/Knowledge*, 58.
125 Foucault, *Power/Knowledge*, 58.
126 Foucault, *Archaeology of Knowledge*, 55.
127 Michel Foucault, *The History of Sexuality*, trans. Robert Hurley (New York: Pantheon, 1978) "It seems that the deployment of sexuality was not established as a principle of limitation of the pleasures of others by what have traditionally been called the 'ruling classes.' Rather it appears to me that they first tried it on themselves" (122).
128 Diane F. Michelfelder and Richard E. Palmer. *Dialogue and Deconstruction: The Gadamer-Derrida Encounter* (Albany, NY: SUNY Press, 1989), 3.
129 Han-Georg Gadamer, *Truth and Method*, trans. by Sheed and Ward (New York: Seabury, 1975), 200 & 202.
130 Hans-Georg Gadamer, *Philosophical Hermeneutics*, trans. David E. Linge (Berkeley: University of California Press, 1976), 103–4.
131 Gadamer, *Truth and Method*, 445.
132 Immanuel Kant, *The Metaphysics of Morals* (1798), trans. Mary Gregor (Cambridge: Cambridge University Press, 1991), 9.
133 Kant, *Critique of Pure Reason*, 99, 100 & 32.
134 Marx, *Capital*, 57, 578n & 79; "When, therefore, Galiani says: 'Value is a relation between persons he ought to have added: a relation between persons expressed as a relation between things" (79).
135 Karl Marx, *Capital: A Critique of Political Economy* I. trans. Samuel Moore and Edward Aveling (Moscow: Progress Publishers, 1954), 49.
136 Marx, *Capital*, 77.
137 Marx, *Capital*, 79–80.
138 Karl Marx, *The Poverty of Philosophy* (New York: International Publishers, 1903), 114.
139 Marx, *Poverty of Philosophy*, 265 and 107.
140 Marx, *Poverty of Philosophy*, 124 and 193.
141 Marx, *Capital*, 74.
142 Karl Marx, *Grundrisse*, trans. Martin Nicolaus (New York: Vintage, 1973), 307.
143 Christian Comeliau, *The Impasse of Modernity*, trans. Patrick Camiller (London: Zed Books, 2002), 44–45.
144 Richard H. Roberts, *Religion, Theology and the Social Sciences* (Cambridge: Cambridge University Press, 2002), 211.
145 Roberts, *Religion, Theology and the Social Sciences*, 211.
146 Cameliau, *The Impasse of Modernity*, "It thereby promotes mainly individualist and materialist values, and fails to recognize any kind of transcendence" (44).

# BIBLIOGRAPHY

Abela, Paul. *Kant's Empirical Realism*. Oxford: Clarendon, 2002.
Abbott, Andrew. *The System of Professions: An Essay on the Division of Expert Labor*. Chicago: University of Chicago Press, 1988.
Adorno, Theodore. *Minima Moralia: Reflections from Damaged Life*. Trans. E.F.N. Jephcott. London: New Left Books, 1951.
———. *Negative Dialectics*. Trans. E.B. Ashton. New York: Seabury, 1973.
Alexander, Jeffrey. "General Theory in the Postpositivist Mode: The 'Epistemological Dilemma' and the Search for Present Reason." In *Postmodernism and Social Theory*. Ed. Steven Seidman and David G. Wagner, 322–68, Cambridge, MA: Harvard University Press, 1992.
Allison, Henry, and Peter Heath. "Introduction." In *Immanuel Kant: Theoretical Philosophy after 1781*. Ed. and trans. Henry Allison and Peter Heath, 1–27, Cambridge: Cambridge University Press, 2002.
Ameriks, Karl. *Kant and the Fate of Autonomy: Problems in the Appropriation of the Critical Philosophy*. Cambridge: Cambridge University Press, 2000.
Anderson, Martin. *Imposters in the Temple: The Decline of the American University*. Bellevue, WA: S&S Enterprises, 1992.
Ankersmit, F.R. *Aesthetic Politics: Political Philosophy Beyond Fact and Value*. Stanford: Stanford University Press, 1996.
———. "Historiography and Postmodernism," *History and Theory* 28 (1989): 137–53.
———. *History and Tropology: The Rise and Fall of Metaphor*. Berkeley: University of California Press, 1994.
———. *Narrative Logic. A Semantic Analysis of the Historian's Language*. The Hague: Martinus Nijhoff, 1983.
———. "Statements, Texts and Pictures." In *A New Philosophy of History*. Ed. Frank Ankersmit and Hans Kellner. 212–40, Chicago: University of Chicago Press, 1995.
Anscombe, Elizabeth. *An Introduction to Wittgenstein's Tractatus*. Herndon, VA: Books International, 1996.
Antoni, Carlo. *From History to Sociology: The Transition in German Historical Thinking*. Trans. Hayden V. White. Detroit, MI: Wayne State University Press, 1959.
Appigranesi, Richard, and Chris Garratt. *Introducing Postmodernism*. New York: Totem Books, 1995.
Appleby, Joyce, Lynn Hunt, and Margaret Jacob. *Telling the Truth about History*. New York: W. W. Norton, 1994.
Auden, W.H., ed. *The Living Thoughts of Kierkegaard*. Bloomington: Indiana University Press, 1966.
Augustine of Hippo. *The Confessions*. Trans. Maria Boulding. New York: Random House, 1998.
———. *The Confessions*. Trans. E.B. Pusey. London: J.M. Dent, 1907.
Austin, J.L. *How to do Things with Words*. ed. J.O. Urmson and Marina Shisa. Oxford: Clarendon Press, 1975.
Ayer, A.J. *The Central Questions of Philosophy*. London: Penguin, 1973.
———. *Logical Positivism*. New York: Free Press, 1959.

Baldwin, Thomas. "Moore's rejection of idealism." In *Philosophy in History: Essays on the historiography of philosophy.* Ed. Richard Rorty, J.B. Schneewind, and Quentin Skinner, 357–74. London: Cambridge University Press, 1984.

Barash, Jeffrey Andrew. *Martin Heidegger and the Problem of Historical Meaning.* Dordrecht: Martinus Nijhoff, 1988.

Barer, Shlomo. *The Doctors of Revolution.* New York: Thames and Hudson, 2000.

Barzun, Jacques. *Classic, Romantic and Modern.* Boston: Little, Brown and Co., 1961.

Bateson, Gregory. *Steps to an Ecology of Mind.* New York: Ballantine, 1972.

Beard, Charles. *An Economic Interpretation of the Constitution.* New York: Free Press, 1966.

Beck, Lewis White, ed. "Introduction" to *Critique of Practical Reason and Other Writings in Moral Philosophy*, 1-49. Chicago: University of Chicago Press, 1949.

Becker, Carl. *Everyman his own Historian: Essays on History and Politics.* New York: F.S. Crofts & Co., 1935.

———. *The Heavenly City of the Eighteenth Century Philosophers* (1932). New Haven, CT: Yale University Press, 1960.

Beiser, Frederick. "David Hume." In *The Columbia History of Western Philosophy.* Ed. Richard Popkin, 454–61. New York: Columbia University Press, 1998.

———. *The Fate of Reason: German Philosophy from Kant to Fichte.* Cambridge, MA: Harvard University Press, 1987.

Bellah, Robert N., Richard Madsen, William Sullivan, Ann Swidler, and Steven M. Tipton. *Habits of the Heart.* Los Angeles: University of California Press, 1985.

Bergmann, Gustav. "Logical Positivism, Language, and the Reconstruction of Metaphysics," *Rivista Critica di Storia della Filosophia* 8 (1953): 453–81; reprinted "in a truncated form" in Richard Rorty (ed.), *The Linguistic Turn.* 63–72. Chicago: University of Chicago Press, 1967.

Bergmann, Gustav. *Logic and Reality.* Madison: University of Wisconsin Press, 1964.

Bernasconi, Robert. *The Question of Language in Heidegger's History of Being.* Atlantic Highlands, NJ: Humanities Press International, 1985.

Bernstein, Richard J. *Praxis and Action Contemporary Philosophies of Human Activity.* Philadelphia: Unversity of Pennsylvania Press, 1971.

Betanzos, Ramon J. "Wilhelm Dilthey: An Introduction." In *Introduction to the Human Sciences: An Attempt to Lay a Foundation for the Study of Society and History* by Wilhelm Dilthey. Trans. Ramon J. Betanzos, 9–64. Detroit: Wayne State University Press, 1988.

Black, Karen. *Dummett.* Cambridge: Polity Press, 2001.

Bledstein, Burton. *The Culture of Professionalism.* New York: W.W. Norton, 1976.

Blocker, Gene. *The Meaning of Meaninglessness.* The Hague: Martinus Nijhoff, 1974.

Bodéüs, Richard. "Aristotle." In *The Columbia History of Western Philosophy.* Ed. Richard H. Popkin, 52–72. New York: Columbia University Press, 1999.

Bonjour, Laurence. *Epistemology: Classic Problems and Contemporary Responses.* New York: Rowman & Littlefield, 2002.

Borges, Jorge Luis. *Ficciones.* New York: Grove Press, 1956.

Bourdieu, Pierre. *Language and Symbolic Power.* Ed. John B. Thompson. Cambridge, MA: Harvard University Press, 1991.

Brandt, Reinhard. "Kants Anthropologie: Die Idee des Werks und die Bestimmung des Menschen." Paper presented at the Central Division meeting of the American Philosophical Association, Pittsburgh, April 1997.

Butterfield, Herbert. "God in History." In *God, History, and Historians: An Anthology of Modern Christian Views of History*. Ed. C.T. McIntire. 192–204, New York: Oxford University Press, 1977.
———. *Herbert Butterfield: The Ethics of History and Politics*. Ed. Kenneth W. Thompson. Washington: University Press of America, 1980.
———. *Man on his Past*. Cambridge: Cambridge University Press, 1955.
———. *The Whig Interpretation of History*. New York: Norton, 1931.
———. *Writings on Christianity and History*. Ed. C.T. McIntire. New York: Oxford University Press, 1979.
Canguilhem, George. *The Normal and the Pathological* (1966). New York: Zone Books, 1991.
Caputo, John, ed. *Deconstruction in a Nutshell: A Conversation with Jacques Derrida*. New York: Fordham University Press, 1997.
———. *Heidegger and Aquinas. An Essay on Overcoming Metaphysics*. New York: Fordham University Press, 1987.
———. *The Prayers and Tears of Jacques Derrida. Religion without Religion*. Bloomington: Indiana University Press, 1997.
Carty, Anthony. "Post-Modernism in the Theory and the Sociology of Law, or Rousseau and Durkheim as read by Baudrillard." In *Post-Modern Law. Enlightenment, Revolution and the Death of Man*. Ed. Anthony Carty. 71–89, Edinburgh: Edinburgh University Press, 1990.
Cassirer, Ernst. *Kant's Life and Thought* (1918). Trans. James Haden. New Haven, CT: Yale University Press, 1981.
———. *Language and Myth*. New York: Harper, 1946.
Chia, Robert, and Ian King, "The Language of Organization Theory." In *The Language of Organization*. Ed. Robert Westwood and Stephen Linstead. 310–28, London: Sage, 2001.
Chomsky, Noam. *Aspects of the Theory of Syntax*. Cambridge, MA: MIT Press, 1965.
———. *Powers and Prospects: Reflections on Human Nature and the Social Order*. Boston: South End Press, 1996.
Cochrane, James, ed. *Rudyard Kipling: Selected Verse*. New York: Penguin, 1977.
Code, Lorraine. "Statements of Fact: Whose? Where? When?" In *Moral Epistemology Naturalized*. Ed. Richard Campbell and Bruce Hunter; *Canadian Journal of Philosophy* 26, 2000 (Supplementary), 175–208.
Coffa, J. Alberto. *The Semantic Tradition from Kant to Carnap*. Cambridge: Cambridge University Press, 1991.
Colodny, R.B., ed. *Frontiers of Science and Philosophy*. Pittsburgh: University of Pittsburgh Press, 1962.
Comeliau, Christian. *The Impasse of Modernity*. Trans. Patrick Camiller. London: Zed Books, 2002.
Cooper, Robin. "Modernism, postmodernism and organizational analysis 3: The contribution of Jacques Derrida," *Organizational Studies* 10, no. 4 (2005): 479–502.
Copp, David. "Normativity and the Very Idea of Moral Epistemology." In *Southern Journal of Philosophy*, ed. Mark Timmons. XXIX (1990), Supplement (*Proceedings of the Spindel Conference*, 1990), 189–210.
Culler, Jonathan. *Framing the Sign: Criticism and Its Institutions*. Norman: University of Oklahoma Press, 1988.
———. *Saussure*. London: Harvester Press, 1976.

Cumming, Robert Denoon. *The Dream is Over.* Vol. I, *Phenomenology and Deconstruction.* Chicago: University of Chicago Press, 1992.
Darnton, Robert. *The Kiss of Lamourette: Reflections in Cultural History.* New York: Norton, 1990.
de Beaugrande, Robert. *Linguistic Theory: The Discourse of Fundamental Works.* New York: Longman, 1991.
de Boer, Karin. *Thinking in the Light of Time: Heidegger's Encounter with Hegel.* Albany: State University of New York, 2000.
Darwall, Stephen. *Philosophical Ethics.* Boulder, CO: Westview Press, 1998.
Davis, Michael. *The Autobiography of Philosophy.* Lanham, Maryland: Rowman & Littlefield, 1999.
Deleuze, Gilles. *Foucault.* Trans. Sean Hand. London: The Athlone Press, 1988.
———. *The Logic of Sense* Trans. Mark Lester. New York: Columbia University Press, 1990.
de Man, Paul. *Aesthetic Ideology.* Theory and History of Literature, Vol. 65. Minneapolis: University of Minnesota Press, 1996.
———. *Allegories of Reading: Figural Language in Rousseau, Nietzsche, Rilke, and Proust.* New Haven, CT: Yale University Press, 1979.
———. "Sign and Symbol in Hegel's Aesthetics," *Critical Inquiry* 8 (Summer 1982): 761–75.
Derrida, Jacques. *Limited Inc.* Trans. Samuel Weber. Evanston, IL: Northwestern University Press, 1988.
———. *Of Spirit.* Trans. Geoffrey Bennington and Rachel Bowlby. Chicago: University of Chicago Press, 1989.
———. *Memoires: For Paul de Man.* Trans. Cecile Lindsay, Jonathan Culler and Eduardo Cadava. New York: Columbia University Press, 1986.
———. *Of Grammatology* (1967). Trans. Gayatri Chakravorty Spivak. Baltimore: Johns Hopkins University Press, 1974.
———. *On the Name,* ed. Thomas Dutoit. Stanford: Stanford University Press, 1995.
———. *Points ... Interviews, 1974–94.* Ed. Elisabeth Weber; trans. Peggy Kamuf. Stanford: Stanford University Press, 1995.
———. *Spectres of Marx.* Trans. Peggy Kamuf. New York: Routledge, 1994.
———. "'To Do Justice to Freud': The History of Madness in the Age of Psychoanalysis." In *Foucault and his Interlocutors.* Ed. Arnold I. Davidson, 57–96, Chicago: University of Chicago Press, 1997.
———. *Writing and Difference.* Trans. Alan Bass. Chicago: University of Chicago Press, 1978.
Dilthey, Wilhelm. *Dilthey's Philosophy of Existence: Introduction to Weltanschauungslehre.* Trans. William Kluback and Martin Weinbaum. Introduction by Kluback and Weinbaum. London: Vision Press, 1957.
———. *Pattern and Meaning in History,* edited and trans. H.P. Rickman. London: George Allen & Unwin, 1961.
Donagan, Alan. "Explanation in History," reprinted in *Theories of History.* Ed. Patrick Gardiner, 402–7, New York: Free Press of Glencoe, 1959.
Dray, William H. *Laws and Explanations in History.* London: Oxford University Press, 1957.
———. *Philosophy of History.* Englewood Cliffs, NJ: Prentice-Hall, 1993.
Dreyfus, Hubert L., and Jane Rubin. "Kierkegaard, Division II, and Later Heidegger." In *Being-in-the-World: A Commentary on Heidegger's Being and Time, Division I.* Ed. Hubert L. Dreyfus, 283–340. Cambridge, MA: MIT Press, 1992.

Dummett, Michael. "The Justification of Deduction," *Proceedings of the British Academy* 59 (1973): 201–32. London: Oxford University Press, 1975.
———. *Truth and Other Enigmas*. Cambridge, MA: Harvard University Press, 1978.
During, Simon. *Foucault and Literature*. New York: Routledge, 1992.
Edwards, James C. *Ethics without Philosophy: Wittgenstein and the Moral Life*. Gainesville: University Presses of Florida, 1974.
Eldridge, Richard. *Leading a Human Life: Wittgenstein, Intentionality, and Romanticism*. Chicago: University of Chicago Press, 1997.
Ermarth, Michael. *Wilhelm Dilthey: The Critique of Historical Reason*. Chicago: University of Chicago Press, 1978.
———. "The Transformation of Hermeneutics," *Monist* (April 1981): 175–94.
Farias, Victor. *Heidegger and Nazism*. Philadelphia: Temple University Press, 1989.
Findlay, J.N. *Hegel: A Re-examination*. London: Allen & Unwin, 1958.
Flew, Antony. "On Not Deriving 'Ought' from 'Is.'" In *Ethics: The Big Questions*. Ed. James Sterba, 43–47. Oxford: Blackwell, 1998.
———. *Philosophy: An Introduction*. Buffalo: Prometheus, 1980.
Flynn, Thomas. "Foucault as Parrhesiast: his last course at the college de france." In *The Final Foucault*. Ed. Manes Bernauer and David Rasmussen, 102–18. Cambridge, MA: MIT Press, 1988.
Förster, Eckart. *Kant's Final Synthesis*. Cambridge, MA: Harvard University Press, 2000.
Foucault, Michel. *The Archaeology of Knowledge*. Trans. A.M. Sheridan Smith. New York: Pantheon, 1972.
———. *The History of Sexuality*. Trans. Robert Hurley. New York: Pantheon Books, 1978.
———. *Madness and Civilization: A History of Insanity in the Age of Reason*. Trans. A.M. Sheridan Smith. New York: Pantheon, 1965.
———. *Order of Things* (1966). London: Tavistock, 1970.
———. *Power/Knowledge: Selected Interviews & Other Writings, 1972–1977*. Ed. Colin Gordon; trans. Colin Gordon, Leo Marshall, John Mepham, and Kate Soper. New York: Pantheon, 1980.
———. "Questions of Method," *I & C 8* (Spring 1981): 3–14.
———. "The Subject and Power," *Critical Inquiry* 8 (1982): 777–95.
Gadamer, Hans-Georg. *Philosophical Apprenticeships*. Trans. R.R. Sullivan. Cambridge, MA: MIT Press, 1985.
———. *Philosophical Hermeneutics*. Trans. David E. Linge. Berkeley: University of California Press, 1976.
———. *Truth and Method* (1960). New York: Seabury Press, 1975.
Gardiner, Patrick, ed. *Theories of History*. New York: Free Press of Glencoe, 1959.
Gay, Peter. *The Science of Freedom*. Vol. II, *The Enlightenment: An Interpretation*. New York: Alfred Knopf, 1969.
Gellner, Ernest. *Language and Solitude: Wittgenstein, Malinowski and the Habsburg Dilemma*. Cambridge: Cambridge University Press, 1998.
Gilbert, Felix. "Intellectual History: Its Aims and Methods." In *Historical Studies Today*. Ed. Felix Gilbert and Stephen R. Graubard, 141–58. New York: W. W. Norton, 1972.
Gillespie, Michael Allen. *Hegel, Heidegger, and the Ground of History*. Chicago: University of Chicago Press, 1984.
Goodman, Nelson. *Ways of Worldmaking*. Indianapolis, Indiana: Hackett, 1978.

Gorner, Paul. *Twentieth-Century German Philosophy*. Oxford: Oxford University Press, 2000.
Gould, Stephen Jay. *The Hedgehog, the Fox, and the Magister's Pox: Mending the Gap between Science and the Humanities*. New York: Harmony Books, 2003.
Guyer, Paul. "Introduction: The starry heavens and the moral law." In *The Cambridge Companion to Kant*. Ed. Paul Guyer, 1–25. Cambridge: Cambridge University Press, 1992.
Guyer, Paul. *Kant and the Experience of Freedom: Essays on Aesthetics and Morality*. Cambridge: Cambridge University Press, 1993.
Guyer, Paul. *Kant on Freedom, Law and Happiness*. Cambridge: Cambridge University Press, 2000.
Haakonssen, Knud. *Natural Law and Moral Philosophy: From Grotius to the Scottish Enlightenment*. Cambridge, MA: Cambridge University Press, 1996.
Habermas, Jürgen. *Moral Consciousness and Communicative Action* Trans. Shierry Weber Nicholsen. Cambridge, MA: MIT Press, 1990.
———. *The New Conservatism: Cultural Critcism and the Historians' Debate* Ed. and trans. Shierry Weber Nicholsen. Cambridge, MA: MIT Press, 1989.
———. *The Philosophical Discourse of Modernity* Trans. Frederick G. Lawrence. Cambridge, MA: MIT Press, 1987.
———. *Postmetaphysical Thinking* Trans. William Mark Hohengarten. Cambridge, MA: MIT Press, 1992.
———. *Theory of Communicative Action*. Vol. I. Boston, Beacon Press, 1984.
Hacking, Ian. *Historical Ontology*. Cambridge, MA: Harvard University Press, 2002.
———. *Why does Language Matter to Philosophy?* Cambridge: Cambridge University Press, 1975.
Hacohen, Malachi Haim. "Leonard Krieger: Historicization and Political Engagement in Intellectual History," *History and Theory* 35, no. 1 (1995): 80–130.
Halle, Louis. "The Historian as Philosopher." In *Herbert Butterfield: The Ethics of History and Politics*. Ed. Kenneth W. Thompson, 1–18. Washington: University Press of America, 1980.
Harvey, Irene. *Derrida and the Economy of Différance*. Studies in Phenomenology and Existential Philosophy. Ed. James Edie. Bloomington: Indiana University Press, 1986.
Hawkes, Terence. *Structuralism and Semiotics*. Berkeley: University of California Press, 1977.
Hegel, G.W.F. *Faith and Knowledge*. Trans. Walter Cerf. Albany, NY: SUNY Press, 1977.
———. *Lectures on the Philosophy of Religion*. Ed. and trans. P. Hodgson. Berkeley: University of California Press, 1984.
———. *The Phenomenology of Mind*. Trans. J.B. Baillie (1910). New York: Harper, 1967.
———. *The Phenomenology of Spirit*. Trans. A.V. Miller and J.N. Findlay. London: Oxford, 1979.
———. *The Philosophy of History*. Trans. J. Sibree. Buffalo: Prometheus, 1991.
———. *The Science of Logic*. Trans. W. H. Johnston and L.G. Struthers. London: Allen & Unwin, 1961.
———. "The Spirit of Christianity." In *Early Theological Writings*. Trans. T.M. Knox, 209–16. Philadelphia: University of Pennsylvania Press, 1975.

Heidegger, Martin. *Being and Time*. Trans. John Macquarrie and Edward Robinson. New York: Harper & Row, 1962.

———. "Duns Scotus's Doctrine of Categories and Meaning." In *Supplements: From the Earliest Essays to Being and Time and Beyond*. Ed. John van Buren, 61–68. Albany: SUNY Press, 2002.

———. *Kant and the Problem of Metaphysics*. Trans. Richard Taft. Bloomington: Indiana University Press, 1990.

———. "Letter on Humanism." In *Basic Writings*. Ed. David Farrell Krell, 189–242. New York: Harper and Row, 1977.

———. *Nietzsche: Nihilism*. Trans. Frank A. Capuzzi. New York: Harper & Row, 1982.

———. "Only a God Can Save Us: The *Spiegel* Interview." In *Heidegger: The Man and the Thinker*. Ed. Thomas Sheehan, 45–72. Chicago: Precedent, 1976.

———. "The Concept of Time in the Historical Sciences." In *Supplements: From the Earliest Essays to Being and Time and Beyond*. Ed. John van Buren, 49–60. Albany: SUNY Press, 2002.

———. "The Word of Nietzsche: 'God is Dead.'" In *The Question Concerning Technology and Other Essays*. Ed. and trans. William Lovitt, 53–114. New York: Harper, 1977.

Hempel, Carl. "Explanation in Science and in History." In *Explanation*. Ed. David-Hillel Ruben, 30–52. Oxford: Oxford University Press, 1993.

———. "The Function of General Laws in History," *Journal of Philosophy* 39, no. 2 (1942): 35–48.

———. *Pathmarks*. Cambridge: Cambridge University Press, 1998.

Higham, John. "American Intellectual History: A Critical Appraisal," *American Quarterly* 13 (1961): 219–33.

Holdcroft, David. *Saussure, Signs, System and Arbitrariness*. Cambridge: Cambridge University Press, 1991.

Holston, James. "Spaces of Insurgent Citizenship." In *Making the Invisible Visible*. Ed. Leonie Sandercock, 30–45. Berkeley: University of California Press, 1998.

Horkheimer, Max, and Theodore Adorno. *Dialectic of Enlightenment*. Trans. John Cumming. New York: Seabury, 1972.

Howe, Irving. *The Idea of the Modern*. New York: Horizon, 1967.

Hoy, David Couzens. "Nietzsche, Hume and the Genealogical Method." In *Nietzsche, Genealogy, Morality: Essays on Nietzsche's On the Genealogy of Morals*. Ed. Richard Schacht, 251–68. Berkeley: University of California Press, 1994.

Hume, David. *Dialogues Concerning Natural Religion*. Ed. Norman Kemp Smith. Indianapolis: Bobbs-Merrill, 1947.

———. *An Enquiry concerning Human Understanding*. Ed. Antony Flew. Chicago: Open Court, 1988.

———. *An Enquiry concerning the Principles of Morals*. Ed. Tom Beauchamp. Oxford: Oxford University Press, 1998.

———. "The Skeptic." In *Essays, Moral, Political and Literary*. Ed. Eugene F. Miller, 159–80. Indianapolis: Liberty Classics, 1987.

———. *A Treatise of Human Nature*. Ed. L.A. Selby-Bigge. Oxford: Clarendon Press, 1978.

Husserl, Edmund. *The Crisis of European Sciences and Transcendental Phenomenology*. Trans. David Carr. Evanston, IL: Northwestern University Press, 1970.

Husserl, Edmund. *Logical Investigations*. Trans. J.N. Findlay. London: Routledge, 2001.

Ingraffia, Brian D. *Postmodern theory and biblical theology*. Cambridge: Cambridge University Press, 1995.

Isaacson, Walter. *Kissinger: A Biography*. New York: Simon & Schuster, 1992.

Jacoby, Russell. "A New Intellectual History?" *American Historical Review* 97 (1992): 400–412.

Jameson, Fredric. *Postmodernism, or, The Cultural Logic of Late Capitalism*. Durham, NC: Duke University Press, 1991.

——. *The Prison-House of Language*. Princeton, NJ: Princeton University Press, 1972.

Jaspers, Karl. *Kant*. Ed. Hannah Arendt; trans. Ralph Manheim. New York: Harcourt, Brace & World, 1962.

——. *Nietzsche: An Introduction to the Understanding of His Philosophical Activity*. Trans. Charles F. Wallraff and Frederick J. Schmitz. Chicago: Henry Regnery Co., 1965.

——. *Philosophy*. Vol II, Trans. E.B. Ashton. Chicago: University of Chicago Press, 1970.

Jencks, Charles. *The Language of Post-modern Architecture*. New York: Rizzoli, 1977.

Kamuf, Peggy, ed. *A Derrida Reader*. New York: Columbia University Press, 1991.

Kant, Immanuel. *Anthropology from a Pragmatic Point of View*. Trans. And Ed. Robert B. Louden, Cambridge: Cambridge University Press, 2006.

——. *Concerning the Ultimate Ground of the Differentiation of Directions in Space*. Trans. David Walford and Ralph Meerbote. London: Cambridge University Press, 1992.

——. "The Conflict of the Faculties (1800)." In *Kant: Religion and Rational Theology*. Ed. and trans. Allen W. Wood and George Di Giovanni. 233–328, Cambridge: Cambridge University Press, 1996.

——. "Conjectural Beginning of Human History (1786)." In *Kant on History*. Ed. Lewis White Beck; trans. Lewis White Beck, Robert E. Anchor, and Emil L. Fackenheim, 53–68. Indianapolis: Bobbs-Merrill, 1963.

——. *The Critique of Pure Reason* (1787). Trans. Norman Kemp Smith. London: MacMillan, 1927.

——. *The Critique of Practical Reason* (1788). Trans. Lewis White Beck. New York: MacMillan, 1993.

——. *The Critique of Judgment* (1790). Trans. Werner S. Pluhar. Indianapolis: Hackett, 1987.

——. *Groundwork of the Metaphysic of Morals* (1785). Trans. Mary Gregor. Cambridge: Cambridge University Press, 1996.

——. "Idea for a Universal History from a Cosmopolitan Point of View (1785)." In *The Philosophy of Kant: Immanuel Kant's Moral and Political Writings*. Ed. Carl J. Friedrich, 116–31. New York: Modern Library, 1949.

——. *Lectures on Metaphysics*. Ed. and trans. Karl Ameriks and Steve Naragon. Cambridge: Cambridge University Press, 1997.

——. *The Metaphysics of Morals* (1798). Trans. Mary Gregor. Cambridge: Cambridge University Press, 1991.

——, *On the Form and the Principles of the Sensible and the Intellgible World*. Trans. David Walford and Ralph Meerbote (London: Cambridge University Press, 1992).

———. *On the Old Saw: That may be Right in Theory but it Won't Work in Practice* (1783). Trans. E.B. Ashton. Philadelphia: University of Pennsylvania Press, 1974.
———. "Perpetual Peace. A Philosophical Sketch (1785)." In *Critique of Practical Reason and Other Writings in Moral Philosophy*. Ed. Lewis White Beck, 306–45. Chicago: University of Chicago Press, 1949.
———. *Prolegomena to any Future Metaphysics* (1783). Ed. Lewis White Beck. Indianapolis: Bobbs-Merrill, 1950.
———. *Religion within the Limits of Reason Alone* (1793). Trans. with an Introduction and Notes by Theodore M. Greene and Hoyt H. Hudson. New York: Harper Torchbooks, 1960.
———. "What is Enlightenment (1785)." In *The Philosophy of Kant: Immanuel Kant's Moral and Political Writings*. Ed. Carl J. Friedrich, 132–39. New York: Modern Library, 1949.
Kaufmann, Walter, ed. *The Portable Nietzsche*. New York: Penguin, 1976.
Kenny, Anthony, ed. *The Wittgenstein Reader*. London: Blackwell, 1994.
Krell, David. *Intimations of Mortality*. University Park, PA: Pennsylvania State University Press, 1986.
Krieger, Leonard. "Comments on Historical Explanation." In *Philosophy and History*. Ed. Sidney Hook, 136–42. New York: New York University Press, 1963.
———. *The German Idea of Freedom*. Boston, Beacon Hill, 1957.
———. *Ideas and Events/Professing History*. Ed. M.L. Brick. Introduction by Michael Ermarth. Chicago: University of Chicago Press, 1992.
———. *Kings and Philosophers: 1689–1789*. New York: W.W. Norton, 1970.
———. *The Politics of Discretion: Pufendorf and the Acceptance of Natural Law*. Chicago: University of Chicago Press, 1965.
———. *Ranke: The Meaning of History*. Chicago: University of Chicago Press, 1977.
———. *Time's Reasons: Philosophies of History Old and New*. Chicago: University of Chicago Press, 1989.
Kuehn, Manfred. *Scottish Common Sense in Germany, 1768–1800: A Contribution to the History of Critical Philosophy*. Montreal and Kingston: McGill-Queen's University Press, 1987.
Lacan, Jacques. *The Four Fundamental Concepts of Psychoanalysis*. Trans. Alan Sheridan. New York: Penguin, 1977.
Lakoff, George, and Mark Johnson. *Metaphors We Live By*. Chicago: University of Chicago Press, 1980.
Leitch, Vincent. *Cultural Criticism, Literary Theory, Poststructuralism*. New York: Columbia University Press, 1992.
Leiter, Brian. "The Paradox of Fatalism and Self-Creation in Nietzsche." In *Willing and Nothingness*: Schopenhauer as Nietzsche's Educator. Ed. Christopher Janaway, 217–57. Oxford: Clarendon Press, 1998.
Lessing, Gotthold Ephraim. *Laocoon* (1766). Trans. Robert Phillimore. London: George Routledge and Sons, 1874.
Levin, Harry. *Refractions: Esssays in Comparative Literature*. New York: Oxford University Press, 1966.
Lewis, C.I. *The Ground and Nature of the Right*. New York: Columbia University Press, 1955.
Luft, David S. "Being and German History: Historiographical Notes on the Heidegger Controversy," *Central European History* 27, no. 4 (1994): 479–502.
Luther, Martin. "On the Councils and the Church." In *Luther's Works: American Edition*. Ed. Eric W. Gritsch. Vol. 41, 100–104. Philadelphia: Fortress Press, 1966.

Lyotard, Jean-François. *The Postmodern Condition: A Report on Knowledge*. Trans. Geoff Bennington and Brian Massumi. From the series *Theory and History of Literature*. Ed. Wlad Godzich and Jochen Schulte-Sasse. Minneapolis: University of Minnesota Press, 1984.

———. *The Postmodern Condition: A Report on Knowledge*. Cambridge: Polity Press, 1998.

Macey, David. *The Lives of Michel Foucault*. New York: Pantheon Books, 1993.

Magee, Glenn Alexander. *Hegel and the Hermetic Tradition*. Ithaca, NY: Cornell University Press, 2001.

Makkreel, Rudolf. *Dilthey: Philosopher of the Human Studies*. Princeton, NJ: Princeton University Press, 1975.

Mandelbaum, Maurice. *The Problem of Historical Knowledge: An Answer to Relativism*. New York: Liveright, 1938.

———. *Purpose and Necessity in Social Theory*. Baltimore: Johns Hopkins University Press, 1987.

Marx, Karl. *Capital: A Critique of Political Economy* I. Trans. Samuel Moore and Edward Aveling. Moscow: Progress Publishers, 1954.

———. *Grundrisse*. Trans. Martin Nicolaus. New York: Vintage, 1973.

———. *The Poverty of Philosophy*. Trans. Martin Nicolaus. New York: International Publishers, 1903.

McAdams, Dan P. *The Stories We Live By*. New York: Guilford Press, 1997.

McIntire, C.T. *Herbert Butterfield: Historian as Dissenter*. New Haven, CT: Yale University Press, 2004.

Mehlman, Jeffrey. "Introduction to Derrida's essay 'Freud and the Scene of Writing,'" *Yale French Studies* 48 (1972): 74–117.

Merleau-Ponty, Maurice. *Phenomenology of Perception*. Trans. Colin Smith. London: Routledge & Kegan Paul, 1962.

Michelfelder, Diane F., and Richard E. Palmer. *Dialogue and Deconstruction: The Gadamer-Derrida Encounter*. Albany, NY: SUNY Press, 1989.

Mink, Louis O. "The Autonomy of Historical Understanding." In *Historical Understanding*. Ed. Brian Fay, Eugene O. Golob, and Richard T. Vann, 61–88. Ithaca, NY: Cornell University Press, 1987.

———. "The Divergence of History and Sociology in Recent Philosophy of History." In *Historical Understanding*. Ed. Brian Fay, Eugene O. Golob, and Richard T. Vann, 163–81. Ithaca, NY: Cornell University Press, 1987.

Moore, G.E. *Principia Ethica*. Cambridge: Cambridge University Press, 1993.

Munzel, G. Felicitas. *Kant's Conception of Moral Character*. Chicago: University of Chicago Press, 1999.

Nagel, Gordon. *The Structure of Experience*. Chicago: University of Chicago Press, 1983.

Naugle, David K. *Worldview: The History of a Concept*. Grand Rapids: Eerdmans, 2002.

Nietzsche, Friedrich. *The Gay Science; with a prelude in rhymes and an appendix of songs*. Trans. Walter Kaufmann. New York: Random House, 1974.

Norris, Christopher. *The Truth about Postmodernism*. Cambridge, MA: Blackwell, 1993.

———. *What's Wrong with Postmodernism*. Baltimore: Johns Hopkins University Press, 1990.

Norton, David Fate and Richard Popkin, eds. *David Hume: Philosophical Historian*. Indianapolis: Bobbs-Merrill, 1965.

Oakeshott, Michael. *The Politics of Faith and the Politics of Scepticism*. Ed. Timothy Fuller. New Haven, CT: Yale University Press, 1996.
Ogden, C.K., and I.A. Richards. *The Meaning of Meaning*. London: Routledge, 1985.
Orr, Leonard. "The Post-Turn: Derrida, Gadamer and the Remystification of Language." In *Deconstruction: A Critique*. Ed. A. Rajnath, 197–212. New York: Macmillan, 1989.
Ortega y Gasset, José. *Concord and Liberty*. Trans. Helene Weyl. New York: Norton, 1946.
Palmer, Richard. *Hermeneutics*. Evanston, IL: Northwestern University Press, 1969.
Paton, Hebert James. *The Categorical Imperative*. Chicago: University of Chicago Press, 1948.
Pocock, J.G.A. *The Machiavellian Moment: Florentine Political Thought and the Atlantic Republican Tradition*. Princeton, NJ: Princeton University Press, 1975.
Pöggeler, Otto. *Martin Heidegger's Path of Thinking*. Trans. Daniel Magurshak and Sigmund Barber. Atlantic Highlands, NJ: Humanities Press International, 1987.
Polt, Richard. *Heidegger: An Introduction*. Ithaca, NY: Cornell University Press, 1991.
Popkin, Richard H. *The History of Scepticism from Erasmus to Spinoza*. Berkeley: University of California Press, 1979.
Popper, Karl R. *The Logic of Scientific Discovery*. London, 1971.
———. *The Poverty of Historicism*. London: Routledge & Kegan Paul, 1957.
Priest, Stephen, ed. "Introduction," *Hegel's Critique of Kant*, 1–48. Oxford: Clarendon Press, 1987.
Putnam, Hilary. *Meaning and the Moral Sciences*. London: Routledge & Kegan Paul, 1978.
———. *Words and Life*. Ed. James Conant. Cambridge, MA: Harvard University Press, 1994.
Quine, Willard Van Orman. "Epistemology Naturalized." In *Naturalizing Epistemology*. Ed. Hilary Kornblith, 15–30. Cambridge, MA: MIT Press, 1985.
Randall, John Herman. *The Career of Philosophy*. New York: Columbia University Press, 1962.
Rapaport, Herman. *Heidegger & Derrida: Reflections on Time and Language*. Lincoln: University of Nebraska Press, 1989.
Recki, Birgit. "Das Gute am Schönen: Über einen Grundgedanker in Kants Äesthetik," *Zeitschrift für Äesthetik und allgemeine Kunstwissenschaft* 37 (1994): 15–31.
Rey, Jean-Michel. "Commentary." In *Nietzsche's New Seas: Explorations in Philosophy Aesthetics and Politics*. Ed. Michael Allen Gillespie and Tracy B. Strong, 75–96. Chicago: University of Chicago Press, 1988.
Richardson, William J. *Heidegger: Through Phenomenology to Thought*. The Hague: Martinus Nijhoff, 1967.
Roberts, Richard H. *Religion, Theology and the Social Sciences*. Cambridge: Cambridge University Press, 2002.
Rorty, Richard, ed. *The Linguistic Turn*. Chicago: University of Chicago Press, 1967.
———. *Philosophy and the Mirror of Nature*. Princeton, NJ: Princeton University Press, 1979.
———. *Philosophy and Social Hope*. New York: Penguin, 1999.
Royle, Nicholas. *After Derrida*. Manchester: Manchester University Press, 1995.
Sandercock, Leonie, "Framing Insurgent Historiographies for Planning." In *Making the Invisible Visible: A Multicultural Planning History*. Ed. Leonie Sandercock, 1–33. Berkeley: University of California Press, 1998.

Sartre, Jean-Paul. *Being and Nothingness.* Trans. Hazel E. Barnes. London: Methuen, 1957.

———. *Les chemins de la liberté.* Paris Gallimand, 1946.

———. *La nausée.* Paris Gallimand, 1938.

———. "Preface." In Frantz Fanon, *The Wretched of the Earth.* Trans. Constance Farrington, 7–31. New York: Grove Press, 1998.

———. *The Words.* Trans. Bernard Frechtman. New York: Braziller, 1964.

Saussure, Ferdinand de. *Course in General Linguistics.* Ed. Charles Bally and Albert Sechehaye, in collaboration with Albert Reidlinger, trans. Wade Baskin. New York: Philosophical Library, 1959.

Schlick, Moritz. "Meaning and Verification," *Philosophical Review* 45 (1936): 339–69.

Schorske, Carl. "Leonard Krieger," *Journal of the History of Ideas* 52 (April/June 1991): 340.

Seuren, Peter A M. *Western Linguistics: An Historical Introduction.* Malden, MA: Blackwell, 1998.

Sheehan, Thomas. "Heidegger's Early Years: Fragments for a Philosophical Biography." In *Heidegger the Man and the Thinker.* Ed. Thomas Sheehan, 3–30. Chicago: Precedent Pub. 1981.

Silverman, Hugh J., ed. *Philosophy and Non-Philosophy since Merleau-Ponty.* Evanston: Northwestern University Press, 1988.

Skinner, Quentin. "The idea of negative liberty: philosophical and historical perspectives." In *Philosophy in History: Essays on the historiography of philosophy.* Ed. Richard Rorty, J.B. Schneewind, and Quentin Skinner, 193–221. Cambridge: Cambridge University Press, 1984.

———. *Liberty before Liberalism.* Cambridge: Cambridge University Press, 1998.

———. *Reason and Rhetoric in the Philosophy of Thomas Hobbes.* Cambridge: Cambridge University Press, 1996.

Sluga, Hans. *Heidegger's Crisis: Philosophy and Politics in Nazi Germany.* Cambridge, MA: Harvard University Press, 1993.

Smith, Neil. *Chomsky.* Cambridge: Cambridge University Press, 1999.

Spivak, Gayatri Chakravorty. *A Critique of Postcolonial Reason: Toward a History of the Vanishing Present.* Cambridge, MA: Harvard University Press, 1999.

Strawson, P.F. *The Bounds of Sense: An Essay on Kant's Critique of Pure Reason.* London: Methuen, 1966.

———. *Individuals: An Essay in Descriptive Metaphysics.* London: Methuen, 1959.

Sykes, Charles. *The Hollow Men: Politics and Corruption in Higher Education.* Washington: Regnery Gateway, 1990.

———. *ProfScam: Professors and the Demise of Higher Education.* New York: St. Martin's Press, 1988.

Taylor, Charles. *Human Agency and Language.* New York: Cambridge University Press, 1985.

———. *Sources of the Self: the Making of the Modern Identity.* Cambridge, MA: Harvard University Press, 1989.

Toynbee, Arnold. *A Study of History.* Oxford: Oxford University Press, 1939.

Tregenza, Ian. "The Sceptical Idealist: Michael Oakeshott as a Critic of the Enlightenment," *History of Political Thought* 24, no. 4 (2003): 705–21.

Tucker, Robert C., ed. *The Marx/Engels Reader.* New York: Norton, 1972.

Tully, James. *An Approach to Political Philosophy: Locke in Contexts.* Cambridge: Cambridge University Press, 1993.

Vann, Richard T. "Turning Linguistic: History and Theory and *History and Theory,*

1960–1975." In *A New Philosophy of History*. Ed. Frank Ankersmit and Hans Kellner, 132–56. Chicago: University of Chicago Press, 1995.

Venturi, Robert, Denise S. Brown, and Steven Izenour. *Learning from Las Vegas*. Cambridge, MA: MIT Press, 1972.

Voltaire. *An Essay on the Age of Louis XIV*. Trans. Mr. Lockman. London: J. & P. Knapton, 1739.

Walker, Margaret Urban. "Naturalizing, Normativity, and Using What 'We' Know in Ethics." In *Moral Epistemology Naturalized*. Ed. Richard Campbell and Bruce Hunter, 103–38. *Canadian Journal of Philosophy* Supplementary Volume 26. Calgary: University of Calgary Press, 2000.

Whitehead, Alfred North. *Process and Reality*. Cambridge: Cambridge University Press, 1929.

Wiener, Philip. "Herbert Butterfield," *Journal of the History of Ideas* 41, no. 1 (1980): 157–58.

Wilshire, Bruce. *The Moral Collapse of the University*. Albany: SUNY Press, 1990.

Wittgenstein, Ludwig. *Lectures and Conversations on Aesthetics, Psychology, and Religious Belief*. Berkeley: University of California Press, 1966.

———. *Philosophical Investigations*, trans. G.E.M. Ascombe. Oxford: Oxford University Press, 1958.

———. *Tractatus logico-philosophicus*. New York: Harcourt, Brace, 1922.

Gordon S. Wood, "Conspiracy and the Paranoid Style: Causality and Deceit in the Eighteenth Century," in *Knowledge and Postmodernism in Historical Perspective*. Ed. Joyce Appleby, Elizabeth Covington, David Hoyt, Michael Latham, and Allison Sneider, 94–104. New York: Routledge, 1996.

Wright, Crispin. "Realism, Antirealism, Irrealism, Quasi-Realism," *Midwest Studies in Philosophy* 12 (1988): 25–49.

Young, Robert Maxwell. *White Mythologies: Writing History and the West*. London: Routledge, 1990.

Yovel, Yirmiahu. *Kant and the Philosophy of History*. Princeton, NJ: Princeton University Press, 1980.

Zinn, Howard. "The Politics of history in the era of the Cold War: Repression and Resistance." In *The Cold War and the University*. Ed. Noam Chomsky. 35–72. New York: New Press, 1997.

# *INDEX*

Abela, Paul
   Kant's empirical realism, 40–42
Abelard, Peter, 116
Adorno, Theodore, 17–18
Alexander, Jeffrey, 125
Arendt, Hannah, 213
Aristotle
   dialectics, 88
   Kant on, 44
   on phenomena, 219
   theory of primary cause, 87, 288n100
Arnold, Matthew, 71, 126, 243
Augustine
   Becker cites, 159
   epistemology, 135
   on language, 128–30, 133, 141, 149
   on time, 138–41
   Wittgenstein's similarity to, 152
Austin, J.L., 9
   on Hume's Fork, 20
   Rorty on, 113
Ayer, A.J., 20
   Rorty on, 113

## *B*

Barash, Jeffrey
   on Heidegger, 211, 231
Barzun, Jacques, 268
Bauer, Bruno, 265
Beard, Charles
   new historians, 160, 163–65. 188
Beattie, James, 36
Beck, Lewis White
   influence of Cassirer, 277n91
   influence on Krieger, 189
Becker, Carl
   The Enlightenment, 155–56
   Mandelbaum on, 163ff.
   Mr. Everyman, 161–62
   on Locke, 158
   theory of history, 157–60
   Wilkins on, 286n16
Bentley, Michael, 154
Berger, Peter, 127
Bergmann, Gustav, 113
Betanzos, Ramon, 97
Bolzano, Bernard, 134
Bonjour, Lawrence
   epistemology, 75–76

Bosanquet, Bernard, 126, 243
Bourdieu, Pierre
   Heidegger's language, 225, 290n36
Brinton, Crane, 160
Butterfield, Herbert, 161, 166, 171, 193
   *Whig Interpretation of History*, 153–55

## *C*

Caputo, John,
   on Heidegger, 211
   on Enlightenment, 240
Carnap, Rudolf,
   Rorty on, 113
   Wittgenstein meets, 174
Carty, Anthony
   on postmodernism, 211
Cassirer, Ernst, 126, 138
   influence on Beck, 277n91
Chia, Robert
   criticizes Dilthey, 92
Chomsky, Noam
   language scandal, 280n41
Coffa, J. Alberto, 134
Coleridge, Samuel Taylor, 126, 243
Comeliau, Christian
   logic of modernity, 267
Cooper, Barry
   on Dilthey, 92–93
Copp, David
   moral epistemology, 249, 291n106
Croce, Benedetto, 126, 165, 243
Culler, Jonathan
   on Saussure, 121
Cumming, Robert DeNoon
   Heidegger's *dummheit*, 225

## *D*

Danto, Arthur, 188
Darnton, Robert, 187
Darwall, Stephen
   Hume's challenge, 23
Darwin, Charles
   Rorty's encounter with, 114–15
De Beaugrande, Robert, 122
De Boer, Karin
   on Heidegger, 221–22
De Man, Paul
   *Metalepsis*, 84
   on Hegel, 74, 84
   on Nietzsche, 119, 280n45
Deleuze, Gilles
   on Foucault, 244–48

Derrida, Jacques, 233
　anti-structuralism, 235
　*Aufhebung*, 238–39, 241
　*Deconstruction*, 233–34
　*Différance*, 236–37, 240–42
　Gadamer meets, 255–70
　Hegel nauseates, 239ff.
　Hegel's language, 239–40
　nothing-outside-the-text, 238
　on Saussure, 123–24
　on Heidegger, 226
Descartes, René
　Deleuze on, 244–45
　epistemology, 273n2
　Foucault on, 240, 247–48
Dickey, Lawrence
　on Hegel, 77
Dilthey, Wilhelm, 74, 127, 143, 188, 211–12, 243
　Hegel's influence, 104, 108–9
　Heidegger's critique, 218
　'lived experience," 106–7
　loss of faith, 94–95, 281n74
　metaphysics, 96
　"objective mind," 105
　philosophical realism, 109–10
　spectator theory of ethics, 92–93
　*Verstehen*, 98–103
　worldviews, 97
Dray, William H., 182, 188
　on Hegel, 76
　on Hempel, 181, 286n32
Dreyfus, Hubert L.
　on Foucault (with Paul Rabinow), 246
　on Heidegger (with Jane Rubin), 220–21
Dummett, Michael
　on language, 20
　philosophical realism, 109–10, 113
During, Simon
　on Foucault, 246

## E

Eliot, William Yandell, 277n92
Ermarth, Michael
　on Dilthey, 105

## F

Farias, Victor
　on Heidegger, 224
Feder, J.G.A.
　reviews *Critique of Pure Reason*, 54
Feuerbach, Ludwig, 265
Field, Hartry
　on language, 11, 17

Flew, Antony
　on Hume, 55–56
Flynn, Thomas
　on Foucault, 234
Förster, Eckart
　on Kant, 56
　on Wittgenstein, 56
Foucault, Michel, 242
　archaeology of knowledge, 292n91
　discourse, 251–53
　Heidegger's influence, 246–47
　homosexuality, 244
　on history, 243, 249–53
　on Kant, 244–46
　on Marx, 254–55
　on Sartre, 14
　on sexuality, 295n127
　the Other, 247–48
Franklin, Benjamin
　Marx credits, 264
Frege, Friedrich Ludwig Gottlob, 136
　and Nazis, 276

## G

Gadamer, Hans-Georg
　Derrida meets, 255–70
　on Heidegger, 213–14
　on History, 256
　Rorty on, 114
Garvé, Christian
　reviews *Critique of Pure Reason*, 54, 276n72
Gay, Peter, 47
Gilbert, Felix, 160, 288n67
Gillespie, Michael Allen
　on Heidegger, 230–31
Goodman, Nelson, 9, 113
Gould, Stephen Jay, 107

## H

Habermas, Jürgen
　*Aufhebung*, 238
　Semantics, 4
Hacking, Ian
　on Hume, 42, 275n55
　on Locke, 19
Hacohen, Malachi Haim
　on Krieger, 189, 195
Halle, Louis
　on Butterfield, 155
Hawkes, Terence, 124
Hegel, G.W.F., 16, 34
　cunning of reason, 75, 82
　dialectic, 88

Hegel, G.W.F. (*continued*)
  ethics, 85, 89, 107, 222, 279n33, 280n54
  external realism of, 37, 74–76, 109–11
  "God, himself, has died," 65–70
  happy consciousness, 85
  "infinite grief," 2–4
  idealist, 6
  influence on: Dilthey, 100; Heidegger, 214, 217, 221, 229; Mandelbaum, 172; Ranke, 90; Rorty,114–15
  loss of faith, 77–78
  on history, 87, 109, 223, 280–81n47
  on language, 70–74, 77–84, 87, 222, 279n30, 281n58
Heidegger, Martin
  *Abbau*, 234
  *Alethes*, 217
  *Being and Time*, 214
  death of God, 210
  discourse, 219
  "Greek way of seeing," 223–25, 229
  Hegel influences, 221–22
  influence on Foucault, 246
  Kant, 213
  Kierkegaard influences, 221
  language, 217–20, 225, 228–29
  *Logos*, 215, 290n24
  and Nazism, 225, 290n36
  negative dialectic, 217
  on history, 230–32
  on Nietzsche, 227–28
  on Plato, 119, 222, 228, 232
  ontological difference, 212
  *Physei*, 216
  piety, 211–12, 232
  Rorty on, 113
Heine, Heinrich, 84
  on Kant, Fichte, and Hegel, 280n44
Hempel, Carl, 174
  covering law hypothesis, 174, 188, 206, 286n32
  criticisms of, 182–83
  on Hume, 174–75, 178
  on Mandelbaum, 174–80
Higham, John, 160
Hirsch, E.D., 119
Hume, David, 15
  Becker on, 156
  custom, 24, 28, 34
  common sense, 33
  human nature, 22–23
  Hume's fork, 20ff.
  Hume's law, 36

Hume, David (*continued*)
  on language, 31–32, 35
  on history and necessity, 25–27, 83
  on taste, 49–50
  sentiment, 28–41, 274n31
  theory of virtue, 31
Husserl, Edmund, 216
  Heidegger's mentor, 211–14
Hutcheson, Francis, 34

## I-J

Ingraffia, Brian
  death of God, 115
Jacoby, Russell
  on Dilthey, 101–2
James, William, 9
Jaspers, Karl. 229
  on Nietzsche, 118–19
Johnson, Mark, 9

## K

Kant, Immanuel, 15
  categorical imperative, 16, 49, 42, 275n53, 277n91
  "The Conflict of the Faculties," 61–62
  Copernican Revolution, 7
  *Critique of Judgment*, 44–52, 135–38
  *Critique of Practical Reason*, 39, 43–44, 275n53, 276n61
  *Critique of Pure Reason*, 7–9, 42–43, 148
  dialectics, 263
  discursive principles, 47, 52–53, 58–60, 243
  Foucault's Thesis, 244–45
  Good Will, 257–58
  *Groundwork of the Metaphysics of Morals*, 57–59
  influence on Vienna Circle, 134, 137
  maxims, 56
  metaphysics, 278n100
  on Hume, 38–47, 49–50
  *On the old Saw: What works in theory won't work in practice*, 54–55, 276n72
  Rousseau corrects, 58
Kierkegaard, Søren, 53, 71, 111, 270
  despair, 117
Kissinger, Henry, 277n92
Krell, David, 210
Krieger, Leonard, 160
  combines Kant and Marx, 204–7
  Hegel's influence on, 76, 184, 205
  historical method, 190–95
  on Foucault, 242

Krieger, Leonard (*continued*)
   on Hempel, 183–84
   on Hume, 191–93
   on Kant, 200–203
   on Marx, 197–200
   on Nazism, 188–89
   on Plato, 279n13
   on Pufendorf, 188, 193–96
   on Ranke, 199–200
   on Sartre, 184–86
   "politics of discretion," 183, 187ff.

## L

Lacan, Jacques, 126, 236, 284n51
Lakoff, George, 9
Langer, Susanne, 126
Leibniz, Gottfried Wilhelm, 46, 116, 214, 226, 273n2
Lessing, Gotthold Ephraim, 79
Lévi-Strauss, Claude, 126, 236
Lewis, C.I.
   "action orientation," 9–10
   Hume's fork, 20
   skepticism, 10
Locke, John
   inner objects, 149
   psychological perspective, 274n2
Löwith, Karl, 211
Luckmann, Thomas, 126–27
Luther, Martin
   death of God, 1, 278n2
Lyotard, Jean-François, 210, 289n2

## M

Magee, Glenn Alexander
   on Hegel, 81
Makkreel, Rudolf
   on Dilthey, 98–100
Mandelbaum, Maurice
   correspondence theory of knowledge, 286n26
   on Hume and Kant, 169–70
   on relativism, 164–65
   temporal framework as law, 166–68, 286nn27–28
   *The Problem of Historical Knowledge*, 163–64
   the science of culture, 165–66
Mandeville, Bernard de
   Marx credits, 264
Marx, Karl, 232, 244, 263–64
   commodity fetish, 264–66
   credits Locke and Mandeville, 264

Marx, Karl (*continued*)
   on Hegel, 89
   on language, 266–67
   on Proudhon, 265
McAdams, Dan, 18
McIntire, C.T., 154
Meillet, Antoine, 120
Merleau-Ponty, Maurice
   on the *cogito*, 247, 294n107
   Schneider's apraxia, 293n79
Mersenne, Marin
   epistemology, 273n2
Michelfelder, Diane, 256
Mink, Louis O.
   on Hempel, 182–84, 188, 286n32
Misch, Georg, 94
Montaigne, Michel de, 158
Moore, G.E., 74, 128, 138–40, 143
   Bloomsbury Group, 278n13
   influence on Wittgenstein, 128, 138–40, 143–44, 151
   on Hegel, 73
Morris, Charles, 9
Munzel, G. Felicitas
   Kant's aesthetics, 47, 276n64

## N

Nietzsche, Friedrich, 53, 71, 111, 153
   cause and effect, 119
   death of God, 2, 60, 115–17
   will to power, 119, 227

## O

Oakeshott, Michael, 194
Ogden, C.K. with I.A. Richards
   on Hegel, 71–73
Ortega y Gasset, José
   on Dilthey, 92
Oswald, James, 38

## P

Palmer, Richard
   meeting between Gadamer and Derrida, 256
   on hermeneutics, 119
Pater, Walter, 71, 126, 143
Petrarch, 9
Pflanze, Otto, 188
Pierce, Charles Sanders, 9
Plato, 15
   formalism, 73
Pocock, John
   "Machiavellian Moment," 4

Pöggeler, Otto
   on Dilthey, 96
   on Hegel, 279n33
Popkin, Richard
   on Hume, 21–22, 27
Popper, Karl, 280n41
Priest, Stephen
   on Hegel, 88
Priestley, Joseph, 38, 151
Proudhon, Pierre-Joseph, 265
Pufendorf, Samuel. *See* Krieger, Leonard: on Pufendorf
Putnam, Hilary, 9
   after Lewis, 11
   on language, 11–12, 113
   on Wittgenstein, 128

## Q

Quine, Willard van Orman, 9
   holism, 113
   on Hume, 20
   Quine-Duhem thesis, 88

## R

Rabinow, Paul (with Hubert Dreyfus)
   on Foucault, 246
Ramus, Peter, 116
Ranke, Leopold von
   Hegel's influence, 90–92, 101–2, 109
   loss of faith, 91
   philosophical realism, 37, 109–11
Reid Thomas, 34, 38
Richards, I.A. with C.K. Ogden
   on Hegel, 71–73
Roberts, Richard, 267–68
Robinson, James Harvey, 160, 164, 168
Rorty, Richard
   "Conversation of the West," 282n3
   linguistic turn, 113–15
Rousseau, Jean-Jacques, 47, 256n13, 292n78
Rubin, Jane (with Hubert Dreyfus)
   on Heidegger, 220–21
Ryle, Gilbert, 126

## S

Sartre, Jean-Paul. *See also* Krieger, Leonard: on Sartre
   humanism, 14
   nausea, 13–14
Saussure, Ferdinand de
   axis of simultaneities, 121
   *Cours Linguistic*, 121
   diachronic, 122, 124–25

Saussure, Ferdinand de (*continued*)
   inner duality of value, 120
   *Langue* and *parole*, 122–23
Schiller, Friedrich, 71
Schlick, Moritz, 174
Schorske, Carl
   on Krieger, 188
Schutz, Alfred, 127
Scotus, Duns, 116
Seuren, Peter
   Hegel's language, 72–74, 83
Skinner, Quentin
   contextualism, 282n89
   politics, 103, 187
Skotheim, Robert, 160
Sluga, Hans, 226
Smith, Adam, 38, 93
Spivak, Gayatri Chakravorty
   on Heidegger, 225
Steward, Dugald, 34
Strawson, P.F.
   on Kant, 41–42
   on Kant and Wittgenstein, 39
Sykes, Charles, 187

## T

Taylor, Charles
   on language, 77
Thompson, Robert
   on Saussure, 125
Trilling, Lionel, 126

## V

Valla, Lorenzo, 116
Voltaire, 26, 83
   inner objects, 149
   "pack of tricks," 159

## W

Walker, Margaret Urban, 74
Whitehead, Alfred North, 282n89
Wittgenstein, Ludwig
   cites Augustine, 128–29, 139
   discursive duck-rabbit, 184, 186, 199, 207–8
   duck-rabbit, *147*, 147–49, 151
   grammatical form, 141
   inner objects (critique), 149–50
   Kantian judgment, 133–38, 142–43, 149
   language-games, 128–29
   modern university, 285n64
   motto, 282n89
   pointing to (ostension), 130–31, 145–47

Wood, Gordon, 5
    non-paranoid style, 284n45
Wright, Crispin
    Kant's empirical realism, 40

## Y

Yorck, Count, 218
Young, Robert Maxwell, 127

## Z

Zinn, Howard, 187